A HIDEOUS MONSTER OF THE MIND

A HIDEOUS MONSTER OF THE MIND

American Race Theory in the Early Republic

BRUCE DAIN

Harvard University Press

Cambridge, Massachusetts, and London, England · 2002

Library of Congress Cataloging-in-Publication Data

Dain, Bruce R., 1967–
  A hideous monster of the mind : American race theory in the early republic /
Bruce Dain.
    p. cm.
  Includes bibliographical references and index.
  ISBN 0-674-00946-0 (alk. paper)
  1. Race—History. 2. Race—Philosophy. 3. Racism—United States—History.
4. Racism in anthropology—United States—History. 5. Race discrimination—
United States—History. 6. Eugenics—United States—History. 7. African
Americans—Public opinion. 8. Public opinion—United States. 9. United States—
Race relations. 10. United States—Moral conditions. I. Title.
GN259 .D34 2003
305.8′009—dc21   2002027299

CONTENTS

For my parents

European Americans classified the New World as they conquered it. They carried magnifying glasses and taxonomic charts into the wilderness. The new United States, they declared, would be a nation grounded in the visible truths of nature. But those truths would not be self-evident. Subtle processes, internal mechanisms, and hidden springs would appear beneath everything.

Where black people stood in the natural order was unclear. Self-evident, visible, perceptible truths would not be able to capture this thing called race. Race itself was a monster if ever Americans conceived one, but a monster hidden in their minds, not, as many of them came to think, in the reality of a nature behind the appearances. That reality was obscure, shifting, and complex. From the Revolution to the Civil War, Americans first made race intensely real by making it natural in new ways. Their concepts of nature mattered deeply to their understandings of race and vice versa.

Racial concepts did not move tidily from a shallow Enlightenment environmentalism to a deep biology; nor were the two positions mutually exclusive. Nurture and nature intertwined. No linear progression led from essentially ethnocentric, superficial Enlightenment egalitarianism to an unequivocal, candid—and politically expedient—nineteenth-century "hard" racism. New work in the history of science teaches us that a sharp distinction between nineteenth-century biology and eighteenth-century natural history is not tenable. Our understanding of the course of racial thought should follow suit in abandoning such clean divides. That lesson applies also to framing racial thought in black/white dichotomies or dialectics.

The study of the intellectual history of race in the nineteenth century has often been an exercise in explaining and excoriating the rise of "hard" biological racism. That is surely important, but it is insufficient. Intellectually, racism is not the same thing as racial categories describing human diversity. The influential "scientific" racism that arose in the mid-nineteenth century United States was neither unchallenged nor the only racial theory around. And it was not, even by the standards of the day, scientifically incontestable. Other, sometimes antiracist, theories were advanced that were as meaningful and resonant as the well known biological racist ones, and no more illogical or absurd, if not less so.

All sides in slavery and race debates, from the early days of the republic and including African Americans, were addressing the basic issue of whether slaves and ex-slaves were capable of citizenship in a republic. Had slavery and prejudice too deeply formed and damaged blacks? The question was usually posed in terms of supposed environmental effects on a plastic human nature, a subject that European naturalists and philosophers had been pondering for years. Science increasingly focused on classification and the problem of reproduction, heredity, and variation, while American culture and politics focused on race, sexuality, and race mixing. Beneath apparent disparities, science and society converged. In the United States, the convergence yielded, besides hard racist theories, conceptualizations of races as historically and culturally constructed.

This book is an integrated intellectual history of the emergence in the United States, from the American Revolution to the Civil War, of these first major rationalizations of race. It aims to go beyond polarization of the history of racial thinking into the two sides of the great nineteenth-century American racial divide, the "black" or the "white." I read key published writings on race, by both black and white Americans together, and informed by the insights of recent historians of science. I argue that ideas on race did not fall into neat, self-contained, racially determined categories. Such ideas encompassed more than racism and are just as interesting and significant, if not more so. Their history transcends the musings and prejudices of a white intellectual elite with scientific pretensions. Ideas of race were interrelated aspects of the attempt to classify and explain human difference, all in the wake of a revolution fought in the name of a universal liberty that existed only on parchment.

My work is indebted to Winthrop Jordan's interweaving of continuity and change in the understanding of antiblack prejudice. From the Renaissance forward, if not before then, "black" signified sin and evil among Europeans: hostility to dark-skinned peoples preceded significant contact between Europe and West Africa. The expressions and the intensity of such prejudices varied greatly, Jordan showed, in relation to the demographics of slavery, political ideology, revolution, and sometimes sheer coincidence. In leading off my own work with the post-Revolutionary era, I am not dismissing as unimportant the earlier antiblack prejudices first analyzed by Jordan. I would say, rather, expanding on George Fredrickson's work on white images of blacks in the nineteenth century, that no race theory, no systematic attempts to define race, existed in America until after the American Revolution. Only then was antiblack prejudice seriously challenged, and only then did the idea of universal emancipation become "thinkable," as shown in David Brion Davis's majesterial studies of the problem of slavery in Western thought.

All these books, as important as they are, dealt only with the "white" mind. Subsequent social histories did consider both blacks and whites. That work, however, has usually seen ideas as instrumental, subordinate to day to day life, to how Americans created and defined one another, on the ground, so to speak, as blacks and whites. In this approach, African American racial consciousness responds to the horrors of the Middle Passage and New World slavery as well as to the unfulfilled promise of "all men are created equal." Blackness becomes a form of "double consciousness," as W. E. B. Du Bois put it long ago, a sense of being both African and American, insiders and outsiders, different and equal.

In a sense, then, if antiblack prejudices among whites were ancient, black people's *own* sense of blackness may be seen as a new thing under the sun in the eighteenth-century Atlantic world. So was race theory.

This book began as an undergraduate thesis at Yale University directed by David Brion Davis, whose guidance and encouragement were invaluable. I would also like to express my appreciation to Melvin P. Ely and Eugene D. Genovese for helpful comments on my early work. At Princeton University, my dissertation director, James M. McPherson, dispensed sound advice and unflappable reassurance throughout. His lucid lecturing style, outstanding scholarship, and clear, vigorous prose have been an inspiration. Among the Princeton faculty, I would also like to thank Sean Wilentz, John Murrin, the late Gerald Geison, and William Jordan, as well as the Shelby Cullom Davis Center for Historical Studies. Eric Foner's comments on my work were greatly appreciated. At Princeton, several organizations provided the means for me to work full-time on my dissertation: the University Center for Human Values, the Princeton Society of Fellows at the Woodrow Wilson Foundation, and the Whiting Foundation. At the University of Wyoming, I want to thank in particular William Howard Moore and Ronald Schultz for their support, and at the University of Utah, Ray Gunn. The people at Harvard University Press—Aida Donald, Kathleen Drummy, Kathleen McDermott, Colleen Lanick, and Susan Wallace Boehmer—have been a pleasure to work with from start to finish.

Among my friends and family, I thank especially Andre Arnold, Elizabeth Carls, Margaret Croyden, Darin Dockstader, David Igler, Ellen Greenstein Millender, Michael Millender, Isabel Moreira, Jay O'Connor, Hyungi Park, Raul Ramos, Kimberly Mack Rosenberg, David Schiminovich, Jason Scorza, Marcia Travers, Robert Travers, and Cynthia Willard. Clifford Rosenberg and Laura Wilcox Yavitz read and improved several early drafts. Margaret Harper's love provided something more important. To my parents, Norman and Phyllis Dain, whose love and help were invaluable, this book is dedicated.

The negro *"with us" is not an actual physical being of flesh and bones and blood, but a hideous monster of the mind, ugly beyond all physical portraying, so utterly and ineffably monstrous as to frighten reason from its throne, and justice from its balance, and mercy from its hallowed temple, and to blot out shame and probity, and the eternal sympathies of nature, so far as these things have presence in the breasts or being of American republicans! No sir! It is a constructive negro—a John Roe and Richard Doe negro, that haunts with grim presence the precincts of this republic, shaking his gory locks over legislative halls and family prayers.*

James McCune Smith, *Frederick Douglass's Paper* (1852)

The Face of Nature

Again, gay Phoebus, *as the day before*
Wakes ev'ry eye, but what shall wake no more;
Again the face of nature is renew'd,
Which still appears harmonious, fair, and good.

Phillis Wheatley, "Thoughts on the Works of Providence,"
Poems on Various Subjects (1773)

Nineteenth-century science came to see change as the order of nature. Thomas Jefferson, apostle of the American Enlightenment, did not. Neither did the first major "black" writer in the Anglo-American world, Phillis Wheatley, the precocious young Boston slave, famous in North America and England for her wit and learning, whose poems Jefferson dismissed—and implicitly responded to—in his famous statements on race and slavery in his only published book, *Notes on the State of Virginia*. Wheatley's poetry and letters hailed the goodness of Providence, which had created all humans, "all lovely copies of the Maker's plan."[1] Nature was "harmonious, fair, and good." Wheatley's celebrations of rational order, modeled on the Augustan couplets of Alexander Pope and expressing an evangelical Protestant Christianity, were also subtle essays on how slavery, product of unreason and sin, violated God's design.

Jefferson the deist saw nature as a balanced, self-sustaining, and harmonious "natural economy," one readily accessible to the eyes and the mind. A rational republic might reflect that economy and so produce and sustain virtue, for a time anyway.[2] But Jefferson professed to have doubts. He presented slavery and race as problems made insoluble by Negro resentment, white prejudice, and "the real distinctions which nature has made" between black and white.[3] Wheatley would have seen Jefferson's doubts as blasphemous. If a certain Calvinism, a sense of God's perfection and man's loathsome corruption, lurked beneath both

Wheatley's and Jefferson's visions of nature, Wheatley's God forgave and forgot sin. Forgiveness and redemption were built into the scheme of nature itself. Each day, the light of the morning dispelled the dreams, chaos, and "causeless strife" of night, when reason was "suspended" and passion ran rampant.[4] And Africans were children of a proverbially sun-drenched land. Wheatley was careful to use "sable" to describe the African's skin, not "dark" or "black," ancient Christian associations with sin and evil.[5] As she wrote in "On Being Brought from Africa to America," Africa could be seen as dark only as a place of souls "benighted" by unbelief, as she had been. Black skin was not evil. It was irrelevant:

> Some view our sable race with scornful eye,
> "Their colour is a diabolic die."
> Remember, *Christians*, *Negros*, black as *Cain*,
> May be refin'd, and join th' angelic train.[6]

Jefferson did not see Africans as diabolic or sinful exactly. Rather they were the embodiment of animality, lacking reason, imagination, self-restraint, and the ability to make free and rational choices, that ability being the only manner of salvation allowed by his deism. Africans' "blackness without," as the historian Winthrop Jordan put it, their "monotonous veil of black," in Jefferson's words, mirrored Jefferson's own anguished "blackness within," in Jordan's phrase, his fears of his own animality.[7] He tried to exile blacks from the promise of the new republic. In *Notes,* his defense of the New World and the American Revolution against European aspersions, Jefferson not only presented blacks as inferior and unassimilable. He cast corruption bred in whites by slavery as a mortal threat to the young natural republic. Even after emancipation, blacks, Jefferson wrote, would remain marked, hated, and bitter, whites corrupt and tyrannical. Race war would probably be inevitable and disastrous: "God has no attribute which can take side with us in such a contest." Sublimated Calvinism had apparently become fear of a racial apocalypse, nightmare of inevitable fight to the death of race against race, with justice and revenge both on blacks' side.[8]

Jefferson's "playing in the dark"[9] is captured by Wheatley's evocation of the experience of dream and night in perhaps her best poem,

"Thoughts on the Works of Providence," a paean (written a decade before *Notes*) to "this vast machine," creation:

> On pleasure now, and now on vengeance bent
> The lab'ring passions struggle for a vent.

That was Jefferson regarding race and slavery exactly. But Wheatley's God always provided the relief of morning, when His hand again would restore to reason the mastery over passion:

> What secret hand returns the mental train
> And gives improv'd thine active pow'r again?[10]

Jefferson refused that hand. Wheatley, victim of the Middle Passage, secure in her moral stance, could trust a just and forgiving God. Jefferson, guilty master of many Wheatleys, could only fear His justice.

On the subjects of race and slavery, he enjoyed no waking light, or rather wanted none. He claimed to be scientific and look only to nature for truth. Whether realizing it or not, however, he relied on his ingrained feelings as well as his intellect, perhaps more so. His use in *Notes* of the natural classification of the day, his attempt scientifically to fix blacks' place in the vast machine, were equivocal, and I suspect disingenuously so. Intentional or not, his equivocation yielded paralysis, the product of an eighteenth-century Enlightenment mind playing in the dark, not a nineteenth-century hard racist one.

I disagree with the common argument that *Notes* is the starting point for American scientific racism, that Jefferson is its founding father. In my view, these paternity suits are not strong; the DNA does not match. Not only is determining conceptual priority difficult and complicated, but Jefferson's concepts of self, nature, and nation differed too sharply from prevailing outlooks in the nineteenth and twentieth centuries. His perspective, as much as Wheatley's or other eighteenth-century African Americans', rested on the Whig idea of a natural harmony self-evident to the senses and, through the senses, to the mind. This idea, which was philosophical and often simplistically empirical, was central to the American Enlightenment and American revolutionary ideology. It was a notion that nineteenth-century biology and American racial discourse, white and black, focusing on inner structures and substance, would forego.

Nor was refuting *Notes* the starting point of African American race writing. In *Notes,* Jefferson in effect was reacting to a Phillis Wheatley, to her very existence and her accomplishments, however much he denigrated them. Subsequent African American expression in the late eighteenth and very early nineteenth centuries was not a mere response to *Notes*. Instead, such writing reprised Wheatley's brand of universal humanism and religiosity and spoke as she did with the moral authority derived from the sufferings and struggles of black people in a prejudiced and slave-ridden society. The Enlightenment concept of natural harmony structured black people's first attempts to write no less than it did Jefferson's pronouncements. The very idea of writing oneself free was typical of the eighteenth century, when writing seemed to be the visible sign of reason and imagination. Reason acting upon sense experience, according to John Locke, whose epistemology shaped the Ango-American Enlightenment, provided the only source of knowledge about the world. The innate faculties of reason and imagination ordered the testimony of the senses and defined humanity, distinguishing man from beast.

The first black writers—Wheatley, Jupiter Hammon, Ukiasaw Gronniosaw, Olaudah Equiano—believed that reason, imagination, and the capacity for Christian conversion were one and the same.[11] Conversion implied reason, imagination, humanity, and equality. In this view, Africans' capacity to write about conversion did not just prove black humanity but eventually suggested white inhumanity and moral inferiority. In the late eighteenth century, Anglo-African writing moved from presenting the slave trade as a kind of fortunate fall, bringing Africans into contact with civilization and God, to open mockery of slaveholding whites as hypocrites, no true Christians or civilized men. Such writing powerfully repudiated black skin as a natural category. "Blackness" was not seen as natural but as a word that referred to collective experience of the enormities of the Atlantic slave trade combined with the liberating potential of literacy and voice, encounters with the Bible and evangelical Protestantism, and the doctrines of universal equality and the rights of man.[12] Jefferson for his part denied to African Americans the very facul-

ties of reason and imagination; to him, their writing was below consideration, no evidence at all of their capacity for equal citizenship in a harmonious natural republic.

Notes remains the most important and influential eighteenth-century
American statement on race. During the past thirty years Jefferson has
been condemned as a racist, praised as an abolitionist, and psychoana-
lyzed as the founding father of modern white America's racial hang-ups,
guilt, and hypocrisy. A man full of contradictions and not given to revealing his intimate thoughts, he lends himself to these interpretations.
His psyche has proved extraordinarily difficult to reconstruct; in matters
of race and slavery the case regarding the sincerity of *Notes* can be made
either way. Perhaps there was no essential Jefferson, and he constantly
"played hide and seek with himself," as one recent biographer puts it.[13]
Jefferson can be seen as a representative figure in that many European
Americans have played hide and seek with themselves about race, proclaiming universal liberty and at the same time rationalizing their self-interest in denying that liberty to everyone, or at any rate finding ways to
argue that giving up that interest would be just too dangerous. His
words on race and slavery in *Notes* are remembered not only because he
was Thomas Jefferson, slaveholding revolutionary, author of the Declaration of Independence, buyer and seller of men, women, and children,
father to at least one of his slaves' children—but because his words were
in their contradictions profoundly effective.

These words were clearly part of Jefferson's vindication of a slaveholding Virginia and United States, not an un-self-conscious, blind *cri
de coeur.* They were included in a work purporting to be objective science. It is worthwhile to reconsider his dilemmas regarding race and
slavery in terms of the understandings in his time of the facts of nature:
that was the intellectual context for racial ideas, including Jefferson's.
Attention to the theories of the natural historians of his day suggests that
it would have been hard to conceive a more self-serving set of paradoxes
than the ones Jefferson came up with in *Notes.* If Jefferson's essence may
never be known or may not have existed, what might be understood
better than it has been are the language and concepts through which he
said such incongruous things. There have been enough efforts to read
through his words to whatever paradoxes, dilemmas, hypocrisies, or

games may have constituted his psyche. I am not trying to reveal, render judgment on, excoriate, or certainly not excuse or exonerate an essential Jefferson. The goal is to analyze *Notes* in relation to the natural history of its day and begin to present a fresh interpretation of late eighteenth-century Enlightened American discourse on race. From such an analysis can come a rethinking of the transition to nineteenth-century concepts.

Jefferson was prophetic in realizing—or claiming to realize, or deceiving himself into realizing—that race and slavery would corrupt and finally destroy his grand but static and superficial vision of the United States as a natural republic. He partly foresaw, and helped to shape, the future of slavery and race relations. His understanding of natural science, however, was not prescient. It was in fact based on what were becoming, by the 1780s, rather old-fashioned Enlightenment concepts. The future of American racial thought, racist and anti-racist, white and black, lay not in Jefferson's ideas but rather in the conceptual path blazed by naturalists who went beyond immediate sense experience. That path Jefferson did not tread, although he himself showed in *Notes* that all other roads led to a precipice.

☉ THE START OF "RACE"

The roots of European and American prejudices against Africans are ancient, preceding the introduction of slavery to the New World and much before then too. Rationalized languages of race are something else again. They are the product of eighteenth-century "natural history," which was the first systematic modern attempt to describe and understand living nature on the basis of observation and reason operating upon sense experience.

Long before the eighteenth century, the Western tradition had seen the existence of differentiated human groups marked by physical attributes. These attributes were sometimes understood as innate but more often as a function of climate. The Old Testament refers to the hot sun as related to African blackness. It also asks the seemingly innatist rhetorical question that racists have loved to quote: "Can the Ethiopian change his skin, or the Leopard his spots?" Homer ascribed the curly hair and black skin of the Ethiopians to the heat of the African sun, and theories for how the skin darkened in response to heat appear in classical sources, Roman geographical and natural tracts like the works of Pliny, and some early Christian and medieval discourses.[14] Notions that strangers and foreigners are different or inferior—"barbarians," as the Greeks said—carry an equally ancient pedigree. If the Bible said that all humans descended from Adam and Eve—the doctrine of "monogenesis"—there were also longstanding arguments for the separate origins of geographically distinct peoples, "polygenesis," a doctine that eventually came to mean that the races were distinct, separately created species.

Something about dark skin may have especially disturbed Europeans, whose heritage painted the devil black, and even more so northern Europeans, living through long dark nights. In English before 1600 the word "black" could mean, as seen in the early usages illustrated in the *Oxford English Dictionary:* "Deeply stained with dirt; soiled, dirty, foul" and "Having dark or deadly purposes, malignant; pertaining to or involving death, deadly; baneful, disastrous, sinister" and "Foul, iniquitous, atrocious, horrible, wicked."

But "blacks" only became a "race" in the fifteenth or sixteenth centuries, when animal breeding terminology seems to have fused with ancient ideas about aristocratic familial legacy and "blood." A noble house had long been referred to as a race, a usage sometimes broadened to the whole nation ruled by an aristocratic house; the first such broad national usage is cited in the *Oxford English Dictionary* from a source in 1600. That was the Age of Exploration, of conquest, and lineage understandings of race became intertwined with uses of the term to refer to varieties of shape, size, and color among different kinds of dogs, horses, cattle, and sheep. New "breeds" of men had been discovered by European explorers and conquerors circumnavigating the globe, setting up colonies in strange and distant places. Hence "race" connoted roughly geographical groups of people marked by supposedly common physical characteristics.[15]

In the eighteenth century "race" was also used to characterize all human beings, as distinct from the animal world. For instance, in several poems Wheatley made analogies between a single species of plant and all human beings, the latter seen emphatically as one "race," indeed a "blooming race" bending to the sun, evidence of God's creation. Here she did more than follow Milton—along with Pope, the poet she most revered—who in *Paradise Lost* had rumors in Heaven deem earth "the happy seat of some new Race call'd man." In "Thoughts on the Works of Providence" Wheatley in effect connected this (single species) use of "race" with eighteenth-century natural classification:

> All-wise Almighty providence we trace
> In trees, and plants, and all the flow'ry race;
> As clear as in the nobler frame of man
> All lovely copies of the Maker's plan.[16]

She put all humans together in a single species in sharper language in "To the University of Cambridge, in New England," her rebuke to Harvard College students for dissolutely squandering their opportunity to "scan the heights" of creation. That advantage was denied to "an Ethiop," a slave, and a woman. But such a person knew about the effects of sin:

> Ye blooming plants of human race divine,
> An *Ethiop* tells you 'tis your greatest foe;
> Its transient sweetness turns to endless pain,
> And in immense perdition sinks the soul.[17]

The "blooming plants of human race divine" is a natural classification. "Blooming" referred in many of her poems to all humanity's or an individual's fulfilling humankind's rational nature and recognizing God's glory. Her use of the term "sable race" was a national or lineal use of the term "race," like the "British race," with no natural connotations. It was an example of the variable, unresolved meanings of "race" in literary and public discourse, of how "race" was not inevitably understood as a natural category.

Yet as Wheatley knew, natural classification seemed essential to knowledge, to understanding and appreciating God's vast machine. Formed intellectually by Pope's mechanistic Newtonianism, she seems to have understood classification as most eighteenth-century Anglo-Americans did, as the process of naming a real, divinely ordained scheme or plan of natural creation, a scheme most easily discerned in the "flowr'y race."

Actually, modern natural classification, which originated in the early eighteenth century with the work of the great Swedish botanist and founder of plant and animal taxonomy, Carl von Linné, known as Linnaeus, broke with previous assumptions about a perfectly lawful natural order.[18] Linnaeus had not intended to discover a divinely ordained scheme. His method was in some respects deliberately arbitrary, his cosmology no confidently drawn picture of benevolent design thwarted only by human passions and perversity. Natural historical classification arose out of a growing awareness of the unique complexity of the living world. Yet order did obtain. Although thousands of species of trees had been discovered across the world and no two trees anywhere grew exactly alike, most trees were identifiably trees. Why and how? The sublunary realm of rocks, soil, birds, beasts, trees, and even men and women seemed to be not the same as the heavens, where moons and planets moved along paths that could be perfectly predicted. The new physics could even plot the path of a cannonball here on earth, but not the flight of a sparrow. But why not, and did it have to be so? Might not there be laws of living nature somehow equivalent to Newton's laws of motion, the great intellectual accomplishment of seventeenth-century Europe?[19] After a spurt of seventeenth-century optimism and failed attempts to reduce absolutely everything in the natural world to mathematical system, the answer often came to seem no.

When Jefferson and other major white intellectuals of the American Enlightenment recognized natural complexity, however, they tended to throw up their hands and retreat to confident statements about the natural truths that presumably could be perfectly grasped by man. Such truths, if derived, in Lockean theory, from sense experience, would be treated as if they were axioms deduced by a priori reasoning, as in mathematics. This contradictory pattern characterized Anglo-American science of the day, and it also can be seen in ideas about society. The British Glorious Revolution of the late seventeenth century led to a kind of compromise in form of the marriage of social hierarchies with reason and the notion of certain basic rights for all humans. The growing recognition of the enormous complexity of nature was mitigated by this compromise and did not much affect understandings of human nature and society. By the eighteenth century, even the somewhat anti-establishment tendencies of followers of the Scottish Enlightenment, especially its dissenting Protestant wing, did not abandon the British compromise entirely; they only charged the Anglican establishment with having violated self-evidently true universal rights and freedoms.[20]

On the European continent, the politics of nature and nation were rather different. Especially in France, the complexity of nature seemed overwhelming, to the point where certainties eroded, as the microscope opened up new worlds of tiny, marvelously constructed living beings and explorers and colonists in the Americas and Asia described an increasingly vast array of animals, plants, and people. "Physics" connoted the study of causes. Natural "history" to eighteenth-century scientists at first meant pure description of the natural world: the idea was that the natural world was too complicated, intricate, mysterious, and messy to admit of mathematical precision or perhaps even of causal analysis.[21] "History" became a process of naming the visible and then of tracing shifts in the visible over time due to changes in environment.

In our own time, Michel Foucault, despite or perhaps because of his hatred of the Enlightenment's attempt to use observation and reason to denominate not just an objective natural order but a universal norm of "man" and a normative social order, evoked the natural historical project incisively: "Natural history is nothing more than the nomination [naming] of the visible. Hence its apparent simplicity, and that air of näiveté it has from a distance, so simple does it appear and so obviously imposed by things themselves." In this view, the taxonomic schemes of natural history became possible only through the deliberate exclusion of almost everything that had made the world comprehensible and livable to previous ages. "One has the impression that with Tournefort, with Linnaeus or Buffon, someone has at last taken on the task of stating something that had been visible from the beginning of time, but had remained mute before a sort of invincible distraction of men's eyes. In fact, it was not an age-old inattentiveness being suddenly dissipated, but a new field of visibility being constituted in all its density." Natural history was the attempt to discern the order of the visible world by trying to ignore all the divine and magical depth earlier ages had perceived in words and things, or rather, in words-as-things.[22]

By contrast, the nineteenth century may be said with only slight exaggeration to have heralded the emergence of "life" and "history," as well as a newly self-conscious understanding of language. In biology, organisms were now dissected to discern their internal functioning instead of observed to tabulate their external characteristics into a system of nature, as eighteenth-century natural historians had supposedly done. One now had a concept of an "inside" of anatomical relations and physiological and psychological processes, and an "outside" of physical elements in which the organism resided and out of which it constituted and maintained itself. This conception was resolutely not "innatism." Nature and nurture still intertwined. Indeed, they intertwined more fully than ever before, to yield ideas of qualitative change over time in a single direction—not mere deviation from a norm. The organism came to be seen as growing, living, and dying in relation to and as part of its environment; entire species, races, and civilizations might themselves grow, change, and die or pass into new forms. Before the biological period, the idea of such organic transformation as qualitative development appears to have been almost inconceivable, because internal structure was not seen to develop in one direction over time. Instead, natural systems were dynamic equilibria that oscillated around a norm, so to speak, the oscillations produced by changes in external circumstance. Time, to quote Foucault, "is never conceived as a principle of development for living beings in their internal organization; it is perceived only as the possible bearer of revolution in the external space in which they live."[23] If somewhat overdrawn, this characterization captures Enlightenment environmentalism and suggests its differences from a nineteenth-century biological view in a way that avoids a nurture/nature dichotomy.

Yet this view does not fully recognize how complex and proto-historical were certain natural historical perspectives on classification and nature, such as those of Georges Louis Leclerc, Comte de Buffon, who was Linnaeus's main adversary and the greatest critic of the New World (and hence Jefferson's major adversary in *Notes* as well).[24] The "flat" taxonomy of Linnaeus (which was not in fact completely ahistorical) is taken as the eighteenth-century rule, and it is seen in excessively flat terms. By the same token, because Jefferson in *Notes* followed Linnaeus and repudiated Buffon, natural history in the United States has typically been read as a superficial taxonomic business that, with respect to race, merely codified white narcissism and perceptions born of slavery.[25] Jefferson was not so simple, however, and neither was Linnaeus.

Linnaeus did not enlist rationalism, a new sense of language, and the insights born of exploration and colonialism in the service of any version of "all men are created equal." Instead, he tried to preserve what he regarded as the hallowed, timeless, natural social hierarchies of his own Sweden. When Linnaeus began his studies as a provincial student at Uppsala University, he understood nature in basically medieval terms as a limited, neatly governed realm in which the names and uses of things were inscribed in their very nature. He expected to be able himself to examine and name every existing plant. It was his students' frustrating experiences grappling with nature's diversity as they fanned out across the globe on trips with the Swedish East India Company that alerted Linnaeus to nature's complexity and spurred him to attempt an arbitrary, tabulating method. He reasoned, in effect: look at a plant, name its parts. Patterns emerge in its particulars, in the small differences between it and similar plants. Set up a table of characteristics and compare them; if sufficient comparisons are made, the result will be a coherent and useful, if greatly arbitrary, set of terms defining species.

Once he had the insight to create such an arbitrary scheme, Linnaeus and his students tried numbered systems, trinomial classifications, and several other arrangements before he settled on his now-familiar genus/species binomials. For plants, the binomials were based on the number and shape of pistils and stamens; nipples and teeth eventually sufficed for animals. He hoped that this simple, practical, shorthand mode of classification would help to make Sweden prosperous and its elites secure and powerful. New forms of husbandry and local economic self-sufficiency would arise, as the fruits of European exploration led not to some far-flung Swedish empire but rather to new expertise to be applied at home to recreate nature's stupendous plenitude in full in and around Sweden itself. As Lisbet Koerner puts it, Linnaeus envisioned "Lapland cinnamon groves, Baltic tea plantations, and Finnish rice paddies," all rationally managed by and for the gain of king, aristocrat, cleric, and farm owner.[26]

Linnaeus boasted that anyone could quickly learn his system from his brief, well-organized, simply written Latin instruction manuals (the most famous and influential of which was the 1758 edition of his *Systema Naturae*). But his stress on the useful stemmed in part from cynicism about man's capacity ever to act really rationally. In the preface to the

1758 *Systema Naturae,* he warned readers that if theologically the final goal of creation was to produce man, man was, naturally considered, an animal, naked and frail. As Koerner shows, Linnaeus wavered between seeing nature as a paradise for man's rational use and seeing man as a weak and contemptible thing, no better than a monkey. His classification of the genus *Homo* reflected that basic ambivalence. Sometimes he divided between man and ape merely in terms of night versus day, *Homo diurnus* versus *Homo nocturnus;* elsewhere he would contrast thinking to unthinking, *Homo sapiens* to *Homo troglodytes.* But he would also often say that apes had language, fought wars, executed criminals, and sang in choirs, and that the two species blended into one another imperceptibly through intermediate forms.[27] Within *Homo (sapiens) diurnus,* he counted five unranked categories, *ferus, americanus, europaeus, asiaticus,* and *afer,* plus one category for "monstrous" freaks of humanity, *monstrosus.*

That Linnaeus treated *ferus* (meaning "wild men" who grew up alone in the wilderness) as equivalent to geographical classifications like *americanus* or *europaeus* shows how arbitrary the scheme was. Linnaeus never arranged creation in an ordered "Great Chain of Being" with glorious man at the top. And Linnaeus did not see species, even man, as fixed and ordained but changeable both by environment and especially interspecies hybridization, which created new species over time. In private, he mocked man, God, and the very idea of benevolent design: "Oh what kind of marvelous animals are we, for whom everything else in the world is created. We are created out of a foaming drop of lust in a disgusting place . . . We grow up in foolishness like apes and guenon monkeys. Our daily task is to prepare from our food disgusting shit and stinking piss. In the end we must become the most stinking corpses."[28]

Jefferson would not have echoed these sentiments. In *Notes,* he used the fairly common idea that chimpanzees mated with African women not as Linnaeus would have used it, as testimony of human animality and closeness to apes, but as proof of the Negro's bestial distance from the rationally governed white man. Essential nature, not a history of circumstance, explained differences between black and white. African American writers like Wheatley presented all human beings as standing at the pinnacle of earthly creation. These writers did not present sin as animality, nor fear the encroachment, sexual or otherwise, of animalistic nature into a human realm. For them, sin, like reason and imagination, was entirely a human affair. There was no animal/rational axis, and classification was unproblematic as applied to all men and women: all were human.

Jefferson had some inkling of the epistemological doubts behind natural historical method, an inkling which he used to cast as overblown nonsense European theorizing about nature. Thus he justified his stance of naive empiricism in *Notes,* and flatly listed, in what he took to be the Linnaean spirit, the glories of Virginia's flora, fauna, institutions, and virtue. This was his repudiation of Buffon, the most philosophically sophisticated and dynamically-minded of eighteenth-century naturalists, and the New World's most important critic. In the early portions of Buffon's classic *Histoire Naturelle,* which appeared in forty-four volumes from 1749 to 1804 (five volumes published by his assistant, Daubenton, after the author's death in 1788), he deemed the uncivilized New World cold, wet, and unhealthy, harboring only undeveloped, savage beasts and men without sexual desire, all very inferior to the "mature," developed, civilized, intensely sexual Old World peoples and their moderate, cultivated environment. The cosmopolitan Buffon was contemptuous of moralizing and conventional piety and traced human drive and human progress, civilization, and refinement to sexuality: he posited no opposition between reason and passion. He also took an exalted view of all humans as capable of great refinement and improvement, and he espoused egalitarianism and the abolition of slavery. He hated slavery and despised the word "race" as a classificatory term applied to humans, always preferring to use "people" or "nation."

➌ NATURE AS A LIVING WORK: BUFFON

Buffon based classification and his whole natural system on human perceptions of change and stability in nature over time. Nature, he proclaimed, was "a perpetually living work, a constantly active worker . . . The springs that she uses are living forces, which space and time can only measure and limit without ever destroying: forces that balance one another, merge, and oppose each other without ever destroying one another."[29] These forces were perhaps not so different from those in physics. According to Buffon, who began his scientific career as a mathematician and physicist, Newton's law of gravity was fundamentally incomprehensible, an "occult force." Gravity involves action at a distance, in the human imagination a contradiction in terms. But if nothing seemed to connect apples on trees to the earth, in all human experience they always fell down, and always at the same measurable and predictable rate: thus Newton's laws of motion took on, in Buffon's terms, "a probability so great that it is equivalent to certitude." Nothing of "physical truth," nature's basic reality, the world beyond the human mind, was knowable or as self-evident in the same way as "mathematical truths," based as they were entirely on human reason, which Buffon took to be the self-sufficiency and self-evidence of logic. Yet physical truths, in so far as they could be discovered through human observation of change over time, were superior because not mere tautologies.[30]

Buffon took Locke's conviction that the mind functioned only by combining sensory impressions as a call for a "general" natural history: a bona fide system like Newton's laws that, if not nearly so mathematical, would go beyond the purely arbitrary. Working out such a system required broad comparisons of diverse species from diverse environments, so that the mind could "little by little form lasting impressions, which soon are linked in our intelligence through fixed and invariable relationships, and from there we reach more general views," yielding laws of nature.[31] A "matière vivante" or vital force seemed to cause "organic molecules" to organize themselves into living beings. If Buffon could not explain exactly how such organization took place, and the theory had problems, as an admiring reviewer succinctly put it in 1750, Buffon had achieved much: "He shows that it is necessary to have recourse to *an ever-active, organic matter, always given over to shaping itself,* to making itself, and to producing beings similar to those which house it."[32]

This historical, forces-acting approach led to a new system of classification, based on reproduction. Species, Buffon said, was "an abstract and general term," an invention of human minds. All individuals in nature were each separate beings, detached from other beings, with nothing in common at any one point in time except that they strongly resembled certain other individuals. But it was actually "the constant succession and renewing of these individuals which constitute them [species]. It is by comparing the present state of nature with that of the past, and actual individuals with former, that has given us a clear idea of what is called species." Although the donkey resembles the horse more than the barbet the greyhound, the latter two, since they produce fertile offspring, are varieties within a single species; the horse and ass are different species, since their offspring are "vicious and unfruitful individuals." And (contra Linnaeus) since no one had ever observed one variety give rise to another that could not breed fertile offspring with the original, the environment never created new species, only varieties.[33]

By the same token, since all the varieties of man could propagate together, all humans were and would always remain unquestionably a single species. More important to Buffon, taking a view of living beings over the life cycle made plain the chasm separating humankind from all other species, none of which had ever displayed human ingenuity or built civilizations. Looked at on an anatomist's slab, a human might seem no more than a hairless ape, as Linnaeus had wryly observed. For Buffon, however, broad comparisons taking time into account clearly showed that human beings were unique in nature and that they had existed and struggled in time more than any other species. Only humans possessed advanced language and complex memory, could combine sensory impressions in creative ways, and had cleared the land, tilled the soil, and built cities and states.[34] But circumstances sometimes prevented them from using their capacities to the full and improving their lot. For instance, "Negroes," a term Buffon applied mainly to the inhabitants of West Africa, were inferior to other varieties of mankind as a result of the effects over time of the marshy, foul air, sweltering heat, and the rank, overgrown fecundity of the worst of the African tropics. Yet Negroes bred true with whites, and it testified to man's nobility as a species that the Negro type quickly disappeared as the worst African regions became more temperate. For Buffon, most Africans were definitely not "Negroes."[35] And his discussion of Negroes included a powerful antislavery sermon. Almost everywhere, he was sure, people could improve their circumstances and themselves.

Over time, watery, fetid swamp lands subject to extremes of temperature gradually had given way to dry, hospitable, temperate terrain—as the internal fires of the globe subsided after creation, and as human civilization cleared the land, further moderating the climate. Animals and plants became larger, more healthy, more vigorous, and humans became bigger, stronger, more vital. Human libido increased; civilization emerged as an outgrowth of sociability and family feeling based on sexuality.

But the New World was just that, new—immature, recently raised from the deeps. Its environment and its flora and fauna, humans included, were undeveloped, greatly inferior to their counterparts in the Old World. For Buffon, Native Americans—although still human because they could breed true with Old World peoples—were probably not originally Old World men and women who had migrated to the New World and degenerated there. Native Americans seemed indigenous to the Americas, sharing the New World's weakness and immaturity. Buffon wrote, in a passage that so infuriated Jefferson that he translated and reprinted it in *Notes:* "The [American] savage is feeble, and has small organs of generation; he has neither hair nor beard, and no ardor whatever for his female . . . he is also less sensitive, and yet more timid and cowardly; he has no vivacity, no activity of mind; the activity of his body is less an exercise, a voluntary motion, than a necessary action caused by want; relieve him of hunger and thirst, and you deprive him of the active principle of all his movements; he will rest stupidly upon his legs or lying down entire days."[36]

Jefferson seemingly did not see the resemblance between Buffon's view of Indians and his own view of blacks as passive animals who could not be moved but by compulsion. Sexuality did not strike Jefferson as the very basis for society and civilization. He had blacks as coarsely sensual but animalistic (unrestrainedly lustful) and sluggish, while Buffon had Indians as cold and sexless and therefore incapable of love, family, or civilization: "their heart is frozen, their society cold, their empire cruel."[37] Buffon privileged heat, force, and drive. The rather squeamish Jefferson, himself a professed deist but of an essentially Calvinist background, fearful of the passions and apparently suffering the psychosexual complexes of the white male slaveholder, prized reflection, harmony, and balance. Those he claimed to find only in whites.

Buffon did attribute heat, force, and drive to the European colonists in the New World. Possibly taking the idea from Montesquieu, and influenced by Benjamin Franklin's 1755 *Observations Concerning the Increase of Mankind, Peopling of Countries, etc.,* which reported geometric population growth in the North American colonies, Buffon argued that the European colonists, as ambassadors from a "mature" environment and high civilization, could bring civilization, prosperity, and a quick maturity.[38] Most of Buffon's readers scarcely noted this part of the *Histoire*'s comments, so powerful and prominent were his earlier assaults upon the harsh stepmother American Nature and her stunted, feeble children. Like Europeans, educated Americans read the *Histoire*. Next to Linnaeus's *Systema Naturae* the most popular natural historical work of the day, the *Histoire* was brilliantly written, often sensationalist, and the model for the genre of natural description and also for French prose style. (In 1795, when newly founded Union College in Schenectady, New York, decided to allow students to elect to study a "living" language rather than Latin or classical Greek, Buffon's *Natural History* provided the text for French studies.)[39]

Buffon's reputation as a thinker fared less well, especially in North America. In Europe, the late eighteenth century saw a trend among European naturalists away from generalization and nebulous, essentially untestable hypotheses like "organic molecules" and toward concrete, smaller-scale studies of discrete organisms or types of organisms or ecosystems. D'Alembert contemptuously dismissed Buffon as "le grand phraseur."[40] American readers could not see the forest of his sophisticated historical approach for the trees of his depictions of exotic people and beasts. And Buffon had inspired other European writers like Peter Kalm, Cornelius de Pauw, and the Abbé Raynal to malign the New World environment as one aspect of their broad attack on the European conquest of the New World as a story of greed, slavery, and extermination, and the American Revolution as a fraud.[41]

Americans had to reply, and "the Dispute of the New World," as historian Antonello Gerbi terms it, was in full swing by the 1780s. Several refutations of Buffon, Raynal, and de Pauw, most by physicians and based on concrete examples and statistical compilations, appeared in the American Philosophical Society's *Transactions*.[42] And Jefferson's *Notes* was written to reassert North America's value and independence when both—not to mention his own political career—seemed in dire peril. In 1779, the head of the French legation in Philadelphia had sent a questionnaire to prominent Americans about conditions and prospects for trade in their respective states. In *Notes* Jefferson attempted to frame comprehensive answers and describe and champion the New World in natural historical terms. The French legation dispatched its questionnaire, and Jefferson began compiling materials, at the time of the disastrous Battle of Camden, North Carolina, where a unit of Virginia militia had disgraced itself. In Virginia itself, the state assembly was starting to question Jefferson's handling, as governor, of the state's war effort. The French had sunk millions of francs into the American war. Would it be worth it, with the Americans on the verge of defeat? If Buffon was right about the New World, what immediate benefits could be expected from the United States, even if the Americans did the impossible and won the Revolution? At home, having finished his term as governor and recuperating from a riding accident and the death of his infant daughter, Jefferson completed *Notes*. Written largely in 1780 and 1781, printed privately in Paris in 1784 and for the public in London in 1787, *Notes* was "probably the most important scientific and political book written by an American before 1785."[43] It was also the most prominent contribution by an American to the Dispute of the New World.

❧ BLACKNESS AS AN OLD WORLD DISEASE

The Dispute emerged just as some Americans were first beginning to believe that the systematic study of nature mattered to their lives. Franklin, as Esmond Wright has shown, embodied this shift from a fatalistic Calvinist determinism, seeing nature as part of God's inexorable, inscrutable will, to the deist belief in a somehow balanced system of nature wherein God had no immediate place and upon which human beings could act for the better.[44] Such a perspective was a good way to address the contradictions of the conquest of the New World, including slavery. A certain naturalism could seemingly resolve the contradiction of the American idyll or new Eden as also a place of extremes of savagery and death, of avarice, disease, slavery, cannibalism, and torture.

Was all nature or society like the harmoniously designed economy of parts of an individual organism, or did natural and social equilibrium result instead from what Linnaeus himself termed nature's constant "war of all against all," a dynamic process of competing forces? Either way, blacks would be given little place in a natural republic. Indeed, their presence could seem to threaten a kind of Hobbesian state of war inside the United States itself.

Peter Onuf has recently argued that Jefferson saw blacks as a captive "nation" at war with the United States, or rather a captive nation created by the experience of slavery, just as British tyranny had engendered national consciousness among "Americans." And this incipient black "nation" would of course hate white Americans. Without black emigration, race war would be inevitable. According to Onuf's Jefferson, blacks hated and suffered too much to become citizens of the republic: they were a separate, implacably inimical people in their own right. Emancipation hence had to be followed by transportation to some land that they could call their own, where, he wrote in *Notes,* they could become a nation in themselves. Virginia might send them out "with arms, implements of household and of the handicraft arts, seeds, pairs of the useful domestic animals, &c. to declare them a free and independent people, and extend to them our alliance and protection, till they shall have acquired strength." Jefferson's discussion of blacks' (to him mostly inferior) characteristics followed this passage, as an explanation for why blacks could never be assimilated into Virginia. Psychologically he perhaps needed one beyond the resentments generated by slavery.[45]

In Jefferson's presentation in *Notes,* black slaves became a kind of Hobbesian threat posed to the otherwise harmonious natural republic by the Old World's machinations. Jefferson cast whites and potentially reds as the healthy human norm and a republic of transplanted Europeans and assimilated Indians as a healthily functioning whole with little strife, at least so long as an agrarian mode of society maintained. Yeoman virtue and proper social institutions could prevent base passions and strife from gaining control. Bring blacks into the New World, though, and vicious competition, corruption, and violence ensued—the Old World's awful gift to the New. It was for him not so much a matter of dynamic competition among peoples but of the introduction of a disruptive, resentful, and inferior alien force into an otherwise harmonious balance of nature and society. Jefferson thus used the Dispute once again to shift responsibility for slavery from himself and his class to Old World greed. In his landmark revolutionary tract *Summary View of the Rights of British America,* written in 1774, and then two years later in the original draft of the Declaration of Independence, he had blamed slavery in British America on Europe, especially the British king, a passage that the Continental Congress, balking at such blatant hypocrisy, excised.[46]

It is in Franklin rather than Jefferson that we have the first great American champion of the philosophy of replacing divine commands with natural imperatives, God's terrors and ineffable will with nature's knowable, manipulable design. Franklin did not start out this way. When the horrors of smallpox ravaged Boston in the 1720s, James Franklin and his younger brother Benjamin Franklin, in their *New England Courant,* had assailed Cotton Mather's and Zabdiel Boylston's inoculation campaign as ungodly and absurd: by impeding the spread of disease, inoculation interfered with God's designs and His righteous punishment of sinners. Disease had little to do with maintaining health, much less dynamic equilibrium. But by the 1760s, inoculation had fully caught on, and few Americans, including Franklin, took seriously worries about tampering with divine provenance by preventing plague.[47] By then, to men like Franklin, raw nature need not be either brutally, desperately conquered or left alone but rationally tamed, by and for human civilization, by clever, ambitious, yet virtuous men. Just as smallpox could and should be prevented, clearing forests and draining swamps would quickly reduce disease and moderate the climate, making America even more healthy and populous and Americans ever more robust exemplars of individual success and self-restraint.

American analyses of the mainland climate, mostly written by physicians, discussed climatic changes as the result of a reparable imbalance in the properly harmonious natural economy of fluids or humors, a conception tracing back to Galen and Aristotle. In 1770 the physician Hugh Williamson sent a paper to the American Philosophical Society, "An Attempt to account for the CHANGE of CLIMATE, which has been observed in the Middle Colonies in North America." The Philosophical Society, founded by Franklin in 1743 and presided over by men like the distinguished physician Benjamin Rush and later the scientist David Rittenhouse and Jefferson himself, was the scientific center of Philadelphia, itself the intellectual capital of America, "the pineal gland of the republic," as John Adams put it.[48] According to Williamson, in the Middle Atlantic colonies "our winters are not so intensely cold, nor our summers so disagreeably warm as they have been." Human cultivation of the land moderated the climate, a process that he had worked out on what he granted were "trite and general reasonings" about the action of sun and wind on cleared and cultivated land as opposed to wild and overgrown land.[49] Williamson asked other physicians to keep track of clearing and climate to provide detailed proofs, concretely and commonsensically reasoned out.

Jefferson himself did not abjure modifying nature to achieve a better balance of forces. At Monticello he was forever experimenting, often wildly, with new crops and farming methods. His schemes also went further afield. In a 1786 letter to a member of the Académie des sciences, he proposed to dig a canal through the "isthmus of Panama," which would supposedly provide an easy passage to the Pacific and enhance trade, make the Gulf of Mexico more navigable by mitigating strong currents, and stop the Gulf Stream, thus making navigation easier across the whole Atlantic seaboard.[50] Rather than conceding that the New World was intrinsically any more extreme in climate than the Old, Jefferson cast his Panama canal project as merely pragmatic, a simple cure for a set of obvious problems.

When it came to social issues, tinkering with the status quo was a mistake to believers in "harmonious" (static) natural equilibrium.[51] Poverty, for instance, could not be cured by legislation. In a 1753 letter on immigration to the New World, Franklin compared English and German immigrants: although from the same stock and similar climates, the English sometimes became lazy and feckless in America, while hardworking Germans prospered. Franklin wondered if the poor laws "peculiar to England, which *compel the rich to maintain the poor,* have not given the latter a dependence, that very much lessens the care of providing against the wants of old age." Providing too much relief for the poor upset the "scheme of Providence" and did "more harm than good." (Similarly, Jefferson, when he argued against taking any direct action against slavery, would fall back on the "more harm than good" line in defensive, fatalistic terms.) Equating natural and social economies, Franklin compared the poor laws to attempts by New England farmers to destroy the blackbirds that ate the corn; the result was that a "kind of worm" fed upon by the blackbirds "increased prodigiously," leading to much greater losses in grass than savings in corn; the farmers "wished again for their black-birds."[52] Franklin did not see the increase in worms as a result of dynamic equilibrium that could change and adjust, and hence could be substantially manipulated: to him the farmer's actions had wrecked the natural system. One might equate Franklin's reasoning with Williamson's or the other Philosophical Society writers about improving the climate. Strong and virtuous effort was required of man to clear the land and create salubrity, a kind of natural process on the order of requiring poor people to support themselves, and Franklin had the New World as a poor white man's free labor paradise, which for a time it was, especially in the Middle Atlantic states. That paradise only seemed possible, however, if humans struggled to improve themselves, such struggle being their appointed role in the natural order. If they did not, it would be like killing the blackbirds: the system would be upset.

In *Observations Concerning the Increase of Mankind,* Franklin had wanted to keep blacks out of North America, a desire he presented as natural, because people want to be with their own esthetically pleasing and familiar compatriots (among whom he included Native Americans).[53] He did not cast a black presence as wrecking the natural economy of society. By the end of his career, partly through contact with radical antislavery French physiocrats, the increasingly cosmopolitan Franklin, who met Wheatley in London in 1773, no longer saw blacks even as ugly. He affirmed the intellectual ability and rights of African Americans.

Other enlightened, antislavery white Americans, applying a medical model, anticipated an easy cure for the Old World plague. Williamson, Rush, Benjamin Smith Barton (a prominent Philadelphia physician who wrote an important defense of the American climate for the Philosophical Society), and others expected blacks actually to turn white in temperate America, once they acquired their freedom. Medical explanations were concocted to explain the coming change, seen as both cure and beautification. A craze developed to discover instances of "white Negroes," persons of African descent with so-called Negroid features but whitened skin, who were sometimes understood as evidence that all northern free blacks would soon whiten up.

Rush, perhaps North America's staunchest eighteenth-century adherent of Scottish Enlightenment doctrines, was the American to search hardest for white Negroes. The connection was not accidental.[54] Scottish commonsense philosophy built upon Locke's ideas to argue that since the mind was a passive *tabula rasa* (blank slate) impressed upon by sense experience and since all humans received sense impressions the same way, God must have given all of them as a species the ability to understand clearly and to reason correctly about the world. There existed a "moral sense" and an "aesthetic sense," so that moral and aesthetic judgments, and hence beauty and religious truth, were objectively real and the same for everyone. Classification as well was a natural human ability: any classificatory system that relied upon the senses, as Linnaeus's supposedly did, would accurately describe reality. Thomas Reid, a leading figure in the Scottish Enlightenment, reproached Buffon for attacking Linnaeus's system as too arbitrary and dismissed Buffon's scheme as pure and pernicious atheistic materialism. According to Reid, whatever Linnaeus's intent, the Linnaean or any other system built upon plain human observation would inevitably approach truth.[55] Rush, following the ideas of Reid and David Hartley, founder of associational psychology, believed that faith and reason were fully compatible: the world was perfectly designed and comprehensible, both spiritually and physically. To Rush, God had indeed so providentially made the world that the antidote for rattlesnake venom would inevitably exist in some plant native to the rattlesnake's environment.

Rush spent a desperate ingenuity, both before and after the Revolution, working out what the ready cure for blackness might be. His first effort came in a famous paper of 1773 defending Negro intelligence and humanity in a most cosmopolitan way (and citing Phillis Wheatley as proof). Rush went so far as to argue that the notion of Negro ugliness was mere chauvinistic partiality. His foray into aesthetic relativism was brief, however. By the late 1780s he was developing his well-known theory that West African miasmas caused an endemic leprosy that blackened the skin, a condition perpetuated in America by the awful conditions of slavery. Rush believed that American physicians would find a remedy. Until then, however, intermarriage between Negroes and whites had to be strongly discouraged, for reasons of public hygiene (and presumably beauty).[56] The natural republic was a glorious, God-given harmony that the presence of black-skinned people disturbed, but to Rush the sickness did not seem fatal. Freedom and nature would triumph.

A supposed case in point was the celebrated Henry Moss, an African American from Maryland who seems to have known a profitable thing when he saw it in the mirror: mottled white spots spreading across his body. In 1795 he appeared in Philadelphia, where Dr. Charles Caldwell, a protégé of Rush, established Moss at an inn and helped put him on exhibit for a fee as a natural historical curiosity. Philadelphia's naturalists turned out in force. Moss did well: according to various accounts, he purchased his family's freedom, moved to Virginia, bought a farm, and turned completely white. In the 1790s some of Moss's patrons, still imbued with the idea of the American natural republic as a healthy white body, could claim to believe that all free African Americans might quickly experience such a whitening "cure" and have a place in American society that they could not have if they were free but still black.[57]

Joanne Melish has recently argued that in what would become the American "North," especially New England, late eighteenth-century European Americans were already coming to see their society as both "free" and "white." During and after the American Revolution, northern states enacted gradual emancipation schemes, with slaves generally having to earn their freedom through decades of continued service. In this hesitant, gradual "first emancipation," to use Arthur Zilversmit's phrase, northerners began to disown their deep connections with the slave trade and forget about the significant role that slaves, especially domestics, would continue to play for some time in the developing "free labor" northern economy. The desire to find "white Negroes" certainly testifies to this growing exercise in denial.[58] At the same time, the major figures in the white-Negro debate were not really northern amnesiacs but people from the Middle Atlantic states like Rush or Barton who took a national perspective that denounced slavery and conceded its significance —and that of the free black presence—to "free" territory. Nor did the most important such figure, and the early republic's major race theorist, Samuel Stanhope Smith, president of the College of New Jersey, actually predict general short-term Negro whitening in America: to him, Henry Moss was the exception proving the rule of the persistence of blackness in the United States. Like Jefferson, Stanhope Smith perceived the full extent of the problem.[59] As for Jefferson himself, when he discussed white Negroes in *Notes,* he had them as diseased, "an anomaly of nature," instances of albinism with skin "a pallid, cadaverous white, untinged with red."[60] To Jefferson, blackness was healthy for Negroes, who belonged in Africa or anywhere else but Virginia and the United States.

⊛ NOTES ON VIRGINIA: AMERICAN PARTICULARS

That was the lesson of reason operating on the testimony of experience. In *Notes,* Jefferson less exalted abstract reason than clung to particulars in recognition of the precariousness of human knowledge and of the American republic's fate. If the cosmos was as finely tuned as a clock, human reason and observation were for Jefferson too limited to figure out all the parts and their workings. It was a characteristic saying of his, as he put it in *Notes,* that "nature has hidden from us her modus vivendi." Human beings could not discover nature's true essence. Abstract, deductive reason was more limited still.

Decades later Jefferson set down what he described as his "habitual anodyne," in a letter to John Adams: "I feel therefore I exist." For Jefferson, feeling did not here mean emotion, but sensation, as the rest of the passage made clear: "I feel bodies which are not myself: there are other existences then. I call them *matter.* I feel them changing place. This gives me *motion.* Where there is an absence of matter, I call it *void,* or *nothing,* or *immaterial space.* On the basis of sensation, of matter and motion, we may erect the fabric of all the certainties we can have or need."[61] For Jefferson, thinking itself probably had a material basis, and there seemed nothing otherworldly about consciousness (he did not believe in life after death): "Thought may be a faculty of our material organization," he wrote in 1803 to the French physician and naturalist Pierre Jean Georges Cabanis.[62]

Jefferson seems to have discussed the abstract problem of natural classification only once, thirty years after writing *Notes,* in a letter to Dr. John Manners concerning gardening. He here expressed a strong nominalism, the view that natural classifications are arbitrary names, mere categories of human language and thought not in any way inscribed in the nature of things. "Nature has, in truth, produced units only through all her works. Classes, orders, genera, species, are not of her work. Her creation is of individuals. No two animals are exactly alike, no two plants, nor even two leaves or blades of grass; no two crystallizations." Buffon would have agreed, but where Buffon went on to argue that all "physical truths" were provisional and depended on human observation of change over time, Jefferson writing to Manners took a static view which assumed that true knowledge of the physical world had to be definite and timeless. Classification in his view did not meet the standard and so had to be seen as a mere language of convenience so that humans could communicate their observations about a real and stable if basically ineffable natural world. For that purpose, Jefferson believed, Linnaean binomial classification, having come into general use and having the virtue of being fairly simple, easy to remember, and, significantly, based on visible characteristics, would do. He rejected the classificatory schemes of the new generation of major naturalists, like the founder of comparative anatomy, Johann Gottfried von Blumenbach, or the great French biologist, Baron Georges Cuvier, as being cumbersome and virtually unusable because they were based too much on internal anatomy and hence dissection. "It would certainly be better to adopt as much as possible such exterior and visible characteristics as every traveler is competent to observe, to ascertain, and to relate."[63]

In *Notes* itself, Jefferson had made no theoretical pronouncements on natural classification. His tables comparing the size of animals common to Europe and America, and of forms unique to each continent, followed Buffon, although he did argue that the American round-horned elk, the American rabbit, and certain squirrels seemed to be distinct New World species because their descriptions could not be reconciled with those given for similar European forms. "These, I think, are the only instances in which I have departed from the authority of Mons. de Buffon in the construction of this table. I take him for my ground work, because I think him the best informed of any Naturalist who has ever written." Yet it seemed obvious to Jefferson that Buffon and Daubenton simply had not actually "measured, weighed, or seen" the buffalo, deer, wolf, and several other American animals, for the weights the French gave were simply too low.[64] Jefferson's list of Virginia's vegetables used the Linnaean binomials, which had by then become the lingua franca of botany. In a listing of Virginia's birds as described in an illustrated work by traveler Mark Catesby, he supplied Catesby's, Linnaeaus's, and Buffon's designations for each species, without comparing or ranking the three.

In Jefferson's presentation, all these supposedly unvarnished facts testified that Buffon's idea of the inferiority of New World nature was absurd, an instance of prejudice and over-theoretical imagination running away with the facts. Rejecting all attempts, including those by Buffon and Voltaire, to explain the presence of what seemed to be fossilized sea creatures in rocks in the high Andes, Jefferson pronounced: "Ignorance is preferable to error; and he is less remote from the truth who believes nothing, than he who believes what is wrong."[65] He acknowledged that certain parts of America were as cold and wet as Buffon said, but observation showed that some useful animals, like cattle, were largest and healthiest in cold and damp climates, in America as well as Europe: Buffon's equation of small animals with coldness or extremes of climate had to be rejected, and in any case climatic extremes were greater in Paris than in Williamsburg, the warmest spot in Virginia. Enormous bones had been discovered in the Ohio country, and since according to Jefferson extinction violated the economy of nature and was therefore impossible, the mammoth probably still roamed somewhere on the American continent. Contra Buffon, Jefferson also reiterated Franklin's arguments about North American population growth and praised what he saw as the many instances of American genius.

As for Native Americans, Jefferson took great exception to Buffon's bleak assessment; Jefferson gave American Indians considerably more sympathy and reasonable, if romanticized, understanding than he gave to African Americans. As Jordan put it, Jefferson's might be seen as a "dichotomous view of triracial America." He declared that familiarity with Indians taught that they were anything but Buffon's "automatons." Any coldness in demeanor or listlessness among American Indians resulted from the hardships of their savage life, which they bore stoically, with courage and honor, as witnessed by the magnificent, passionate orations given by the Indian chiefs. By implication, although Jefferson did not say it openly in *Notes* (he would do so later in his career), Indians might in time be completely incorporated into white society and republicanism. Analysis of Indian languages revealed many similarities to Asian tongues. Repudiating Buffon's view of Native Americans as probably indigenous to the New World, Jefferson reasoned that the Indians' forefathers had emigrated to the New World from Asia in ancient times. "More facts are wanted" in order to judge the Indian's mental capacity fairly, and when the facts were in, and allowance was made for the circumstances of Indian life that called for display of only certain talents, "we shall probably find" that Native Americans "are formed in mind as well as body, on the same module with the 'homo sapiens Europeaus.'" (Here Jefferson inserted a note citing "homo sapiens Europeaus" as Linnaeus's "Definition of a Man" in the *Systema Naturae*.) He here finally touched upon the species/variety question: "I do not mean to deny, that there are varieties in the race of man, distinguished by their powers both of body and mind. I believe there are, as I see to be the case in the races of other animals."[66] But animals' "bulk and faculties" did not depend on which side of the Atlantic they inhabited: nature did not take sides. Note the vagueness of "races" here—did Jefferson mean species or varieties?

Only in the most impassioned complaint against what he saw as Buffon's pointless and destructive abstractions did Jefferson directly approach the species problem, albeit in equivocal terms. In a passage that was probably meant to recall Shylock's "Do I not bleed?" speech Jefferson wrote: "As if both sides [of the Atlantic] were not warmed by the same genial sun; as if a soil of the same chemical composition, was less capable of elaboration into animal nutriment; as if the fruits and grains from that soil and sun, yielded a less rich chyle, gave less extension to the solids and fluids of the body, or produced sooner in the cartilages, membranes and fibres, that rigidity which restrains all further extension, and terminates animal growth." All life grew in the same basic way, and size did not matter fundamentally: "The truth is, that a Pigmy and a Patagonian, a Mouse and a Mammoth, derive their dimensions from the same nutritive juices." It did not much signify how or why the nutritive juices worked or were limited, and humans could probably never know anyway, for the difference in increment in growth "depends on circumstances unsearchable to beings with our capacities." "Certain laws of extension" imposing an upper and lower size limit were given to "every race of animals" at creation, laws somehow built into organic structure. "What intermediate station they shall take may depend on soil, on climate, on food, on a careful choice of breeders. But all the manna of heaven would never raise the Mouse to the bulk of the Mammoth."[67] Hence even if American nature was smaller (and careful consideration of what limited evidence as yet existed testified that it was not), it would not mean to Jefferson any great inferiority, any basic "immaturity." One must wonder if Jefferson understood or even knew of the overarching historical theory of classification and development that framed Buffon's attack on the New World.

And here, in his most general and sweeping condemnation of Buffon, Jefferson did not use the formal term "species" but instead what was in his usage the vague, undefined "race." That usage came as part of his testimony to the inadequacy of human reason. He was less race theorist than racial obscurantist. As Jordan showed, Jefferson's use of blackness harked back to thinking previous to the advent of natural history, to the idea of evil and sin as inscribed in black skin. Blackness to him was not a word, a figure of speech, a mere description, or historical construct, but a God-given natural entity. Jefferson's deliberate obscurity regarding "race" in a purportedly scientific discussion was integral to his construction of the American slavery problem as intractable.

❧ RACE AND SENSIBILITY

Observe Jefferson's language at the crucial point in the text: "I advance it as a suspicion only, that the blacks, whether originally a distinct race, or made distinct by time and circumstance, are inferior to whites, both in body and mind. It is not against experience to suppose, that different species of the same genus, or varieties of the same species, may possess different qualifications." These two sentences do not fit together. In the first ("I advance it as a suspicion only"), Jefferson signally did not say that blacks might have become a "distinct species" or "distinct variety." He said that they might have become a "distinct race." Again, he used the equivocal term "race" because "variety" would have meant to his way of thinking superficial environmentally-produced differences in *Homo sapiens,* while "species" would have connoted a permanent, God-given distinction. By contrast, in the second sentence ("It is not against experience"), he broached the unity debate in the formal, definite natural historical terms he eschewed everywhere else in the text except his discussion of Native Americans. The next sentence after "It is not against experience" put the contradiction between the first two sentences into a single, concentrated statement: "Will not a lover of natural history then, one who views the gradations in all the races of animals with the eye of philosophy, excuse an effort to keep those in the department of man as distinct as nature has formed them?"[68] Here Jefferson implicitly treated the Great Chain of Being, and the confidence in human reason and classification the chain implied, as settled facts. Yet again, though, the word "race" stood in for "species"—in this striking blend of confidence (the chain) and equivocal disingenuousness (race, not species or variety) in this key sentence, Jefferson was playing games with his readers, and perhaps with himself.

The rest of the passage left no doubt about his view of the one practical question involved: could Negroes be incorporated into Virginia after emancipation? The answer was no. Even if human, blacks were too inferior and resentful to be citizens of Virginia. Jefferson's discussion of race appeared in "Query XIV" of *Notes,* on "Laws," as a defense of the emigration provisions in the gradual manumission statute then being contemplated by the Virginia legislature. "Deep rooted prejudices entertained by the whites; ten thousand recollections, by the blacks, of the injuries they have sustained; new provocations; the real distinctions which nature has made; and many other circumstances, will divide us into parties, and produce convulsions which will probably never end but in the extermination of one or the other race."[69] These fervid "political considerations," as Jefferson called them, preceded five pages of what he presented as dispassionate discussion of "the real distinctions which nature has made," based on the experience of a lifetime living with blacks and slavery (experience lacked by European savants), all culminating in the equivocal "suspicion only" of black inferiority.

Jefferson's litany of blacks' characteristics was a natural historical classificatory table. Jefferson defined membership in *Homo sapiens* (a Linnaean binomial he did not actually use here, however) in conventional Lockean terms, by possession of imagination and reason, which he clearly thought blacks lacked. His list of black characteristics began with "the first difference that strikes us," color. He dismissed the much debated question of the anatomical structure and causes of difference in complexion in favor of the much more important issue of aesthetic effects and implications. *Notes* barely discussed blacks' anatomy. To Jefferson, anatomical considerations were less sure than the clear visual, surface testimony of the aesthetic sense—and more than anything else, this primacy of the aesthetic sense shows how deeply he was an eighteenth-century elite Anglo-American man, not a nineteenth-century European American racist. Where whites had infinitely varied hues and expressions, blacks, he declared, remained swathed seemingly forever in an "eternal monotony, which reigns in the countenances, that immoveable veil of black, which covers all the emotions of the other race." Given Jefferson's assertion that black women were so universally repugnant, he reasoned that it was only natural for black men to prefer white females to those of their own race, "as uniformly as is the preference of the Oranootan [sic] for the black women over those of his own species."[70] By orangutan, Jefferson meant what we would call chimpanzee.

There he finally used the term "species," and with the unstated but plain implication that blacks were a distinct species from whites and that they lacked beauty and fine sensibility. Blacks' desire for their own women Jefferson deemed mere lust, rather "than a tender delicate mixture of sentiment and sensation." According to Wheatley, Negroes, "black as *Cain*," could be "refin'd" and "join th' angelic train": the desire for "refinement," for sanctification through the development of sensibility by means of reason and faith together, was to Wheatley the essentially human trait. Jefferson, by contrast, believed that the (white) human aesthetic sense taught that blacks occupied an inferior place in creation, and that the very desire of black men to improve themselves by choosing white women was no human quest for refinement but proved their bestial inferiority and their terrible sexual threat. Blacks had intense sense impressions but little reason, little sense, and no sensibility, that refined ability to discriminate sense impressions which especially the English-speaking eighteenth century made the basis of human sympathy, love, and imagination.

Sensibility, though, was an unstable trait, especially when involved in relationships of power, as between master and slave or, to lesser degree, man and woman, as depicted in Jane Austen's *Sense and Sensibility* (begun 1797, published 1811). Elinor, the older of the two protagonists, has sense (that is, common sense), reason, and self-restraint; her sister Marianne has sensibility—emotionality, refined tastes, love of the arts. But Elinor, passionate underneath her reserve, is too controlled for her own good. Marianne is too passionate; her over-refined albeit charming sensibility leads to misplaced affections and intellectual superficiality. Both sisters are deceived by men. Neither sense nor sensibility alone could provide reliable knowledge of the world; neither works very well in catching a husband—the chief aim of young women of their class and time. For getting a man is at base venal, a matter of power and wealth, money and houses. Overmuch sensibility (fine feeling) will lead to revulsion at the marriage market, withdrawal into desperate fantasy, and lack of self-restraint, judgment, and taste—and in the end the destruction of the capacity for refined love, which was in Jefferson's words "a tender delicate mixture of sentiment and sensation." Too much sense (reason) leads to bitterness and possibly cold manipulativeness and cynicism.[71]

More dangerously, sense that is touched by sensibility can produce paralysis, knowledge without possibility of action: Elinor is often a Cassandra—and Cassandra is really Jefferson's role regarding slavery, as expressed in *Notes*.[72] His implicit professions of sense—but not cold sense—are opposed throughout the text to the excesses of Buffonian "vivid imagination and bewitching language" and, in discussions of race and slavery, to the Negro's animalistic lustfulness.[73] Buffon could be refuted, his over-imaginativeness reproved, but nothing could be done about blacks and slavery.

This paralytic state of affairs Jefferson cast as more tragic for whites than for blacks, since the latter, without sense and true sensibility, did not suffer very badly. "Their griefs are transient. Those numberless afflictions, which render it doubtful whether heaven has given life to us in mercy or in wrath, are less felt, and sooner forgotten with them."[74] Hence they did not express their grief in writing, sculpture, or painting, although often exposed to the highest examples of the arts, and occasionally (as with Wheatley) "liberally educated" by abolitionists or benevolent masters. By contrast, Indians, with none of the same advantages, carved figures "not destitute of design and merit" and would "astonish you with strokes of the most sublime oratory," strokes proving "their reason and sentiment strong, their imagination glowing and elevated." Far different with the Negro: "But never yet could I find that a black had uttered a thought above the level of plain narration, never see even an elementary trait of painting or sculpture."[75] Blacks could have religious feeling, as Wheatley did, but that was different from reason and imagination.

Jefferson had to dismiss a Wheatley. One instance of substantial black reason or imagination would upset his whole scheme. "Misery is often the parent of the most affecting touches in poetry—Among the blacks is misery enough, God knows, but no poetry. Love is the peculiar oestrum of the poet. Their love is ardent, but it kindles the senses only, not the imagination. Religion indeed has produced a Phillis Whatley [sic]; but it could not produce a poet. The compositions published under her name are below the dignity of criticism. The heroes of the Dunciad are to her, as Hercules to the author of that poem." The *Dunciad* was the crippled Pope's scathing satire on literary hacks: evidently Jefferson knew of Wheatley's debt to Pope and abolitionists' associations of the two. The black African writer (and composer) Ignatius Sancho's letters, Jefferson continued, "do more honour to the heart than the head. They breathe the purest infusions of friendship and general philanthropy, and shew how great a degree of the latter may be compounded with strong religious zeal." If Sancho (who worked in England) "is often happy in the turn of his compliments, and his stile is easy and familiar," his imagination "is wild and extravagant, escapes incessantly from every restraint of reason and taste, and, in the course of its vagaries, leaves a tract of thought as incoherent and eccentric, as the course of a meteor through the sky . . . we find him always substituting sentiment for demonstration."[76]

Yet slavery was still wrong, and Jefferson believed that blacks could be more moral than their masters. They could be equally or more generous, feeling, loyal. But not intelligent or imaginative. The slaves of the Romans, according to Jefferson less well treated than Virginia's Negroes, produced both artists and scientists: "Epictetus, Diogenes, Phaedon, Terence, and Phaedrus, were slaves. But they were of the race of whites." The conclusion seemed sure: "It is not their [blacks'] condition, then, but nature, which has produced the distinction" between black and white.[77]

Jefferson, like most of his contemporaries a follower of Baconian faculty psychology, could view faculties as discrete: he could see a strong moral faculty side by side with a weak intellect. And in asserting Negroes' moral sense, Jefferson was not insisting in spite of himself on their fundamental humanity.[78] He did not draw on Scottish moral sense philosophy to the point of judging humanity based on the heart, not the head; indeed, neither did most Scots. Furthermore, it was common in his day to attribute the moral sense to certain higher animals like horses and dogs.

Reason and imagination, though, mattered less to Jefferson than color. Repulsion to blackness was primordial, even if blacks' mental inferiority might not be. Whatever science finally concluded as to the species question, he declared, the "lover of natural history" would want to keep Negroes as distinct from whites as nature originally made them. Dark skin, an arbitrary surface characteristic, Jefferson himself granted might not suffice to prove blacks were not human. Yet he took whites' intense repulsion to black skin as axiomatic: ultimately it alone precluded immediate emancipation and assimilation. Jefferson concluded his discussion of race in the "Laws" section with this statement: "this unfortunate difference of colour, and perhaps of faculty, is a powerful obstacle to the emancipation of these people." Blacks' very advocates themselves were "anxious to preserve" the "dignity and beauty" of human nature, and hence reviled a black presence in America, so much so that they sometimes joined those opponents of emancipation "actuated by sordid avarice only." Where emancipation in Rome required but one effort, since the freedman "might mix with, without staining the blood of his master," emancipation in the United States necessitated a second effort, "unknown to history." When freed, the slave "is to be removed beyond the reach of mixture."[79]

Jefferson was not professing polygenism in conventional, religious terms of his day. His views of race little resembled those the Scots philosopher Henry Home, Lord Kames, who had famously espoused polygenism and whose work Jefferson admired. According to Kames, the races were self-evidently distinct species, for they differed from one another much more than many closely allied animal forms that all naturalists agreed were distinct species; and such species, like hares and rabbits or goats and sheep, could produce fertile crosses, so Buffon's fertility definition of species had to be rejected. At the same time, Kames granted that the Bible was the literal Word of God, something Jefferson would not have avowed. Since Holy Writ said that all humans were one, God, Kames said, must have miraculously differentiated among them, creating several distinct species of humans, as part of the "confusion of tongues" after the fall of the Tower of Babel. Kames took faith in the natural human ability to classify so far as to denounce not only Buffon for needless complexity but Linnaeus for needless arbitrariness. It was plain to the eyes, Kames argued, that God had enabled humans to distinguish among species if they but used their eyes and their reason. Classification was completely unproblematic.[80] Jefferson knew better than that, and besides, he would have had no use for miracles.

Jefferson's treatment of race was a bravura ideological performance, as he equivocally and self-reproachfully doubted Enlightenment environmentalist orthodoxy as applied to West Africans, an orthodoxy that in a Buffon's hands had had nothing good to say about the United States and the New World. To Jefferson, African chattel slavery in the New World, product of the Old World's greed, corrupted the ideal young republic. Blackness seemed an indelible stain.

☙ EFFECTIVE PARALYSES

That stain was the subject of the famous "Query XVIII," "On Manners and Customs," the most impassioned and now best known passage in *Notes.* The experience of owning slaves brutalized whites, with every white child absorbing the spirit of tyranny from the crib: "The whole commerce between master and slave is a perpetual exercise of the most boisterous passions, the most unremitting despotism on the one part, and degrading submissions on the other . . . The man must be a prodigy who can retain his manners and morals undepraved by such circumstances." Beyond being degraded, blacks could have no love for the country that had enslaved them. What was to be done? In a society still ruled by that great swindle of history, the idea that the authority of kings, nobles, and priests flowed from God, it might be possible to fight one tyranny, slavery, with another, divine right. If priests and kings could convince the people that God commanded emancipation, then slavery might end. It was all very well for French savants mired in a Catholic monarchy to glibly demand immediate emancipation of African slaves. But in a society that had won a glorious victory against superstition but had not at the same time ended slavery, emancipation might prove impossible.[81]

But God could not be forgotten, Jefferson cried in what has struck many readers as the most important antislavery jeremiad in American history:

> And can the liberties of a nation be thought secure when we have removed their only firm basis, a conviction in the minds of the people that these liberties are the gift of God? That they are not to be violated but with his wrath? Indeed I tremble for my country when I reflect that God is just: that his justice cannot sleep for ever: that considering numbers, nature and natural means only, a revolution of the wheel of fortune, an exchange of situation, is among possible events: that it may become probable by supernatural interference! The Almighty has no attribute which can take side with us in such a contest.[82]

Jefferson here grasped that in order to end slavery, Americans had to abandon notions of a clockmaker, deist divinity in favor of a wrathful Old Testament God who could scourge the land with blood. Perhaps white Americans could do nothing about the dilemma that their toleration of slavery created. Still, God would make them pay in the end.

The deist Jefferson's lapse into fear of that God was only momentary. He never abandoned his faith in the economy of nature and in North America (and especially Virginia) as a self-contained natural, bucolic paradise in service to a republic governed by a natural aristocracy. The Dispute of the New World preoccupied him for years, as he inspected purported saber toothed tiger bones and predicted great discoveries from Lewis and Clark's expedition.[83] Regarding slavery, Jefferson, who had initially not intended *Notes* to be issued for the public, felt that public discussion of the subject would be counterproductive. No, it would be the "rising generation" of younger Americans who would come to see the evil of their forefathers' ways and enact universal manumission.

Rather than being a founding document of a new American "scientific racism," *Notes* was a home-grown interpretation of an increasingly obsolescent natural philosophy. It was an astute if limited and probably partly disingenuous exploration of the excruciating dilemmas race and slavery posed to elite eighteenth-century Enlightened white Americans caught in a narcissistic trap.

That trap was of its time. Never before and never since could an American be simultaneously a slaveholder, revolutionary leader, and standard bearer of democracy and "all men are created equal." Jefferson realized that race and slavery would corrupt and destroy his vision of America as the natural republic. It is not clear whether he understood how remarkable his times were and that such a vision represented a possibly unique, particular instance in history, not an epochal moment of the discovery and enactment of timeless, universal, self-evident truth. He could only wring his hands and predict a catastrophe that almost no one (white) yet really believed possible. Jefferson played eighteenth-century Cassandra; he was not a nineteenth-century Everyman.

Unlike early African American writers, who did cast themselves as Christian Everymen, Jefferson did not regard great suffering as redemptive. Just the reverse. Suffering created consciousness of injury and intractable resentments; if blacks were human in the first place, it had also led to irremediable inferiority. Jefferson was fatalistic. Environmental effects might permanently mar or embitter humans, in priest and caste-ridden Europe or in the slave quarters at Monticello (provided blacks were human to begin with). The question of monogenism versus polygenism proved secondary, a distraction. It became one, anyway, to Jefferson's white critics, who reviled his quasi-polygenism, but mostly ignored or shared his powerful and perhaps calculated confession that white sins guaranteed that blacks could never become citizens of the American republic.

Environmentalism was intertwined with the great problem in revolutionary era thought—the tension between revolutionary upheaval in pursuit of perfection and the effort to constitute a stable if less than perfect society. Nature, and the intertwining of nature with history and circumstance, seemed more and more on the side of the latter; from the white perspective, free blacks were not whitening and increasingly seemed little less degraded than slaves. Perhaps blacks were innately distinct.

Among whites, the persistence of blackness in temperate America meant that environmentalism's logic would consume itself, leading to denials of human unity and common nature. Among black people, by the early nineteenth century, a Wheatley who assumed a perfectly ordered vast cosmic and natural machine would no longer be possible either.

In Jordan's classic analysis, Jefferson's evident psychosexual complex towards blacks and guilt over slavery drive the convolutions of *Notes*. The Jefferson deconstructed here is perhaps more calculating. He seems to have consciously built an argument for European naturalists and savants, but one in which his discussion of blacks and race—if always in service to that argument—drew special force from displacement of unresolved personal feelings and dilemmas. If perhaps a slave to his passions, Jefferson proved master of his reactions. The Jefferson of *Notes*, as one of my students once put it, was not naturally cool but thoroughly air-conditioned.

2

Culture and the Persistence of Race

We often see among the children of Africa both in insular and continental America, heads as finely arched, and persons as handsomely formed, as are ever seen among the descendants of Europeans. And it was remarked of the army of Toussaint in St. Domingo that many of his officers were not exceeded in elegance of form, and nobleness of aspect, by any in the army of Rochambeau, or Le Clerc.

Samuel Stanhope Smith, *Essay on the Causes of the Variety of Complexion and Figure in the Human Species,* 2d ed. (1810)

The first American writer to give blackness significant this-worldly depth appears to have been Samuel Stanhope Smith. Calling upon reason and observation, not damnation or salvation, in his 1810 *Essay on the Causes of the Variety of Complexion and Figure in the Human Species,* a revised edition of the widely known first edition of 1787, Stanhope Smith tried to reconcile monogenism with the persistence of blackness in America, egalitarianism with race, and God with science and a certain environmentalism.[1]

By the turn of the eighteenth century slavery had not petered out, African Americans had remained black, racial apocalypse had not come to the United States. Instead, the number of slaves rose by nearly three quarters from 1790 to 1820, the number of free blacks tripled, and the total number of African Americans nearly doubled. Blackness had to be reconceived to reflect these conditions. Leading the way intellectually was Stanhope Smith, who haltingly began to accept blackness into the natural, rational republic, with the qualification that there were blacks and blacks. On the one hand were degraded, stupid, repugnant, possibly malevolent Negroes (by which he meant West Africans), seen in a newly rationalized version of the idea of blackness as sin. On the other hand were the nobly formed Haitian rebel soldiers and the full-featured, dark-skinned, highly civilized inhabitants of ancient Egypt and Ethiopia. Blacks could constitute a distinct people, persistently black but still human, capable of improvement and degradation, depending on circumstances.

The 1810 *Essay*, the most important and influential American statement of monogenism of the nineteenth century, even after the Civil War, would become racist ethnology's foil. The ethnologists' self-serving and inaccurate dismissal of Stanhope Smith as a hidebound religious anachronism has also shaped historians' understanding of his resolutely rationalist and even secularist outlook. His work can usefully be reinterpreted in context of both the polygenism and the African American writing of his own time, as well as the sophisticated, relativist racial aestheticism of his contemporary and main scientific source, the German naturalist Johann Gottfried von Blumenbach, inventor of the term "Caucasian." Stanhope Smith's rejection of ineffable faith and grace uninformed by reason and his repudiation of epistemological doubt in the power of science both limited and defined him.

Stanhope Smith's position was almost the mirror image of the recourse beyond reason to faith and right that is found in much early African American writing. There, "blackness" would become an ironic, humble moral superiority, born of suffering, like that of Job before his sophistical friends, whose cleverness counseled despair. Early African American writers saw blackness as related to skin color only incidentally and as a concept deriving from Africans' experiences in the Atlantic world after the beginnings of the transatlantic slave trade. These writers, focusing on Christian morality, interpreted blackness in terms of an abiding religious messianism. Stanhope Smith rejected messianic and evangelical "heart" religion.

ᔕ THE 1787 ESSAY: ADAPTATION VERSUS DEGENERATION

In beginning to reconceive blackness as a kind of substance, Stanhope Smith set out to prove the compatibility of reason, sense experience, and godliness (the rational kind), which would affirm the truth of monogenism. Early in his career he thought to do so would be a simple matter.

His first *Essay* was a brief, assured performance, not too different from Rush's environmentalist lecture against slavery of 1773. The later,

1810 edition, written against Jefferson and three more recent polygenists, was so changed and expanded, and so much less hopeful, that it should be considered a different book, one creating something new in defense of an old idea. Stanhope Smith always remained a disciple of the Scottish common sense philosophy that both he and Rush learned as undergraduates at the College of New Jersey (later Princeton University) from his mentor and eventual father-in-law, John Witherspoon. A major Scottish figure who sailed to America to take the presidency of the college, which had foundered since Jonathan Edwards's untimely death as sitting president a decade before, Witherspoon had become an American patriot. (Not only had he signed the Declaration and served in the Continental Congress, but he also coined the term "Americanism.") He presided over the College of New Jersey until his death in 1794 and was succeeded by Stanhope Smith.

Stanhope Smith developed Scottish common sense principles into a comprehensive educational vision. Especially in the South and West, his teachings would popularize moderate Calvinism, Baconian inductive natural philosophy, and especially the highly developed social theory of the later Scottish Enlightenment, particularly that of Thomas Reid. Stanhope Smith's vision tried to confront the thorniest problems at the intersection of Calvinism and Enlightenment naturalism. The latter ruled. To Witherspoon and then Stanhope Smith, the testimony of reason and the senses was radically distinct from the entirely personal and nonrational experience of revelation. All principles of society, duty, conduct, and organized religion could and had to be deduced entirely from observation of human nature.[2]

In America Witherspoon had tried to stamp out the immaterialism of a Bishop Berkeley and the epistemological skepticism of a David Hume. The priority Witherspoon gave to natural philosophy left no room for the continued influence at the college of Edwards's pietism and complex inquiries into the problems of free will and salvation. To be sure, for Witherspoon and Stanhope Smith the testimony of the senses organized by reason always corresponded to biblical teachings. Yet, as Mark Noll writes in his study of Princeton and the American republic during Stanhope Smith's lifetime, "Witherspoon exalted a value free science of ethics to the place in morality that Edwards reserved for grace."[3] Stanhope

Smith would tell Princeton's graduating seniors in the curriculum's capstone course on moral and political philosophy that although humans could not unravel "the mystery of things," ethics, the rules of moral conduct, could be made into a science, based on perception and reason, which powers all members of society possessed.[4] Hence polygenist principles, Stanhope Smith charged in the 1787 *Essay*'s conclusion, "tend to confound all science, as well as piety; and leave us in the world uncertain whom to trust, or what opinions to frame of others. The doctrine of one race, removes this uncertainty, renders human nature susceptible of system, illustrates the powers of physical causes, and opens a rich and extensive field for moral science."[5]

Stanhope Smith seems to have first laid out his proofs of monogenism during conversation with Witherspoon and another of Witherspoon's sons-in-law, David Ramsay, Princeton graduate, student of Rush, historian of the Revolution, and member of the American Philosophical Society. Impressed, Ramsay arranged for Stanhope Smith to present his ideas at the society's annual oration, which he did in two lectures in January and February 1787.[6] This first version of the *Essay* was published as a book later in the year at the society's request, together with a new section that Stanhope Smith added, "Strictures on Lord Kaim's [sic] Discourse, on the Original Diversity of Mankind." The 1787 *Essay* became, with Jefferson's *Notes,* one of the few American literary or scientific writings of the day to receive positive notice in Europe and was reprinted in both Edinburgh and London.[7]

The 1787 *Essay* boiled down to a Scottish common sense version of the ancient Judeo-Christian idea of human uniqueness in creation. Stanhope Smith argued that human beings were unique in nature, not mystically but self-evidently to the senses, that is, physically. The human soul might not be material: Stanhope Smith dismissed this fundamental question as impossible to resolve by reason and science. But the soul did seem to occupy a material housing that was unique in nature but fully part of it: like humans, all animals and plants had a finely balanced natural economy, but in humans that economy was tuned especially delicately, which explained why humans alone in nature could have consciousness and a sense of moral accountability before God.

Understanding this uniquely sensitive human natural economy was also the key to understanding human diversity, as far as that could be rationally comprehended. Stanhope Smith dismissed quibbling among physicians about what actually caused observed physiological effects and confined his reasoning to established ideas in the medical profession and among respectable, that is, monogenist, naturalists. Physicians all agreed, he said, that hot climates increased the production of bile, one of the major fluids of life and a crucial one in humans, according to theories going back to Galen and Aristotle. Common experience taught that overexcitement or tension could be fatal in hot climes. A state of extreme "relaxation," leading to increased fluid discharge, was necessary for the body to cope with extreme heat. As the bile's "aqueous parts" evaporated in tropical or desert heat, some of the excess bile accumulated in the middle layer of the skin and darkened it.

Stanhope Smith went remarkably far toward a positive view of human diversity as neutral adaptation. The uniquely fine human natural economy, he wrote, allowed mankind to conquer the globe. He repeatedly rejected as impious and absurd Kames's notion that each race was miraculously fitted to its region at the dispersion from Babel. Instead, God had self-evidently made the human natural economy uniquely flexible so that mankind could survive, adapt, learn, explore, and conquer the globe: "The goodness of the Creator appears in forming the whole world for man, and not confining *him*, like the inferior animals, to a bounded range, beyond which he cannot pass either for the acquisition of science, or, for the enlargement of his habitation. And the divine wisdom is seen in mingling in the human frame such principles as always tend to counteract the hazards of a new situation."[8] Humans always traveled, migrated, learned. It was their nature; it made objective, postlapsarian knowledge of God possible. By contrast, if polygenism was valid, then morality, law, religion, and policy would all fall into confusion, and "human nature, originally, infinitely various, and, by the changes of the world, infinitely mixed, could not be comprehended in any system. The rules which would result from the study of our own nature, would not apply to the natives of other countries who would be different species; perhaps, not to two families in our own country, who might spring from a dissimilar composition of species."[9]

Stanhope Smith's praise for exploration and expansion led him toward a remarkable Christian version of a certain cultural relativism.

> If the advocates of different human species suppose that the beneficent Deity hath created the inhabitants of the earth of different colours, because these colours are best adapted to their respective zones, it surely places his benevolence in a more advantageous light to say, he has given to human nature the power of accommodating itself to every zone. This pliancy of nature is favourable to the unions of the most distant nations, and facilitates the acquisition and the extension of science which would otherwise be confined to few objects, and a very limited range. It opens the way particularly to the knowledge of the globe which we inhabit; a subject so important and interesting to man.—It is verified by experience. Mankind are forever changing their habitations by commerce. And we find them in all climates not only able to endure the change, but so *assimilated* by time, that we cannot say with certainty whose ancestor was the native of the clime, and whose the intruding foreigner.[10]

Stanhope Smith used the word "culture" to explain diversity, through an analogy with the rearing and preservation of new varieties of domestic plants and animals. He presented this analogy in a key passage that he would repeat verbatim in the 1810 version of the *Essay:* "It is well understood by naturalists that various races capable of propagating their kind, may be formed out of the same original stock of animals, or of plants, and that, by proper culture and care, they may forever be preserved distinct." In the case of man, this process allowed dominion over the earth, as well as accounted for the persistence of "old" racial traits (adaptations) in new environments. However, as applied to mankind in the late eighteenth and early nineteenth centuries, the word "culture" conventionally also meant degree of "cultivation" in the sense of refinement, education, and sensibility. Individuals, nations, societies, and races could all be more or less "cultivated" in this sense. From this perspective, difference connoted inferiority. Here lay the faultline in both editions of the *Essay,* a tension between seeing human diversity as the fruit of positive adaptation or of moral and mental degeneration.

This tension related directly, I think, to fundamental anxieties surrounding European expansion and the conquest of the New World. The European encounter with the New World led many writers and thinkers to environmentalism and nascent relativism. Such attitudes emerged not merely from ambivalence at the horrors of conquest but from an often contradictory desire for the security of assuming that all the new peoples encountered during exploration and conquest were human and could be expected to share common feelings and reason with Europeans.[11] Such security was much the gist of the 1787 *Essay,* assuaging anxiety that exploration and migration might have destroyed the very possibility for religion, statecraft, and a stable republic. Stanhope Smith projected those dangers not onto European corruption and African animality, as did Jefferson, but onto polygenism, irreverence, and carrying reason beyond the bounds of common sense. He would eventually argue that Jefferson's polygenism and Buffon's attacks on the New World had led them into the same error in logic. He told his students, "From a few facts imperfectly observed a rash and unfair judgment is pronounced on the whole party, or a whole nation. With the same confident precipitancy have we sometimes heard the natives of Africa, who have been contemplated only in a state of savagism or of slavery, pronounced to be destitute of the best faculties of human nature; and the American continent judged to be unfriendly equally to corporeal vigor, and to mental talent."[12]

If Stanhope Smith in theory praised diversity, he still denigrated blackness as the mark of savagery and degradation, a corrupted version of the white archetype: to him as to his compatriots like Jefferson, most nonwhites were plainly morally, physically, spiritually, and intellectually inferior. A kind of neutral adaptation might be involved there, but it was for the most part adaptation to the conditions caused by savagery, sin, and wandering into very hostile environments—all products of free but bad human choice. "The vapours of stagnant waters with which uncultivated regions abound; all great fatigues and hardships; poverty and nastiness, tend as well as heat, to augment the bile. Hence, no less than from their nakedness, savages will always be discoloured, even in cold climates." Poverty, savagery, nastiness, and sin changed the natural economy and in a heritable way—the poor, nasty, and savage, in Europe and

America as well as Africa, were greasy, stupid, and dark, qualities passed on to and often intensified in their descendants. Negroes, subject to a tropical sun, miasmas, and savagery, were "degenerate." The only black people Stanhope Smith did grant to be civilized, the Abyssinians (or Ethiopians), were, he believed, comparatively recent migrants from Asia; they were a straight-haired people with "tolerably regular features," whose combination of attainments, form, and color was "as a prodigy in the torrid zone of Africa."[13] The poor and their children were ugly and stupid; savages and their offspring were even worse off; and Negroes were the most debased of all.

How persistent might such adaptation, mostly sin's wages, be? What hope was there for savages? Here Stanhope Smith began to make the kind of distinction that would be crucial for nineteenth-century monogenism and especially antislavery and African American thinking. Blacks, he reasoned, did not have to whiten up to be redeemed and thus slough off the legacies of millennia in savagery and centuries in thralldom. Whatever climate a people in ancient times first encountered after wandering off from Ararat would produce physical effects that would become so deeply incorporated into the system that they would become a permanent "ground." Subsequent adaptations would all be superimposed over that ground. Blacks might never whiten up; black skin was their ground. Yet their other inferiorities might quickly be erased were they freed and allowed to live unmolested in a temperate climate in a free republic. Indeed, Princeton's free blacks displayed straightened hair, sharpened features, and improved minds, as did many house servants in the South, who were much better treated than field slaves. Emancipated blacks could easily become fit citizens for the republic: whitening was not required. After all, he said, poor whites were not the equal of aristocrats or the wealthy. Such well-favored people typically displayed superior beauty, intelligence, and nobility, all derived from circumstances that put refined thoughts in their minds and from a heritage of privilege allowing them for generations to marry the most beautiful and accomplished mates. Stanhope Smith expressed sympathy for the poor and degraded of whatever locale and makeup: backwoods cabins, slave quarters, Indian tepees in America, huts in "miasmatic" West Africa, or London's wretched factories and hovels. Backwoodsmen and mill workers alike were capable of reason, faith, virtue, citizenship, and improvement. The same held true for Negroes.

Stanhope Smith had himself achieved membership in what seemed to be a secure, stable northern American elite. Handsome, personable, fastidious, and decorous, he admired Pope, Swift, Addison, and Steele and "affected the neoclassical pose."[14] His own brother quipped that Samuel preached "not Christ crucified, but Sam Smith and him dignified." Samuel Stanhope Smith's own experiences would seem to have confirmed Witherspoon's teaching that reason and the moral and aesthetic senses were universally improvable faculties, especially in the New World. Stanhope Smith was connected with the Indian missions sponsored by New Side Presbyterians in New Jersey and his home state of Pennsylvania, where his father had been a devout schoolmaster. After graduating from the College of New Jersey in 1769, he taught for a year in his father's school, then tutored at Princeton until 1773, when illness sent him to a warmer climate. As he arrived in Virginia to work as an itinerant Presbyterian minister, a new Presbyterian institution, Hampden-Sydney College, in Farmville, was being founded; he was named president and built up the college over the next six years. He also saw life in a slave society first hand. Slavery, he reported in the 1787 *Essay,* if unfortunate, was not nearly so awful as most of its critics claimed, and in any case eventually it would end. Not being directly involved in slavery's "boisterous passions," he did not suffer the anguish of a Jefferson. Stanhope Smith always presented human reason and composure as much less corruptible than did Jefferson, who in *Notes* depicted humans as limited beings adrift in a sea of sensations and passions that the faculties of reflection and imagination could never calm but might barely navigate. In the 1787 *Essay* Stanhope Smith sounded sure that if the nation followed his own devout yet systematically rational and empirical course, it would reach safe waters.[15]

In 1779 Witherspoon called Stanhope Smith to the professorship of moral philosophy at Princeton. The year after Witherspoon died in 1794, Stanhope Smith, his academic reputation well established by the 1787 *Essay*'s positive reception in Europe, and his administrative skill, personal grace, dignity, and magnanimity evident to the college's board of trustees, was appointed acting president and, in 1802, president. He quickly liberalized the curriculum, establishing the first chair of chemistry at an American university and allowing students to choose advanced courses in the sciences instead of in Latin and Greek. His, and Witherspoon's, plan to make the College of New Jersey into a bastion of common sense training for the republic's leading citizens seemed well under way.

⌁ PUT YOUR SOUL IN THEIR SOULS' STEAD

The few African Americans writing on the subject at the turn of eighteenth century did not share Stanhope Smith's conception of blackness as a meaningful entity resulting from adaptation to environment. They proceeded from the assumption that in terms of nature, all humans were equal and skin color was an incidental difference. These writers, unlike Stanhope Smith, saw no dichotomy between Christian revelation on the one hand and reason and sense experience on the other. If Stanhope Smith was driven to see and rationalize blackness, that is, sense it and reason about it, they were driven to imagine it as a mere word signifying faith and experience understood in spiritual terms.

As evangelical Protestantism swept the Anglo-American world, more and more Christianized African Americans believed that personal revelation was necessary for creation to make sense. Protestant evangelicals believed that the testimonials to conversion and God's will by ordinary folk, even slaves, demonstrated God's work and the fulfillment of His promise. From African Americans' perspective, evangelical Christian conversion and faith could lend meaning to their great and undeserved suffering, transform it into a realization of God's greatness, glory, and purpose, beyond human schemes and full knowledge. In African American writing, "blackness" more and more came to represent such suffering and the hope for meaning and redemption.

Literacy held a special place in African American faith, as the key to understanding the special power of the Bible. The very first black Atlantic writings, conversion stories, had recognized that power; "blackness" was quickly transfigured from a sign of sin, ignorance, and inferiority to one of redemptive suffering and experience. Ukiawsaw Gronniosaw's *Narrative,* first published in 1770, presented blackness as a mark of sin or at least pagan ignorance, to be erased by contact with Christianity and European civilization, especially through literacy and Bible reading. The Bible, Gronniosaw recalled, would not at first "speak" to him as to whites, and it refused because of his skin; he eventually became fully European, figuratively white, and not only learned to read the Bible but led Calvinist prayer meetings. Subsequent African American writing would mock whites' pretensions to Christianity and liberty and conceive blackness as a symbol of humanity, liberty, and righteousness. As Henry Louis Gates has shown, Gronniosaw's "talking book" would be successively modified in major Anglo-African writings. The Bible would come to "speak" through blacks and then would speak only to and through nonwhites. Hence black writing exposed to whites and the world the white man's hypocrisy and lack of real Christianity, civilization, and spirit of liberty.[16]

Moral judgment was rendered on whites. The African American Jupiter Hammon proclaimed in 1787: "That liberty is a great thing we may know from our own feelings, and we may likewise judge so from the conduct of the white people in the late war. How much money has been spent, and how many lives ha[ve] been lost, to defend their liberty? I must say that I have hoped that God would open their eyes, when they were so much engaged for liberty, to think of the state of the poor blacks, and to pity us."[17] Petitions before and during the Revolutionary War had often militantly proclaimed blacks' natural rights to liberty, and tens of thousands of slaves fled to the British lines in hope of promised freedom.[18]

Accounts of African life could become parables of true civilization ruined by the slave trade, as in Olaudah Equiano's *Narrative,* first published in London in 1789, a widely read work that became the prototype for the nineteenth-century slave narratives. The text presented Equiano's preliterate self as an innocent, and Africa as a kind of Eden, in contrast to the mature voice of his adulthood. The adult Equiano, having mastered writing and Christianity and because of his misery as a slave to Europeans, revealed the deceitfulness of European pretensions to civilization and Christianity and of European assaults on supposed African heathenism and sin. African civilization was relatively simple, but that signified virtue. Here, in a repudiation of associations of purity with whiteness and Europe, a third factor was introduced into the classic Old World/New World dichotomy of the Dispute, as Africans in the Atlantic world claimed the authority, based on bitter experience, to fix the meaning of the principles of the Age of Revolution on both sides of the Atlantic. Rather than anything intrinsically African, blackness signified that transatlantic experience and judgment. Interestingly, it now seems that Equiano was likely born in South Carolina and perhaps had never even been to Africa.[19] As Vincent Harding has written, in America it would be "the children of Africa, whose freedom the Constitution makers sacrificed on the altar of a tenuous and limited white unity," who pushed the United States hardest to live up to its own creed and create a more perfect union.[20]

In black writing in the United States, the moral authority lent by suffering was central, as it became increasingly clear that liberty applied to whites only. James Madison rose in Congress to quash a 1797 petition presented to Congress by the Philadelphian Absalom Jones, co-founder of the first independent black church, on the part of several fugitive slaves from North Carolina protesting against the Fugitive Slave Law passed by Congress in 1793. Madison pronounced that free blacks had "no claim" on Congress's attention. In the same year, Prince Hall, founder in Boston of the first African American Masonic lodge, asserted that blacks could not safely walk the streets on public holidays. In 1805 a Philadelphia crowd drove blacks away from a Fourth of July celebration, and there were proposals to stop any more blacks from moving into the city, which already had the largest and most vocal and active free black community in the nation. By then free blacks had formed independent black churches and mutual aid, improvement, and relief societies. There were protest writers, groups arguing both for and against emigration out of the United States, and several successful and well-to-do businessmen. And black restiveness grew alongside white hostility. With the state emigration restriction laws strengthened, resubmitted to the Pennsylvania state legislature, and nearing passage, in 1813 the Philadelphia black sail-maker James Forten, perhaps the most prosperous African American in the nation and a man once thoroughly apolitical and silent but now politicized, militant, and vocal, produced an influential series of protest letters. In the first, he said of blacks: "And let me here remark, that this unfortunate race of humanity, although protected by our laws, are already subject to the fury and caprice of a certain set of men, who regard neither humanity, nor law, nor privilege. They are already considered as a different species, and little above the brute creation."[21] Forten's letters and other black protests succeeded; the laws failed to pass.

Forten and other African American spokesmen of the time were obviously cognizant of what might be called Jeffersonian views of black people, but they did not theorize about the origins or significance of black skin or concede more than figural and ironic significance to blackness. Environmental or any other explanations for skin color remained conspicuously absent in eighteenth- and early nineteenth-century African American writing. Arguments about the effects of circumstance, or "condition," as it was called, were concerned with exposing the unjust constraints imposed by slavery and prejudice; they did not invoke natural history environmentalism or address skin color or any form of natural racial diversity. All humans were the same—good and bad, clever and mediocre, and everything in between. Their physical traits were merely superficial, connoting no substantive difference.

On January 1, 1813, the fifth anniversary of the closing of the African slave trade, George Lawrence, a New York City free Negro, told an audience at the African Methodist Episcopal Church that arguments asserting blacks' inferiority to beasts "are lighter than vanity, for vacuous must the reason of that man have been, who dared to assert that genius is confined to complexion, or that nature knows difference in the immortal soul of man: No! the noble mind of a Newton could find room, and to spare, within the tenement of many an injured African." However laudable Phillis Wheatley's accomplishments, given her circumstances, Lawrence continued, in a vein typical of early African American writing, she was not Shakespeare, and Benjamin Bannaker was not Newton.[22] The so-called exceptions do not prove the rule. In an 1809 "Address" to the New York African Society, a black uplift association, William Hamilton, a pioneering black minister and intellectual in New York City (and reputed to be Alexander Hamilton's son), referred to Jefferson's statement that the white man "must be a prodigy who can retain his manners and morals undepraved" by slaveowning. Hamilton asked rhetorically, "But what station above the common employment of craftsmen and labourers would we fill, did we possess both learning and abilities; is there aught to enkindle in us one spark of emulation: must not he who makes any considerable advances under present circumstances be almost a prodigy?"[23]

Benjamin Bannaker wrote to Jefferson in 1792 to advance himself as proof that blacks were not intellectually inferior and that God had "afforded us all the same sensations and endowed us with the same faculties; and that however variable we may be in society and religion, however diversified in situation or color, we are of the same family, and stand in the same relation to him." Finding the faith and the means to end slavery peacefully would be a simple matter of "wean[ing] yourselves from those narrow prejudices which you have imbibed with respect to them [blacks], and as Job proposed to his friends, 'put your soul in their souls' stead;' thus shall your hearts be enlarged with kindness and benevolence towards them; and thus shall you need neither the direction of myself or others, in what manner to proceed herein."[24] An exercise in honest sympathy and humility before God would remove all of Jefferson's vaunted obstacles to emancipation.

African Americans, then, would have from the start an ironic relationship to "blackness," a word that could mean sin but also be refigured as righteousness, even beauty. Such positive blackness would also necessarily remain a sardonic commentary on whiteness and the whole idea of racial difference. Early "black" writing embodied several paradoxes, virtually assuring that blackness could not at that point become too real. If it appeared essential to proclaim individual examples of black intellectual and imaginative capacity, these individuals could not be exalted too highly, lest the "condition" argument no longer seem valid and Wheatley and Bannaker become exceptions proving a rule of black inferiority. Although they cast the slave trade as satanic, African Americans committed to Christianity could not overstate notions of Edenic African innocence, could not present Africa as a sun-drenched paradise, because Africa was not Christian.

Furthermore, early African Americans had a problem when they began to invoke a "black" Egypt, as Hamilton and others did in various ways, apparently on the basis of information appearing in European travel literature and other contemporary European writings. African Americans could not overdo that, because they also saw Egypt in Exodus terms as the House of Bondage, whites as "the modern Egyptians," as Wheatley had put it in a letter, and the Israelites as themselves, awaiting a new Exodus.[25] However, as Albert J. Raboteau observes, black Exodus imagery had its limits too, since African Americans believed in the principles of the American Revolution and also hoped whites would repent and that all America would become a true Israel, a promised land. But whites seemed now complacently to believe that their own actions, even regarding slavery, necessarily embodied God's will, that America was the new Israel no matter what. This was a far cry from the humility of a John Winthrop and the Pilgrims who landed at Plymouth Rock, for whom, Raboteau writes, "God's will was the measure of America's deeds, not vice-versa." After the American Revolution, "of course, no American preacher or politician would have disagreed, but as time went on the salient features of the Exodus story changed. The farther Americans moved from the precariousness of Egypt toward the security of the promised land, the greater the danger of relaxing the tension between America's destiny and God's will."[26] Blacks' sufferings reestablished that tension, taught the true meaning of the Exodus story, and hence of the American Revolution. The great slave rebellion and ultimately successful revolution in the French slave colony of St. Domingue provided a sterner lesson still.

African American Christians expressed a growing evangelical conviction in the literal truth of God's word, and they believed that God's hand would be required to open whites' minds to grasp that word and to deliver blacks. Reason alone would not suffice; reason, sense experience, and the experience of faith were all of a piece. At the same time, ideas were being floated among influential white men, American and European, professing to be scientific, monogenist, rationalist, and godly, that fixed racial classifications. These classifications, based on appearances that were supposedly determined by circumstances, gave a new reality to blackness. They also grappled with events in Haiti and offered the example of ancient Egypt as a positive model for difference. Although these theories and the men who propounded them were not irreligious—far from it—they privileged reason above evangelical faith in the contemplation of nature, including human nature.

◊ CAUGHT BETWEEN DEISM AND IRRATIONALIST PIETY

The leading North American figure in this appeal to reason rather than evangelical fervor was Samuel Stanhope Smith. By 1810, facing a new world of zealous evangelical Protestantism and passionate party politics, he was in crisis, intellectually and personally. The new *Essay* was his counteroffensive, proclaiming that his rational, Christian, republican way was the only one, that it alone could reasonably encompass all humans, rich and poor, superior and inferior, white and black, into a single system promising hope for all while avoiding social anarchy, over-enthusiasm, and error on all fronts. He would aid the cause of religion by refuting in the case of human unity those "self-dubbed naturalists, vain of their own faint shadow of knowledge, because they know so little . . . Genuine philosophy has ever been found the friend of true religion." He would leave the "interior fortresses" of religion, where he had labored most of his life, and join "those who are defending her outworks, and carrying their attacks into the enemy's camp."[27] This metaphor would have struck him as absurd in 1787, when the unity of reason and revelation could be taken for granted.

The "interior fortresses" were in a shambles as far as Stanhope Smith was concerned. Students at the College of New Jersey had become boisterous, evangelical, even Jeffersonian-Democrat. In 1802, part of Nassau Hall, the college's main building, went up in flames, the fire set, many thought, by rebellious students. (We now know that the fire was almost certainly accidental.) Rather than benevolent parental control, Stanhope Smith's rigorous moral stewardship over the students seemed to be tyranny, like King George's abuse of the colonists, and Stanhope Smith stood dumbfounded as students demanded their "rights." During the severe winter of 1807, the weather kept the students confined inside, where hallway hockey games got out of hand; several rowdy boys were expelled; declaring their independence, the students rebelled *en masse.* Stanhope Smith and the board of trustees expelled scores of them, but the board ultimately blamed the rebellion on what it saw as Stanhope Smith's over-liberal policies: the college had become too free thinking and rationalistic. It would have been fairer to say that the world had become enthusiastic. In 1808, several evangelical Christians, trusting the heart over the head in matters of faith, were elected trustees of the college, and soon the evangelicals came to dominate the board; in 1812 Stanhope Smith was forced out of the presidency. Three years later he suffered an apoplectic stroke; he died in 1819.

Rational deference and moderation went out of fashion in the Jeffersonian and evangelical 1800s. Jeffersonians increasingly feared hierarchy and deference as mere aristocratic, urban corruption; Stanhope Smith's determined moderation and belief in deference had led him to High Federalism. Yet as his experiences at the college showed, defeat had split the anti-Jeffersonian camp, and a moderate course was now impossible. Many High Federalists who would not call themselves evangelicals now suspected science, especially natural history, as an irreverent, materialistic, Jeffersonian business.

Notes on Virginia took much of the blame. For his scientific interests Jefferson was deemed a "howling atheist" and "confirmed infidel." His supposed discovery of mammoth bones came in for particular ridicule. John Quincy Adams quipped that Jefferson's protégé Merriwether Lewis on his Western expedition "never with a Mammoth met, / However you may wonder; / Nor even with a Mammoth's bone, / Above the ground or under."[28] One Federalist pamphleteer railed at Jefferson for his apparent polygenism: "Sir, we excuse you not! You have degraded the blacks from the rank which God hath given them in the scale of being! You have advanced the strongest argument for their state of slavery! You have insulted human nature! You have contemned [sic] the word of truth and the means of salvation!"[29]

Notes seemed yet another instance of the hypocrisy of the Virginian slavemongers who unfairly dominated national politics because of the invidious 3/5th clause that they had managed to force into the Constitution: each slave was to be counted as 3/5ths of a person for purposes of fixing the number of seats states received in the House of Representatives and hence also for determining representation in the Electoral College. Actually, the 3/5ths clause resulted more from demands by South Carolinians and Georgians, and Jefferson had disapproved of it. Without the clause, though, he would have lost the 1800 presidential election. New England Federalists in particular assailed Virginians for twisting Scripture, misinterpreting nature, and manipulating the Constitution, not just in the 3/5ths clause but by purchasing the Louisiana territory by presidential fiat, when Congress was supposed to vote on all treaties. Federalists also harped no end on the rumors of Jefferson's involvement with Sally Hemings.

The whole idea of natural history, which *Notes* was seen to exemplify, now struck many Federalists as hypocritical, impious, and absurd. The New York City minister and Federalist Clement Clark Moore (later of "The Night before Christmas" fame) wrote an anti-*Notes* pamphlet in 1804. The human mind, Moore said, echoing Jefferson without seeming to know it, could never perfectly order the vast complexity of God's creation. But Moore was a frank irrationalist in his piety: all creation was unfathomable and mankind was not really part of nature. Such a gulf existed between man and beast that "modern philosophers" like Jefferson invented absurd theories of Negro animality and cross-breeding with orangutans to bridge the gap and preserve the faulty, arrogant human idea of a "chain of beings."[30]

Stanhope Smith, although separating man from beast, would have abhorred Moore's irrationalism as much as Jefferson's quasi-polygenism, if not more so. Stanhope Smith's moderate, rational approach was equally at odds with the way that the American Academy of Arts and Sciences in Boston, originally begun as a New England rival to the American Philosophical Society, had become so anti-Jeffersonian that it rejected natural history as nonsense. Only supposedly firmly founded and pious fields like mathematics and astronomy were true science.[31]

The 1810 *Essay*, then, had a double aim. It would shoot down the so-called scientists whose polygenism and deism and sometimes downright atheism so frightened and alienated the faithful, driving them into irrationalist religious excess (and threatening Stanhope Smith's college presidency). At the same time the new *Essay* would uphold true science and rational thinking: its arguments about human diversity were resolutely secular, restricted to natural history. The *Essay* would attack "heart" religion and defend true science. In doing so, Stanhope Smith was implicitly defending his own religious stance, his enduring belief, following Witherspoon and the Scots, in a universal God-given moral science, grounded in monogenism, as the only true human certainty.

Stanhope Smith did not here appeal much to the creed of common sense experience. Visceral self-evidence was out: his readers' common responses could no longer be taken for granted. Instead, he relied on scientific authorities and even speculations about causation. In spite of himself, he had been forced partly to confront the complexities of late natural history. His major scientific source was Blumenbach, whom Stanhope Smith's friend, Benjamin Smith Barton, the Philadelphia physician and botanist, had encountered at the University of Göttingen while studying for his medical degree. Aware of Stanhope Smith's interest in the natural history of man, Barton brought to him from Germany a copy of the renowned third edition, published in 1795, of Blumenbach's *Natural Variety of Man* (in Latin), the most influential work of the time on human diversity. Stanhope Smith raided this book for evidence, arguments, and sources, many of which he took without attribution, making him appear more erudite than he was. (There would have been nothing unethical at the time about this kind of borrowing; most scholars and scientists did the same.)

One thing in Blumenbach especially gratified Stanhope Smith and he let his readers know it: Blumenbach in the 1795 *Natural Variety* advanced the same argument about the effects of climate on bile production and hence skin color that Stanhope Smith's 1787 *Essay* had done. This, Stanhope Smith said, was independent invention of the same theory by himself and the greatest authority of the era on the subject, who had not read the 1787 *Essay*.

Most of what Stanhope Smith took from Blumenbach was out of context and used in the service of his own beleaguered common sense faith. Blumenbach's scientific perspective was, compared to Stanhope Smith's, thoroughly naturalistic, and his vision of human diversity derived from his broad theory of natural diversity, a theory that rejected the degeneration line almost entirely, for plants, animals, and humans alike. And Blumenbach thought better of Africans, including West Africans, than any other major naturalist of the era. Still, if nothing could seemingly make a dent in Stanhope Smith's blithe rejection of epistemological doubt—and he does not seem to have fully grasped Blumenbach's outlook—Blumenbach's ideas did lend themselves to the much more nuanced concept of human diversity that Stanhope Smith advanced in 1810, compared with his 1787 *Essay* or with what any American had yet espoused.

Blumenbach's ideas were central to the nineteenth-century ethnology debate, particularly controversies about racial skull shape and the idea of a black ancient Egypt. Often seen as the founder of modern comparative anatomy, Blumenbach began the study of "craniology," according to which skulls are calibrated for "racial" characteristics. Drawing on craniology, nineteenth-century ethnology put itself through convolutions to rewrite Blumenbach's comparative anatomy in terms of an inevitable logical emergence of biological racial innatism. Anthropologists today still accept Blumenbach's basic thesis that skin color and features can be reasonably guessed from skull shape. But Blumenbach's race theory and nineteenth- and twentieth-century approaches, including ethnological polygenism, part company there.

For, despite the various definitions of race and blackness that would appear in the nineteenth and twentieth centuries, one thing would seem sure in the United States. Someone with very dark skin and full features was "black." Although dark skin repelled him, Blumenbach would have found that designation largely irrelevant. He invented the term "Caucasian" in 1781, but to him it did not mean exactly "white." The first edition of *On the Natural Variety of Mankind* appeared in 1775 as Blumenbach's doctoral dissertation. Therein he observed in a survey of human varieties based on skull shape: "and so we will go on to the third variety of mankind, that is, the African nations, about whom we may be brief, since what there is to be said about their skulls is of small importance. Those skulls of mummies which I have seen are round and spherical, but still of elegant and symmetrical form."[32] "Round and spherical" (eventually called "brachiocephalic") skulls corresponded to dark skin and full features. But "elegance and symmetry" of skull form, seen as evidence of intelligence and capacity for high civilization, would matter more to Blumenbach than skull shape or skin color or features per se.

In the second edition of *Natural Variety* (1781), Blumenbach set forth his exemplar of humanity, the "Caucasian," based upon beauty, which he believed that the people inhabiting the Caucasus Mountains displayed in greatest measure. They probably resembled mankind's pristine original form most closely. Yet no people by Blumenbach's time, he realized, could be absolutely pure. Harmony and intelligence, not some impossible absolute identity with the original humans, now mattered more than any particular shape or conformation, even the Caucasian. He soon concluded that study of additional ancient Egyptian skulls, reported in the 1795 *Natural Variety* and more fully in subsequent works, showed that a third of the ancient Egyptians were Negroid, presumably hailing from sub-Saharan Africa, another third a relatively dark-skinned version of the Caucasian, like the Hindus in India, and the final third a mixture of these two types.

In the 1805 *Contributions to Natural History,* which discussed Egyptian head form at length, Blumenbach also assembled an entire chapter of examples of intelligent and accomplished Negroes, including Wheatley and Bannaker. He declared that "there is no so-called savage nation known under the sun which has so much distinguished itself by such examples of perfectibility and original capacity for scientific culture, and thereby attached itself so closely to the civilized nations of the earth, *as the Negro.*"[33] Comparisons between the most beautiful Europeans and the most miserable and degraded Africans were unfair. Not all Europeans were shining examples of the Caucasian ideal, and great variety obtained among Africans. In the 1795 *Natural Variety,* Blumenbach's example of the Negro type was not the supposedly debased West African savage usually given as the Negro exemplar but rather the brilliant early eighteenth-century black theologian, missionary, and ex-slave Jacobus Elisa Joannes Capitein (who worked in the Netherlands and West Africa).

To Blumenbach, more Europeans than individuals from other regions were harmonious, but then Europeans were the most highly civilized. Still, if the most beautiful people on earth were whites living in the Caucasus mountains, a beauty more original than that of other peoples, other kinds of harmony were pleasing, and other peoples, even supposed savages, were capable not just of beauty but of science. And consider this passage from the 1805 *Contributions:*

> Amongst the negroes and negresses whom I have been able to observe attentively, and I have seen no small number of them, as in the portrait-like drawings and profiles of others, and in the seven skulls of adult negroes which are in my collection, and in the others which have come under my notice, or of which I have drawings and engrav-

ings before me, it is with difficulty that *two* can be found who are
completely like each other in form; but all are more or less different
from one another, and through all sorts of gradations run imperceptibly into the appearance of men of other kinds up to the most pleasing
conformation. Of this sort was a female creole, with whom I con-
versed in Yverdun, at the house of the Chevalier Treytorrens, who had
brought her from St. Domingo, and both whose parents were of
Congo. Such a countenance—even in the nose and the somewhat
thick lips—was so far from being surprising, that if one could have set
aside the disagreeable skin, the same features with a white skin must
have universally pleased, just as Le Maire says in his travels through
Senegal and Gambia, that there are negresses, who, abstraction being
made of the colour, are as well formed as our European ladies.[34]

Blumenbach's approach, for all its reliance on comparative anatomy,
remained essentially visual, in the Enlightenment mode. Perceptible,
visual harmony were always essential to being human. And as with
both Jefferson and Stanhope Smith, some perception of especial "fineness" was key to what harmony meant, some basic distance between refined or refinable man and supposedly coarse beast. Although he found
black skin repugnant, Blumenbach could see fineness in relative terms.
Round-headed, black, full- featured people could be beautifully, finely
made, hence highly intelligent. If quite different from the Caucasian
standard, perhaps in many cases anatomically far removed from that
standard and therefore in some sense quite "degenerate," Africans were
nevertheless not inferior. But neither were they the same. For all Blumenbach's patent Eurocentrism, "degeneration" had become disentan-
gled from value; it had become tantamount to divergence. Blumenbach
did not discuss blacks' whitening up, nor did he require whitening to be
possible in order to prove black humanity or capacity. Negroes were
themselves, and acceptable that way.

This was so because, for Blumenbach, degeneration had basic limits.
It would not become transformation; change did not mean that nature
would collapse into anarchy, or humans would become beasts. Blumenbach's anthropology could see Negroes as something other than degraded white people, could even refrain from demanding that they

change in progress's name, because of his broad and thoroughgoing vision of an essentially stable if variable nature. His perspective on race was interwoven with his developing attempts to frame broad theories of natural variation and classification. In an important conceptual innovation, Blumenbach came to hypothesize a vital force without some sort of mysterious, mystical vitalism, without a notion of the essence of a species as a kind of resilient, God-given entity beyond human comprehension. As a result, there could be difference without deformation of some essential entity.

Blumenbach was able, Kant wrote, to combine "the physio-mechanical and the purely teleological kind of explanation of organized nature, which one had previously believed impossible."[35] If one explains the world only in terms of physical processes of forces acting on passive matter as did Newtonian physics, then there might seem to be no way to explain how or why species remained constant at any one point, as they seemed to do, whether or not there was any long-term change. Many naturalists resorted to teleological explanations. It was somehow in the nature of each individual species to become its type, to develop and behave in a characteristic, preordained specific manner. Aristotle, the father of biology, did not face this problem because in several respects he had all matter, living and dead, behaving teleologically. Newton's laws of motion disproved that, or so it seemed. Hence the difficulty of reconciling living nature with physics except by saying that God had somehow made living matter different or by hypothesizing some sort of ultimately mechanical process that acted—probably on a level too minute to be observed—to make living beings reproduce themselves accurately. Buffon's "organic molecules" (or vital force) were entities that through an invisible, incomprehensible, but supposedly mechanical process replicated themselves. Another approach was to say that reproductive cells contained an infinite or enormous number of successively small but perfectly complete individuals, like an endless series of Russian dolls—the doctrine of preformation. Both Buffon and Blumenbach rejected this as too static and argued that growth had to be seen as a process of articulation and qualitative change, subject to environmental influences, from germ cell to embryo to infant to adult—the theory of epigenesis.

Many naturalists, Linnaeus included (although he leaned toward preformation), basically ignored these abstractions and took it for granted that a real, if possibly gradually changing order existed in nature, even if the best that humans might do was to make up mere species names that only poorly approximated or might never approximate that order. Blumenbach did rather better, and in a Linnaean rather than Buffonian sense.[36] He realized that the idea of some sort of active vital principle would eventually lead to the notion of the radical transformation of species over time. How could a vital force allow some variation yet somehow still restrain itself from fundamental transformations that would yield such a chaos of change that nature would collapse into disorder? One could no longer define species by their physiological capacity for reproduction, as had Buffon, whose intra-fertility definition of species turned out to have too many problems. For one thing, Kames had been right that closely related species that seemed to maintain themselves constant, like sheep and goats or hares and rabbits, could breed fertile crosses. But if so, why had the original species not merged into something new long ago? Was there any escape from teleology? Late in his career, Buffon himself adopted the idea that all species had some sort of innate but limited capacity for heritable variation that could cumulate only so far.

Blumenbach's notion of a formative force addressed the issue. There were, he hypothesized, many different "local" vital forces for different kinds of tissue, like muscle, bone, and nerves. These were marshaled together and directed in growth by a kind of master plan, the formative force, inherent in the "generative fluid." Thus life. The formative force was more like a template than an active, causative power; it regulated the growth of muscle, bone, and nerve in a way distinct to each species. As with Buffon's vitalist principle, Blumenbach saw the formative force as equivalent to a Newtonian law, an "occult" way of explaining effects a posteriori, the true cause of which could never be known and remained shrouded, he wrote, "in Cimmerian darkness as the cause of gravitation or attraction." Even if the formative force itself could be thought of as having a goal, a telos, which never fundamentally changed, the environment might still affect its operation, perhaps even its constitution. By the 1805 *Contributions*, Blumenbach was reasoning that the formative force had built into it a certain adaptability, a capacity for certain variations in order for the species to survive different conditions. These potentials for variation, however, were limited and interrelated: as a given set of potentials was brought out by the environment, a certain other set of potentials was closed off. Some environmental effects would become permanent and heritable, but species would never transform into something new as a result. Blumenbach had no mystically living entity behind species, no special resilient balance, only a template with built-in directions for growth and potentials for change.

In the 1795 *Natural Variety of Man,* which Stanhope Smith saw, Blumenbach discussed in only two paragraphs the formative force, which could be affected by the environment and was the only plausible explanation for natural variety in the midst of stability. He proposed his own definition of species, which Stanhope Smith quoted and followed in the 1810 *Essay:* "Animals ought to be ranked in the same species when their general form and properties resemble one another, and the differences which subsist among them may be derived from some degenerating cause."[37] For Blumenbach, then, degeneration meant the effects of environment on the formative force. The basic neutrality of "degeneration" in Blumenbach's scheme was not obvious from this passage, however, and he had not yet much developed his idea of potentials for variation. His discussion here of the formative force was so brief and cautiously phrased that it appears to have enabled Stanhope Smith to dismiss the idea as the sort of dubious and too quickly outdated reasoning that a careful thinker should avoid: the naturalists were quibbling pointlessly about causation again. The rest of Blumenbach's work, more solidly grounded, might be trusted.

In any case, since all pious naturalists agreed that environmental effects could become hereditary, Stanhope Smith reasoned, just how the process worked did not really matter. He stayed with the idea of the inheritance of acquired characteristics in its classic form, not realizing that such a mechanism could lead to the breakdown of the very notion of species. Probably Stanhope Smith's view that human beings, because finely constituted to be intellectual and moral actors, explorers and masters of nature, were in essence much more variable than animals and plants prevented him from recognizing the possibility of transformation of species to the point of disorder. He recognized that amalgamation, environmental effects, and migration had made any neat racial classification impossible, but the notion that the same could be said about any idea of an originally created species order seems not to have entered his mind. In his view, only human varieties were extremely different from one another and only because of the uniquely human combination of special susceptibility to environment and capacity for both reason and sin.

Stanhope Smith failed to grasp that for Blumenbach there had been so many changes over the course of human history, so many environmental effects, that to speak of any contemporary people as more than relatively pristine and undegenerate was absurd. The original form had no resilience, or staying power; the essence of the original was only an organizing principle, with great and heritable variability built in. In the present, all that might really be judged was the beauty or harmony of elements in each individual. Then a notion of the true original or at any rate the most harmonious human form might be arrived at. Hence "Caucasian"—a category that meant significantly less to Blumenbach than "white" meant to Stanhope Smith.

For Blumenbach, high intelligence did not signify the existence of a superior, undegraded white form but rather the product of the potentially random conjunction of elements. There was no vital thing here, no specially undegraded presence, that made a beautiful or smart Negro that way, no special human entity, not even civilization, that such blacks had, or to which they had somehow managed to return and that others lacked or had lost. In his discussion of Negro equality, Blumenbach disparaged the idea of classifying human beings in terms of savagery or civilization. His classificatory scheme had a different function, part of a broad attempt to understand the history of nature, man included. In his system, no pitched battle ever raged between human civilization and a hostile, threatening nature.

☙ REJECTING RACIAL CLASSIFICATION

In the 1810 *Essay,* Stanhope Smith aimed to show that deism or irrational piety meant suicidally abandoning civilization and reason, mankind's weapons in the fight against nature and sin: humanity, not to mention the College of New Jersey and the United States, would be destroyed.

Beings with sufficiently fine natural economies to possess reason and moral perception could not be like beasts and survive. Stanhope Smith's idea of nature remained in more or less the Jeffersonian mode: a vision of timelessly checked and balanced forces, forces so stable that the equilibrium could hardly be called dynamic. But nature, although beautiful and balanced and worthy of study and contemplation in its own right, was also the enemy of humankind. Nature threatened human beings every moment with a fall into savagery, degradation, and stupidity.

Bereft of horn, hide, and tusk, men and women could never have survived in nature without spear, cloth, thatched roof, knife, and fire. To argue that human beings somehow developed such skills on their own was absurd: "Hardly is it possible that man, placed on the surface of the new world, in the midst of its forests and marshes, capable of reason, indeed, but without having formed principles to direct its exercise, should have been able to preserve his existence, unless he had received, from his Creator, along with his being, some instructions concerning the use and employment of his faculties, for procuring his subsistence, and inventing the most necessary arts of life."[38] From this beginning, advanced civilization emerged and humans became increasingly beautiful and intelligent and increasingly able to reason and perceive beauty, which Stanhope Smith defined as regularity and grace in structure that afford "striking indications of design in their author, or suggest their peculiar aptitude to some useful end."[39] For Stanhope Smith reason and aesthetic perception, unlike instinct, were improvable faculties. Yet those faculties would become degraded as humans fell into savagery and sin.

The struggle of reason and virtue against unreason, heathenism, and savagery had to frame any consideration of human diversity. Counting and naming "races" was not only impossible because the gradations were so fine and juxtapositions of different characteristics so varied, but it was useless as well. By contrast, contemplating the vast diversity and often great misery produced by sin in concert with hostile nature was worthwhile. Stanhope Smith tried to prove that since there were two variables in human diversity—climate and state of society—that could mesh in myriad ways, racial classification could never work. As he saw it, this proof constituted the book's main contribution. Blumenbach had counted five races (categories still in use today after a fashion), Buffon six, Linnaeus four; Kant, Cuvier, and others had their own different schemes. Where such discrepancies taught Blumenbach the significance as well as the difficulty of the classification problem, Stanhope Smith saw confusion and futile Jesuitical speculations. If thoughtful, godly people could not agree on the answer, the problem had to lie in the question: racial classification itself made no sense.

Witness the Negro, supposedly the most extreme instance of human variety. In truth, Stanhope Smith said, any such thing as a pure Negro hardly existed. Instead, a complex continuum of characteristics stretched across Africa, ranging from intensely black skin, tightly curled hair, and very full features in the hottest, most miasmatic, nasty, and savage regions (such as the West African coast, from whence African Americans came) to copper skin, straight hair, and fine features in the African mountains and other relatively temperate zones. And there were Africans with full features and light skin, straight hair and dark skin, and so forth. Although Africans differed most from the white original, Negro as a category still meant almost nothing. If that was so, then polygenism, claiming that the "races" were obviously distinct species, was nonsense.

Stanhope Smith reiterated his belief that blacks would not whiten up any time soon if at all. The 1810 *Essay* said nothing in the main body about Negro whitening and repeated the old "ground" argument for why whitening might never take place. Stanhope Smith indeed expressed great annoyance that he had been misrepresented in an encyclopedia as predicting Negro whitening in the 1787 *Essay*. In a footnote in the 1810 edition, he proclaimed that he had earlier "assigned reasons why no very sensible effect of the kind [whitening] should yet be expected. But, that time will efface the black complexion in them I think very probable, as it has done in the colony which, according to the testimony of Herodotus, was anciently transferred from Egypt to Colchis."[40] That is, whitening would take many centuries or millennia—if its prospect testified to human unity, it provided no answer to the slavery and race problem in the present or foreseeable future. And in any case, Stanhope Smith was now sure that a black skin did not necessarily connote inferiority.

Stanhope Smith directly refuted Jefferson's argument that there were no great black writers and artists. Nobody ever asked, Stanhope Smith said, why hardscrabble American whites or the European poor never wrote verse: "When have we seen the miseries of Newgate or the gallies [sic] produce a poet?" Moreover, America had not as yet produced any real white geniuses, Jefferson's hosannahs to Franklin or Rittenhouse notwithstanding. Perhaps Wheatley was not much of a poet, as Jefferson charged, but how many white slaveowners could write grammatical sentences, much less poetry, however bad? Ignatio Sancho displayed, as Jefferson conceded, elements of an easy, even excellent prose style, a great accomplishment given his circumstances. The ancient Greeks founded the Western tradition, yet "Turkish despotism" had reduced their modern descendants to utter degradation, and the modern Copts, "a people more dull and stupid than the negroes of Angola," descended from "those Egyptians who were once the masters of the Greeks themselves." Stanhope Smith did not, however, claim any kinship between the Egyptians and African Americans. Although he observed that the Egyptians had about the same features and skin color as modern African Americans, he saw them as quite a different people. At any rate, the evidence seemed clear to Stanhope Smith that the Negro's "dullness" was only "apparent" and best attributed "principally to the wretched state of his existence first in his original country, where he is at once a poor and abject savage, and subjected to an atrocious despotism; and afterwards in those regions to which he is transported to finish his days in slavery and toil."[41]

By the same token, that a Wheatley or Sancho had appeared at all proved to him that slavery was not so horrendous as abolitionists claimed. Stanhope Smith reported that on the basis of his stay in Virginia it gave him "great pleasure to be able to say that, except in a very few instances, I have generally witnessed a humane treatment exercised towards that dependent and humiliated race of men." Blacks had not yet been emancipated due to "political considerations beyond the scope of the present work" and in any case, "the public safety necessarily prevents a speedy accomplishment of an event so desirable to humanity."[42]

☙ AFTER THAT I HAVE SPOKEN, MOCK ON

Thus Stanhope Smith resembled Jefferson in his political impotence regarding slavery. Natural history provided no solution. Stanhope Smith expressed utter contempt for defenses of the practice but offered no plan for emancipation. In one of his lectures to the Princeton students, "On the Relation of Master and Servant," he rejected every current proslavery argument.[43] One might have expected him at least partly to endorse the idea that slavery, if unfortunate, had the one positive effect of civilizing and Christianizing heathen African savages. Far from it: "This is making the prejudices of our self-love the judge of their [the blacks'] happiness, while at the same time our own interest is the advocate.—There is no country, however severe the climate, and however barren the soil, from which a native is not unhappy to be exiled."[44]

Still, human nature being selfish, whites would never end slavery on their own. The slaves were worth so much money that the public coffers could not be used to buy them from their masters. One option remained, and one with the dual benefit of ending slavery and training freed slaves in the discipline of earning their own bread. Sharing the conventional prejudice that many freed slaves would not know how to work on their own, Stanhope Smith proposed to allot each slave a plot of land and some free time to work it, with the proceeds going toward buying that slave's freedom, at a fair price set by an impartial court. The industrious would win freedom. Even then, he continued, white prejudice would probably persist, weakening free blacks' motivation to improve further, so that they would remain forever marked as an inferior group. The persistence of blackness would plague the republic.

Stanhope Smith could think of one solution: to create a colony of freed slaves in the Western territories of the United States, where the government would reward racial amalgamation. "In order to bring the two races nearer together, and, in course of time, to obliterate those wide distinctions which are now created by diversity of complexion, and which might be improved by prejudice, or intrigue, to nourish sentiments of mutual hostility, every white man who should marry a black woman, and every white woman who should marry a black man, and reside within the territory, might be entitled to a double portion of land."

Although Stanhope Smith was bold enough to say this openly, he knew very well that most white Americans would never accept such a plan. The "obstacles" were "hardly to be surmounted." Something had better be done, though, for "the time must come when these slaves will feel their force; and there will be not wanting among them men of a daring and enterprising genius to rouse it into action, to the great hazard of the public safety." Not all slaves were so very degraded. The image of the degenerate African savage or American slave stupefied by suffering had metamorphosed into that of the noble Spartacus, man of enterprising genius: "The servile war at Rome was one of the most dangerous which ever agitated that republic; and we have lately seen with horror the convulsions of St. Domingo." Stanhope Smith called on his students to treat their slaves well and to Christianize them, for the more Christian they became, "the greater security will you have for your own safety, and the safety of the republic."[45] This was Jefferson without the hate and the sexual anxiety.

An interesting contrast is offered in the leading African American minister (and ex-slave) Daniel Coker's "Dialogue between a Virginian and an African Minister," a pamphlet published also in 1810, and like Stanhope Smith's *Essay* having to walk a fine line. One of the few pieces of African American protest writing written and published in the slaveholding South, Coker's "Dialogue," although aiming to try to convince white slaveowners to enact emancipation, could not condemn slavery too loudly and could show little rancor. He cast himself, and all African Americans, in the role of the suffering and morally superior Job reproving his friends, and he cast whites into the role of those godless and arrogant friends. Lines from the Book of Job furnished the epigraph: "Suffer me that I may speak; and after that I have spoken, mock on" (Job 21:3).[46]

Coker's "African Minister," disputing with a Virginia planter who defends slavery, dismissed the major proslavery arguments in three main ways: by displaying superior knowledge of the Bible as an antislavery text, by evoking sympathy for the slave's horrible afflictions, and by asserting that Jefferson was slavery's foe and that his gradual emancipation scheme should be put into practice. Coker ignored Jefferson's attacks on the Negro's faculties and his arguments for black inferiority. Nor did he mention Jefferson's conviction that emancipated slaves, marked by their skin, could never become free and equal citizens. And although the whole question of black capacity found no explicit place in the dialogue, it was implicit in the unschooled black minister's knowledge of the Bible, his rational argument in debate, and his absolute moral superiority over the complacent Virginian, who never seriously thought about slavery and hardly knew his Bible.

It was as if ragged Socrates, pleading his own unworthiness, again led some aristocratic boy out of ignorance and into the light. This firm, ironic mastery contrasted strongly with the image the minister painted of Africans in Africa as "innocent, unsuspecting creatures; free living in peace," and of slaves as abject sufferers whose very lives were every moment subject to arbitrary power, even unto death. And they were also subject to corruption, for if slaves sometimes became vicious and immoral, only whites bore the blame: "holding these men in slavery is the cause of their plunging into such vicious habits as lying, pilfering, and stealing; then, I say, remove the cause, that the effects may cease."[47] Coker allowed only that kind of environmental effect.

As far as race theory went, only in treating amalgamation did ideas of natural racial differences emerge, and in what have to be read as sardonic terms. The Virginian asks whether emancipation would not lead to miscegenation, "an unnatural mixture of blood, and OUR posterity at length would all be mulattoes." The minister replies: "This, I confess, would be a very alarming circumstance, but I think your conclusion is entirely wrong; for it is a rare thing indeed, to see black men with white wives; and when such instances occur, those men are generally of the lowest class, and are despised by their own people. For Divine Providence (as if in order to perpetuate the distinction of color) has not only placed those different nations at a great distance from each other; but a natural aversion and disgust seems to be implanted in the breast of each." But the matter of amalgamation "is already gone beyond recovery; for it may be proved with mathematical certainty, that if things go on in the present course, the future inhabitants of America will be much checkered." This was white men's fault, "which you know is an undeniable truth."[48]

Coker's "Dialogue" might be read as the inverse of the 1810 *Essay* or Stanhope Smith's slavery lecture. Coker relied on the Bible's literal truth, rejecting the question of human unity and black capacity as beneath the dignity of debate. He proved willing even to grant amalgamation an evil, race a natural reality, and Jefferson's equivocation praiseworthy and also to accept a very gradual emancipation plan. Implicitly, Coker made proof of black equality (and utter rejection of *Notes*) the only issue. Stanhope Smith in 1810 focused on the ever-present horrors of nature and a fall into savagery and (nonwhite) inferiority, although all humans were basically the same and could be improved.

Historians' typical charge that nineteenth-century monogenists like Stanhope Smith put God above reason and relied on narrow-minded absurdities seems unwarranted. If anything, Stanhope Smith's repudiation of enthusiastic faith limited him. His rationalist, common-sense assumption of a transparent, coherent world and his conservative outlook led in effect to impotence and pessimism in considering ways out of the racial dilemmas of his time. He also could not escape from the narrow esthetic standards of his culture. Still, although he hardly compares intellectually with a Blumenbach or in sensibility with a Coker, his attempt to analyze human diversity compares well to the polygenists of his day, who were not the consistent, rational secularists they claimed to be. Instead they sank into irrationalism and narcissistic raptures over whiteness.

⟣ IRRATIONALIST NARCISSISM: POLYGENISM IN THE EARLY NINETEENTH CENTURY

Consider Charles Caldwell, Rush's protégé who set up the "white Negro" Henry Moss in Philadelphia but who also ultimately became a polygenist and member of the intensely racist antebellum American School of Ethnology. Caldwell, by 1810 a prominent physician, wrote two long reviews, published in 1811 and 1814, of Stanhope Smith's *Essay*. Claiming that reason could never defend human unity, Caldwell declared that monogenists' only legitimate resort was to miracle. He even defended Kames's resort to the Tower of Babel story and tacitly argued that the Bible should be abandoned as a source of natural truth.[49]

Suppose, he said, that naturalists discovered a tribe of men identical to Europeans but covered with wool like sheep. Because their brains would be exactly the same, this people would be morally and intellectually equal to whites. Yet on account of their wool, European naturalists would almost certainly class them as a distinct species. According to Caldwell, Negroes resembled whites less than this tribe would: Negroes' skeletons differed in the legs and spine, their natural economies were different, as were their skulls and hence their brains and minds. Furthermore, the inheritance of acquired characteristics could not explain the differences, and in any case he rejected the notion to begin with. What he was trying to say was that internal characteristics affecting the natural system and the intellect should matter more to naturalists than conspicuous but essentially irrelevant external ones, that skin color by itself did not count. The implication was that black skin did not prove polygenism but rather served only to mark categorically significant mental inferiority and anatomical difference.

Jordan sees Caldwell (and Stanhope Smith's other critics) as testimony to a turn toward defining race via internal biology, one against which Stanhope Smith was basically helpless. On one level, I might agree. On another, from the viewpoint of the history of science, such a reading verges on anachronism. Caldwell and Stanhope Smith's other critics had no good theory of biology; in their own terms their position was incoherent. They were driven toward internalist polygenism because Stanhope Smith and especially Blumenbach, the reigning scientist of human diversity, had discredited the more coherent external, classificatory versions. Rather than nascent biological racism, the polygenism of Caldwell and company was a reactive ideological movement bucking the scientific and religious trends of the time.

In his reviews of Stanhope Smith, Caldwell actually got himself into serious trouble by bringing in physiology, and he should have known better. He himself had translated into English in 1794 Blumenbach's *Elements of Physiology*, which had partly laid out the formative force idea. Attacking Stanhope Smith, Caldwell declared that there was an "ever active principle" of living beings "which offers resistance to the impressions of new and unfriendly causes, and so completely accommodates itself to the existing state of things, as finally to paralyze and even completely destroy all susceptibility to their actions." That explained why the body developed a tolerance for poison. By the same token, Caldwell reasoned, the sun could darken the skin of a white man only so far before the white man's system responded and counteracted the process. Stanhope Smith, according to Caldwell, had failed to discriminate "between the laws of living and those of dead matter—the laws of mechanics and those of physiology."[50] In this sense, neither did Blumenbach. Cald-well misread Blumenbach's physiology in too vitalist, resilient terms, and then criticized Stanhope Smith for not being a vitalist. Stanhope Smith at least realized that making natural processes fully material meant rejecting the idea of a special form of matter constituting living beings, especially human beings, in favor of the idea of living beings as matter organized by a particular natural process. Caldwell believed that noth-ing prevented God from creating some special living matter. Stanhope Smith realized that the very existence of such matter would mean that human beings could not understand the rest of the world or be con-verted to a rational Christianity in which the entire world, God's cre-ation, could be comprehended. Caldwell did not care: polygenism ap-parently counted more to him than making sense. He always relished controversy. He reported with glee in his autobiography that many peo-ple attributed Stanhope Smith's apoplectic stroke of 1815 to the force of Caldwell's critiques of the 1810 *Essay.*

Most early polygenists or quasi-polygenists were more irrationalist than Caldwell. Jefferson's confessions of human inadequacy had had a certain brilliance, with human beings caught in the web of their passions and self-interest and unable fully to comprehend natural harmony. His contradictory perceptions about blacks did not allow him to decide whether they were fully human. He finally admitted that blacks repelled him but also expressed frank guilt over slavery. Such self-consciousness of paradox and language was unusual. Most early polygenists were just sloppy thinkers. They studied anatomy to find material to put into badly constructed notions of a hierarchical chain of beings.

A case in point is British physician Charles White, whose *Account of the Regular Gradation in Man* (1799) was at the time the last word in polygenist race theory. Like Jefferson's "suspicion only" or "I tremble" passages in *Notes,* the following passage from White's book appear in virtually every historical treatment of late eighteenth-century nascent "racism": Where but in Europe, White asked, might be found "that no-bly arched head, containing such a quantity of brain . . . ? Where that variety of features, and fullness of expression; those long, flowing, grace-ful ring-lets; that majestic beard, those rosy cheeks and coral lips?" And "in what other quarter of the globe shall we find the blush that overspreads the soft features of the beautiful women of Europe, that emblem of modesty, of delicate feelings, and of sense? Where that nice expression of the amiable and softer passions in the countenance; and that general elegance of features and complexion? Where, except on the bosom of the European woman, two such plump and snowy white hemispheres, tipt with vermilion?"[51]

In effect, White was saying (as Jefferson had) that Negroes were so ugly, animalistic, and inferior that they simply had to be a distinct group of beings intermediate between Europeans and apes. Europeans had various anatomical differences, including "such a quantity of brain," White said, meaning bigger skulls, which likely correlated with higher intelligence, but in White's view noble brows and majestic beards for the men, blushes and beauteous breasts for the women mattered more. Unlike Jefferson, who hardly discussed anatomy, White did not have slavery as a serious problem. He maintained that his work had no bearing on slavery. Equality, even membership in *Homo sapiens,* did not matter; blacks deserved human rights. For most Negroes were at least "equal to thousands of Europeans, in capacity and responsibility; and ought, therefore, to be equally entitled to freedom and protection. Laws ought not to allow greater freedom to a *Shakespear* [*sic*] or a *Milton,* a *Locke* or a *Newton,* than to men of inferior capacities."[52] But if so, one could ask, would it not make the most sense and be simplest to say that the circumstances explained any differences from whites?

Stanhope Smith had little trouble dismissing White's attempt to detach race from questions of citizenship, salvation, and slavery. The last several pages of the 1810 *Essay* went to refuting White and a well-known lecture by New York College of Medicine Professor of Surgery, John Augustine Smith, that attacked the 1787 *Essay* and reiterated White's supposed comparisons between Negro and European anatomy.[53] To disprove White and J. A. Smith, Stanhope Smith produced his own tables of black versus white anatomical measurements and characteristics and explained any differences environmentally and culturally. Here he had less to prove than his critics did. Stanhope Smith just had to show what White indeed freely granted—that most blacks were equal to some white people—and then invoke Occam's razor to have the power of degradation and slavery as the simplest and best explanation.

❧ THE MASTERS OF THE GREEKS THEMSELVES

Refuting the new polygenism, Stanhope Smith produced his own aesthetic response to blacks, as a counter to White's gushing about white womanhood: "I have now before me a young black woman, the property of a female relation, who has a heel as well formed as that of the fairest lady." This sentence might appall the twenty-first-century reader for its blithe acceptance of the fact of one person owning and commanding the display of another, but Stanhope Smith regarded this enslaved woman with more propriety than White regarded European women.

As far as the nobility of black men was concerned, Stanhope Smith went far for a white man of his day. Dealing with anatomy, polygenists stressed the so-called "facial angle," a measure of prognathism developed by Dutch anatomist Peter Camper (actually a monogenist), who had speculatively arranged human skulls in a series, from the European down to the Negro, who seemed only slightly less prognathous than the ape. White had invoked the facial angle in support of polygenism. So did J. A. Smith, who further cited Blumenbach's authority, although, as Stanhope Smith observed in the 1810 *Essay,* Blumenbach had rejected and indeed demolished the reasoning behind Camper's facial line.[54]

Still, Stanhope Smith found appealing the notion that intelligence bore a relationship to skull shape, and he pointed to Haiti: "We often see among the children of Africa both in insular and continental America, heads as finely arched, and persons as handsomely formed, as are ever seen among the descendants of Europeans. And it was remarked of the army of Toussaint in St. Domingo that many of his officers were not exceeded in elegance of form, and nobleness of aspect, by any in the army of Rochambeau, or Le Clerc."[55] (Rochambeau and Le Clerc were the generals in the expeditionary force Napoleon sent to reestablish French control in St. Domingue.) The black rebels were not, Stanhope Smith said, wild ape-like madmen, as so many white Americans believed. They were nobly formed, honorable soldiers and patriots. Although long subject to "atrocious despotism" and a bad climate in the New World and the Old, the Haitians did not seem to be inferior, stupid, and badly formed children of sin. Stanhope Smith apparently hoped they might become even more; perhaps he envisioned their reaching the grandeur of the ancient Egyptians, who, he wrote, had had full black skin and full features.

This admission by a European American that a great, civilized people could have not just black skin but also full features was remarkable. In Stanhope Smith's scheme, an extremely hot but dry climate could explain blackness as a neutral adaptation. In torrid zones, the most advanced civilization could offer limited defenses against the sun. Dark but civilized peoples in torrid climes were basically whites in black skin with systems somewhat "relaxed" to survive the heat. But in the rest of the 1810 *Essay*, full features signified degradation, brutishness, and stupidity, usually born of a combination of sin and "miasma," as in West Africa. Stanhope Smith's aestheticism did not extend below the Sahara. Blumenbach himself had said that only a third of the ancient Egyptians people resembled Negroes; the rest were people resembling the natives of India, who were probably Caucasians, or a mixture between this "Hindu" type and the Egyptian Negroid one. Stanhope Smith might have echoed that argument and concluded that most of the Egyptians were basically white, with the Negroes their slaves (which is what the American School of Ethnology would later say). But he did not do that.

Furthermore, in having the Egyptians as both black-skinned and full-featured he cited with approval the observations of a deist and arch-rationalist with connections to Jefferson and the Jeffersonians in America and whose writings he elsewhere reviled as prejudiced, atheistic nonsense. Along with Blumenbach, Stanhope Smith referred to Constantine Volney, a skeptic, critic of religion, and *philosophe* with connections to the physiocrats, as the major source for the idea of Egyptian Negroidness. In his *Travels through Syria and Egypt* (1784), Volney declared it astonishing that "when we reflect that to the race of negroes, at present our slaves, and the objects of our extreme contempt, we owe our arts, sciences, and even the very use of speech; and when we recollect that, in the midst of those nations who call themselves the friends of liberty and humanity, the most barbarous of slaveries is justified; and that it is even a problem whether the understanding of negroes be of the same species with that of white men!"[56] Blumenbach quoted this sentiment approvingly in the 1795 *Natural Variety*. Volney, in his most famous work, *The Ruins; or, Meditations on the Revolutions of Empires: and the Law of Nature*, had the ancient Ethiopians as archetypes of reason's triumphs and of the inevitable decline into superstition and corruption.

Volney basically rejected natural history and the whole idea that human variety—and especially Christianity—had any fundamental importance or relationship to intelligence. Much like Montesquieu, whose work greatly influenced his own, Volney approached human variety and climate from the perspective of political theory, not natural history. He was not interested in physiology but in how circumstance shaped society and institutions.[57] Volney drew not only no "racial" distinctions between ancient Ethiopians and sub-Saharan Africans, but no distinctions between ancient Ethiopians and African Americans. No persistent reality, whether innate or a product of a history of interrelationship between environment and heredity, lay in or beneath dark skin and full features. The Ethiopians and New World Negro slaves were the same: he attributed no significance to visible diversity. A human being was a human being. Climate or degree of civilization made no difference, and degeneration theory was, by implication, nonsense. For Volney, nothing was prior to inclusion in rational society. Everyone, everywhere could be like the Ethiopians of old if they but embraced reason and eschewed religious superstition.

Stanhope Smith would discountenance such an attack on religion. Yet his own rationalist theology did not perhaps differ so very much, especially when faced with the irrationalist enthusiasm of the Second Great Awakening, except that for him superstition and debasement carried heritable physical effects. Stanhope Smith's own commitment to reason may help explain why he trusted Volney's account of Egypt. Elsewhere in the 1810 *Essay* he dismissed Volney's widely read account of life in the United States, written while Volney was a refugee from the Terror and often a guest of Jefferson's, as shot through with ridiculous errors and baseless generalizations. On Egypt, however, perhaps because Blumenbach did, Stanhope Smith trusted Volney. On Volney's authority, Stanhope Smith said that the copper-colored "mixed race" now populating Egypt was distinct from Egypt's ancient population, which had been much closer to that of tropical, sub-Saharan Africa than at present: "And in proof of this opinion it is ingeniously remarked by Mr. Volney, that the face of the Sphinx, which exhibits a strong expression of the negro countenance, and was probably copied from the standard of face which chiefly prevailed, and consequently was chiefly admired among those who sculptured it, is a standing monument to the ancient

Egyptian visage, and of its conformity, in many of its lineaments, with that of tropical Africa, with which region they must have had the most intimate relations."[58]

Beyond this implication of amalgamation with tropical Africans, Stanhope Smith provided no explanation for Egyptian Negroid features, though he did cite Volney's explanation approvingly in a footnote: "'The countenance of the negroes,' says he [Volney], 'represents precisely the state of contraction which our faces assume when strongly affected by heat;—The eye-brows are knit, the cheeks rise, the eye-lids are drawn together, and the mouth pouts out. This state of contraction to which the features are perpetually exposed in the hot climates of the negroes is become the peculiar characteristic of their countenance.'"[59] Such "contraction" (and "contractivity" was the most important of Blumenbach's "local" vital forces) would be adaptation, yes, but without connoting mental inferiority.

In one of his Princeton lectures, Stanhope Smith connected in proto-relativist terms ancient Egyptians and contemporary Africans. He was reprising his argument of the 1787 *Essay* (repeated verbatim in the 1810 version) that a "particular habit of body" responding to climate or behavior could become, "at length, incorporated into the system." "Thus," he said, "the harsh features of a Tartar are the natural result of the corrugations, and distortions created by the climate." And more to the point: "that silly and idiotic countenance which we frequently observe in the wretched natives of Africa, seems to be a compound effect of the pain, and the faintness created by the intense rays of a vertical sun immediately beating on the head exposed to their stroke without covering." Volney's observations of the Sphinx corroborated this idea: the Sphinx "exhibits, he supposes, a type of the countenance of the ancient inhabitants of the country, who resembled more the natives of tropical Africa than the present population, which is a degenerate compound of Greeks, Romans, Asiatics and Turks."[60] Climate alone had produced Negroidness: "that silly and idiotic countenance which we frequently observe in the wretched natives of Africa" related to state of civilization only in that Negroes did not wear hats. And if not hat-wearing Anglo-Americans, the Negroid ancient Egyptians were not savages. Stanhope Smith here implicitly conceded that there could be Negroid peoples who were not inferior, and could be "the masters of the Greeks themselves."

Turn the point around and put it positively and Stanhope Smith's treatment of Egypt, Haiti, and even possibly his trust of Volney, becomes more comprehensible. Even if blacks in the United States could not become whites in black skin, blackness, under the right conditions, might still be or become something other than a moral blight or a threat of revolution.

As slavery and the free black population did not just persist but grew, the basic tension in the environmentalism of a Stanhope Smith between neutral adaptation and moral degeneration could be applied in different, opposing ways. His ideas could be used to justify white cultural and, in effect, racial supremacy, based on the regrettable staying power, through neutral adaptation, of racial caste in the United States. His brand of environmentalism could also legitimate black cultural and racial distinctiveness as moral superiority, based on blacks' cruel experience of exploitation in the New World and on the existence of the supposed true monotheism, civilization, and lack of caste exploitation in African life (most especially ancient Egypt), and hence the supposedly redemptive character of African Americans. Environmentalism's duality, then, could make race into a potential language for both the inevitability of racial caste and its overturn.

3

The Horrors of St. Domingue

[African American emigrants] arrive with the impression that where there is no prejudice against color there is no difference in the ranks of society, but they have the mortification to find that they are as distinctly marked here as elsewhere.

American commercial agent at Port-au-Prince (1825)

In the 1810s and 20s, ideas of distinctive blackness become evident in public discourse about the meaning of the Haitian Revolution and the merits of African versus Haitian emigration for African Americans. These discussions raise a key question. To what extent did the new conceptions of blackness emerge out of ideas exchanged across racial lines? Running arguments about race now took place between black and white thinkers, but the story is more complex. What, after all, is a "black idea" or a "white idea"? Certain patterns of black/white or white/black intellectual calls and responses, or thrusts and parries, may be identified. But the intellectual genealogies are more intricate and cross-racial, and more interesting, than formulations like black idea, white idea, or black/white dialogue allow.

The debates over Haitian versus African emigration brought to the fore powerful images of blackness as somehow essential to American national success. Protean ideas crossed and recrossed ideological and racial boundaries in often contradictory ways.

We see this in the implications of the ideology associated with the American Colonization Society. Founded in 1816, an organization of ministers and prominent politicians, North and South, the Colonization Society was dedicated—at least in theory—to sending all African Americans, starting with the free men and women, "back" to Africa. Colonizationists held that blacks were inevitably and always would be miserable slaves, criminals, and paupers in the United States, product of a vicious cycle of degradation and intractable white prejudice. This rhetoric of conservative environmentalism promised that a Haitian-style race war was not actually inevitable in the United States. Fears of race war had taken on complex racial overtones, based on American readings of the racial complexities of Haitian society, before, during, and after the revolution there.

Were pure black slaves or free mulattoes the danger? Who, racially, made better freedmen? Colonization ideology, engaged in the disputes over these questions, eventually shifted in reaction to free blacks' response to those disputes. African American protest ideology became in some ways self-consciously "blacker" as a result of the Haitian Revolution and its aftermath. Expressed preferences among African Americans interested in emigration for resettlement in what they called a black Haiti rather than Africa was countered by Colonization Society ideology. The society invoked environmentalism and ancient Ethiopia as a black paragon, source of Egyptian grandeur, and West Africa as ripe for redemption by Christianizing African Americans. Haitian emigration failed. Eventually, in arguments to remain in the United States as free citizens, virtuous and capable of succeeding there, major African American writings had ancient Egypt, rather than the more clearly black Ethiopians, as the major icon of black greatness. Politically and culturally, all Egyptians or African Americans might be black, but that did not imply that blackness was a hard and fast pure natural category, opposed to whiteness.

We cannot say that these new and thereafter highly influential racial concepts were white ideas or black ideas. They were both and in a larger sense neither. They were mixed and contingent, coming out of an involved, ironic, and cross-racial debate that cannot be adequately grasped in segregated terms.

A more separatist approach has more validity in considering racial ideas before the Haitian Revolution. Then race had been less significant in public discourse and less utilized for complex instrumental political purposes. Emigration schemes had not yet taken on any organized, explicit form, to the point where white colonization advocates had to take African Americans' opinions into account to some extent. Emigration ideology could not succeed if most free blacks refused to go, or, if they considered leaving, they wanted to choose where to go. These cross-racial disputes gave African Americans their first major public voice as a group. The specter of the Haitian Revolution fundamentally changed and heightened American public discourse regarding race. Blacks had acted on a world stage in the most dramatic way possible. They had agency as never before. To many European Americans this was terrifying; to African Americans, inspiring.

In the parlance of the day, the terms "St. Domingue" and "Haiti" often served as code words for attitudes toward events on the island and their implications for the United States. "St. Domingue" or sometimes "the French West Indies" connoted the great slave-based French sugar and coffee colony and the horrific revolution and war that destroyed it. "Haiti" signified the post-revolutionary, post-emancipation society on the island, at first triumphant, soon riven by civil war, and, as far as Americans, white and black, were concerned, if in different ways, a failure.

⤺ FIRST RESPONSES

Slave revolts increased noticeably in the United States after the first rumors of the uprisings in 1791 in St. Domingue. American slaveholders strove to protect themselves thereafter by limiting or eliminating manumission, restricting the freedom of free African Americans, and denying entry in some states to those persons of African descent who might sow the seeds of rebellion. Any serious abolition movements in major slave states were doomed. A complex exercise in specifically American hypocrisy tended to blame unrest and slave rebellion on "mixed" free African Americans, who had no place in the United States, and portrayed black slaves as docile when not stirred up by free African Americans or white abolitionism.

In every New World slave society but the United States, complex hierarchical gradations of black/white mixture had already evolved. These societies were not replicas of European life. Sugar and coffee cultivation quickly became so profitable that large-scale plantation agriculture became the norm. Vast numbers of African slaves greatly outnumbered Europeans. Mixture would inevitably be widespread and longstanding.

Sharp black/white distinctions proved impossible even for the Europeans who desired them. Nor was the master/slave line clear. An involved and immensely diverse Afro-Caribbean culture was created by the large numbers of African slaves and the many masterless free people of varied descent—African, European, and African European—teeming throughout the Caribbean. They passed from place to place and in and out of slavery and other forms of labor, as well as piracy and rootless, often desperate, independence. The American Revolution and the more radical French notions of liberty, equality, and fraternity mobilized masterless and slave society in a furor of rumor and convulsion.

The roots, character, and racial implications of the Haitian Revolution remain in question. It is clear that in pre-revolutionary St. Domingue, although there were formal terms designating racial mixture down to the 128th part, island society in practice broke down into four main racial caste divisions, the first two a small minority of the population: *grands blancs,* great white planters; *petits blancs,* Europeans lacking great property; *gens de couleur* or *affranchis,* free people of color, often of mixed ancestry and sometimes substantial merchants or planters; and hundreds of thousands of slaves, *noires,* most of pure African ancestry, being worked to death in atrocious conditions and suffering more than a 5 percent annual mortality rate (not counting plague years or war).

Throughout the eighteenth century, as a booming sugar market swelled the number of slaves, the *affranchis*' legal, political, and social status declined (much as the "mulatto" castes in New Orleans and Charleston would do under King Cotton in the nineteenth-century), until, inspired by events in Paris, the *affranchis* in 1791 demanded the rights of man (for themselves, not the slaves). The planters resisted, and a "colored" rebellion followed but was quickly subdued; wholesale slave revolts erupted, guerrilla bands formed, and both the Spanish and the British occupied parts of St. Domingue and tried to take control. The ex-slave guerrilla leader Toussaint Louverture (he spelled his name "Louverture," not "L'Ouverture"), who eventually became the dominant rebel figure and hero of the revolution, himself bought and sold slaves until 1793. And during the conflict, for all that he often acted as an independent agent and opposed or fought against the *grands blancs* and the French, Toussaint maintained nominal allegiance to France and attempted at least on paper to conciliate the great planters and to keep up sugar and coffee production, eventually by imposing a forced labor code that gave the laborers a third of the profits of their labor. Throughout, *affranchis* and even ex-slaves fought on different sides—for the British or the Spanish or the French, sometimes in the name of republicanism and the French Revolution and sometimes not, sometimes in the name of blackness, whiteness, or mulatto, sometimes against slavery and sometimes not.[1]

European Americans seem to have understood little of this. Their reactions to events in St. Domingue broke down along hardening party lines but with both Federalists and Jeffersonians seeing the revolt as black. Once it became clear that the planters in St. Domingue would not quickly regain power, the Federalist administrations of both Washington and Adams supported the rebels, as a check to the French in the New World and also to keep up trade with St. Domingue, the United States' second largest trading partner. Southern newspapers and members of Congress echoed these views. In a remarkable exercise, Federalists celebrated the Haitian Revolution as a coherent movement mounted by black slaves in the supposedly restrained, rational style of the American Revolution—a revolution that would supposedly check the anarchy of the French Revolution in the New World.[2] The New England Federalist minister Abraham Bishop proclaimed as early as December 1791 (when unrest in St. Domingue still centered on the *affranchis*) that the "black" rebels had "a right to expect our effectual assistance. They are pursuing the principles which we had taught them, and are now sealing with their blood, the rights of men."[3] Federalist support for the Haitian Revolution gained votes for the party from most enfranchised free blacks.

Jeffersonians were conflicted. Being democrats in principle, and committed to self determination and equality, they nevertheless wanted France to regain control in St. Domingue, although they did not generally favor re-enslavement of what they too seem to have at first seen as the Haitian blacks. Still, in the Republican press, especially in the deep slave South and as refugee planters from St. Domingue streamed into southern ports, atrocity stories quickly spread about the black St. Dominguan savages massacring women and children and eating white babies.[4] Upon assuming the presidency in 1801, Jefferson broke off relations with the Toussaint Louverture government and asked Congress, unsuccessfully until the Haitian civil wars began in 1806, for a ban on all trade with the island. He also offered to help Napoleon Bonaparte, who moved against Toussaint in 1802, subdue the rebels.

Napoleon, proclaiming slavery forever banished from the French colonies, had sent a massive expeditionary force to St. Domingue, led by his brother-in-law Charles Leclerc, with secret orders to recapture the island and put the blacks back on the plantations. Toussaint was betrayed and captured and sent off to die in a French dungeon, but soon his chief lieutenant, an ex-slave and ferocious fighter, Jean Jacques Dessalines, rallied all the different Haitians to fight an all-out war on the French and on any remaining white planters. In the United States, Jefferson tendered aid against Toussaint and then Dessalines, but he realized that if France won, Napoleon would send troops from a reconquered St. Domingue to garrison New Orleans and take control of the Mississippi Valley, all as part of a great French New World slave empire centered in St. Domingue. As it turned out, the St. Domingue expedition was devastating for the French, and impending war with Britain made untenable the prospect of holding Louisiana against British naval power. Jefferson took advantage of the situation to buy the Louisiana territory from Napoleon in 1803. Historians have speculated a good deal about Jefferson's recognition that American power and American expansion and the preservation of agrarian virtue in the New World depended, ironically, on the success in St. Domingue of his greatest fear for his own Virginia: slave rebellion.[5]

As far as African Americans were concerned, although conditions in the United States were different from those in the Caribbean, there were connections with Afro-Caribbean culture and support for the rebels of St. Domingue. Many African Americans had not been brought to the United States directly from Africa but had toiled for a time in the Caribbean and been "seasoned" to the New World environment; the slave grapevine carried word of the great events in St. Domingue. Gabriel Prosser's rebellion plot in Charleston in 1800 was apparently modeled upon Haitian events. Prosser, a free man probably born a slave, planned to capture Charleston's prominent citizens, and if a general slave revolt failed, possibly trade their lives for a ship to sail to Haiti. He enlisted two Frenchmen into his scheme on account of their revolutionary republican ardor. According to Douglas Egerton, Prosser did not see his rebellion as a race war but rather as a republican revolution.[6] At Prosser's trial, one of his co-conspirators testified that he had nothing more to say in his defense "than what General Washington would have had to offer, had he been taken by the British and put to trial by them." Throughout the nineteenth century African Americans would idolize Toussaint as a black George Washington.[7]

The earliest African American source that substantially discussed events in St. Domingue appears to have been Prince Hall's 1797 "Charge" to the African Masonic Lodge he had founded in Charlestown, Massachusetts. Like Benjamin Bannaker before him or Daniel Coker after him, Hall identified African Americans' awful plight with Job's. The satanic stealers and traders of men who abused blacks would reap the rewards they had sown, "to their shame and confusion: and if I mistake not, it now begins to dawn in some of the West-India islands; which puts me in mind of a nation (that I have somewhere read of) called Ethiopians, that cannot change their skin: But God can and will change their condition, and their hearts too; and let Boston and the world know, that He hath no respect of persons." Hall also wept for lives being lost in war. He set up a tension between Christian benevolence and Old Testament wrath.

As he warmed to his subject and denounced the godlessness of prejudice against blacks, even in Boston, he more directly invoked "the French West Indies." There, but six years before, "nothing but the snap of the whip was heard from morning to evening; branding, broken on the wheel, burning, and all manner of tortures." But now, "blessed be God, the scene is changed." Whites had seen the evils of slavery and prejudice and accepted blacks as brothers. (Perhaps Hall here meant the British occupation of St. Domingue or the French decree of universal emancipation by which a French council of deputies had tried to regain control of St. Domingue in 1794.) He pronounced: "Thus doth Ethiopia begin to stretch forth her hand, from a sink of slavery to freedom and equality." The warning to whites was obvious, as also was Hall's sense of providential closure to the great events of this world, events which always carried eschatological meaning. Wrath was turning to universal redemption.

Hall's "Charge" was unprecedented in its sharp juxtapositions of wrath and benevolence. Consider one paragraph, in which he began with praise for the innate intelligence of so many ordinary black men, like the unlettered sailor he knew who had observed a solar eclipse and quickly deduced the proper explanation. Such instances of native intellect testified that "God can out of the mouths of babes and Africans shew forth his glory." Blacks should therefore love and adore God and be content. God would take vengeance on their enemies: "therefore let us kiss the rod and be still, and see the works of the Lord."[8] That rod would smite whites.

Events in St. Domingue seem to have emboldened and changed Hall, if an earlier charge by him to the African Masonic Lodge is any indication of his former views. In 1792 he had counseled humility, love, and benevolence as the Mason's duties above all, even in the face of the worst injustices. War was so horrible, he said, that its sufferings could never be wished upon blacks' worst enemies, for all men were brothers. Masons should "have no hand in any plots or conspiracies or rebellion, or side or assist in them." Human brotherhood was foremost. Hall also pointed to great instances of African Christian self-sacrifice and contempt for worldliness and worldly suffering: Tertullian, Cyprian, Augustine, and Fulgentius. He did express indignance at the prejudice that had opposed an African Masonic lodge and had tried to keep African Americans out of the patriot armies in the Revolutionary War. "He that despises a black man, for the sake of his colour, reproacheth his Maker."[9]

In 1797, under St. Domingue's influence, it was as if Hall now desired in a single brief address to capture the intense violence, perils, passion for justice, the swings of fortune and trials of faith, and unforeseen deliverances and rewards of blacks' New World existence. This was a more confident charge delivered to inspire African American Masons not just to endure but to judge and to hope, to combine humility with a new righteousness—not merely that of patient self-sacrifice but of stern moral judgment, secure in their faith in God's coming wrath against the oppressor. God would defend blacks "against all our enemies" and "no weapon form'd against us shall prosper; only let us be steady and uniform in our walks, speech and behaviour, always doing to all men as we wish and desire they would do to us in the like cases and circumstances."[10]

Hall used "black" as a descriptive term. All humans were one race, and skin color was as irrelevant to him as to Wheatley. It might not be too much to speculate that Hall found St. Domingue a promise of liberation from blackness conceived as suffering and endurance. His speech ended with a poem he had written, a set of six rhymed Augustan couplets. The poem began by dismissing "blind admirers" who praised beauty and "the glories of the red and white." "I know no beauty but in holiness," for God was the perfect idea of beauty that could not be created as matter in this world. Thus the greatest human beauty, nearest to God, had to be invisible, intangible, spiritual: holiness and goodness. "May such a beauty fall *but to my* share / For *curious* shape or face I'll never care."[11]

Hall had pulled together the major strands of early African American writing, weaving them around events in Haiti with a vehemence new in black discourse of the time. To Hall, French West Indian events uniquely confirmed African American faith and moral perception. Like Jefferson's *Notes*, Hall's 1797 charge occupied a perhaps unique moment, when revolution, this time in St. Domingue rather than Virginia, had not yet been completed, much less soured.

✑ THE DANGER: FREE MULATTOS OR ALL BLACKS?

To many American whites, the Haitian Revolution had become a frightful racially charged affair that exacerbated their racial feelings and fears. European Americans preferred mulattos to pure blacks because they were more like themselves but also feared them for exactly the same reason. In this view, rational, masterful whites would never submit to slavery but animalistic blacks required it; hence the partially white mulattos were dangerous, conflicted between animal submission and rational mastery. As Alfred N. Hunt shows in his study of American responses to the Haitian Revolution, Dessalines's rise to power seems to have marked a turning point. The new Republic of Haiti was, according to its own constitution, for blacks only. Those few Europeans remaining on the island, mostly Dutchmen who had supported or fought for the rebels, were granted status as blacks and allowed to stay. This may have been the first purely ideological usage of the term black in world history.[12] It was also propaganda meant to defuse tension between ex-slaves and ex-affrachis and present a united front to the world. Atrocity stories about the barbarity of Haitian blacks now swept through the North American press. Dessalines was portrayed as a bestial Negro madman, bloodthirsty and out of control. The best that Federalist supporters of the Haitians could say now was that whites had begun the bloodshed and were reaping what they had sown. For Jeffersonians, Dessalines was a nightmare, although his victory made the Louisiana Purchase possible.[13]

Dessalines seems to have been so frightening that many American whites turned to a form of denial: on their own, blacks could never launch or lead a slave rebellion. European Americans, particularly pro-slavery advocates, tended to lay blame for the St. Dominguan uprisings and violence, and especially the rebel victory, on the St. Dominguan affranchi caste, increasingly seen in the United States as almost uniformly "mulatto." Haitian mulattos, it was said, discontented with their lot and inflamed by dangerous French ideas, had roused the St. Dominguan pure black African slaves, who would never on their own have thought to rebel but who, once begun, had shown their irrational animal nature. By implication, American slaveholders had little or nothing to fear, since most African American slaves were pure blacks. Only the free blacks, potential instigators of rebellion, were conceded to be mixed to any large degree: vicious *agents provocateurs* of revolt, they had to be severely restricted or expelled.

Along these lines, several prominent southern newspapers painted glowing portraits of Toussaint Louverture as the black George Washington—but also as unique, an exception who in the abstract and in his own person proved the rule of Negro inferiority and incapacity for freedom. Hence his forced labor code. But after Toussaint, Dessalines and black savagery had wrecked Haiti.[14] This configuration of ideas, turning Toussaint and the history both of St. Dominguan horrors and Haitian post-emancipation problems into proslavery arguments, persisted for many years. The staunch southern firebrand Edmund Ruffin, who would have the "honor" of firing the first shot at Fort Sumter, lauded Toussaint in his *Political Economy of Slavery* (1857), a synthesis of major proslavery arguments. According to Ruffin, the black slaves had worked content-edly in St. Domingue until the free mulattos had managed to stir their sluggish brute passions, and the world's richest colony was laid waste in an orgy of murder and rapine. To restore order after putting down the mulatto rebellion in the south, Toussaint had to impose a labor system that was tantamount to slavery, according to Ruffin. The "only truly great man yet known of the [N]egro race," Toussaint, "after suppressing the civil war, assumed and exercised despotic and severe authority, com-pelled the former slaves to return to the plantations, and to labor, under military coercion, and severe punishments for disobedience."[15]

Only sporadically did Ruffin and other Americans like him recognize how sugar and coffee cultivation and the society it produced differed from American cotton culture and racial demographics. Only when de-siring to paint themselves as benevolent masters would men like Ruffin note the great mortality rate in the Caribbean, where masters worked slaves to death and then imported more. No need had existed to create conditions for the slave population to reproduce and grow on its own, as had to be done in the nineteenth-century United States, where wildly expanding cotton production was never sufficiently profitable to follow the awful Caribbean example even had large-scale slave importations continued beyond 1808. Much less did American proslavery advocates see how all these factors, combined with the response to St. Domingue and Prosser, had intensified the hard and fast American black/white dis-tinction, with mulattos as an anathematized and increasingly legally un-recognized middle ground.

Jefferson had seen more clearly. In 1801, understanding that even Ne-groes, whatever their supposed inferiority, would strike for liberty when the chance appeared, he proposed, without result, to dispatch all Afri-can Americans to Haiti, a much closer and more practical destination than Africa. There, "beyond the reach of mixture," as he had put it in *Notes*, they could play out whatever low destiny awaited the Negro race. Jefferson did not expect their independence in Haiti to be much of a success or to last except as a degraded caricature of white society.[16]

It has been argued that black/mulatto tension became the central problem in post-emancipation Haitian history.[17] The civil war there cer-tainly involved racialized propaganda campaigns that affected racial discourse in the United States. An elite formed by mercantile, urban, ex-affrachis centered in Haiti's southern port cities opposed an elite of agrarian ex-slaves whose strongholds were in northern lands once occupied by the sugar and coffee plantations of the *grands blancs*. Soon after independence, Dessalines (who in practice severely exploited black laborers) had proposed redistributing land among ex-slaves as well as ex-affrachis, a plan that helped get Dessalines assassinated in 1806 by a cabal of his own lieutenants urged on by the mulattos. Then the effort of Henri Christophe, Dessalines's chief lieutenant, to step into Dessalines's shoes plunged Haiti into fourteen years of civil war between what became Christophe's black Kingdom of Haiti in the North and what became the mulatto general Alexandre Pétion's Republic of Haiti in the South (Pétion had led the 1799 uprising against Toussaint).

Unlike Dessalines, Christophe tried to maintain the great plantations and install a black landlord aristocracy. Pétion bought security for his regime by distributing land in small lots to his soldiers: subsistence farming became the norm in the Republic of Haiti. In racial propaganda to curry favor with foreign powers, especially the United States and Britain, Christophe and his fellow generals portrayed Toussaint as Haiti's savior and Pétion's cadre as dupes of the French. Pétion's propaganda reviled Christophe and attacked Toussaint as loath to share power with mulattos.[18]

American slaveholders liked neither side, and they and the dominant Republican party opposed relations with either regime. Which side African Americans would or could take is unclear. Some antislavery whites in the North expressed strong preference for Pétion. They assumed that "pure" blacks (Negroes) lacked self-restraint and required the modulating influence of white blood, so to speak. Where an unrestrained, impassioned people could never become republican citizens, mulattos might be trusted to govern Negroes, even in freedom. Like the proslavery view, the white antislavery view also had blacks as bestial and mulattos as partly sharing in white masterfulness, only now those qualities were being interpreted vis-à-vis their relevance for freedom, not slavery. What made mulattos dangerous slaves also made them good freedmen.

The Quaker Hezekiah Niles, editor of the influential *Niles' Weekly Register* and an antislavery man, voiced this view at length. From its inception in 1812 to the end of the first African American emigration to

Haiti in 1825, the *Register* covered Haiti extensively, printing some 140 pieces on Haitian affairs. Niles heaped praise on the "mulatto" Pétion and piled abuse on the "black" Christophe, portraying him as a willful child aping the corrupt manners of royalty. For instance, an 1816 piece charged Christophe with murdering thousands of "colored" women after a single "colored" officer betrayed him. Here and elsewhere, Niles predicted that the "tyrant" Christophe would soon fall. Loathing monarchy and aristocracy, Niles ridiculed what he portrayed as "King Henry's" monarchical, apish black pretensions, his tyrannical lack of self-control, and the barbarity and gaudiness of his "court." If Niles's attitude was not openly antiblack, he did choose to attack Christophe in racialized terms, and he plainly favored mulattos over Negroes.[19]

Most of the substantial pieces on Haiti in the *Register* came after 1815, when both northern and southern Haitian regimes had become sufficiently stable to focus on foreign relations. Haiti was discussed also because of the warm relations between Christophe's increasingly Anglophilic regime and British abolitionist leaders; these relations brought an ambitious and remarkable young African American, Prince Saunders, to prominence in Haitian affairs.

☙ ENGLISH LIBERTY AND BLACK DOCILITY

Saunders compiled and published two versions of *Haytian Papers,* a collection of pro-Christophe, *noiriste* documents and testimonials, including a history of the Haitian Revolution and civil wars from Christophe's perspective. The first version, issued in 1816, was aimed at Britain, not America, and its reception reflected the differences between antislavery in the two countries. Saunders, who seems to have been the American-born son of immigrants from St. Domingue, had been educated at the Moor and Indian School connected to Dartmouth College, after which he taught at Boston's African School. An illness caused him to travel to a mild climate. In 1815, on his way to Africa, he stopped in London to obtain aid from the British abolitionists Thomas Clarkson and William Wilberforce in a well-organized and fairly widespread venture, led by the prosperous New England free black shipbuilder and whaler Paul Cuffe, to transport African Americans to settle in Sierra Leone.[20]

Wilberforce and Clarkson, who had been in close contact with Christophe, convinced Saunders to go instead to Haiti, where he became one of Christophe's agents. Personable, ambitious, and fluent in French, Saunders would be deeply involved in Haitian politics for the rest of his life and would travel to both England and the United States to promote the cause of one or another Haitian regime. In 1815 the British Privy Council was debating recognizing Christophe's Kingdom of Haiti, and Christophe, corresponding extensively with Clarkson, presented his regime as moving toward English social norms, Protestant Christianity, and even use of the English language. Saunders put himself in Christophe's good graces by quickly assembling *Haytian Papers* as part of the effort to convince the British that Christophe was a model ruler whose government deserved full diplomatic recognition.

Haytian Papers featured most prominently Saunders's translation of Christophe's most important enactment, his forced labor code, the Code Henri. This stipulated that plantation laborers had to stay on the land, where they would get a fourth of their gross product, the state would receive another fourth, and the remaining half would go to a new landlord aristocracy. The code aimed to promote stability and progress by training ex-slaves in the self-discipline of free labor. That Christophe would give them back less of their labor than Toussaint did was not remarked, and in fact Toussaint's name went almost unmentioned in the whole book. That under Pétion there was no forced labor was ignored.

Saunders, certainly aware of anti-French sentiment in England, depicted Christophe as valiantly continuing the struggle to defeat the evil forces of the French Revolution in the person of Pétion, who became Napoleon to Christophe's Wellington. That Britain had attempted to take over Haiti as a slave colony in 1793 was overlooked, as was Christophe's own intrigue with Leclerc and his betrayal of Dessalines. In Saunders's portrait, Christophe stood as the black race's ideal warrior, benevolent ruler, civilizer, and modernizer, the shining example of black capacity. Like the British monarchy itself, Saunders wrote, Haiti under Christophe embodied both tradition and modernity, Old World and progress. Christophe's Haiti was forward-looking but well fortified against all revolutionary excess. At Christophe's 1811 coronation, the Haitian Council of State had proclaimed, in a statement reprinted in *Haytian Papers:* "Though we appear in the same hypothetical situation as the Americans, being a new people, still we possess the wants, the manners, the virtues, and we will add, the vices of the old states. Of all the modes of government, that which has appeared to us most justly deserving of a preference, is the one of middle tenor, between those hitherto put into practice at Hayti."[21]

Saunders's efforts (along with those of the Haitian Council of State) played well in London. They impressed Joseph Banks, privy councillor and member of the prestigious African Institution, the British anti-slavery society established in 1807 to oversee the abolition of the British slave trade. Banks deemed the Code Henri "the most moral association of men in existence; nothing that white men have been able to arrange is equal to it." Because it gave black laborers "a vested interest in the crops they raise," the code secured "a proper portion of happiness to those whose lot in the hands of white men endures the largest portion of misery." It was a shame that white governments would not recognize Haiti. "Perseverance, however, in the line of conduct laid down in the Code Henri cannot but in due time conquer all difficulties, and bring together the black and the white varieties of mankind under the ties of mutual and reciprocal equality and brotherhood, which the bountiful Creator of all things had provided for the advantage of both parties."[22]

Banks seems to have been unaware that Toussaint's code had offered workers greater incentive than the Code Henri, and Saunders did not enlighten him. Saunders understood that Banks and his friends were involved in a debate over abolishing slavery in the British West Indies that concerned the question of whether ex-slaves could, or would, learn to work in a disciplined manner, and that the Code Henri, as presented in *Haytian Papers,* provided a model for the transition from slave to "free" labor.[23] Moreover, from *Haytian Papers,* British and American readers who were sympathetic to abolitionism and were likely to be Protestant, anti-Papist, and anti-French, would not know that the majority of Haitians embraced Roman Catholicism or that Haitian culture represented a complex syncretism of Africanisms and French customs and attitudes.

Soon Saunders, ever adroit, would win praise from European Americans. In late 1816 or early 1817 he became Christophe's Minister of Education. His educational program quickly garnered for Christophe's regime the only positive notice it would ever receive from *Niles' Weekly*

Register, which commended Saunders's work and especially his attempts to establish Protestant churches and schools. Perhaps, Niles conceded, Christophe was not totally wicked.[24] Saunders, however, soon lost Christophe's favor, apparently for using the royal bank account for his own amusement, and he left Haiti for Philadelphia, site of the largest and most active free black community in the United States. There he retrenched and tried to regain Christophe's regard by drumming up African American emigrants for the war-torn Kingdom of Haiti, which badly needed skilled laborers and craftsmen.

Here Saunders showed that he understood the differences between American and British audiences. He realized in particular that the strategy he adopted in the London edition of *Haytian Papers* would probably fail to inspire African Americans, who admired Toussaint and would tend to be anti-monarchical. In the American edition, which Saunders arranged to have published in Boston in 1818 and which sold poorly, the market apparently having already been saturated with the British version, a chapter extolling monarchism and a section eulogizing the African Institution were both omitted. He also took a lead role in free black activism against the American Colonization Society.[25]

In 1818 when Saunders addressed the Pennsylvania Augustine Society, a black literary society, on the virtues of education, he praised Haiti's system of instruction. Indeed, he said, nowhere but in the northern United States, "some portions of Europe," and "the island of Hayti" was there such a strong sense of the importance of education. Yet he refrained from making Christophe into the perfection of human virtue.[26]

That same year, advocating Haitian emigration in a major speech before the American Convention of Abolition Societies, a national group including both European Americans and African Americans (and not excluding slaveholders) that met bi-annually in Philadelphia, Saunders walked even more carefully. He understood that both black Philadelphians and the most committed white abolitionists deplored the Haitian civil wars and had also come to reject African emigration and the ACS. Saunders not only refrained from attacking Pétion as he had done in *Haytian Papers* but lamented the Haitian civil war and asked the Convention of Abolition Societies to mediate a peace settlement. Both Haitian regimes, he declared, were "arbitrary and somewhat allied to military despotism," and corrupted by avarice and idolatry. In divided Haiti, husbands were tragically separated from wives, parents from children. Yet both regimes might be improved and reconciled by men so benevolent and disinterested as Philadelphia's abolitionists. Saunders further exploited northern free blacks' apprehensions about a rumored surge of black migrants up from the South, which would supposedly threaten both white and free black jobs and bring even more hatred down on the black community. Were Haiti unified, such blacks could emigrate there instead.

Saunders's only advocacy of Christophe's kingdom was by implication. He praised at some length the great British abolitionists whom he knew and finally read Banks's letter concerning Christophe and the Kingdom of Haiti. According to Banks, Christophe's regime was stable and virtuous, anchored by the Code Henri, and would never be reconquered by France.

Nowhere in his American speeches did Saunders raise the black/mulatto issue. Instead, he insisted to the Convention of Abolition Societies that in Haiti emigrants would be entirely free from race prejudice and European influences or presence. Haiti was all black, with no Europeans whatsoever, and the Spanish were on the verge of selling the eastern portion of the island to Christophe. Saunders implied through Banks's letter that the Code Henri would protect emigrants from any other exploitation as it schooled them in the discipline of free labor.[27]

Saunders's efforts in the United States seem to have regained Christophe's favor, but the emigration campaign proved ill-fated. Not only did Saunders damage his reputation among African American leaders by what seems to have been his compulsive philandering, but in 1820, on the verge of granting Saunders a ship and $25,000 to transport African American immigrants, Christophe suffered a stroke. Within weeks rebellion broke out and Christophe committed suicide. Another emigration project, promoted by an African American who settled in Haiti, Silvain Simonisse of South Carolina, likewise failed during the tumultuous events of 1820. Two years later, Pétion's successor in southern Haiti, General Jean Pierre Boyer, finally managed to reunite northern and southern Haiti and capture the Spanish eastern part. Christophe's estates were broken up and the land divided; subsistence farming became the norm everywhere. Saunders, ever the opportunist, would move permanently to Haiti in 1823 as Boyer's attorney general.[28]

❧ BLACK BENEVOLENCE: NEW WORLD OR OLD?

Boyer revived the emigration scheme. He did it primarily to appeal to American whites. The French, who still claimed "St. Domingue" as their own, were threatening to launch another re-enslavement expedition. Haiti needed international support and diplomatic recognition as an independent state. American power was on the rise; Boyer also probably realized that some American whites preferred his regime to Christophe's or to an island reconquered by an imperialist-minded France. His attempts to contact James Monroe's administration in Washington had all been ignored or rebuffed, but Boyer knew that many prominent Americans concerned about slave insurrection and race war, including Henry Clay, Bushrod Washington (George Washington's nephew), and Andrew Jackson, wanted somehow to remove free blacks from the United States, and that these men supported the American Colonization Society. In 1821, the society would found the colony of Monrovia (the next year renamed Liberia) in West Africa, to which the black settlers from America would supposedly bring civilization and Christianity. But the colony had severe problems with disease and with native African relations, and more important, most American free blacks now intensely opposed African emigration as a plot to shore up slavery by getting rid of free blacks. Thus in 1824, Loring C. Dewey, a New York City agent of the Colonization Society who was having a hard time persuading free blacks to go to Liberia, opened a correspondence with Boyer regarding the possibility of the society setting up a new colony there.

At first, one of the Colonization Society's founders, Robert Finley of New Jersey, had tried to establish good relations with free blacks. He sought out Paul Cuffe, who welcomed the society's participation in his emigration effort, and men like James Forten and Richard Allen, who had supported Cuffe's original plan and were friendly to Finley's organization. Daniel Coker himself would lead a group of eighty-six African Americans to West Africa under the Colonization Society's auspices in 1820. But from the start many ordinary African Americans questioned the Colonization Society's motives and its accounts of life in Africa.

A testimonial from an 1817 Philadelphia protest meeting attended by thousands of free blacks proclaimed that the whole scheme was calculated to produce nothing but "MISERY and sufferings and perpetual slavery." Forten, who had presided over this meeting, at first strongly disagreed. His experience told him that neither wealth nor education could give blacks social equality in the United States. They "will never," he wrote to Cuffe, "become a people until they come out from amongst the white people." But as Finley's organization grew to include more and more slaveholders and as its policy statements increasingly testified to its unwillingness to interfere with slavery in the United States, free black leaders like Forten about-faced (and in retrospect it is clear that proslavery motives drove several of the society's founders, if perhaps not Finley). By 1818, Forten was the society's loudest critic.[29]

It is unclear that Boyer knew much about this growing opposition to the Colonization Society or would have cared had he known. He certainly was not aware that Dewey had contacted him without asking permission from the society's leadership. Jumping at this chance perhaps to win diplomatic recognition from the United States, Boyer corresponded with Dewey at length, touting Haiti's virtues for African Americans and promising free land and provisions to groups of emigrants, plus travel money for those who needed it. In contrast to the "barbarous shores of Africa," Haiti was civilized, healthful, and welcoming.[30]

The Colonization Society leadership, including slaveholders who wanted nothing to do with the place that they, like the French, still insisted on calling "St. Domingue," saw African American emigration to Haiti as a threat. The society officially repudiated Dewey and condemned Boyer as a repressive despot.[31] Boyer lost any chance of American diplomatic recognition and ended up on the side of colonization's critics. But, like Christophe before him, he still needed laborers and craftsmen and so went forward with the emigration scheme. He sent a dashing mulatto officer, Jonathan Granville, to the United States to contact Dewey, meet with philanthropic whites, and make arrangements with prospective settlers. Within weeks, African American community leaders were applauding Granville, producing pamphlets stating Boyer's terms, and organizing Haitian emigration societies.

Ideological patterns crystallized during the Haitian/African emigration debate, lending increasing force to racial theories. Colonization ideology developed in a way that allowed its adherents to keep slavery, at least for the present, and to see American liberty as being for whites only but still escape guilt over slavery or prejudice. These whites often cast themselves as angels of practical benevolence. With slavery expanding daily, cotton production growing exponentially, and the example of St. Domingue before them, most slaveholding whites probably found it too disturbing to concede openly that the whole great, burgeoning, profitable system rested on pure coercion so despised by its victims that they would choose freedom at a moment's notice. The slaveholders chose to believe that slaves were passive if no one agitated them; free blacks were the true peril. They must go. Still, the idea persisted that slavery was in some sense an evil, even if one so longstanding, entrenched, and profitable that whites could hardly be blamed for maintaining it. Though docile, blacks were still probably human and deserved human rights. But whatever they might once have been or might someday become, they seemed very inferior now, and how could slavery be done away with overnight, especially when free blacks seemed so degraded and white prejudices ran so strong—and the system so profitable? Sending blacks to nearby Haiti, hotbed of rebellion, would only increase the chances of an American race war.

Colonization thought cleverly resolved these tensions. Prejudice, if regrettable, was understandable and intractable. One could not expect it to disappear because a few accomplished blacks existed, and white contempt made accomplishment impossible for all but a few. The exception proved the rule. Prejudice, black criminality, and poverty had become a vicious cycle. As a result, whites could not be held responsible for their attitudes, which, if perhaps sinful, constituted a social fact, just as blacks could not be blamed for the persistent degradation that sustained white hatred. The only solution was for free blacks to leave the United States immediately. In Africa, free from prejudice, these African Americans would become self-reliant colonists, redeemers, and civilizers of an entire continent, restorers of a race. The slaves might follow the freedmen, but only gradually. Like prejudice, slavery was a regrettable but profoundly entrenched social fact; no one now living bore the guilt of the original sin. Freeing at once all the slaves would probably destroy the

United States unless provision were made for their immediate emigration and unless all the inevitably degraded, resentful free blacks had already been shipped off. The slaves were expensive property: the economy of half the United States could not be overthrown in a day, and race war could not be risked. Emancipation had to be gradual, compensated, and linked to emigration, and it could begin only after the free blacks had departed. The American Colonization Society managed to keep the politically divisive slavery issue mostly out of national politics—and several recent historians have argued that such suppression was the main intention of the society's most powerful supporters like Clay. Opponents of the society like John Quincy Adams found its political clout too great to buck: once he assumed office as President, Adams reversed his former opposition to providing the society with federal money.[32]

Supporters of Haitian emigration for African Americans, by contrast, wanted to keep abolitionism alive and bring the slavery issue forward. They made no professions that slaves were content and only free blacks restive and rebellious. Moral sympathy characteristic of much eighteenth-century abolitionism lay at the core of this view. In the white pro-Haitian emigration view, slaves passionately desired freedom and had the will to fight for it: they had to be removed as soon as possible. Africans were men and brothers deserving sympathy, freedom, and philanthropic aid, but brothers capable of fratricide if their situation became hopeless. To show why the slaves were not docile and had to be removed along with free blacks, white champions of Haitian emigration for all African Americans had to paint scenes of horrible black vengeance. They had to make slavery seem so dangerous and evil that whites would not hesitate to forgo all the profit to be had from slavery. That is, they had to invoke the horrors of St. Domingue at the same time as saying that somehow sending blacks to Boyer's new Haiti would guarantee American safety. But if slavery was not immediately ended everywhere in the United States and if the slaves were so dangerous that a new St. Domingue loomed in America, would the prospect of some day being settled in Haiti really quell American slaves' resentments? Would a Haitian emigration plan stop the Haitians from working to overthrow American slavery?

There was a way to sidestep these objections, but an implausible one:

placing one's faith in the moderation of Boyer's regime. For instance, Niles in the *Register* praised Boyer for liberality, in contrast to the history of atrocities perpetrated by Christophe. True, Niles conceded, the Haitians were indomitable fighters who had defeated the combined armies of Europe, but to Niles that only proved that the United States should take them seriously and establish good relations with them, especially now that they were governed by a responsible, self-restrained (mulatto) leader. Niles first made this argument in September 1823, before Dewey had even written to Boyer.[33] He would repeat it throughout the mid-1820s. His contradictions show how hard it was, despite the St. Domingue/Haiti distinction, to have one place be both carrot and stick.

Still, Haitian emigration might seem the ideal solution if one hated and feared slavery enough. Yet the contradictory pressures of the effort drove its adherents, including those who, unlike Niles, at first attributed no meaning whatever to race, toward expressions of race theory and invidious racial comparisons.

America's foremost abolitionist of the 1810s and 20s, the Baltimore Quaker saddlemaker and editor Benjamin Lundy, William Lloyd Garrison's mentor, literally walked up and down the United States denouncing slavery, fearlessly imploring emancipation to audiences of slaveholders and warning of the coming race war that would be God's judgment on white America and deliverance for blacks. "Yea," he pronounced in 1824 in the pages of his influential *Genius of Universal Emancipation,* "all nature cries aloud that something must be done to appease the kindling wrath of outraged humanity and violated justice, ere the fate of ancient Egypt, or of modern St. Domingo, shall be ours."[34] Lundy rejected the whole idea of race. "The odious distinctions between white and black have been created by tyrants," he said, "for the express purpose of acquiring and preserving their *unjust authority.* That is the Alpha and Omega of it."[35] At first he espoused emigration only as a practical expediency for those blacks with no prospects in the United States, especially manumitted slaves in the South.[36] Lundy, who worked extensively with free blacks, found the Colonization Society's motives increasingly suspect because African colonization was so self-evidently impractical on every level: transporting large numbers of African Americans, slave or free, to Africa was prohibitively expensive and difficult.[37] Moving them to nearby Haiti, by contrast, would be comparatively cheap, cost-ing, Lundy calculated at one point, a mere $500,000 per year for fifty years to transport America's entire black population, and Boyer's gov-ernment welcomed emigrants and even declared a willingness to subsi-dize them. Generosity alone, Lundy wrote in June 1825, motivated Boyer, who would become history's "second Moses."[38] Several times Lundy himself traveled with emigrants to Haiti to ensure their fair treat-ment.

How Lundy managed this position intellectually and psychologically is hard to say. In his presentation, Haiti apparently belonged to a kind of post-revolutionary, post-millennial dispensation, radically distinct from St. Domingue's horrors. Sending African Americans to Boyer's Haiti would vault the United States into this dispensation with no need to en-dure St. Domingue's or Pharaoh's fate.

Perhaps some sort of race theory underlay this vision. Lundy had been reading Niles, starting perhaps with his piece asserting the Hai-tians' indomitability, which was reprinted in the *Genius* as testimony to "the Negro Character" in October 1823. In November 1824, Lundy de-clared that blacks were meant to live in a tropical climate and whites in a temperate one: "There can be no doubt that the whole of the African race in this country might, in time, be elevated to the rank that nature designated they should hold, and sent to people a clime more congenial to their constitution than that in which they now drag out a miserable existence, in degradation and chains."[39] Were blacks to be "elevated" by whites in the United States or in the "more congenial" clime of Haiti? Lundy's sentence seems to have been a strange amalgam of Coloniza-tion Society social environmentalist and social engineering rhetoric and Boyer's Haiti-as-black-Eden propaganda. Lundy almost had to make such a juxtaposition, since, unlike the Colonization Society, he could not call upon a set of splendid images and myths to argue for blacks' be-ing in Haiti.

Colonization Society members could do so. They pointed to the an-cient myth of the Christian empire of Prester John hidden somewhere in central Africa, the early flowering of Christianity in North Africa, and ancient Ethiopian or Egyptian splendor and high civilization. These im-ages could be coupled with a sense of evangelical Christian mission among religious white abolitionists, who could cast themselves as furthering the promised redemption of a continent, a race, even the world. Compared with Africa, Haiti offered white antislavery of the 1820s not only no glorious black past but also little by way of a larger, transcendental mission, other than that of white America saving its own sinful skin. Sincere or not, believed or not, Colonization Society propaganda appealed powerfully to religious and benevolent motives—particularly once that propaganda shifted toward evangelical messianism in response to free blacks' and Lundy's attacks. Moving African Americans to Haiti, colonizationists said, would constitute mere "emigration" and fail to serve the great cause of African redemption. African "colonization" had this grand purpose. By shipping off restive free blacks and mulattos, African colonization promised not only security at home in the United States but the restoration of civilization and Christianity to an entire benighted continent.

There was little that white advocates of African American emigration to Haiti could say in response to such an argument. Lundy and other white advocates, such as Dewey or Niles, had to concentrate on Haiti's benevolence under Boyer and on its practical advantages (including an appropriate climate for blacks) as the only way to ward off race war in the United States.

☙ ETHIOPIA IN AFRICA

Colonization Society ideology was potent, especially when coupled with evangelical benevolence. In 1825, a Connecticut clergyman became the society's secretary. Bringing colonization into line with the broad spectrum of evangelical benevolent reform, Ralph Gurley stressed universal salvation over and above expediency. Actually, this new benevolence was nothing if not expedient. Lundy's or Niles's criticisms were bad enough, but free black denunciations of African emigration threatened to discredit the Colonization Society entirely. Free blacks had to want to go to Africa in substantial numbers. A show of benevolence and redemptive mission was positively required.

David Brion Davis has argued that historians have dealt too harshly with the American Colonization Society, whose estimate of the persistence of prejudice in America turned out to be not far wrong.[40] I would say that colonization and the whole 1820s emigration controversy merits new scrutiny for another reason. Colonization's very social conservatism helped lend redemptive visions of race a new force in the United States. In colonization thought, race became part of a sweeping yet gradual drama of world history as the story of universal salvation. Responding to various white abolitionists, to free black critiques and pro-Haitian sentiment, and to black and white messianism, certain sincere colonizationists became the first major American figures explicitly and unequivocally to see blacks as in effect fully equal and undegenerate, in Africa and as Negroes—that is, as distinct, different, and separate, but still equal, and connected to the West and Christianity.

This development should be seen less as a logical outgrowth of the colonization position than as a contingent product of a complex debate in which perceptions of events in the French West Indies took center stage. The colonizationist attempt to fuse race with what was cast as social realism appears decisive in hindsight only because it was the most important and ideologically successful American attempt once again to tame the radical potential of the Age of Revolution for slavery and race relations. That potential was symbolized to colonizationists and defenders of slavery not just by St. Domingue but now seemingly by a threatening Haiti swelled by African American emigrants as well.

Under Gurley's leadership and as part of the effort to convince free blacks to go to Liberia, not Haiti, the Colonization Society began in 1825 a monthly journal, the *African Repository,* that trumpeted the great work supposedly under way in West Africa. The first issue, in March 1925, provided historical context. "Observations on the Early History of the African Race," by "T. R.," portrayed the Ethiopians as the world's first great people. They were conquerors and also teachers who brought the arts and sciences of civilization to the world, establishing colonies in places as far off as Japan. They overcame and taught the Egyptians, the Mesopotamians, and the Chinese. Proclaiming themselves gods, they were worshipped across Asia and Africa. Surviving tales and superstitions told of their grandeur: "It is supposed that they are the Giants that invaded Heaven, on the plains of Babylonia—the Magicians of Egypt, the Magi of the east, the Titans of Greece and Rome, the Cyclops of Sicily, and the fabulous Heroes of the world: invincible in war, and yet preeminent in all the arts of peace; distinguished above other men for learning, enterprize and valour—at once the tyrants and instructors of mankind!"[41]

The "mutability of human affairs"—time and chance—laid this great people low. T. R. cited Volney's *Travels* and quoted his famous tirade against prejudice. The great Ethiopians fell as did all they had built and shaped, T. R. continued in a Christian vein that Volney would have despised, for "the civilization which was derived from this venerable source, was of the earth, and transitory." Africa was now prostrate, its greatness, once the height of worldly power and knowledge, forgotten, its children bought and sold and maligned as beasts devoid of reason. Where Volney had superstition and religion as the culprits in the fall of empires, T. R. had Christianity as the only defense against the vagaries of fortune. After their New World sojourn, T. R. wrote, African Americans now could return to Africa, bringing a new kind of civilization in the history of the world, one "blended with the light that came down from Heaven—that can never be extinguished—the light of immortality!"[42]

There was little answer to such an argument that the pro-Haiti faction could make. Most slave country in the United States was warm, so Haiti's climate offered little difference, and of course African Americans originally hailed from Africa, not Haiti. Lundy did his best to present Boyer's regime in a positive light, but the effort was feeble. Lacking grand images like Egypt and Ethiopia and with little but self-preservation to offer whites, Lundy offered a redemption based on fear and threat, and the more Lundy made people afraid of race war the more they would also likely fear Boyer's Haiti itself. T. R., by contrast, offered benevolent motives and promises of black racial redemption and universal salvation that African American colonists would bring to the benighted natives in Africa. A once great and mysterious, then fallen, but now potentially blessed and divinely guided Ethiopia was the key. T. R.'s vision of a restored African greatness drew upon various sources: quotations and paraphrases on Egypt and Ethiopia from Volney; an article in the prestigious *North American Review* on Champollion's 1821 decipherment of the Rosetta Stone; the writings of Herodotus and Diodorus Siculus; antislavery tracts; traditional biblical commentaries tracing the nations of the earth to Noah's sons Ham, Shem, and Japeth;

and of course Psalm 68:31, "Princes shall come out of Egypt and Ethiopia shall soon stretch forth her hands unto God." Psalms 68:31 would also be probably the single most important biblical passage for nineteenth-century African Americans.

But most Europeans saw Egypt as grander than Ethiopia. This was partly because the Egyptian ruins were larger and more familiar and partly because of the Attic Greeks' renowned reverence for Egyptian profundity. Preference for Egypt also perhaps derived from disbelief that full Negroes—"Ethiopian" remained a synonym for Negro—had founded Western civilization. A writer excerpted in the *African Repository* itself professed such doubts.[43] In the 1820s, Egyptian majesty—usually not directly connected to race—was beginning to come into vogue in Europe and the United States. Egypt would be especially useful for racial debate because it was mysterious and portentously vague, even frightening and tomblike, associated with the mysteries of death and fate. Still, much more was coming to be known about Egypt than Ethiopia. Napoleon's 1798 Egyptian Expedition had included an army of scholars and chroniclers, whose majesterial *Description de l'Égypte* was published in four volumes in the 1810s and 20s. Vivant Denon, leader of Napoleon's scholarly army, pronounced the Egyptians to have been black or dark, if not identical to what he saw as debased West Africans; like Volney, however, Denon did not lend any deep reality to race and saw all humans as essentially the same. The *Description* confirmed Volney by including engravings of a Great Sphinx with Negroid features. Spurred by Napoleon's discoveries, and especially by Champollion's achievement, an Egyptian revival began in American architecture and decoration in the 1820s and 30s. Starting in 1826, as touted in the *New York Evening Post* and elsewhere, three Egyptian mummies were on view for several years at Rembrandt Peale's New York Museum. Highbrow periodicals like the *North American Review* and the *American Quarterly Review* ran hundreds of pages of articles on Champollion and Egyptian greatness, but these pieces mostly concerned the relevance of Egyptian records to disputes over biblical chronology and the literal truth of Holy Writ.[44]

Given how much more highly regarded Egyptian civilization was than Ethiopian and how Egypt but not Ethiopia was seen as being in the

Western tradition, African Americans' laying claim to Ethiopia, however great, as black would accomplish little for their own pride or for their elevation in the eyes of European Americans. Besides, except in weak efforts, like Stanhope Smith's, to have the inhabitants of the Upper Nile be "Abyssinians" from Asia, African Americans' Ethiopian ancestry was not in much doubt. But it was not as usable as the Egyptian connection. Furthermore, Egypt's perceived status as "mixed," a combination of Ethiopians, native Egyptians, and Mediterranean Europeans, would appeal to African Americans. They could say that the Egyptians' mixed but nevertheless predominantly black appearance and character corresponded to their own, a claim challenging and repudiating the idea of blackness as a natural category. Antebellum African Americans would venerate Egyptian more than Ethiopian civilizations of the past.

ℑ RACIAL CASTE AND THE COLLAPSE OF HAITIAN EMIGRATION

Until after both T. R.'s piece in the *African Repository* and the failure of Haitian emigration, however, African Americans invoked a black ancient Egypt primarily in Ethiopian terms, that is to say, terms defined by Christianity and the experiences of the post–slave-trade black Atlantic world. Egypt was read early on as another site of past black Edenic virtue and innocence despoiled by whites but soon once more to be exalted. African Americans up to then had seemingly found little need for a black Egypt as the fount of European civilization. No evidence I know suggests that they saw post-emancipation Haiti as the quintessential embodiment of a distinct blackness. St. Domingue and Haiti symbolized deliverance in the by-then conventional Exodus terms of the fruit of the experience of redemptive suffering. Whites had reaped the seeds of their own inhumanity in St. Domingue, and blacks had been delivered to found Haiti. That was all: humanity was still universal. African Americans who wrote about emigration presented Haiti as a land without prejudice or at any rate as a far better place than the United States.

Pro-Haitian emigration rhetoric among African Americans was relatively cautious and primarily stressed economic prospects. Free black people would not want to echo the Colonization Society claim that they would inevitably be degraded in America and could never belong there. A laudatory letter from Haiti by Thomas Paul, a Boston Baptist African

American minister missionizing there with Boyer's permission, can be read between the lines to reveal prospective African American immigrants' concerns. Haiti, according to Paul, was healthful and safe; he had never encountered hostility there when preaching or professing a Protestant faith; farm provisions were cheap; and the arts and crafts were making such progress that jobs for skilled craftsmen were plentiful. Paul also found it reassuring to live among "an enterprising population of several hundred thousands of active and brave men, who are determined to live free or die gloriously in the defense of freedom."[45]

Black leaders like Allen or Forten again supported emigration to Haiti, especially for those poor blacks or fugitives who could not succeed at all in America. Black people also appreciated negotiating with Boyer's regime directly, without having to deal with whites of such dubious motives as Colonization Society agents. Educated and respectable African Americans regarded themselves as having mastered the arts of civilization and truths of Protestant Christianity during their sojourn in America but having been prevented by prejudice from fully showing their mastery. Civilization and faith might be fulfilled when brought to Haiti's aid. This would be a minor redemption, the Haitian rebels having already given the greatest hope, black freedom and self-determination, to African Americans.[46]

At an August 15, 1825, meeting in Baltimore to celebrate French recognition of Haiti, the African American orator William Watkins declared, in an address reprinted in Lundy's *Genius*, "I view, in the existence of that Republic, a practical and ostensible realization of the prophecy—'Ethiopia shall stretch forth her hand.'" Boyer had purchased French recognition by promising an indemnity to the French government of one hundred million francs over twenty years, payments that would kill the already crippled Haitian economy. According to Watkins, Haitian independence provided "an irrefutable argument that the descendants of Africa were never designed by their creator to sustain an inferiority, or even a mediocrity, in the chain of beings." All that was required, Watkins said, was education and there would arise in Haiti "as great and as wise men, among the people of our colour, as ever preceded us on the stage of human existence."[47] The Republic of Haiti was not millennially perfect now, but with a little help it would quickly refute the calumnies of prejudice and recapture ancient African (that is, Ethiopian) grandeur. Respectable African Americans sought to provide that help.

The more prosperous African Americans turned out to be the only ones to benefit from emigration. The American commercial agent at Port-au-Prince observed that African Americans came "with the impression that where there is no prejudice against color there is no difference in the ranks of society, but they have the mortification to find that they are as distinctly marked here as elsewhere."[48] Very dark skin may have been a hindrance in Haiti, where there certainly was color and caste prejudice or at least a hierarchy of value based on both color and wealth. Literary historian J. Michael Dash points out that early nineteenth-century Haitians often protected their self-esteem by identifying with Europe and portraying Americans as "a coarse, immature and materialistic people."[49] Whether or not color played a role, relatively well-to-do African Americans could join the refined Haitian club: most of them found good places and jobs and wrote glowing letters home. Poor and unskilled African Americans, Haitian officials complained, did not enjoy the drudgery of sugar cultivation and drifted to the cities, where they caused trouble.

Here was an ironic correspondence indeed between "colored" and "white" thought. The Haitian mulatto elite proved about as badly impressed with the mass of free African Americans as was the Colonization Society. Lower-class African Americans were seen as a social danger. Boyer published warnings in *Niles Weekly Register* and elsewhere that only the frugal and industrious should apply to emigrate. Emigration to Haiti was effectively suspended in May 1825 when, citing "improper speculations by the emigrants, and by agents of foreign vessels," Boyer stopped paying transportation costs.[50] Ravaged by the years of civil war, Haiti was not the wealthy colony it had been as St. Domingue, nor was it the color and caste-blind workers' paradise its leaders claimed. Out of several thousand emigrants (estimates range from six to thirteen thousand), a large proportion (perhaps two thousand or more) returned to the United States, and many who remained in Haiti resented its class and color-conscious culture. Its attractions for African Americans declined.

Attempted again on small scale in 1838 and then finally before the

American Civil War, Haitian emigration proved a fiasco both ideologically and practically.[51] Emigration to Africa from the United States continued into the twentieth century. If relatively few African Americans settled in Africa, the redemptive ideology surrounding African emigration, in part drawn initially from American Colonization Society propaganda, persisted among them.

Haiti could not easily serve as an epitome of black society. Its economic plight seemed particularly telling. Many African Americans and almost everyone else saw Haiti's ability to equal or surpass the sugar output during colonial days as a major test of black capacity and self-government. After a reasonably good start under Toussaint's labor code, sugar production—the main source of the island's wealth and of its economic importance to the United States during colonial days—began to fall off, although Christophe's Code Henri actually did fairly well economically speaking. In the 1820s, when the fragmented landholding patterns begun under Pétion became almost universal after Boyer's reunification, the sugar yield declined precipitously and Haiti's major economy became subsistence farming. Proslavery propagandists exploited this downturn and seeming economic irrationalism no end.[52] No American writing, not even by African Americans, recognized that the Haitian state had, in effect, and at the heavy price of economic decline, rural impoverishment, and militarism, assured its independence. Giving the people land, which Afro-Caribbean traditions saw as the domain of the gods, gave them a stake in the nation.[53]

For American antislavery propaganda purposes post-revolutionary Haiti as a symbol became both dangerous and counterproductive. As a model for black rebellion and racial apocalypse, as St. Domingue, it went mostly underground, serving as a major subtext, a threat that was sometimes stated, rarely discussed at length, but always there. For African Americans in particular, ancient Egypt became a new exemplary text whose explication proceeded in terms of messianism, environmentalist natural history, and concepts of prejudice, caste, and social environment that developed during the emigration debates.

4

The Mutability of Human Affairs

I aver, that when I look over these United States of America, and the world, and see the ignorant deceptions and consequent wretchedness of my brethren, I am brought oftimes to a stand, and in the midst of my reflections I exclaim to my God, "Lord, didst thou make us to be slaves to our brethren, the whites?" But when I reflect that God is just, and that millions of my wretched brethren would meet death with glory—yea, more, would plunge into the very mouths of cannons and be torn into particles as minute as the atoms which compose the elements of the earth, in preference to mean submission to the lash of tyrants, I am with streaming eyes, compelled to shrink back into nothingness before my Maker, and exclaim again, thy will be done, O Lord God Almighty.

David Walker, *Appeal . . . to the Coloured Citizens of the World* (1829)

It is difficult to say exactly when African Americans first engaged directly with race theory. When and how did African Americans begin to describe their skin color as the mark of a biological entity, a thing, with its own history and life, perhaps not fully reducible to climate or circumstance? Should such descriptions be taken at face value or as ironic table-turning on race theories that were emerging among white commentators? When and how did black discourse first begin to reject or modify the environmentalism of natural history? For that matter, when did African Americans begin to invoke environmentalist, natural historical arguments, and evidence for human unity and black capacity or degradation in the first place? Lacking voluminous sources, and given the difficulty of determining authorial intent or tracing the spread of ideas or intellectual influences, we may never know for sure.

My strong guess is that African Americans first openly attempted to come to grips with natural history on their own terms and in their own

words in 1827, with the publication of the first African American newspaper, the weekly *Freedom's Journal,* which ran several long original
pieces on racial themes. Two years later these themes received fuller and
somewhat different expression in David Walker's *Appeal . . . to the Coloured Citizens of the World,* the most radical black protest pamphlet of
the nineteenth century. Although other African Americans, both earlier
and contemporaneously with the *Journal* writers and Walker, discussed
what blackness meant (or did not mean) and tried to conceptualize reversing the effects of slavery and prejudice and uplifting their brethren,
I have not found instances of African American use of natural history,
albeit such usages may exist. In any case, the *Journal* material and
Walker's *Appeal* were the most important African American expressions
of their time (just before the advent of militant abolitionism) on the nature of blackness, the future of African Americans, and the history and
nature of black people in Africa. These expressions were fundamentally
engaged in the cross-racial emigration debates and also encompassed
African Americans' enduring redemptive Christianity and sense of race
as defined by exploitation and suffering in the modern Atlantic world.
These black writers presented the natural reality of race as an open
question as they tried to figure out the meaning of their people's and
whites' character and changing fortune. There were no certainties. As
Raboteau observes, the single most important biblical passage for nineteenth-century African Americans, Psalm 68:31, "Princes shall come
out of Egypt and Ethiopia shall soon stretch forth her hands unto God,"
"was not so much a prophecy as it was a prayer."[1] Black questionings
about race were also complex prayers and meditations on the shifts of
fortune in a fallen world.

Hence, although the *Journal* writers and Walker broached the issue
of race and nature, it would be wrong to see their ideas as a black race
theory to answer growing white certainties. A "black race theory" rubric
implies a more monolithic and purely reactive approach to race among
African Americans and a greater level of conceptual segregation than actually existed. The historian Mia Bay has recently written of the birth of
a "black ethnology," which seems both anachronistic and overly segregated as applied to Walker or the *Journal.*[2] The word "ethnology," connoting "the science of races," came into use in British intellectual circles

only in the late 1830s as a subset of the natural history of man, and became popular in the United States only in the 1840s. If anything, the "black ethnology" rubric runs influence quite the wrong way. The questioning and unresolved black "mutability of human affairs" argument, drawn partly from natural history and colonization propaganda, would help provoke the rise both of white radical abolitionism and American ethnological polygenism. Just as Walker and the *Journal* writers drew on earlier debates across racial lines, some whites would quickly pick up on language and ideas in the *Journal* and especially the *Appeal*, and white ethnology would be obsessed not just with beating down radical abolitionism but with proving the Egyptians white. Walker and the *Journal* writers' most un-"ethnological" bitterness at having to broach naturalized concepts of race testifies to their achievement and self-consciousness.

Race was not simply an unthinkingly accepted language or a mask for these black people's concerns about justice and right. As early African Americans well knew, judgment of people by their color and facial features was also mostly nonsense. Hence characterizing early black engagements with natural history is quite difficult. One gets little feeling of Linnaean hollowness or flatness from these engagements. Yet what provides a sense of depth and flavor, what indeed makes free blacks' historical and racial vision seem familiar and alive, was not exactly a modern, organicist conception of life, and certainly not hard ethnological innatism.

☙ THIS DELIGHTFUL PICTURE HAS LONG SINCE VANISHED

Educated free black people doubtless early became aware of the various racial theories current among white writers. Excerpts from polygenist or quasi-polygenist works that asserted permanent black inferiority, especially Jefferson's *Notes on Virginia,* appeared in major magazines and newspapers of the early republic. African Americans also read Samuel Stanhope Smith's monogenist, environmentalist *Essay* of 1810 and that same year had available to them a work that disdained racialism, *An Enquiry Concerning the Intellectual and Moral Faculties and Literature of Negroes* by Abbé Henri Grégoire, member of the French Revolutionary abolitionist society, *Amis des Noires,* who had corresponded with

Toussaint Louverture. This compendium of the careers and accomplishments of blacks, first published in French in 1808, served as an encyclopedia for pro-Negro thought, black and white, throughout the nineteenth century. Grégoire dismissed as nonsense the natural historical controversy over the characteristics and status of the Negro. In his view, all sides, monogenists included, employed at best tenuous science and reasoning and excessive great distinctions between Africans and Europeans. "All systems" that assumed major differences between black and white were evil, adopted "by those who, by every means seek to materialize man, and to rob him of the dearest hopes of his heart," by those seeking to argue against the truth of Genesis, and "by men, who, interested in colonial culture, seek, in the supposed want of the moral faculties of the negro, another reason for treating him, with impunity, like a beast of burden."[3] Grégoire told readers to forget natural historical debate over race as hopelessly corrupt and focus on the plain facts of instances of great black achievements, past and present. To these he devoted nearly two hundred pages, including examples of black intelligence, piety, progress, and morality not just in Europe but in Africa, Haiti, and ancient Egypt (which he saw as black or dark). Yet blackness was no more an entity for Grégoire than for Volney, whose *Ruins* had appeared in five separate American editions by *Freedom Journal*'s day and had helped to spread Freemasonry and to inspire radical free thought and Romantic poetry and philosophy.

Eighteenth-century environmentalist racial theory had rested on the belief that living things, perhaps especially humankind, changed fairly quickly in response to their surroundings. West African "miasmas" and savagery, not innate qualities, produced the "degenerate" Negro. If degeneration might acquire great weight over time via the force of habit and mode of life intertwining with biology through the inheritance of acquired characteristics, the experience of civilization and salubrity could soon produce health and intelligence, if perhaps not whiteness. This environmentalism differed from a conventional Christian concept of fall and possible redemption, and differed again from the mutability idea implicit in the idea of ancient Egypt, black or otherwise, as having once ruled the known world then fallen into ruin. Everything thus passed away in an endless melancholy series of cycles of rise and decline.

Volney's intensely secular *Ruins* saw as the "causes and principles" behind the "rise and fall of empires" religious fanaticism and greed, which always threatened reason and science. Jefferson for his part feared that the "wheel of fortune" would turn and destroy white America for the sin of slavery; he did have the perspicacity and honesty to see that appeals to a timeless nature could provide no solace when confronted by the enormities of slavery and race in the New World.

Colonization Society propaganda took what may be called a social environmentalist view, or, sociologically speaking, a structuralist-functionalist view that rationalized the current situation. Slavery and prejudice and their awful effects, long established, were by now nobody's fault; they constituted a social system that could not be swayed or ameliorated except very slowly. The reality of American life meant that even if blacks were human and thus *de jure* equal, they were and would remain *de facto* inferior. Benevolent solutions to this difficult problem required time, and meanwhile nothing should be said or done to rouse slaves or harass slaveholders. The latter had to be allowed to act voluntarily, or race war might destroy the republic. This perspective subordinated salvation and benevolence to the inertia of social environment and, what amounted to the same thing, the political expediency of not meddling with slavery.

By the time of the *African Repository,* however, the Colonization Society was proclaiming the Liberia project as a means to help redeem the world, albeit gradually. Blacks' return to Africa would slowly lift both Africa and America out of sin. This argument was tied to some kind of pluralistic race theory with redemption coming as each race perfected civilization and Christianity in its appointed zone. The abolitionist Benjamin Lundy reasoned much the same way, although he remained unassuaged by the colonizationists' social environmentalist excuses for slavery and feared a racial apocalypse as much as Jefferson had. But the intrinsic inadequacy of emigrationist arguments as practical solutions for the problem of slavery, plus black hostility to African colonization and the difficulties of advocating Haitian emigration for African Americans, drove Lundy also to dabble in a comforting racial pluralism as a way to avoid fully facing slavery's enormity.

African Americans could not escape the terrible reality of their life in

America, and they well understood the reality of prejudice. They tended to link blackness with messianism in a sort of cyclical history, beginning with an almost prelapsarian Africa. The prominent African American Methodist minister, New Yorker Peter Williams, Jr., observed ironically in his "Oration on the Abolition of the Slave Trade," delivered in 1808, "Before the enterprising spirit of European genius explored the western coast of Africa, the state of our forefathers was a state of simplicity, innocence, and contentment. But alas! this delightful picture has long since vanished; the angel of bliss has deserted their dwelling; and the demon of indescribable misery has rioted, uncontrolled, on the fair fields of our ancestors."[4] Past African greatness was less political and cultural than innocent and pristine, prior to modern history and "black" identity. That identity was usually seen as having its origin in the horrors and desolations of the Atlantic slave trade and given liberating potential by literacy and encounters with the Bible, evangelical Protestantism, and the American Revolutionary doctrines of universal equality and the rights of man.

Early African Americans invoked a dark-skinned Egypt in terms of original African innocence despoiled by vicious outsiders. William Hamilton, in his "Oration, on the Abolition of the Slave Trade," delivered in New York in 1815, said that because Africa lay "immediately under the fostering care of the sun," it was originally pure and Edenic and had given shape to the world's first civilizations. Except for the desert lands, the fertile soil of Africa produced its fruits with a minimum of human labor, so that the early Africans had to have been happy and virtuous. "Egypt was anciently settled by an honest, industrious, peaceable and well-developed people," who were eventually scattered across the earth by two successive invasions of "wicked" nations. The refugee Egyptians, Hamilton reasoned, since they had fled Egypt to escape invaders and to continue their peaceful way of life, "must have remained the same peaceable, just and honest people for a long series of time."[5] From this point of view, it could be argued that these ancestors of people whom the Atlantic slave trade would make "blacks" had been driven out of Egypt before the time of the Hebrew captivity: Pharaoh did not count as an African.

Not that pre-Egyptians would necessarily be seen as perfect; nor would Pharaoh necessarily be cast as European. In an 1810 sermon on the abolition of the slave trade, the African Methodist minister William Miller praised pharaonic Egypt as highly civilized: "The inhabitants of Africa are descended from the ancient inhabitants of Egypt, a people once famous for science of every description." This people had fallen due to their own sins, going from monotheism to idolatry and then enslaving the Hebrews.[6]

One of the first black expressions of a mutability philosophy of history rather than a sinful fall from true religion or pristine innocence appeared in *Haytian Papers,* both the British and American editions, by Prince Saunders. In a passage that may have derived from Volney's *Ruins,* which Saunders, a sophisticated traveler familiar with both French and British culture, would have known about, he declared:

> in the irresistible march of the affairs of this world, every thing paints the instability of sublunary concerns: empires rise and fall, flourish and decay. The light of knowledge follows the impulse of revolutions, and travels, successively, over the surface of the globe. Greece, Germany, and Gaul, were not originally the seats of learning. Our traducers pretend to have forgotten what the Egyptians and Ethiopians, our ancestors, were . . . The testimony of Herodotus, of Strabo, and of other historians of antiquity, confirm these facts. More recent proofs bear evidence in our favour, and yet our enemies, with signal incredulity, feign to doubt all this.[7]

"More recent proofs" probably referred not only to Volney's book but also to the testimony of Napoleon's Egyptian Expedition. It is not clear that any race theory, environmental or otherwise, informed Saunders's statement. Given the black/mulatto conflicts of Haitian history, open proclamations by either side in the Haitian civil wars tended to attribute little natural reality to race, especially as both regimes sometimes tried to apply the term "blacks" to all Haitians regardless of skin color.

Although educated African Americans might well have read *Haytian Papers,* nothing like the mutability approach expressed by Saunders seems to have emerged in their writing until the late 1820s. Other African Americans had, like the young Saunders, contemplated or undertaken African emigration but seem not to have written of a glorious Egyptian past. Saunders was a Freemason, and Freemasonry became a kind of civil religion in post-revolutionary Haiti. Perhaps a black Egypt was frequently spoken of in Haitian Masonic lodges, but it seems not to have been discussed in public statements connected to African American ones like New York's black Masonic Lodge (named for Boyer), Prince Hall's African Lodge No. 1 in Charlestown, Massachusetts, or Boston's Lodge No. 459, to which David Walker would belong.[8]

✺ TO PLEAD OUR OWN CAUSE

We see a turn toward the difficult promise of mutability and the influence of natural history and environmentalism, with religious overtones, in the pages of *Freedom's Journal*, published in New York City from March 1827 to March 1829. At first the Reverend Samuel E. Cornish, an important antebellum leader later to edit several other papers, served as senior editor. Born free in Delaware in the late 1790s, Cornish preached to Maryland slaves, then attended and taught school in Philadelphia, and in 1821 became pastor of the First Colored Presbyterian Church in New York City; he gave up his pulpit to edit the *Journal*.[9] The *Journal*'s junior editor, John B. Russwurm, seems to have been the second African American to receive a college degree, from Bowdoin in 1826. After six months Cornish dropped out, and Russwurm became sole editor.

The 1827 inception date was not arbitrary. It celebrated the imminent formal end of slavery in New York State. In 1799 the state legislature had passed the so-called Gradual Manumission Act, which provided for the gradual emancipation of all slaves born after July 4, 1799 (men born after that date would remain slaves until age 28, women until age 22); those born before would remain in bondage forever. Eventually, in 1817, black industriousness and self-manumissions persuaded the free-labor-minded governor and legislature in 1817 to set July 4, 1827, as the date on which all remaining slaves (of whatever age) in the state would be free.[10]

There was cause for concern as well as celebration. Several of New York City's white editors and politicians used the occasion to echo the Colonization Society's charge that African Americans had made nothing of freedom and were all criminals and paupers. Prejudice had escalated dramatically, as the spread of the suffrage to virtually all white men, especially in the increasingly free labor northern states, was accompanied by increasing restrictions on free blacks, seen by then as unfit for citizenship. In New York State, Federalists had supported black voting rights, but Republicans had been trying since the Revolution to take those rights away, which the demise of Federalism during the War of 1812 made possible. New York City restricted black voting in 1814, and in 1821 the state constitution went even further, eliminating property qualifications for white male voters but requiring black men to own more than $250 worth of property and to have resided in the state for at least three years. These conditions meant that in 1825 only 298 black men could vote out of a statewide black population of 30,000; in New York City only 16 out of more than 12,000 African Americans were eligible to vote.[11] Similar exclusions went on the books in Maryland (in 1783 and 1810), Connecticut (1814 and 1818), Rhode Island (1832), and Pennsylvania (1838). Laws were changed in Rhode Island and Maryland to exclude blacks from the militia, and Maryland also barred blacks from running for public office.[12] Anti-black riots erupted in the 1820s and 30s, and African Americans were driven into lower and lower occupations.

Recent historical research has indicated that anxiety caused by the market revolution and urban industrialization drove this increasing hostility to blacks and intensified "whiteness" as a potent political ideology. The disappearance of free land in the countryside, the improvement of farm equipment, and the construction of new canals and roads all lessened the need for agricultural workers and glutted urban labor markets not just with men but with more and more women. Whites and blacks and men and women competed in the cities for lower and lower skilled and paid jobs. The men among immigrant groups like the Irish who had often been treated as virtual animals in Europe found that not being female or of African descent entitled them to enter the fold of "white" manhood with all its privileges, as voting opened up to all white men and political parties vied for immigrant support. Consequently, many immigrant men became staunchly anti-black. As David Roediger shows, women were considered too undisciplined and emotional to be full citizens, unlike self-sufficient, virtuous "working men." Worse still, blacks were deemed utterly unworthy of rights, innately "lewd and lascivious."

Hence the great cry of many nineteenth-century urban working men facing lower wages or bad working conditions not to be "white slaves." Only servile, animalistic "niggers" could be so treated.[13] Yet, in a remarkable act of what Eric Lott describes as "love and theft," droves of these same white men attended minstrel shows both to mock and to identify with supposedly oversexed, unrestrained, animalistic "black" characters. As well as animalistic inferiority, blackness came culturally to symbolize what white men had to surrender in order to become virtuous citizens and workers.[14] Of course, not all northern workingmen had these deep prejudices and displaced feelings or at least did not display them, and color prejudice predated the 1820s. Still, the changes wrought by the advent of the industrial revolution were real enough and disturbing enough, and life did become harder than ever for free black people.

White Americans in important leadership positions accepted the idea that democracy was for whites only. This included the elitist, conservative American Colonization Society, with its roots in High Federalism and its support from major Republican politicians. The society's self-proclaimed benevolence notwithstanding, its analysis of the damage that slavery had done to blacks fed the prejudice that it claimed to deplore. Furthermore, the society's plans to rid the United States of free blacks and then slaves were designed to appeal to a broad spectrum of white men north and south and to suppress antislavery activism.[15] And the national symbol of democracy, the southern slave owner Andrew Jackson, albeit disdaining the notions of social hierarchy and the organized, aristocratic benevolence that people like the colonizationists represented, would be staunchly anti-black and would further the political strategy of suppressing sectional differences over slavery.

Freedom's Journal grew out of the concerns of free African Americans about the heightened prejudice and discrimination they now faced. At a meeting of prominent free blacks in New York City convened to address recent newspaper attacks upon them, it was decided to give black people a new voice. Thus was born the first national forum for African Americans and the first comparatively extensive published source to emerge from the African American community. As Cornish put it in a mission statement in the first issue, "We wish to plead our own cause.

Too long have others spoken for us."[16] Cornish presented the paper's goals as promoting education, civil rights, and free black uplift and as providing accurate news of Africa, Haiti, and especially free blacks' true position in the United States. Read surreptitiously in slave states and openly throughout the free states, often aloud at churches, barber shops, and taverns, the *Journal* truly was national. Along with responses to prejudice or exhortations to virtue and respectability, it ran advertisements from black businesses as well as a few carefully worded accounts of escapes from slavery or notices from families trying to find relatives who might have made it up north or to Canada. At its height the *Journal* had more than thirty agents nationwide, including David Walker in Boston. Subscriptions during the first year ranged from eight to eleven hundred, an average number for a New York-based weekly of the day.[17]

The *Journal*'s inception, coming so soon after the failure of the Haitian emigration project, was also a declaration that free blacks were in America to stay. Cornish despised the American Colonization Society and had been deeply involved in the negotiations with Boyer and no doubt felt disappointment when the venture soured.[18] Cornish made the *Journal* into the scourge of the ACS. In editorials and through material from other sources that he chose to reprint in full or in part (a practice common in periodical publications of the time), he reiterated his conviction that African emigration was at best a pipe dream and at worst a proslavery plot. Advocates, white and black, of the Liberia project were invited to debate the issue; several took up the offer. Free blacks were exhorted to pursue education, sobriety, thrift, and virtue, "to use all diligence to form ourselves a virtuous and intelligent character. This will disarm prejudice of the weapons it has too successfully used against us; and it will also strengthen the hands of our friends in their efforts on our behalf."[19] Blacks' professed friends had to be made to shake off the ACS's influence and to stop assuming, contrary to any firsthand knowledge, that blacks were in as bad a condition as the society contended. Such friends, Cornish wrote, were "actually living in the practice of prejudice, while they abjure it in theory, and feel it not in their hearts."[20]

Cornish reprinted a pro-Colonization editorial from the *Georgetown Columbian* that said that blacks ought to remove themselves to Africa, "to render themselves distinguished and honoured in that clime for which Nature had so emphatically fitted them"; they never could achieve the privileges of equality in the United States. Cornish replied: "We do not believe it. Is he ignorant of the history of nations? Has he never read in his Bible that the Lord reigneth? We are unwavering in our opinion, that the time is coming (though it may be distant) in which our posterity will enjoy equal rights. The idea that the free population of the North are more fitted to the climate of Africa than the whites, is perfectly futile—acts evince the contrary." As for African redemption, a few well trained and placed missionaries would do more to Christianize that continent than an ill-conceived "colony" ever could.[21]

Another Cornish editorial pointed to census returns to counter ACS claims about black degradation: New York City had one colored pauper to every 185 blacks, as compared with one white pauper to every 115 whites.[22] Cornish printed William Watkins's exposé of a pro-emigration memorial supposedly by Baltimore free blacks as actually having been written by two prominent white colonizationists.[23]

Ironically, the ACS was probably the decisive influence on *Freedom's Journal*'s interest in race history and theory—in invoking a knowledge of nature and "the history of nations." In the American slavery debate, the ACS was first to assume the relevance of a great, civilized, ancient Africa. This idea, advanced in an attempt to fend off emigration to Haiti, was most notably developed in T. R.'s "Observations on the Early History of the African Race," in the *African Repository*. Russwurm would reprint this article verbatim in the *Journal* in 1828. Earlier, in April 1827, Cornish published the first African American writing that might possibly be considered race theory and the most important piece in the *Journal* under his aegis. This original three-part article was entitled "The Mutability of Human Affairs," a direct quotation from T. R.[24]

⚙ HAITI AND EGYPT IN THE JOURNAL

Freedom's Journal editors, contributors, and readers showed great concern with mutability and ancient Egypt, significant pride in Haitian independence, and a good deal less interest in the problems of post-independence Haiti. Cornish had been involved with Haitian emigration, and Russwurm's graduation address at Bowdoin had optimistically treated "The Condition and Prospects of Hayti."[25] But by the late 1820s

Haiti's luster had dulled, and new conditions in the United States, along with the new vogue for things Egyptian, had pushed ancient Africa, especially Egypt to the fore among African Americans searching for the lessons of history and for a usable past in the struggle to deal with the present. Furthermore, Cornish had become disenchanted with any kind of emigration, and Russwurm had become enchanted with the African colonization version.

During Cornish's tenure as chief editor, the *Journal* ran six major pieces on ancient Egypt and four pieces of consequence, all excerpts from other sources, that discussed Haiti. Only two of these four, one a reprint of an article in the *British Quarterly Review* on the life of Toussaint Louverture (eulogized as the noble antagonist of perfidious Napoleon) and the other an account of the Haitian Revolution (under the pseudonym "Africanus") from the *Christian Watchman,* were actually about the black island and both skirted the civil wars and their aftermath.[26] The other two pieces were really about ancient Egypt.

One of the latter was a long extract from *America; or, A General Survey,* a new important and widely reviewed book written anonymously by the editor and diplomat Alexander Everett of the distinguished Everett family of Boston.[27] In his chapter concerning European colonies in America, Everett discussed Haiti (which in his view had still not yet achieved full independence) and recounted African history as proof of black equality. From the Flood until the Persian conquest, a period far longer than the reign of the Roman Empire or the modern hegemony of Western Europe, Africans had "enjoyed a decided predominance throughout the whole ancient western world." Indeed, Everett attested, blacks were "even not without some plausible pretensions to a claim of superiority."[28]

Everett soon put this conclusion to uses that Cornish and Russwurm no doubt would have found objectionable. Yet *Freedom's Journal,* editorially honest, excerpted the whole of *America*'s remarks on blacks, Haiti, Egypt, and America, including a claim that even when Haiti won full independence and recognition from other nations, it would probably always remain a mediocrity. A biological analogy explained why. According to Everett, each race resembled an individual person or a nation, with a lifespan going from vigor to senescence: "Nations and races, like individuals, have their day, and seldom have a second. The blacks had a long and glorious one; and after what they have been and done, it argues not so much a mistaken theory as sheer ignorance of the most notorious historical facts, to pretend that they are naturally inferior to the whites." Given what they had once achieved long ago, the prejudice now arrayed against them, and their degradation in the "white" dominated world, blacks might never prosper again: the "most that can reasonably be expected of them" would be self-government and some degree of improvement and learning from their (white) neighbors.[29]

Freedom's Journal also ran Everett's argument that Haitian emigration, by siphoning off the brightest and most ambitious free blacks, provided the best safeguard against racial unrest in the United States. Everett here denounced the Colonization Society's rhetoric as dangerously radical, "inasmuch as it keeps up in the public mind, an impression, that the situation of the slaves can be violently and suddenly altered for the better, by this expedient of emigration." Blacks were so degraded and whites so powerful that no general slave revolt could possibly succeed, and in practical terms all the slaves could never be sent to Africa in any case. "Finally, it may be questioned whether we ought to wish to remove from amongst us, if we could do it peaceably and easily, so large a portion of the working class." Means might eventually be found to elevate African American slaves, but for that to be possible it was crucial now "to discourage in every possible way, the idea that any thing can be effected immediately and at once."[30] In an editorial following the final extract from *America,* Cornish challenged "the advocates of Slavery, to disprove any thing in the foregoing extract. To them, our columns are open to a candid investigation of the subject."[31]

The other Haiti-related excerpt in *Freedom's Journal,* entitled "Africa," came from a book-length vindication of the capacities of the Negroes written upon Grégoire's model by the Haitian Baron de Vastey (Pompée Valentin Vastey), who had been Henri Christophe's chief propagandist and sometime chief courtier. Like Saunders, De Vastey proclaimed that "every body [sic] knows that the Greeks, so celebrated for the polish of their manners, and the refinement of their taste, were in a state of the grossest ignorance and barbarity, living, like the beasts, upon herbs and acorns, till civilized by colonies from Egypt."[32] Like Everett,

De Vastey simply assumed Egyptian blackness, although he gave far less natural reality to race than Everett's *America*. *Freedom's Journal* original material, however, would not take the Egyptian Expedition's finding of Egyptian blackness so easily for granted.

⑨ EGYPT AND THE BIBLE

Proofs of Egyptian blackness could become a major counterargument to the most important conventional defense of African chattel slavery in the New World, the so-called Curse of Canaan or Curse of Ham. Black writing had usually avoided the Curse, but it now proliferated in the *Journal* refutations, and "black" biblical genealogies for Africans appeared.

The basic story of the Curse, from Genesis, had been variously used to justify all manner of exploitation, from the Israelites' seizure of the land of Canaan, to European serfdom and treatment of Slavs as captive forced labor (hence the word "slave"), to African chattel slavery in the New World. In the Old Testament, after Ham had mocked his father Noah's drunkenness and nakedness (and sometimes Ham's sin was seen as sodomy or even castration of his father), Noah condemned Ham's youngest son, Canaan: "Cursed be Canaan and a servant of servants shall he be unto his brethren" (Genesis 9:25).[33] Free blacks and white southerners, and especially southern ministers harping on the supposed implications of that particular verse of scripture well into the late twentieth century, interpreted the Curse of Canaan according to the long tradition of what has been called "chronological" history, for almost two thousand years the main way Judeo-Christians had seen the past, and subject to endless different readings. As well as the *Freedom's Journal* articles, the *African Repository, American Quarterly Review,* and *North American Review* material on Champollion and Egypt all dealt heavily in biblical chronology, which basically sought to order a cosmic, God-given series of events rather than a purely human one; human causation was unimportant; dates and sequence, especially of biblical events, were paramount. Chronology traced human diversity back to the time of the Flood, to Noah's three sons, Ham, Shem and Japheth, seen as the progenitors of Africans, Asians, and Europeans, respectively. Applications of the Curse to Africans were ancient: as punishment for Ham's sin, all the Canaanites, or sometimes all Ham's descendants, had their minds degraded, their skin blackened, their features thickened and coarsened, and even, as a Talmudic scholar put it in the fifth century A.D., their penises "shamefully elongated."[34]

These standard versions of the Curse were vulnerable on several fronts. The Bible also had Ham's elder sons Cush and Misraim as, respectively, the founders of Ethiopia and Egypt, a circumstance that abolitionists, white and black, unfailingly pointed out. Defenders of the idea that blackness was the God-given mark of slavish inferiority responded by reiterating the idea that the Curse applied to the Canaanites only. In this view, Cush and Misraim, who were indeed the progenitors of the Egyptian and Ethiopian ruling classes, had been white men; ancient Egyptian and Ethiopian blacks, descendants of Canaan, had been brought to the Nile valley as slaves. In 1806 the English traveler W. G. Browne had even reported that the Egyptians had mummified themselves to ensure that posterity knew that they had been white. African Americans and their advocates dealt with this new calumny by reasserting the standard Greek and Roman, biblical, and French Enlightenment evidence for Egyptian and Ethiopian blackness and then saying that the Canaanites, as attested by many popular biblical commentators, were the forebears of the Phoenicians, a Semitic people. Hence the Curse of Canaan had, they said, no relationship to skin color.[35]

Freedom's Journal printed an excerpt from an anonymous piece making this argument, "The Curse of Canaan," which had appeared in the *New York Observer,* organ of the moderate-to-conservative wings of the Presbyterian Church. The article, which Cornish as a Presbyterian minister of the same persuasion probably read closely, declared that black-skinned people descended from Cush and had built the pyramids.[36] Cornish and Russwurm fully agreed, but other *Freedom's Journal* articles found evidence in the Bible and biblical commentaries to insist that blacks descended from Misraim. A long three-part letter to the editors, "The Genealogy of the African Race," by "S" took this line and had Cush as white. According to S, the Egyptians, progeny of Misraim, had colonized Greece, Carthage, Sidonia, and China, the last after being driven out of Egypt by the Hycksoes, white marauders descended from "wicked Cush." The rest of Misraim's descendants fled into the inhospitable regions of Africa, where they degenerated physically and morally.

Unlike William Hamilton a dozen years earlier, who had also postulated an Egyptian diaspora, S apparently accepted the idea that sub-Saharan Africans were inferior. He also asked his readers to excuse his possible inaccuracies, "when told that the writer is quite a youth."[37]

The *New York Observer* had published another anonymous article, also reprinted in *Freedom's Journal,* entitled "An Apology for Pharaoh," an assault on American slavery and its defenses as being far worse than what Pharaoh did and said regarding the Israelites. And Pharaoh and his armies were swallowed up in the Red Sea. "Yet I say, Egyptian slavery was not as hard as some other cases of slavery; and Pharaoh's excuses are, I think, better than what have satisfied, and now satisfy, many."[38] Such an argument enabled African Americans to identify with the Hebrews and at the same time call upon ancient Egyptian splendor and power as evidence of what Africans could accomplish.

୭ MUTABILITY: WHITENESS AND ASHES

But the Egyptians had been destroyed, and not only by the parting of the Red Sea. Their entire civilization had crumbled, only to be rediscovered millennia later in the desert sands. So went the inexorable tides of history. T. R. in the *African Repository* may have seen African redemption as an easy road to universal salvation, an end to "the mutability of human affairs." But the anonymous author of "Mutability of Human Affairs" in *Freedom's Journal* saw no end in sight, no sure hope that humans would conquer sin.

"Mutability," in a passage reminiscent of Constantin François Volney's *Ruins,* began by likening the Egyptians to slaves on the American auction block. "During a recent visit to the Egyptian Mummy, my thoughts were insensibly carried back to former times, when Egypt was in her splendor, and the only seat of chivalry, science, arts and civilization." The author, "as a descendant of Cush," mourned over Egypt's "present degradation" and reflected on "the mutability of human affairs."

My heart sickened as I pondered upon the picture which my imagination had drawn—like Marius surveying the ruins of Carthage, I wept over the fallen state of my people.—Wherefore is it, that a gloom pervades the mind, while reflecting upon the ages which have passed; and which, like the "baseless fabrick of a vision," have scarcely left a wreck behind them? But such applies not to Egypt: for her obelisks and pyramids, which attest her greatness still remain, amid the grandeur of the desert, full of magnificence and death, at once a trophy and a tomb. But her kings, to preserve whose bodies from sacrilegious hands, they were erected, where are they? Have they not been torn from their "vaunted sepulchers" and exhibited to a gazing world? *Have not they too been bought and sold?* Methinks, the lesson to be learned from this, should warn other potentates, who are lavishing the hard earnings of their industrious subjects upon their costly mausoleums, of the vanity of their labours.[39]

Upon walking into Peale's Museum in New York to view his ancestors, the author had seemingly been stunned by the scene of whites buying, selling, and exhibiting the mummies as white, grand, and mysterious. These dessicated black Egyptian despots hawked by these most unchristian and unrepublican white Christian republicans was a spectacle of utter fallenness, theft, and degradation that encapsulated the sordid and mundane enormities of the Atlantic slave trade and the black Atlantic world—enormities that themselves furnished history's most melancholy example of "mutability."

The change that was the order of this world could also be for good, though, as in the New World, where new towns and cities appeared almost daily "where thirty years ago, naught but the footsteps of the savage had ever disturbed 'the deep solitude of the forest.'" Yet in Europe, the "lenient policy of the government of Napoleon" had been replaced by despotism and the Bourbon restoration, and the great Napoleon now lay "on the rocky shores of sea girt St. Helena."[40]

The author must have seen the placards and displays at Peale's and probably heard the lectures presenting the mummies in secular terms as spoils and scholarly fascinations from a mysterious land of pharaohs and gold. To this sense of the conquest and the unearthing of distant mystery, the author of "Mutability" proposed in counterpoint the intimate familiarity and eschatological significance among fellow Christians with biblical events in Africa: "History informs us that Cush and Menes (the

Misraim of scripture) were the sons of Ham." Those sons and their descendants peopled Africa and the Persian Gulf. A black-skinned Egypt was the first link in the chain of civilization, leading through Greece and Rome to modern Europe and America. If "mankind generally allow" that Egypt founded the arts and sciences, it was not acknowledged that the Egyptians could have any resemblance to present-day Africans, yet Herodotus, "'the father of history,' expressly declares that the 'Egyptians had dark skin and frizzled hair.'" Everything known of the ancient Ethiopians, a people everyone from the Bible forwards granted to be black, argued that their "obscure and mythological" religious language, their priests and social organization, and their remarkable "contempt of death," all matched characteristics of ancient Egypt.[41]

In the second installment of "Mutability" race became the explicit issue, and notions of nonwhite "degeneration" were dismissed. The Ethiopians shared every social form with the Egyptians, their brethren, and had constant intercourse with them, yet appeared black and full-featured in the earliest reports, so how could Negroes be degenerate? In "Mutability's" presentation, the very idea of race became a category imposed by white prejudice on a complex reality defying classification. Still, in the past, whites' ignorance of Africa had probably been for the best. The Greeks and Romans must have known little of remote Ethiopia's glories. Otherwise more Africans would have fallen prey to their rapacity:

> that spirit of conquest which led Alexander to weep because he had not other worlds to conquer, and Julius Caesar to contest with the barbarous tribes of Britain (from whom he could expect nothing but the mere honour) would have prompted the former to have crossed the burning sands of Sahara, even to the far-famed city of Timbuctoo; and the latter, instead of the voluptuous arms of Cleopatra, to have marched his victorious legions (or by the Red Sea to have coasted) into Ethiopia, and added to his present list, the names of a few more cities plundered and burnt, a few more thousands slain, and left to whiten nature's face.[42]

Note the double entendre of "whiten"—meaning both racially to whiten and to reduce to ashes and bones.

This powerful implication that whites rather than blacks were degenerate, perhaps innately, was revealed as sarcasm in the next passage, which resisted the temptation to argue that blacks were the true human standard. What, the author asked, was the original color of the Egyptians and Ethiopians? To Herodotus they were both black, more or less like present-day sub-Saharan Africans. Yet the present-day Arabs, living in the same region as Egypt of old and also a people descended from Cush and Misraim, were copper-colored. "How is this to be explained? Are we to supposed that the present race of Arabs have degenerated, while the original black colour has remained good?" (that is, remained good in us, today's blacks). No: since only the hottest climates had really black people and the coldest regions whites, and since copper-colored peoples inhabited vast portions of the globe, warm and cool, it made most sense to say that Adam had been copper colored and that whites and blacks were both environmentally produced variants of that original type. After all, it took only a century for the people in a Portuguese colony on the African coast to become almost indistinguishable from the native Africans. Heat perhaps explained black skin, as Pliny had believed. At any rate, since appearance was obviously so changeable and it was so very easy, from history, to cast blacks as superior, surely no relationship existed between skin color and intelligence or skin color and degradation.[43]

Whites, however, tried to say that blacks were ignorant and degraded, created to serve their brethren and hardly superior to chimpanzees; furthermore, they supposedly lacked fine feeling, were insensible and ungrateful, and, "the craniologist exclaims," they had to be an inferior and distinct species because of their "retreating foreheads." All this was so patently a case of blaming the victim it hardly deserved notice. It was not rational argument. "Oh, that another Solomon might arise in this age of enlightened reason, and convince the world, *that our people, naturally, are not worse than other men*," that every seeming inferiority stemmed from hatred and abuse, and that such inferiority was exaggerated in any case. Black skin derived from a bit of pigment in a thin layer of the skin, "the *rete mucosem*," and could anyone truly give a rational defense of prejudice based on that?[44]

That time and chance and the omnipresent sins and vagaries of human history afflicted all nations was the theme of the third and final installment of "Mutability." Without the pyramids and ruined temples, the world would have known as little of Egypt's grandeur as it did of Ethiopia's. In a passage reminiscent of Stanhope Smith, the author wrote, "For the present descendants of the ancient Egyptians are an ill-looking and slovenly people immersed in ignorance and sloth." The Macedon of Alexander fell, and Greece itself now suffered under the Turkish yoke. "Popish writers" would have it that nineteenth-century Rome was as great as under the Caesars; this was vain and idle talk. Blacks had been cruelly used, "mutability" had afflicted them the worst, and they were now "as degraded in many parts of this happy land as we can possibly be." If progress and uplift were not inevitable, yet "it must certainly be considered uncommonly miraculous that mutability should attend all other nations," that is, other than blacks. Blacks' time would come: "relying firmly upon the justice of a righteous God, we believe that a fairer day is yet to dawn upon our longing eyes." Meanwhile, prudence and economy, modesty and discretion might ameliorate some of blacks' disadvantages in the United States.[45]

❧ REJECTING DEGENERATION

Colonizationists bitterly resented the *Journal*'s opposition to them. For instance, when the colonization-minded faculty of the Princeton Theological Seminary canceled their subscription to *Freedom's Journal* on that account, divinity professor Archibald Alexander declared, "If I were a coloured man, I would not hesitate a moment to relinquish a country where a black skin and the lowest degree of degradation are so identified that scarcely any manifestation of talent, scarcely any course of good conduct can entirely overcome the contempt which exists."[46] Alexander lacked the imagination, and the will, to perceive the fundamental challenge leveled by the *Journal* at conservative environmentalism.

Under Russwurm's editorship the cause of African colonization and the American Colonization Society itself fared better. As junior editor, Russwurm probably had not fully shared Cornish's feelings about the evils of African emigration, and rumor had it that Russwurm's openness to emigration drove Cornish to resign as editor-in-chief. Russwurm took over at the end of August 1827.

Although continuing to print major critiques of the ACS, Russwurm's editorials progressively replaced these attacks with equivocations on the subject of colonization, indications of receptiveness to ACS ideology, and finally outright praise for the Liberia project.[47] In an early Cornish-era *Journal* piece that profiled New Haven's free black community and white attitudes, Russwurm had shown that he understood very well the mendacity of ACS attacks on free blacks. Yet even then he had expressed respect for several prominent men who supported the society, and he came to laud their motives and share their views of free blacks' possibilities in Africa and perhaps even of their low character in America.[48] This growing sympathy for African colonization, as well as the dwindling number of original writings in the *Journal* by African Americans, meant fewer and fewer subscribers. The paper went into the red and closed in March 1829; the next month Russwurm sailed for Liberia, to work there in the department of education. Cornish attacked him as a traitor to the race for this decision, which shocked New York's African American community.

Russwurm appears to have resembled Saunders: an urbane man with complex transatlantic connections who could seemingly find no place for himself in the United States. In his piece on New Haven, he confessed the pain that segregation and prejudice caused him, especially the slights endured by colored people traveling in public accommodations: "Such things, we know, are mere trifles, and are unworthy of a moment's thought; but as I do not possess neither the humility nor patience of Job [sic], how can I tamely submit to be so treated?"[49] He was fed up with endurance and refused to be defined by suffering.

Russwurm was born in Jamaica of a white Virginia planter and a slave mother whom his father freed and married. He was sent by his father to school in Quebec, then taken to Maine when his now-widowed father remarried and moved North. Later Russwurm returned to Jamaica, where he did not prosper. He relocated to the United States, taught at the Free African Schools in Philadelphia, New York, and Boston, and then enrolled at Bowdoin College in Maine; his father paid the tuition. When Russwurm graduated, his stepmother advised him to go to Liberia to escape the ravages of prejudice. Instead, he signed on as junior editor of *Freedom's Journal*, but that experience did not convince him that black protest could reverse white prejudice or "enlighten" or "improve," as he would have put it, the free black community in the United States. Under Cornish and for the first nine months of his own tenure, the *Journal* had borne the motto "Righteousness Exalteth a Nation." When Russwurm reduced the large-sheet format in May 1828, the motto became "Devoted to the Improvement of the Coloured Population," and pro-colonization outlooks and material dominated editorial policy.

Nor did Russwurm as editor-in-chief champion a strong sense of diaspora blackness. Instead, he heightened the attack on degeneration theory in raceless terms. His "On the Varieties of the Human Race," which appeared in three parts in April, May, and September 1828, saw human diversity as neutral physiological adaptation. Russwurm began in the first installment by attacking the eighteenth-century anthropologist Lord Monboddo's famous association of chimpanzees and Negroes. In the opening of the second installment of "Varieties" he further decried what he wrongly represented as the atheistic materialism of the major natural systems of the eighteenth century: "For while revelation and the Book of Nature, which is daily unfolding before our eyes, admonish us that all mankind are the descendants of Adam, how impious, how inconsistent are the opinions of Linnaeus, Buffon, Helvetius, and Kaims [sic], who wish us to believe that our primogenitor is the Monkey, or that of [Erasmus] Darwin, that the Oyster is the earliest animal." Russwurm did not mention Stanhope Smith or the physical anthropologist Johann Friedrich Blumenbach. Whether he had read Stanhope Smith or knew about Blumenbach is unknown, but his stress on the effects of climate rather than state of society is by implication a refutation of Stanhope Smith's ideas.[50] Too, according to Russwurm, the climate in Africa was unusually uniform, leading to a more or less uniform human appearance there—just the reverse of Stanhope Smith's view.[51] In the third installment of "Varieties," Russwurm discussed differences caused by food and manners and customs, with food receiving the greater emphasis. In treating manners and customs, Russwurm tried to be neutral: "If we compare the wild and the domestic horse, the bison, and the ox, the [illegible] and the sheep, we shall find the difference between each to be really great." The same was true of the aborigine as opposed to the civilized man. Russwurm did not in this connection discuss the influence of climate, in Africa or anywhere else. Diversity for Russwurm just existed, a fact of nature and of no particular significance. It did not (as for Stan-hope Smith) reflect an endless battle between human civilization and a hostile nature or sin. Russwurm concluded with the idea, expressed ear-lier in "Mutability" but now with no reference to ancient African gran-deur, that the original color of mankind had to be copper like that of the Arabs. There was no white human prototype. Russwurm said nothing about Egypt.[52]

In December of 1828, Russwurm replied to readers' complaints that he was not printing enough original material on ancient Africa in the *Journal:* "We acknowledge, that with the exception of the article upon the *Mutability of Human Affairs,* we have not written anything relating to Africa centuries ago; not that the subject was uninteresting, but be-cause many abler pens had handled it in a manner, we had not hopes of attaining, long before the appearance of the Journal." It is unclear whether Russwurm was here claiming authorship of "Mutability" or us-ing the editorial "we"; I would speculate that "Mutability" had been co-authored by Russwurm and Cornish together. It strikes me that "Muta-bility" in some passages resembles Russwurm's bitter erudition and in others Cornish's more patient and righteous exhortations to virtue and patience; or perhaps, if Russwurm was the sole author, he followed in those passages Cornish's editorial line. By "abler pens," Russwurm pos-sibly meant authors like Herodotus, Volney, Grégoire, Denon, and prob-ably T. R. His reply to readers' complaints was defensive, even waspish: he hoped that his critics "will undertake the publication of a paper for the edification of unenlightened brethren. After its appearance, from its original matter, no doubt vice will disappear, and ignorance hide its un-fashionable head from among our community."[53]

Russwurm apparently did not appreciate that his readers had a new, increasingly "black" interest in mutability and Egypt, interest not served by Volney (who wrote only of Ethiopia, deplored religion, and dis-missed the idea of meaningful racial differences), Stanhope Smith (who was torn between a nascent concept of difference and a degeneration view of blackness), or T. R. (who made the Ethiopians into tyrants and thought that blacks could never become equal in America), or really Russwurm himself in a basically raceless piece like "Varieties." His mockery there of degeneration theory and white environmentalism was perhaps lost on most black *Journal* readers, who would likely have been unfamiliar with natural history's intricacies. Cornish perhaps did not care so much about Egypt either: the *Rights of All*, *Freedom's Journal's* successor, which he founded after Russwurm's departure and which lasted less than a year, printed no original material or major extracts on ancient Africa or race theory.[54] But it remains testimony to free blacks' abiding interest in ancient Africa and *Freedom's Journal's* role in spurring that interest that after the *Journal* began publication, educated African Americans throughout the North began, as we will see, to discuss scientific ideas of race, and especially ancient Africa, at length.[55]

⑨ ABORTION SHALL DESTROY THE BIRTH

Sub rosa these discussions likely related to a more forthright willingness to confront the problem of the perpetuation not just of prejudice but of the "black" race itself. A remarkable interpretation of race, contemporaneous with the *Journal* and Walker's *Appeal*, was offered to the public by Robert Alexander Young, who may have been a street preacher in New York City. His pamphlet, *Ethiopian Manifesto, Issued in Defence of the Black Man's Rights in the Scale of Universal Freedom*, published in New York in 1827, was a radical "black" statement that took no notice of the discussions over emigration or of the existence of *Freedom's Journal*, much less invoked Egypt or race theory or any idea of mutability and lost noble African innocence. Nor did it mention Haiti. I would not say that Young was sui generis, however, only fearless. The themes he brought out would be discussed again and may have underlain some of Walker's analysis in the *Appeal*.[56]

A free man born in Baltimore of mixed black and white descent, Young styled himself in *Ethiopian Manifesto* "Rednaxela [Alexander spelled backwards], sage, and asserter to the Ethiopian of his rights." American blacks had a clear claim to the rights of man, earned by the horrific experiences of the Atlantic slave trade. But their suffering, ignorance, and degradation were now so deep that they could not unify and win these rights on their own. Only God's hand and His coming messiah, deliverer of the blacks, could bring all African Americans together.

The core of this vision was the problem of sexuality and childbearing in the awful circumstances of the black Atlantic world. For Young, the "black" race was defined by reproducing itself under conditions of slavery and by the rape of African women. This insightful construction of black self-consciousness transcended previous African American conceptualizations of race in a way that was analogous to Buffon's focus on reproduction and his rejection of the arbitrariness of Linnaean nominalism. Young here broached issues that the *Journal* writers and Walker's *Appeal* would hardly touch.

Disregarding history and environmentalism, Young declared that blacks had no history to speak of. "The Ethiopian" was "nature's untutored son" and presumably always had been. And there was nothing glorious about blacks "in their state of native simplicity" in Africa, where they had no "enjoyment of their rights, as bestowed to them of the great bequest of God to man." Blacks nowhere understood that "imperious duty exacts the convocation of ourselves into a body politic; that we do, for the promotion and welfare of our order, establish to [sic] ourselves into a people framed unto the likeness of that order, which from our mind's eye we do evidently discern governs the universal creation." This gloss on nature and the United States Constitution was according to Young the prophetic teaching of reason that had been revealed to Rednaxela. For him God had miraculously swept away the fogs of ignorance and degradation so that as yet he alone among black people could perceive the meaning of liberty: "Mark me, and regard well these my words; be assured, they convey the voice of reason, dictated to you through a prophetic sense of truth."[57]

Young's messianism indicates how fully he identified what he called "the black people" as a hybridized diaspora nation created by the Atlantic slave trade and white/black mixture: "a mixed race of men, whose shade hath stamped them with the hue of black." A mulatto Messiah, an Old Testament figure with flowing hair, a man born of a black-skinned mother but himself white-skinned with Negroid features, and known further by certain signs and birthmarks, had already been born in the Granada Islands. This man would eventually "call together the black people as a nation in themselves" and vanquish the slaveholders. His most important task would be to break the psychological connection between master and slave, which Young regarded as a "shackle" that had to be "unlinked," whatever the consequences. The coming Messiah

would accomplish that great task: "Death shall he prefer to a continu-
ance of his race:—being doomed to thy vile servitude, no cohabitation
shall be known between the sexes, while suffering under thy slavery; but
should ungovernable passion attain over the untaught mind an ascen-
dancy, abortion shall destroy the birth." By implication, the product of
forced intercourse between white men and black women would also be
destroyed. Even at the cost of race suicide, blacks' terrible experiences
in the modern world must not pass to another generation. Blacks would
have their rights, or the "race" would end. Young proclaimed himself a
"John the Baptist" to the coming deliverer.[58]

Young saw slavery and oppression as sustained by a kind of twisted
sexual logic of debased affinities. Blackness began as a fundamental lack
of personhood and rights, leaving blacks so benighted in mind that they
could not properly observe or reason about their condition, could not
stop themselves from feeling for their masters and bearing children. And
they could not be proper parents or children. Young cast himself, in
bringing them God's revealed word, as the caring and instructive parent
whom they had never had. "We say it, and assert it as though by an ora-
cle given and delivered to you on high. God, in his holy keeping, direct
thee, though poor untaught and degraded African slave, to a full conception of these the words we have written for your express benefit. Our
care and regard of you will be that of a fostering parent toward a beloved
offspring."[59]

Every "black" child born under slavery was born to perpetuate a terrible system of violence and twisted affinity between slave and master, a
system that created "blackness." The chains of slavery were so fundamental that only miraculous deliverance could "unlink" them and make
blacks unite into a "nation unto themselves," the highest expression of
the rights of man, rights that blacks were entitled to more than whites. In
Young's presentation, the slave system could be perfectly observed and
understood, if only by God or the people with the moral force born of
enduring it, yet such a people would be too bound and blinded to have
the full use of their observation and reason. It was a diabolical trap, like
fallenness itself. A John the Baptist and a Messiah were required, and
that Messiah would not preach endurance and peace but celibacy and
death.

⌒ THEY TELL US ABOUT PREJUDICE—WHAT HAVE WE TO DO WITH IT?

Interesting as Young's manifesto is, it could not compare with Walker's fiery *Appeal* in impact and notoriety. Young relied upon an avenging messiah. Walker, prominent in the black community, called upon the oppressed themselves and issued a warning to the oppressors. Although no evidence exists that Walker knew of Young's *Ethiopian Manifesto,* the *Appeal* also described the degradation of black people and claimed to some extent that only prophetic revelation could break their bonds. Walker was more hopeful, though. He saw to some degree Providential design behind blacks' travails, a larger Christian scheme of redemption in which a rational faith in cosmic order remained possible. The text combined northern free black preoccupations with uplift and analyzing the effects of slavery and prejudice with southern African American slave culture's use of the Bible to call for messianic rebellion. Walker believed that even the most miserable blacks could be inspired and instructed by rational argument and by exhortation to fully perceive and finally to reverse what had been done to them. He too predicted a great black deliverer, but in less miraculous terms and from closer to home than Young did. Walker hoped for the emergence of another slave rebel like Gabriel Prosser or Denmark Vesey. The *Appeal* sought to overcome blacks' debilities to the point of creating or helping such a rebel and providing him with a loyal army ready to face death. Blacks could prove that they were men through their own actions. For all the force of his analysis, Walker did not understand (or choose not to understand in print), as Young seemed to do, how profoundly slaves were affected by the pressures of survival and how immensely daunting it would be even to think about mounting active resistance against overwhelming white numbers and resources. Walker also hoped that the *Appeal* would pierce whites' consciousness; Young was uninterested in preaching to whites.

In the third edition of the *Appeal,* which was most recently reissued in 2000 and is the source for my discussion of Walker, Walker would turn to prophecy.[60] His invective and desperation mounted when it became clear to him that his pamphlet's message was not being acted upon throughout the land, even though he had circulated it openly among blacks in the North and secretly in the South. In a footnote addition to the third edition he claimed divine inspiration for his words: "Some of my brethren, who are sensible, do not take an interest in enlightening the minds of our more ignorant brethren respecting this Book, and in reading it to them, just as though they will not have either to stand or fall by what is written in this book. Do they believe that I would be so foolish as to put out a book of this kind without strict—ah! very strict commandments of the Lord?"[61]

Still, he did not reconceptualize blackness as a dark glass through which African Americans could never see without prophetic aid. Nor did he tackle perhaps the worst, and to Young most fundamental, of blacks' experiences. Walker (whose parents were apparently both "black") referred to sexuality and reproduction only three times—in his discussion of the ancient Egyptians as a mixed people who much resembled African Americans of his day, in a reference to the Mongoloid peoples as "the mulattos of Asia," and in a denunciation of any black man who would want a white wife because she was white. All three instances testified to a quasi-biological vision of blackness and whiteness as existing in some timeless way as perhaps real natural entities. This conception was partly provocation, a complex and audacious play on Jefferson's "suspicion only" of black inferiority. At the same time, Walker presented it as a fully open question whether whites were naturally inferior. "Race" was hence more important to his text than to any other black writing up to that time.

If no single idea or argument in Walker's *Appeal* was new, his emphasis and the breadth of his synthesis of earlier thought were strikingly novel. The originality of the *Appeal* lay first, in its being a synthesis of African Americans' experiences, thought, and resistance—slave and free, South and North—and second, in its sweeping and systematic attempt to analyze and undo the psychological effects of that experience everywhere, to spur righteous collective action against slavery and prejudice, and to force whites to confront the true extent of their sins and crimes.

Walker's synthesis, reflecting his own diverse experience and thought, tried to recreate in readers his own successful struggles for mental emancipation. The son of a slave father and a free black woman, born some time in the 1780s or probably 90s in North Carolina and coming of age in the Charleston of the 1810s that produced Denmark Vesey (whom Walker may have known and at whose church he probably worshipped), Walker eventually moved to Boston, where some time in or before 1825 he opened a used clothing store. He brought North the idea that black rebellion organized by the channels of slave resistance and communication was possible, a notion that he combined with the uplift and anti-colonization philosophies of the northern free black community's growing moral reform culture, where he had quickly risen to prominence. He was the keynote speaker at one of black Boston's "African Celebrations" on Beacon Hill, a leader of the newly formed Massachusetts General Colored Association, and the Boston representative of *Freedom's Journal* (for which he also wrote).[62]

The *Appeal* was the gospel of an African American passion. Walker offered himself as an example of what all African Americans had to undergo. In brilliant, oratorical prose, he put himself on the cross, asked if God had forsaken black people, and exhorted them to repeat his own soul-shaking struggles to free himself from the effects of slavery and prejudice. His white contemporaries, not perceiving the self-consciousness of Walker's use of the often heated and emotional rhetoric of the slave preacher and rebel, and in a work meant to be read aloud and understood by every African American regardless of status or education, dismissed Walker's pamphlet as the ranting of a madman.

When it was discovered how he had used black and even white seamen and a complex hidden network of smuggling and distribution to spread the *Appeal* throughout the slave South in just the ways that slave rebels like Vesey and Gabriel Prosser had recruited men for their plots, white panic ensued. A group of Georgians offered a thousand dollars for Walker's corpse and ten thousand if he was taken alive. Several southern state legislatures secretly passed new laws banning seditious literature like the *Appeal*, and black seamen were restricted to their ships in many southern ports. The mayor of Savannah and the governors of Georgia and Virginia urged Mayor Harrison Gray Otis of Boston to suppress the work. Otis refused, saying that "notwithstanding the extremely bad and inflammatory tendency of the publication, he [Walker] does not seem to have broken any laws," and "we think that any public notice of him or his book, would make matters worse." Walker himself was found near

his shop in August 1830, dead of what many African Americans believed were mysterious causes. New research, however, indicates that
Walker probably died of the same pulmonary infection that had a few
days before killed his infant daughter.[63]

Walker's intense anger and emotional outbursts displayed the painful
process of confronting the true extent of white hypocrisy and the damage done to blacks. As Walker's recent biographer Peter P. Hinks observes, he believed that "individual personality tended to move toward
some unified conception of self premised on personal empowerment
and self-esteem or on dependence and self-denigration."[64] Although
Walker understood that blacks might justifiably feign subservience, he
believed that a man could not finally be both a slave and a man. Nor
could a man be both a servile, degraded "free black" and a man. White
statements of prejudice like Jefferson's *Notes on Virginia,* the effects of
whites' preaching submission to slavery as God's will, lack of education
available to blacks, the machinations of the American Colonization Society, and the lack of powerful black institutions—all had made blacks "ignorant, abject, servile, and mean—and the whites know it—they know
that we are too servile to assert our rights as men—or they would not
fool with us as they do."

As evidence Walker pointed to the South or West: there anyone might
see "a son take his mother, who bore almost the pains of death to give
him birth, and by the command of a tyrant, strip her as naked as she
came into the world, and apply the cow-hide to her, until she falls a victim to death in the road! He may see a husband take his dear wife, not
unfrequently in a pregnant state, and perhaps far advanced, and beat her
for an unmerciful wretch, until his infant falls a lifeless lump at her feet!"
Such sons and husbands had to be servile and ignorant. Free blacks
complacent in ignorance and mean occupations while their southern
brethren thus suffered were little better off. An enlightened, sensible
man would never submit in these ways, which the whites knew very
well, and which explained their efforts to keep the blacks as wretched as
possible.[65]

No slaveholding people, Walker declared, no matter how cruel, had
ever before told its slaves they were not human beings. To Walker, that
diabolical attempt to destroy blacks psychologically distinguished New

World slavery, made it the worst form of debasement in the history of the world, and made blacks history's most debased people. He said in the *Appeal*'s very first sentence that extensive travel and "the most accurate observations of things as they exist" had convinced him "that we (coloured people of these United States) are the most degraded, wretched, and abject set of beings that ever lived since the world began; and I pray God that none like us ever may live again until time shall be no more."[66]

This had been said before, but usually in melancholy terms that accepted to some degree the idea of America's irremediably bad social environment, at least for the present.[67] For example, "The Mutability of Human Affairs" in *Freedom's Journal* argued that black self-discipline, sobriety, hard work, in sum "a more discreet line of conduct," might slightly ameliorate prejudice against free blacks, but it would not end slavery. Even eighteenth-century calls among free blacks for respectable conduct as a way to convince whites to enact emancipation saw this as a slow process. Colonization made benevolence glacial. By contrast, Walker's solution radically repudiated static social environmentalism and staked everything on the individual's dramatic confrontation with sin and victimization. In his chapter-long attack on the American Colonization Society as a fiendish plot to strengthen slavery, Walker asked rhetorically: "They tell us about prejudice—what have we to do with it?"[68]

☙ WE CANNOT EXACTLY TELL

If anything, it seemed that nature, not social environment, explained whites' prejudices. Jefferson had perhaps been right to wonder if blacks and whites were naturally distinct—and the question remained open. But any possible racial differences did not prove that slavery could not be meddled with or that emancipated blacks had to be shipped out of the country. For whatever blacks were, whites were worse. Throughout history whites had been "an unjust, jealous, unmerciful, avaricious and bloodthirsty set of beings, always seeking after power and authority."[69] The sin of slavery had been the downfall of Egypt, Greece, and Rome. How could far crueler and more perverse white America, which had heard the Word of Jesus, hope to escape? Slavery was destroying Spain, which God had visited with internal strife, just as He might now divide white America. Perhaps blacks would become free when whites destroyed themselves.

Walker verged on a racial manicheanism. While some African Americans distinguished between northern Europeans, supposedly the forebears of American whites, and the morally better Mediterranean whites, Walker lumped all Europeans—Greeks, Romans, and Anglo-Saxons—together. "Mutability" and Russwurm in "Varieties" had blacks and whites as variations on an originally copper-colored human standard. For Walker there seemed to exist only two distinct racial entities, blacks and whites, the two poles of human virtue and venality. The Mongoloid peoples he called "the mulattos of Asia." If less righteous than the blacks of Africa, they were still incapable of whites' historic level of cruelty and hypocrisy.[70]

Walker summed up whites' character and, in a takeoff on Jefferson, advanced a "suspicion only" about their nature. The atrocities of the Atlantic slave trade showed that they were worse as Christians than as pagans in antiquity, when "they were too ignorant for such barbarity. But being Christians, enlightened and sensible," they became capable of the higher perversities born of knowing higher truths of Christianity, and now in the American republic, of liberty and equality. Were God to give them any more knowledge, would they not "*dethrone* Jehovah and set themselves upon his throne?" Walker pronounced: "I therefore, in the name and fear of the Lord God of heaven and earth, divested of prejudice either on the side of my color or that of the whites, advance my suspicion of them, whether they are as good by nature as we are or not. Their actions, since they were known as a people, have been the reverse. I do indeed suspect them, but this, as I before observed, is shut up with the Lord, we cannot exactly tell, it will be proved in succeeding generations."[71] Walker never claimed to know for sure whether blacks had a distinct nature. But if whites continued on as they had been going, God would surely destroy them.

As far as blacks' servility was concerned, nature had nothing to do with it, as events in Egypt, Carthage, and Haiti all amply proved. Hence American social facts were nothing, the battle for black individual empowerment everything. Walker understood the power of social environment and an established social system, but such power could be overthrown, he said. The stability of slavery was illusory, as the frightened whites well knew. Change was possible through social consciousness and action. African Americans could break the cycle and see that whites had become blacks' natural enemies, as Jefferson had realized. Blacks had to recreate themselves as men and women. Slavery and freedom were both meaningless as social roles: a slave could be free and a freed-man a slave. Self-image made all the difference. The proper self-image and wrestling with Jefferson and slavery would inevitably lead to action. Every free black man in the country ought to buy a copy of *Notes* and give it to his son: "We and the world wish to see the charges of Mr. Jefferson refuted by the blacks themselves." Proving their manhood was blacks' "great work to do" to prepare the coming of the Lord: "You have to prove to the Americans and the world, that we are MEN, and not brutes, as we have been represented, and by millions treated."[72] Blacks could not wait for God, for He only helped those who helped themselves. Enlightenment and action went hand in hand. Walker prayed:

> We believe that, for thy glory's sake,
> Thou wilt deliver us;
> But that thou may'st effect these things,
> Thy glory must be sought.[73]

Walker invoked Egyptian blackness in a way that said that African Americans were like neither the Pharaohs nor the Israelites. As Scott Trafton observes, Walker did not use Exodus as a metaphor for blacks' position or fate in the United States.[74] He rebuked those ignorant blacks who compared whites to the Egyptians of old:

Some of my brethren do not know who Pharaoh and the Egyptians were—I know it to be a fact, that some of them take the Egyptians to have been a gang of *devils*, not knowing any better, and that they [Egyptians] having got possession of the Lord's people, treated them nearly as cruel as Christian Americans do us, at the present day. For the information of such, I would only mention that the Egyptians were Africans or coloured people, such as we are—some of them yellow and others dark—a mixture of Ethiopians and the natives of Egypt—about the same as you see the coloured people of the United

States at the present day.—I say, I call your attention then, to the children of Jacob, while I point out particularly his son Joseph, among the
rest, in Egypt.[75]

Like the "Apology for Pharaoh" excerpt in *Freedom's Journal*, but
with Pharaoh as black, Walker rehearsed all the things Pharaoh had
done for Joseph and the Israelites, which he contrasted point by point to
whites' treatment of blacks in America. Walker attributed Pharaoh's fall
and blacks' subsequent ignorance and divisions to early disobedience to
God (perhaps in enslaving the Israelites), and in a way linking pre- and
post-Atlantic slave trade African history by proving that black degradation was not natural. Ancient Egypt, Hannibal and Carthage, and Haiti,
he said, proved that blacks' "ignorance and treachery one against the
other" were "not the natural elements of the blacks, as the Americans try
to make us believe; but these are misfortunes which God has suffered
our fathers to be enveloped in for many ages, no doubt in consequence
of their disobedience to their Maker."[76]

Such ignorance and treachery, vastly intensified by white perfidy, still
had to be shaken off now. God demanded it and history, ancient and
modern, taught it. Whites said that blacks were "an *inferior* and *distinct
race* of beings." Consider on the contrary a "retrospective view of the
arts and sciences—the wise legislators—the Pyramids, and other magnificent buildings—the turning of the channel of the river Nile, by the
sons of Africa or of Ham, among whom learning originated, and was
carried thence into Greece, where it was improved upon and refined."
This testimony of history reassured Walker, and he professed himself to
be further cheered when he considered "that mighty son of Africa,
Hannibal," who nearly defeated Rome. God would soon give blacks a
new Hannibal, Walker predicted, but they must shed their passivity and
unite around him. They must keep the Carthaginian example in mind,
and also the Haitian. Blacks must remember "the divisions and consequent sufferings of Carthage and Haiti. Read the history particularly of
Haiti, and see how they were butchered by the whites, and do you take
warning."[77]

This was Walker's first mention of the Haitian Revolution or its aftermath. The second came a paragraph later after further preaching on
black unity and warnings to whites. Walker exclaimed: "But what need

have I to refer to antiquity, when Hayti, the glory of the blacks and terror of tyrants, is enough to convince the most avaricious and stupid of wretches—which is at this time, and I am sorry to say it, plagued with that scourge of nations, the Catholic religion; but I hope and pray God that she may yet rid herself of it, adopting in its stead the Protestant faith."[78]

Why did Walker not predict a "new Toussaint"? He did not mention Toussaint's name in the *Appeal*. Toussaint's victory, the specter of his betrayal by whites, and Haiti's decline must have been more vivid than the remote example of Hannibal, of which American slaves could in any case hardly have been aware—and keep in mind that Walker wrote primarily to rouse the slaves. That most Christian African Americans were Protestant would only have strengthened the comparison of African Americans with Haitians. Walker could have said that a coming African American revolt, free of the "scourge" of Catholicism, would surely succeed where Haiti had so far failed and that blacks would build a vital, prosperous, all-black state in a post-race-war America. But Toussaint's betrayal and then post-revolutionary Haiti, with its civil wars so like the strife now plaguing Spain, may have seemed too dismal a failure, too ill-judged by God. Walker may have felt so committed to his Protestant messianism that he could not imagine Catholic Haiti as a model of black deliverance. Or perhaps the Haitian Revolution was too wildly bloody.

Walker did not say whether blacks would be white America's saviors or its destroyers. Whites might yet heed the gospels. Walker reiterated throughout the *Appeal* that many whites might repent and that a few of them already meant blacks well. The English, for example, were blacks' friends, as shown by their antislavery activism and their harboring of fugitives in Canada. It was possible for all Americans, white and black, to someday become "a united and happy people."[79] Walker regarded republicanism and American institutions as, except for slavery, "healthy and even morally righteous," as Hinks puts it.[80] Walker, then, perhaps saw no relationship between slavery and the emergence of the idea of liberty; liberty to him was seemingly a truth born of God and perverted by whites. His inflammatory prose notwithstanding, he offered the possibility of the black redemption of America without racial apocalypse. He called up the image of St. Domingue but did not really name it.

He had blacks as both vengeful and redemptive, both Old Testament and New. They might be as a people benevolent—Walker expressed the conviction that "it is my solemn belief, that if ever the world becomes Christianized (which must certainly take place before long) it will be through the means, under God of the Blacks." That redemption would be far in the future, though, after New World slavery ended. And once blacks began fighting against slavery, they would "glory in death": "It is just the way with black men—eight white men can frighten fifty of them; whereas, if you can only get courage into the blacks, I do declare it, that one good black man can put to death six white men; and I give it as a fact, let twelve black men get well armed for battle, and they will kill and put to flight fifty whites.—The reason is, the blacks, once you get them started, they glory in death." Whites did not know "that there is an unconquerable disposition in the breasts of the blacks, which, when it is fully awakened and put in motion, will be subdued, only with the destruction of the animal existence."[81] Blackness, then, was a thing so real that it could seem to inhere in the very sinews.

Rather, it might be. Walker suspected such a natural blackness; it was a possibility to be verified or negated by whites' behavior in the future. If whites were as good as blacks by nature—and Walker wondered if they were—then most of them would be able to repent and America would prosper in harmony. If not, if race really was innate, then blacks would, he prayed, soon show their special character. This was his complex and thoughtful challenge to whites and also, one suspects, his question to God. Were all humans really the same?

5

Conceiving Universal Equality

In no way should I dedicate myself to the revival of an unjustly unrecognized Negro civilization. I will not make myself the man of any past. I do not want to exalt the past at the expense of my present and my future . . . I am convinced that it would be of the greatest interest to be able to have contact with a Negro literature or architecture of the third century before Christ. I should be very happy to know that a correspondence had flourished between some Negro philosopher and Plato. But I can absolutely not see how this fact would change anything in the lives of the eight-year-old children who labor in the cane fields of Martinique or Guadeloupe.

Frantz Fanon, *Black Skin, White Masks* (1952)

A century and a half before Fanon wrote his influential book, free African Americans invoked ancient Egypt as a great black civilization. They were not making themselves the men of the past at the expense of their present and future, as Fanon said of his black compatriots in still colonized Africa and the West Indies. Cornish, Russwurm, and Walker were not dreamers, searching for self-definition or denying the violence and terror that defined blacks' experiences of the modern world. They invoked Egypt as part of a carefully considered and present-minded justification for emancipation and equal rights for African Americans and people of African descent everywhere in the wake of the Atlantic slave trade. They were trying to deal with what they faced in the North American environment, where they were members of an oppressed and despised minority in a society with an ideology of freedom and equality.

It was rather white men like William Lloyd Garrison who would discount ancient history and racial identity. As several historians have shown, arguments by free blacks helped to convince Garrison and other evangelical white reformers to give up gradualism and see African colonization as a proslavery plot. But, as is clear from their writings, white Garrisonians remained, as Benjamin Lundy, Garrison's mentor, had always been, terrified by God's judgment and the possibility of race war. They wanted emancipation to be a moment of transcendence of invidious, worldly differences. They even tried to de-racialize the greatest perceived eruption of blackness to date, St. Domingue's "horrors." White Garrisonians presented Haitian emancipation as a tale of peaceful cooperation violated only by white perfidy. Properly understood, emancipation everywhere would yield an end not just to racial strife but to difference itself.

In white radical abolitionist thought we find significant instances in which both ancient Egypt and sweeping environmentalism were replaced by the image of British West Indian emancipation, which allowed Haitian history to be rewritten as well. In the 1830s white radical abolitionists, believing that emancipation would be a move outside of history into a new dispensation in which race would play no part, seem to have tried to ignore race theory altogether. They pointed not to the past but to the present: Caribbean slave emancipation. Instead of blackness and a great ancient Egypt, they called upon images of emancipated black men, women, and children in the cane fields of Haiti or especially in the British West Indies, workers whose supposed free labor would do them good and ultimately help redeem the whole world from its sins.

This view was expressed in raceless terms, with blacks seen as absolutely the same as whites. As George M. Fredrickson noted, there were virtually no pronouncements upon race theory by white radical abolitionists during the 1830s. Garrisonianism was the first instance of what would become a familiar white "liberal environmentalist" stance, to use Fredrickson's term, contending that debased by slavery and prejudice, the slave's character could be remade by training in the responsibilities of free labor and republican citizenship. If similar circumstances similarly affected all people, who were equal to start with, then behavioral modification could make blacks equal to whites. Whites, already free, could just renounce sin and become perfect; blacks had to be trained for years to reverse slavery's effects.[1]

Immediatist abolitionism was a complex and often intellectually inchoate movement that has generated a large body of scholarship, but Garrisonian attitudes toward race theory have hardly been investigated since Fredrickson wrote on the subject. True, Garrisonians were, as James Brewer Stewart puts it, "holy warriors," not thinkers. First and foremost, Ronald G. Walters observes, radical abolitionism, heir to the evangelical religious revivalism of the Second Great Awakening, "*was* a church, an appropriate one for men and women who had both a fiercely Protestant morality and a disdain for metaphysics." In aid of their holy crusade against slavery they drew upon natural history or Scottish common sense notions of the moral sense, but these ideas were not systematically articulated or treated: "Quite clearly, if logical and systematic thought about race, environmentalism, or common sense philosophy were all-important, abolitionists would have to be marked as utter failures. And if we operated on the assumption that ideas by themselves brought men and women to antislavery, then we, no less than they, would be left in confusion."[2]

Garrisonians did have arguments, and there were instances of Garrison and several of his colleagues writing on issues of race in the early 1830s that reveal the nuances and even hypocrisies of their arguments. Committed to immediate abolition, they embraced a raceless (and flawed) egalitarianism that is worth examining, and in comparison with the thinking of African Americans of the 1820s.[3]

❧ IMMEDIATE CONVERSION FOR THE OPPRESSOR

Garrison began his antislavery career in 1829 by going to Baltimore to help Lundy publish *Genius of Universal Emancipation.* That same year Garrison gave a major antislavery speech in Boston verging on immediatism and appropriating major strands of African American protest, but he still, like Lundy, supported colonization or emigration of some kind for African Americans. He soon rejected this position, along with all forms of gradualism. As Paul Goodman and Henry Mayer have recently shown, he was convinced to do so after reading Walker's *Appeal* and encountering influential anti-emigration free black men like Baltimore's William Watkins, and by his own aching, evangelized conscience as he sat in a Baltimore jail in 1830 for allegedly having slandered a supporter of the American Colonization Society. Garrison would always say later that he never rose to speak before a black audience without being ashamed of his color.[4]

Back in Boston, Garrison met with free black leaders to gain support for a radical antislavery newspaper, and on January 1, 1831, the first issue of the *Liberator* appeared, bearing his famous declaration: "I am in earnest—I will not equivocate—I will not excuse—I will not retreat a single inch—AND I WILL BE HEARD. The apathy of the people is enough to make every statue leap from its pedestal and to hasten the resurrection of the dead." This was the culmination of free blacks' influence on the transformation of American abolitionism, to use Richard S. Newman's phrase, their pushing it away from elitism and gradualism and toward radicalism and mass action.[5] A large majority of the *Liberator*'s first subscribers were black. In 1832 Garrison published his synthesis of the case against gradualism and emigrationism, *Thoughts on African Colonization,* usually seen as radical abolitionism's manifesto. One-third of the text consisted of black testimonials against the American Colonization Society and demands for full rights as citizens in the United States.

Although this influence of the black community upon Garrison has only recently come to full light, historians had earlier explored the context of the immediatist sensibility. Radical abolitionism was, Lawrence Friedman observed, "the most intense expression of a larger evangelical missionary subculture," the religious revivalism of the 1820s that gave birth to all manner of utopian perfectionist reform movements and missionary societies.[6] Underlying these movements was the ever advancing market revolution that was transforming both work and consciousness, breaking up old ways of living, undermining the patriarchal family, introducing large-scale wage labor, and spurring the rise of a middle class with new ideas about individual capacities and perfection. Slavery outraged those values, for slaves had no incentive to better themselves and, more important, slavery meant that slaves, subject to their master's will, could not have moral responsibility for their actions before God and hence could not undergo genuine conversion. Masters had usurped the Godhead. For many evangelicals, slavery became an absolute model of unfreedom, the "monster vice," as many of them put it, out of which all other evils flowed, a perspective that led to a certain blindness to other forms of constraint and contributed to the characteristic American idea that anyone not a slave is free.[7]

Historians writing more recently stress that immediatists were not necessarily the shock troops of an advancing market capitalism and bourgeois individualism. Rather, they were critics of capitalism who often saw slavery as the quintessence of the avaricious spirit of the age, a spirit that they knew also plagued ordinary men and women in the free labor North (and which led, whether the reformers realized it or not, to intensified competition with and hostility to black people). From the start, many radical abolitionists worked with labor movements struggling against the decline of traditional handicraft skills and the rise of the anarchic wage economy. Garrison regarded slavery and prejudice as integral to the inhuman exploitation characteristic of the whole money-mad nineteenth-century world. Later in his career he devoted so much time to radical communitarian schemes for fighting the grasping individualism of modern life that many of his abolitionist cohorts reproved him for straying from the abolitionist cause.[8]

These broader perspectives on immediatism arose as historians increasingly considered African American perspectives, leading in turn to the current stress on free blacks' role in white conversions to radical antislavery and mass activism. African American leaders at the time preached the virtues of uplift, sobriety, hard work, and godliness, but with acute consciousness of the pernicious power of caste. Black ideologies of "uplift" held that evidence of success and respectability were proof of the moral strength and will required to cast off the impact of slavery and prejudice. This attitude, however, contra some historians, was not the same as early white immediatism.[9] Rather than creating a new world entirely free from sin, uplift was a matter of the grimmest and most desperate struggle against servility, internal and external, to achieve individual respectability. It signified a radical liberation that would lead to emancipation or successful slave rebellion. African Americans, however evangelical, had little sympathy for the romantic utopianism of white immediatists, who saw their own individual conversions to radical antislavery as moments of perfection transcending history, a perfection that might sweep the nation and the world.

And blacks, however fiercely Protestant in morality, could not, to paraphrase Ronald Walters, disdain metaphysics, for their sense of "black" identity rested on a theodicy, a confrontation with the problem of the evils of slavery in a world governed by a just God. Furthermore, since God's existence was announced through language, through the Word of the Bible, African Americans confronted profound issues in speaking or writing themselves and their experiences into the logos of Christianity or Enlightenment rationalism.[10] In Christianity, sin was "black"; to rationalism, human nature was uniform, and reason was progressing. In European culture there were counter trends of colorless Christian evangelical and/or Enlightenment universalism, along with pessimistic notions that slavery defined modernity, especially in the form of New World colonialism. Still, African Americans could not readily describe their terrifying defining experiences as visible objects to be denominated in the language of naturalism and reason, or as salvation dramas in the mode of *Pilgrim's Progress*. To African Americans, if blackness was not, and could not be, a "thing" as Jefferson suspected it to be, a nameable, classifiable, self-evidently visible natural reality, it was in some crucial sense more deeply real than that. Nor was blackness understood as the result of (whites') sins in the sense that the moment of (a black person's) conversion would put an end to sin's regrettable wages, blackness, and erase difference. Individual salvation involved uplift and will, with a consciousness of past suffering always in mind. Salvation and blackness intertwined.

White immediatists, by contrast, because race did not exist for them as a problem, easily described scenes of slavery and emancipation in sharply dichotomous terms of fallenness and salvation. Still, the *Liberator*'s early dual role as Garrison's vehicle and as organ of the free black activist community meant that sensibilities of both free blacks and Garrison found expression within its pages. Garrison's willingness to print black pronouncements of views very different from his own deserves note. Moreover, because he believed in moral suasion and passive resistance and abhorred violence, one might expect him to have repudiated much of Walker's *Appeal,* but he initially avoided seriously discussing Walker.[11] When toward the end of 1831 the *Liberator* did deal with the *Appeal,* the most important publication by an African American up to that time, Garrison delegated the piece to an underling, "V," who took a thoroughly equivocal tone.[12] And although Garrison himself had no interest in black Egyptian grandeur, he reprinted several speeches by African Americans, and also one speech by a white abolitionist, who did.

Inspired by Garrison and the prospect of whites' crusading for immediate emancipation, African Americans now could invoke Egypt in somewhat more optimistic terms than Walker or *Freedom's Journal* had. Uplift, if still difficult, might succeed more quickly than had been thought. There appeared in the *Liberator,* for instance, an 1831 oration by the minister of the African Methodist Episcopal Church in Chillicothe, Ohio, David Nickens, in which he extolled the coming restoration of ancient Egyptian glory. Nickens had spoken on July 5, when free blacks traditionally celebrated, or rather scorned, so-called American Independence; they would not observe Independence Day itself on the Fourth until slavery finally ended. Later Garrison published a eulogy of William Wilberforce, by black activist William Whipper, who expressed the hope that freed blacks' uplift efforts would soon help to recapture the glory of the pyramids.[13] As we will see in the next chapter, the first African American national conventions, in which Garrison participated, would initially say much the same.

In March 1832, Robert B. Hall, a white radical abolitionist, speaking before the New England Anti-Slavery Society on "Slavery and the Means of Removal," discussed the meaning of St. Domingue and ancient Egypt. Reprinted in the *Liberator,* Hall's speech revealed much of what white Garrisonians made, or rather did not make, of history, race, and blackness. Hall took a different tack than Nickens or Whipper. Did color make any difference to the only thing that was unique to man in the first place, his immortal soul? No. History supplied testimony for that answer: Carthage, "one of the greatest and most potent of the cities of the earth—Rome's dreaded rival—the terror of the surrounding nations—the seat of wealth, refinement, and luxury," was in Africa and peopled by the ancestors of African Americans. (Had Hall been reading the *Appeal?*) "Egypt, the head quarters [sic] of learning, the most civilized of all the ancient nations, with all her stupendous monuments, with her statues, her pyramids, her glory and her pomp, her heroes, her men of genius and mighty kings, was an African nation."[14] For Hall, though, morality and godliness were more important than brains or warlike glory, so that there seemed to him nothing so moral about the Egyptians or Carthaginians. The ways of Egypt and Carthage, Greece and Rome, were of a piece and had to be relinquished if humanity were to be saved.

Incredibly, Hall said that the Haitians had managed such a renunciation. Whites had instigated all the "horrors" of the Haitian Revolution; Haiti was now an "orderly, industrious, virtuous, and prosperous nation." Even if all the Haitian terrors that the most timid of American slaveholders imagined were real, emancipation would still be the right course. But the terrors were not real. All the evidence that could be gathered from the Haitian example showed that emancipation in itself was a process of peace and benevolence. Hall blamed Haiti's post-emancipation problems on Europeans. Undisturbed by white perfidy and re-enslavement plots, the freed people would have toiled calmly and contentedly for wages. Since Hall lent no reality to race and cared nothing for Haiti as a site for African American emigration, he did not need Haiti as proof of black capacity for self-government or high accomplishment, and he could readily turn evidence of post-revolutionary difficulties there into evidence against white sin. Properly understood, events in Haiti showed the humanity of slaves at its best and the inhumanity of slave masters at its worst. Race was irrelevant.

Hall had erased the Haiti/St. Domingue distinction, and in a way that placed not only all the guilt but really all the agency on the sinful slave masters. Slaves were passive and plastic, capable of transformation through free labor in the absence of prejudice. Sin tainted great worldly accomplishment. To be a paragon, Haiti did not have to be prosperous or an ideal republic, much less rebuild the pyramids. Post-emancipation Haitian history should not have been a realm defined by struggle and mutability. Except for white meddling, mutability would have been transcended.

Garrison's own writings in the *Liberator* and elsewhere indicate that his view of both Egypt and Haiti resembled Hall's, although it was more sophisticated. Witness Garrison's fanciful dialogue between Toussaint Louverture and George Washington that he wrote in 1832. He had Washington replying to Toussaint's greeting: "Why when we released ourselves from oppression, did we continue oppression! Toussaint! That my example and acquiescence sanctioned this, is the bitterest recollection of my life on earth." Washington praised Toussaint's efforts to help the black race in Haiti, which efforts had now borne fruit: "Your race are free, and enjoy with the blessings of freedom that increasing light and knowledge which give it its true value, and they may now show to the world that the despised African race have immortal souls, are rational beings."[15] Nobody else at that time, not even Walker, would have used troubled post-revolutionary Haiti this way to prove that blacks were "rational beings." That was what Phillis Wheatley, Benjamin Bannaker, and ancient Egypt were for. Toussaint Louverture would often be added to this list (if not by Walker), but Garrison seems to have been unconcerned with Toussaint the accomplished, self-willed individual as proof of black rational humanity. He wanted all Haitian history, past and present, as such proof, with Toussaint as the representative figure, just as Washington embodied and epitomized the American Revolution. Garrison had here fused the "horrors of St. Domingue" with his idea of what the nation of Haiti could have been. He did not deny or disdain Haitian problems so much as combine into a single vision strife born of white betrayals with the potentially peaceful prosperity born of undisturbed black self-determination.

Black rebellion proved black rational humanity but did nothing to further universal redemption. From this perspective, Toussaint Louverture and David Walker were, in effect, brothers. "V" in the *Liberator*'s analysis of Walker's *Appeal* linked Walker to Haiti: "The name of Walker alone is a terror in the south, and it is probable there are or will be more men like him. Negroes have shown their mental capacity in St. Domingo, where, thirty-two years ago, they were as much or more debased than they now are in the United States. That example of bloodshed and misery is before the eyes of our slaves; that tragedy, it seems to me, will soon be enacted on an American stage, with new scenery, unless something is speedily done to prevent it."[16] If slavery continued, whites would force blacks to exact a terrible vengeance. That vengeance would also testify to blacks' God-given equality and possession of reason.

Black mental capacity manifested itself in rebellion or talk of rebellion, in terrifying the South and all white America. In an 1838 Fourth of July oration, Garrison spoke of African Americans' role in convincing him to abandon colonization and adopt immediatism. Reading Walker and speaking to African Americans who condemned colonization helped bring on a crisis of conscience. He came to see that Haiti's convolutions were whites' fault. They were responsible for "the premonitory rumblings of a great earthquake—the lava tokens of a heaving volcano!" Haitian blacks, following Toussaint's restrained example, had proven themselves both noble and rational, which convinced Garrison of his own sins.[17] This could hardly have been more different from Walker's view of blacks, as, once roused, "glorying in death" or of Haiti as plagued by Catholicism and divisiveness.

White abolitionists who rejected emigration for freed blacks had to be able to argue that emancipation would not lead to race war and a nation of Walkers, Nat Turners, and Toussaints. British abolitionists, facing this same problem in the West Indies, had actually pioneered in thus rewriting Haitian history. An 1832 letter on the Haitian Revolution by "S. S." to the *New Hampshire Observer,* reprinted by Garrison in the *Liberator,* relied for its account of events in Haiti on an 1826 *Edinburgh Review* piece advocating emancipation in the West Indies. In 1794, S. S. said, a decree of the French National Assembly emancipated the whole Negro population of St. Domingue in a day. And "what was the result of this hazardous resolution?" In reply, S. S. quoted the *Edinburgh Review:* "'For the first nine months after this great, and we may say, violent change had been effected in their condition, during a season, too, of unexampled convulsions both in the colony and mother country, we find them continuing to work as perfectly as before, upon their old plantations and for their old masters.'" S. S. concluded, "In St. Domingue slaves, half a million in number, were liberated in a day, without preparation, or even warning, and their transition from bondage to freedom was accomplished with safety and ease; and we know not why the result should be otherwise in the United States to adopt a similar humane and judicious course." Only when the whites tried to reimpose slavery did blacks show their mettle. The ensuing years of carnage, with betrayals on all sides, eighteen years of Haitian civil war, and the forced labor codes, were not mentioned.[18]

In *Thoughts on African Colonization,* published in 1832, Garrison pronounced his detestation of colonizationist hypocrisy, the worst of which was the claim that prejudice could never be overcome, that, indeed, Providence had ordained the existence of antipathy to the Negro. In this view, prejudice, as a colonizationist writer whom Garrison quoted with disdain declared, "could no more be changed than the LAWS OF NATURE." Garrison replied in a famous passage: "I ask, are we [white Americans] pagans, are we savages, are we devils? Search the records of heathenism, and sentiments more hostile to the spirit of the gospel, or of a more black and blasphemous complexion than these, cannot be found. I believe that they are libels upon the character of my countrymen, which time will wipe off."[19] Many blacks would have answered with a sardonic yes: most white Americans, as Walker's *Appeal* declared, were pagans, savages, devils, or at any rate the question was very much open and not rhetorical. Walker told whites what they seemed to be and blacks what they should become. He took for granted in a non-perfectionist way that only devils and perhaps savages or pagans, rejecting God's word or never having heard it, were incapable of decency (much less perfection). Real Christian human beings could change to some extent, even if they might not escape sin entirely. The elimination of slavery and prejudice did not require perfection, only humanity, which Walker hoped for but did not count on.

Garrison, believing in coming conversion and perfection, felt sure of the power of the Word to reform everyone. The key passage in *Thoughts* continued: "there *is* power enough in the religion of Jesus Christ to melt down the most stubborn prejudices, to overthrow the highest walls of partition, to break the strongest caste, to improve and elevate the most degraded, to unite in fellowship the most hostile, and to equalize and bless all its recipients."[20] Human beings could renounce all their sins; it was a repudiation of civilization and Christianity to say otherwise, as the Colonization Society did. God would not have laid the task of salvation upon his flock without giving them the power to fulfill it.

✑ GRADUALISM FOR THE SLAVE

A better model than Haiti (or ancient Egypt), the British West Indies, turned up a year after Garrison's book on colonization came out. In 1833, the House of Commons finally passed a plan to end slavery in British colonial possessions in the Caribbean. They did it in a remarkably prudent way, according to white American perfectionists like Garrison. He and his colleagues took the British example as inspiration to found the American Anti-Slavery Society and began their own national campaign for immediate abolition of slavery in the United States.

West Indian emancipation seemed so prudent perhaps because it was not absolute and addressed the perceived need to reconstruct the slave personality. Under the West Indian scheme the slaves had to stay on the plantations and continue to work for their masters for a term of "apprenticeship," which would supposedly teach them the habits and responsibilities of free labor. Sugar and coffee revenues would continue to fill the coffers of the London banks. It did not work out that way. The final result would be the collapse of plantation agriculture and the rise of subsistence farming; poverty would become endemic. But in 1833 "apprenticeship" seemed to American white radical abolitionists to be a fine plan and exemplar for their own country.

In much American abolitionist writing, this one act of Parliament seemed to have banished the "horrors of St. Domingue" from consciousness. Abolitionists on both sides of the Atlantic wrote as if the Haitian Revolution had hardly occurred. The great deed of emancipation had been accomplished by the conservative, monarchical British, not the anarchistic, enthusiastic French, with their deism and destructive radicalism, who in the end had tried to reconquer and reinstate slavery in Haiti.[21] American white radical abolitionists emphasized British stability and wisdom no end, although they did think that the French had shown right good sense in initially proclaiming the formal end of slavery in St. Domingue in 1793–94. But the British had really shown the right way to do things—a way to avoid race war, preserve economic stability, and educate the former slaves in the ways of free labor.

Haitian forced labor codes became instruments of universal benevolence. A Parliamentary speech excerpted in 1836 in the *Quarterly Anti-Slavery Magazine,* the most highbrow American abolitionist journal, typified much of contemporary American white abolitionist thinking as well. The British reformer and abolitionist, instrumental in passage of the 1833 West Indian emancipation act, Thomas F. Buxton, telling the House of Lords of the success of emancipation in Haiti, quoted the 1794 Haitian labor code at length. The *Quarterly* reprinted that part of his speech. The committee of the French Chamber of Deputies that had been sent to Haiti in 1793 to deal with revolutionary Haiti had set forth the terms of work and then made its declaration of principle, which Buxton quoted with praise: "But to give a uniform direction to large bodies, who require to be guided, *but whom no power has a right to com-*

pel" to keep up production, and maintain the peace, "there must be rural laws." The division between laborers and landowners had to be maintained, the committee said, for it provided *"the only means of insuring large incomes to the proprietors,* and freedom and comfort to the laborers; *of preserving the public peace and order, and of maintaining liberty and equality forever."* In 1798 Toussaint Louverture himself found it necessary to enact forced labor; he echoed the language of the 1794 declaration, and Buxton also quoted his words.[22]

According to white abolitionists, blacks cooperated peacefully with such codes, which would have provided a calm, rational transition to freedom had their functioning not been interrupted by perfidious white attempts to restore slavery. When the blacks nobly resisted, striking for freedom with intelligence and restraint, the slaveowners' cruelty and cowardice bred insane stories of black bloodiness. Nothing could frighten slaveholders more than black restraint and rational action or give them greater reason to invent horror stories about rebellious black ferocity. The editor of the *Quarterly,* Elizur Wright, an important white immediatist and the closest thing the early Garrisonian camp had to an intellectual, wrote an 1836 *Quarterly* piece on "The Horrors of St. Domingue." To the extent that they even took place, he said, the so-called horrors could be laid at whites' door. Reports of massacres, rapes, murders, and torture of whites were so much proslavery fancy. Wright presented the Haitian labor codes, this time as seen in Boyer's 1824 Code Rural, as the perfect reconciliation of responsibility, order, and liberty, and one with which blacks peacefully and happily complied.[23]

✨ USING SCIENTIFIC PARALYSIS

As they reimagined Haiti, most white radical abolitionists in the 1830s avoided Egypt and for the most part ignored racial theory. When they needed an answer to race prejudice, they would point to black accomplishments in America or the black Haitians. But Garrisonians did stress a sort of quasi-environmentalist view of blacks' difficulties in the United States, a view that, very differently than Walker or *Freedom's Journal* had done, undercut the "degenerationist" environmentalist theory of Stanhope Smith.

Abolitionists knew that northern intellectuals and mainstream clergymen (often the same people) carried great influence and respect; without enlisting some of them in the cause, abolitionism had no chance. Meant to win over "men of mind" to the immediatist cause, the *Quarterly*, editor Wright told Garrison, would "tell with overwhelming force upon our Seminaries and upon our reading and thinking men." Garrison praised Wright as "a thorough logician, dexterous, transparent, straight-forward." Wright felt the difficulty of his task keenly, especially as he was short of copy and also of time for his editorial duties.[24] He had to convince sophisticated people to take the testimony of naturalists in such a way as to listen to God telling their hearts to make a change. In the process Stanhope Smith and Blumenbach might even be cited as authorities. Mustering such authority on immediatism's behalf was the burden of the only substantial Garrisonian discussion of race and natural history that I know of that was published in the 1830s. This was a dense, nine-page article, entitled "The Diversities of Men," by "M," published in the *Quarterly* in 1837.

In the effort to win over "men of mind," M began with the same questions Samuel Stanhope Smith had asked in 1787 and 1810: do natural causes suffice to explain human variety? Can variety be explained only through observation, logic, and analogies between human diversity and that of beast, bird, leaf, and tree? M started with climate. Hot climates produce dark, intense coloration. Next came several familiar analogies between variations among plants and variations among human beings: poor soil stunted growth; poverty produced inferiority. M had moved on to the state of society thesis. Caste distinctions darkened the skin, coarsened the features, and clouded the mind. M next picked up the standard "rete mucosem" argument about skin color residing in the middle layer of skin: the thicker the layer, the darker the skin. Heat thickened the skin, as did a greasy, rough diet, or sometimes also extreme cold. Thus racial classification made little sense, since every different combination of climate and mode of life produced its own human type. Thousands of such types existed, presenting a hopelessly complex continuum of characteristics impossible to schematize. This all came straight out of Stanhope Smith's 1810 *Essay*. M directly quoted Stanhope Smith's rhetorical question—"How many races shall we count?"—and advocated racial nominalism in terms borrowed from Stanhope Smith. M further quoted a book on the West Indies testifying that white settlers there "are tending fast towards the complexion of the original inhabitants."[25] The Jews do not intermarry, yet vary in color and features depending on their circumstances. And the citizens of the United States were in general darker and leaner than their European forebears.

Then M got down to it: "It is even maintained by Dr. Smith, of New Jersey, that the negroes of this country, *not amalgamated with the whites,* are gradually losing the curled hair and black complexion of their African progenitors." M had apparently been reading Stanhope Smith's footnote in the 1810 *Essay* arguing that time would eventually whiten African Americans, "as it has done in the colony which, according to the testimony of Herodotus, was anciently transferred from Egypt to Colchis."[26] According to M, Herodotus taught that the Egyptians of his day were "woolly headed and black, and were supposed to be a colony from Ethiopia." This observation was confirmed by "the investigations of Professor Blumenbach, who has found Egyptian mummies to possess the features characteristic of the negro." Yet historians writing a few centuries after Herodotus described the Egyptians "as somewhat less black than formerly," and the present-day Copts, "the descendants of the ancient Egyptians," were brown.[27] But such change took a long time, and meanwhile African slavery threatened America's immediate downfall. How African Americans might look in five thousand years could not save the United States from sin now.

M did not recognize that Stanhope Smith saw the Egyptians of old and of the present as different people, not lineally related, and that Blumenbach found the current Egyptians a degraded mixture of ancient Negroid and Hindu Caucasian peoples. M viewed all history up to the present as hopelessly fallen and cyclical: "The Chaldeans, the black Egyptians, the Greeks, the Romans, the Saracens, have each in turn held the supremacy in the literary world; each in turn has sunk into listlessness and ignorance. The Chinese and Hindoos, for many hundred years, have been wasting away their stock of knowledge. Paganism and tyranny combined, have never failed to cover a land with darkness that may be felt. Liberty alone has given a momentary light." Only republicanism married to true Christian conversion gave history direction: "*Liberty and Christianity* will render all men of every shape and every shade intelligent, reasoning, and holy . . . The withering dogma, that no man can gain without another's loss, begins at last to be found a pestilential lie. Soon may equal and exact justice be mutually rendered by all men of every state and nation; then shall liberty, wealth, and happiness bless the world."[28]

In sum, M was saying that since nothing in natural history contradicted the Bible and perfectionist reform, natural history could be ignored and the work of salvation begun. The point was not to prove that blacks would turn white in America any time soon but to show that they could and probably would do so in the distant future. Mankind indeed constituted one human race. To solve problems of slavery and salvation in the present, however, people had to work for and rely on conversion and faith, not natural history. That natural history had no quick and easy solution to perceived problems of race confirmed radical abolitionism as the only way to save America.

M did not convey how inferior most natural historians, including Stanhope Smith but not Blumenbach, thought true "Negroes" were. While seeming to accept the idea that nonwhites were more or less and variously "degenerate," M tried to argue that the very idea of the Negro's inferiority was a mere function of "caste" prejudice. M cared most about getting rid of sin, caste prejudice, and irreligion; then liberty, prosperity, and salvation would benefit all. Natural history was fallen, historical processes were fallen, culture was fallen, the intransigence of intellectuals and proslavery hacks was fallen.[29] None of that mattered, or rather, it could all be changed through immediate salvation.

In the 1820s and 30s, practically everybody in the slavery debates—white radical abolitionists, colonizationists, proslavery writers, free blacks—found a use for the inertia into which natural history had seemingly fallen at the turn of the eighteenth century, when it became clear that nature would not soon solve all the problems of "degeneration," slavery, and race prejudice. The Colonization Society exploited this dilemma first, in its sophisticated propaganda of the early and mid-1820s. Colonizationists managed to combine natural history with the claim that the Ethiopians, "tyrants and instructors of mankind," had been black, and after them, the grand Egyptians. Ethiopia showed what blacks were capable of in Africa, where there was no color prejudice, where God had intended them to live, where their racial distinctions had developed, and where the surroundings suited them. Remaining in America doomed blacks to permanent poverty and degradation in a permanently hostile environment. Negroes would not be degenerate in Africa, only in America. African Americans both rejected and reversed degeneration: blacks might be plagued by caste prejudice, but whites were the moral degenerates. This position did not foresee whites literally turning black but rather hoped that whites might understand, sympathize with, and act to change "black" people's plight.

M opted out of the race theory game. White immediatists had invented a raceless equality. Ideas of degeneration or blackness were not important. In an interesting piece in the radical abolitionist journal the *Emancipator,* William Goodell conceded that different facial angles and brain weights might indeed reveal a difference of intellect between black and white. But the only question to Goodell was whether the two races had the same moral nature. They did, and so both were human and emancipation was right.[30] Eliminate slavery and prejudice and end caste, and society would be perfected, regardless of race and whatever had turned Negroes black and regardless of whatever might happen to them after a thousand years hence in a temperate America free from slavery. Whiteness and blackness did not count, only the immorality of slavery.

⊙ ESCAPING HISTORY

Other *Quarterly* articles held to the line that prejudice expressed mere caste; one piece profiled the free black community from that perspective, and several others refuted the burgeoning proslavery argument. Elizur Wright himself produced a long article in 1836 critiquing proslavery in general and cited West Indian emancipation as a case study in the reasonableness and practicality of abolition. Also in 1836, the jurist William Jay, son of Chief Justice and founder John Jay and a moderate antislavery man and harsh critic of the American Colonization Society, devoted an article to the most significant proslavery tract to date, Thomas Roderick Dew's *Vindication of Personal Slavery.*[31] Dew's work had emerged out of the 1831–32 debates over emancipation in the Virginia legislature in the wake of the Nat Turner revolt in Virginia (for which Walker's *Appeal* was sometimes blamed). Jay's widely read re-

sponse suggests how anti-historical and anti-natural historical Garrisonianism was, why so few radical abolitionists considered race theory,
and why, when they did, they might take the positions expressed in M's
article.

Proslavery writers spilled bottles of ink bewailing or pornographically
retelling the "horrors of St. Domingue." Dew filled several pages re-
counting those horrors and saying that even black leaders had had basically to reestablish slavery on the island in order to make the freed slaves
work. According to Dew, parvenus or Yankees or any group with no experience of command always made bad masters. Black ex-slaves, embittered and vicious, full-grown in body but with the minds of spiteful children, were the worst masters of all. The vast majority of St. Dominguan
blacks now lived worse lives than before the revolt. Haitian sugar production had dwindled to a mere trickle, when before 1791 St.
Domingue, "the pearl of the Antilles," produced more wealth than any
other colony on earth.[32] Those sugar statistics proved hard for white abolitionists to refute. Jay countered Dew's use of Haiti with the example
of emancipation in the West Indies.

Jay noted Dew's claim that free blacks everywhere lied, stole, were
lazy and craven. Dew ascribed this largely to nature: "In free blacks . . .
the animal part of man gains the victory over the moral." Dew, Jay said,
equated white serfs with black slaves. But, Dew asked, what "intrinsic
'principle' distinct from their 'disabilities and disfranchisements'" prevented the serfs' elevation? If a child of one of those serfs was brought to
a New England town, sent to school and church, and taught a respectable trade, "is there any principle, that would necessarily cause him
when a man, to sigh for a master's control, and a master's protection?
Perhaps similar management would counteract 'the principle of idleness
and dissipation' in the children of our free blacks. We should like to see
the experiment made."[33] A frank examination of society led to recognition of strongly marked caste distinctions, but Jay thought they could be
overcome, or hoped so.

Dew had not actually been so unsophisticated or unaware of caste.
He presented his proslavery sentiments as deriving from a catholic and
worldly appreciation for variety and circumstance. He did not avow

polygenism, and he did not see the childlike, faithful, but immoral Negro as the degenerate product of an insalubrious environment, paganism, and barbarism, a white man gone bad over the millennia. Nor was Negro inferiority necessarily God-given. He wrote: "It requires a clear perception of the varying rights of man and all the changing circumstances by which he may be surrounded, and a profound knowledge of all the principles, passions, and susceptibilities which make up the moral nature of our species, and according as they are acted upon by adventitious circumstances, alter our conditions and produce all that wonderful variety of character which so strongly marks and characterizes the human family."[34] The Negro, then, was for Dew part of the human family, in some ways undeveloped but improvable through proper cultivation only under slavery. Dew, like Stanhope Smith, saw civilization and Christianity as long-term historical change agents that could affect "race." Crucially, Dew added slavery into the mix. Slavery was the only possible school for blacks, the only hope for eventual improvement, which would take a thousand years or so for them perhaps to become whites' equals or at least fully fitted for freedom. According to Dew, civilization and Christianity would never "take" in the Negro without such a long period of slavery. Witness St. Domingue and Haiti. Whites would never be able to labor in the tropical South; Negroes could never govern themselves.

That was the lesson of history. Thus for Dew slavery served as the best possible arrangement, providing guidance and possible long-term improvement for Negroes, and for whites, the leisure to cultivate virtue. The great civilizations of the past—Egypt, Greece, Rome—all were warm-weather slave societies, and they had brought at least a modicum of civilization to their slaves and subject peoples. Hence a nuanced environmentalism could easily be used to justify slavery. Dew assumed that a correct appreciation of both nature and society would reveal strongly marked and sometimes qualitative, if also wonderfully and usefully arranged, variety. Qualitative differences in human societies might be changed for the better over millenia. Certainly not in the immediate future.

Jay and Dew both believed in the superior efficiency of free labor.

Dew deplored it, however, contending that slavery restrained the kind of breakneck development that otherwise would turn the North and the whole nation into a realm of pure capitalist exploitation.[35] Jay emphasized that it was a universal law that free workers produced more than slaves, but to him that demonstrated freedom's superior virtue; the West Indies furnished one such proof. In the interests of their belief in universal morality and in the absolute immorality of slavery, Jay and other white radical abolitionists wanted to avoid notions of American sectional particularity, whether based on race, climate, or historical customs and modes of life. Instead, they stressed how freedom's present progress showed that the cycles of exploitation and failure that characterized previous fallen history could be broken. By implication Egypt, Rome, and Greece did not matter. Or rather, particularity and history did make a difference, causing divisions and distinctions among humankind, but such divisions could be swept away by faith, conversion, and free labor.

What probably underlay this Garrisonian raceless vision of redemption may be seen in a remarkable fantasy by "T. T." that appeared in the *Liberator* in 1832. "The mysterious genius of dreams" first gave TT a vision of what would happen in the United States if slavery was allowed to continue: the slaves would rebel. Aided by the Cherokee and by black troops from Haiti, African Americans would destroy the South and throw whites in irons. Such a black victory was essentially a continuation of the sins of fallen existence. The only difference would be that the tables were turned: blacks would be the enslavers. Only whites had the power to end fallenness; only immediate white conversion to radical antislavery could stop the reign of sin in America.

The second dream imagined a post-abolition paradise where the only social standard was respectability and godliness. Whites and blacks frequently intermarried. The new president-elect was black. The "intercourse," both sexual and social, improved both groups: "whites had gained a certain ease and dignity of manners," their "pugnacious" competitiveness had been mollified; blacks, "the milder race," acquired "a more active and enterprising spirit." Universal human equality had been achieved, not through black agency but through whites being persuaded to do the right thing and avoid race war and enslavement.[36]

T. T. had taken and tamed Walker's frightening, apocalyptic vision. Something like Walker's view of whites as "an unjust, jealous, unmerciful, avaricious and bloodthirsty set of beings, always seeking after power and authority," seems to have become for TT white "pugnaciousness." Walker's vision of black moral superiority and sinful passivity, both born of suffering, became black "mildness." The past did not count for much.

6

Black Immediatism

I wonder that I am a man; for though of the third generation from slave parents, yet in body and mind nature has never been permitted to half finish her work. Let all judge who is in the fault, God, or slavery, or its sustainers?

Hosea Easton, *Treatise on the Intellectual Character, and Civil and Political Condition of the Colored People of the U. States* (1837)

With his 1837 *Treatise,* Hosea Easton, a Hartford, Connecticut, blacksmith and minister, became the first African American to articulate a systematic theory of race. African Americans of the 1820s had expressed new racial thinking, but implicitly, almost accidentally, with no concern for originality or system. Possibly the outlines of a racialized "black" sensibility had come into view, but they did so precisely out of the attempt to be more or less conventional, to turn the most familiar arguments of natural history, biblical chronology, and republicanism against Jefferson's *Notes,* the American Colonization Society, and slavery and prejudice. *Freedom's Journal* appeared in an era when newspapers and magazines routinely excerpted or paraphrased other sources. True to form, the "Mutability of Human Affairs" article vindicated the Negro on purportedly widely accepted historical, natural, and commonsensical grounds. David Walker, having absorbed colonization, *Freedom's Journal,* Volney, Grégoire, Lundy, Saunders, probably Stanhope Smith, and the rest on environmentalism, Egypt, and Haiti, went further in the *Appeal.* He saw two kinds of African warmth: blacks as benevolent saviors or terrifying, avenging rebels. Aiming to provoke rather than justify, he did not develop these ideas beyond presenting his own sardonic Jeffersonian "suspicions" about the nature of blacks and whites: he did not directly engage with the natural history of man. That whites feared the tropical black savage and respected ancient Egypt was enough to go on for his purposes in the *Appeal,* which was primarily a sermon and a call to arms.

Matters had become complicated by 1837, when Easton published his 54-page *Treatise,* calling upon whites to act on the basis of an explicit theory of race.[1] African American self-recreation of Walker's sort must then have seemed unlikely. No great slave rebellion had scourged the land with blood; white Virginians had apprehended and hanged Nat Turner; people thought that Walker himself may have been poisoned. For free blacks, as new allies beckoned and new possibilities, arguments, and forums opened, white prejudice rose to unprecedented fury. Haiti's positive image was now useless. Practicality and realism appeared to be the order of the day, especially now that thousands of zealous utopian whites had joined the cause of abolition but had not converted all whites.[2] Instead, backlash—as the abolition question became a major national concern. Southern proslavery statements like Dew's *Personal Vindication* expounded the "positive good" of slavery for both black and white. Major race riots victimized and killed free blacks throughout the free states; Bostonians mobbed William Lloyd Garrison in 1835; a mob shot and killed white abolitionist Elijah Lovejoy in Alton, Illinois, in 1837; and the 1836 Gag Rule squelched abolitionist petitions in the House of Representatives.

Easton's *Treatise* addressed this new situation. He rewrote race theory from an evangelical Christian and black diaspora standpoint. Desperation drove him to it: the *Treatise* joined Walker's *Appeal* as two of the angriest African American outcries of the nineteenth century. The *Treatise* was also the most insightful analysis of prejudice and implicitly of the strengths and weaknesses of radical abolitionism. Unlike Walker, Easton did not invoke ineffable blackness, God's hidden purpose, or a messianic turning of the tide. Instead, the *Treatise* offered imagery of a male God mated to a female nature, with glorious natural diversity as the result. Slavery and prejudice had corrupted, indeed raped, nature and ruined God's scheme. The idea of black inferiority, initially a transparent justification for slavery, bred black inferiority in fact and gave the lie to every claim of American liberty. Blighted, in body and mind, African

Americans could never on their own shatter or fully penetrate the dark glass of their suffering. In them, nature had not been allowed to finish her work.

Easton died young, at age thirty-five, two months after the *Treatise* appeared: he would not share lecture platforms with stars like Frederick Douglass and communicate his intensity to hundreds of audiences, driving home the points that even abolitionists, white and possibly black, found difficult to hear. Although published by Isaac Knapp, who also printed Garrison's *Liberator,* and endorsed by Garrison himself, the *Treatise* did not win Easton a posthumous place in the pantheon of great black abolitionists.[3] The few historians to discuss it have seen the *Treatise* as a mostly simple expression of frustration at the white response to Garrison.

Actually it was, if raw, a primarily conceptual work that treated painful and sometimes embarrassing ideas, one that has not been appraised as the intellectual production that it was. Recently George Price and James Brewer Stewart, based on new research into Easton's family background, have definitively situated Easton's abandonment of black uplift in the *Treatise* in terms of a nuanced understanding of the social history of the racial crisis of the 1820s and 1830s.[4] In my interpretation, by contrast, he was not abandoning uplift in despair or turning decisively to blackness and race thinking. Instead, the *Treatise*'s project, however much Easton's words might offend late twentieth-century visions of African American culture as a vital response to adversity, was to deny the possibility of any positive reading of the effects of slavery and prejudice. If discussing slavery and prejudice with an intensity and rancor surpassing Walker's, Easton was in the end probably less race-minded than any other antebellum American, white or black, to write on race and nature. His significance lies less in revealing the awful, race-obsessed tenor of his times—many other sources do that—than in the intellectual synthesis he accomplished.

Easton was not and did not present himself as a natural historian or a trained intellectual, although he was fairly well educated for his day. He was a Christian minister, a moralist, and an activist abolitionist interested in providing a conceptual framework for understanding and improving the lot of African Americans and confronting white prejudice and inhumanity. Although making use of certain standard natural history ideas, he repudiated the "natural history of man," a more or less accepted and established subfield of natural history, and he cited no advanced natural historical sources. Still, Easton's work stands as the first major African American writing on record to address in an original and systematic manner racial differences and racial history.

Russwurm's "Varieties of the Human Race" article in *Freedom's Journal* tackled those subjects, but that was a quite short piece and did not lay out anything systematic. Russwurm had dismissed "degeneration" but put little in its place. Although somewhat more distinctive views may be apparent in *Freedom's Journal*'s "Mutability" or in Walker's *Appeal*, those works, too, aspired to be largely commonsensical and ironical documents as far as natural history was concerned: prejudice seemed such nonsense that scientific originality was emphatically not required. Easton went beyond that. In context of the heightening of white prejudice, he admitted outright that he was taking controversial positions about the nature of race and character, positions with which many people, including other black men or white radical abolitionists, would disagree. He therefore consciously assembled a provocative theory for racial differences that combined aspects of natural history, biblical eschatology, and common sense notions into a new conception describing blacks' anomalous position in 1837 as he understood it. Slavery and prejudice were sundered from creation. They had no natural persistence or reality in any sense and could be overthrown in a day.

๑ JAMES EASTON AND THE FAILURES OF UPLIFT

Hosea Easton lived in North Bridgewater, Massachusetts, until 1830 and in Boston from 1830 to 1833 and seems to have been in the thick of free black uplift reform in the 1820s, attending meetings of various groups and chairing a meeting to support *Freedom's Journal* at which Walker spoke "at some length" about the need for black unity and respectability.[5] Earning his bread in his own blacksmith shop, as a clergyman Easton rose to prominence in Boston's African Baptist Church, where he led protests against the American Colonization Society. In the early 1830s he participated, along with Cornish—Walker was dead, Russwurm gone to Liberia—in the first national convocations of black people in American history. This activism would have been expected from a man of his background: as Price and Stewart show, Hosea Easton was reared to emulate his father James Easton, a prosperous man whose success and respectability seemed to transcend race and to promise that sobriety and hard work might indeed be able to overcome white prejudice. Easton would have expected his own life to continue the process, especially considering the new collective efforts among African Americans in the 1820s and the advent of white Garrisonian allies. But he could not get beyond the color of his skin. The *Treatise* would explore why.

James Easton, born in or near Middleborough, Massachusetts, in a settlement of Native Americans and African Americans who kept away from the town's whites, served as an engineer in the Continental Army during the American Revolutionary War. In 1780 he moved to North Bridgewater, where he married into one of the town's best "colored" (mulatto) families. His blacksmith's shop grew into a flourishing ironworks that forged plows, sea chains, and anchors and finally into a full-fledged construction company, entrusted with major jobs like laying Boston's Maritime Railroad and building Boston's Tremont Theater. His shrewdness won James Easton the appellation "the Black Lawyer." He inveighed against segregation in Boston's churches and in the community in general, and deeply experienced the rise of prejudice through the fate of a black uplift project into which he sank thousands of dollars: a manual labor school attached to the ironworks that taught twenty boys a year the classics, a trade, sobriety, and self-discipline. Anti-black feeling finally led to the school's demise, as his son Hosea wrote in the *Treatise:* "By reason of the repeated surges of the tide of prejudice, the establishment, like a ship in a boisterous hurricane at sea, went beneath its waves, richly laden, well manned, and well managed, and all sunk to rise no more."[6]

Nine years before the *Treatise* appeared and two years before his father's death in 1830, Hosea Easton, in a Thanksgiving Day "Address: Delivered Before the Coloured Population, of Providence, Rhode Island," observed that whites would not hire even well-educated blacks for decent jobs. "And for what? because it is customary. Leaving law, justice and equity altogether out of the question. And should it become customary to cut off a black man's head (as it is already at the south), then of course we must lose our head, if custom says it is right." Taking up "some low calling," the ambitious black youth became "like the starving man, who, for the want of wholesome food, partakes of that which is poisonous and destructive." All the same, African Americans had to keep trying to better themselves and cast off the effects of slavery and prejudice. Northern free blacks should abandon their jealousies towards one another, improve themselves intellectually and morally, and work together against white hypocrisy. Like Walker, Easton explicitly echoed Jefferson's "Query XVIII" in *Notes:* "I tremble for the fate of this country. O, America! Listen to the cries of two and a half millions of your degraded subjects. Allied to you by birth and blood."[7] Hosea Easton would soon decide that uplift and Jeffersonian rhetoric availed nothing.

☉ DISAPPOINTMENT AFTER GARRISON

At first, the advent of immediatist abolitionist ideology among whites inspired optimism and intensified talk of uplift, exemplified in the proceedings of the first national gathering of African Americans, which Easton attended. This was the initial convention of the American Society of Free Persons of Colour in Philadelphia in 1830, called to discuss the implications of a terrible race riot in Cincinnati, Ohio, that drove hundreds of blacks out of the city, many to Canada. The society, which seated official state delegations plus anybody else who wanted to come (white or black, though only black delegates could vote), would convene annually through 1835, five times in Philadelphia, once in New York. Like Cornish-era *Freedom's Journal* authors, delegates stressed education and the power of social environment along with moralizing about the dangers of irreligion, profligacy, and drunkenness.[8] As Patrick Rael shows, the delegates were, like Hosea Easton, "the cream of free black society," yet they understood and represented the needs and concerns of the mass of African Americans, slave and free, much better than most previous leaders and whites.

The delegates were initially more confident than *Freedom's Journal* writers had been; they displayed neither melancholy nor a resigned "mutability" outlook. For all the desperation of the Cincinnati situation, the existence of a national convocation of upstanding free black people was something to celebrate, especially with the prospect of winning Garrisonian allies. Delegates were sure that Egypt would be reborn in the United States, and they exhorted their fellow free blacks to "live in the constant pursuit of that moral and intellectual strength, which will invigorate your understandings, and render you illustrious in the eyes of civilized nations, when they will assert, that all that illustrious worth, which was once possessed by the Egyptians, and slept for ages, has now arisen in their descendants, the inhabitants of the new world."[9] With each passing year the conventions increasingly disdained emigration—Liberian, Haitian, even to an extent Canadian. In 1832 Easton proposed the final resolution against overseas emigration.[10]

By the fourth meeting in 1833 Easton was serving as chaplain. The next year he sat on the Necessary Business Committee and committees charged with taking appropriate action to reduce prejudice against people of color, contacting trustworthy black people in Liberia to discover what conditions were really like there, and forming a National Society for the General Improvement of Free People of Color. He also proposed a new committee to investigate grievances against racial voting restrictions in the North. Other convention participants spoke and wrote a good deal about prejudice, some of which was reflected in Easton's *Treatise*. In 1832 John B. Vashon proposed that the convention print and distribute gratis three thousand copies of Andrew Jackson's 1814 proclamation to the free colored inhabitants of Louisiana commending them for their actions in the Battle of New Orleans. The convention agreed and added a proclamation by Jackson's aide-de-camp, Thomas Butler. Easton reprinted both in his *Treatise*.[11]

Easton was also involved in the conventions' most important activity, initiated in 1831 when three distinguished white guests—Garrison, the wealthy New Yorker Arthur Tappan, and New Haven abolitionist and minister to free blacks Simeon S. Jocelyn—proposed the establishment of a Negro college. Like James Easton's school, it would teach the classics and practical trades so that black youths could improve their minds, get decent jobs, and refute prejudice by example. Garrison, Tappan, and Jocelyn pledged to raise ten thousand dollars, a sum to be matched by the free black community. The convention appointed Cornish as the general fund-raising agent; Easton served on the Massachusetts fund-raising committee. But the college project, intended for New Haven, where the organizers hoped it might benefit from proximity to Yale College, met the same end as James Easton's school. New Haven's white community would not tolerate an institution for blacks in its midst; people pelted garbage at Jocelyn's house, then raided "new Liberia," the local black neighborhood. The school never opened its doors, and soon Garrison repudiated the whole idea of segregated schools.[12]

Demoralized by the downfall of the college enterprise and the backlash against Garrison, Walker, and Nat Turner, the free black convention movement began to peter out. The "Declaration of Sentiment" for 1834, the year of Easton's greatest involvement, was markedly less hopeful than two years earlier. It proclaimed that "mutability" had afflicted African Americans worse than any other people in history: "We have observed, that in no country under Heaven have the descendants of an *ancestry* once enrolled in the history of fame; whose glittering monuments stood forth as beacons, disseminating light and knowledge to the uttermost parts of the earth been reduced to such degrading servitude as that under which we labour from the effect of *American slavery* and *American prejudice*."[13] This passage reads like Easton's prose, and he might well have written it.

The conventions also suffered from divisions between apolitical African American abolitionists who, like Garrison, focused on moral suasion as the only means to end slavery and prejudice and more practical minded delegates like Easton who were more deeply concerned with free black affairs and the vote. After a sparsely attended 1835 meeting, which Easton missed, the conventions ceased, not to be revived until the mid-1840s.

Easton's own career was going badly. In 1833 he had accepted a pulpit in the Talcott Street African Methodist Episcopal Church in Hartford, Connecticut. The next year, a three-day race riot ensued after one of his parishioners was attacked as he was leaving church. Easton was compelled to abandon an effort to raise money for a literary and improvement society. There were more attacks, and a fire (whether accidental or set by white terrorists we do not know) destroyed the new Colored Methodist Episcopal Zion Church, to which Easton had just moved as pastor.[14] He wrote the *Treatise* during the next few months; proceeds from its sale would go toward rebuilding the church.

By then he had come to the conclusion that blacks could do all the right things—try to become respectable, join white efforts to end slavery and make all of America educated, sober, industrious, and godly, call conventions, and set up schools and improvement societies—but little changed for them. As Price and Stewart say, the failure of his father's school, his own experiences, his work in the antislavery movement, and the fate of his church—all led him to regard himself as a despairing missionary to unredeemed whites. Why, he asked implicitly on every page of the *Treatise*, did immediatist abolitionism rouse such resentment, when its appeal was so reasonable and Godly? Why did prejudice wreck all uplift projects in the middle or before they even began?

He had come to see prejudice as an almost insurmountable barrier, even for Christian human beings, or rather he had come to see American society as having been so defiled by prejudice that it had become quite literally satanic, a total perversion of republicanism and Christianity. Prejudice had become a system of justifications so entrenched that only a direct intellectual assault might succeed against it. Ideas mattered; prejudice had to be disassembled on a conceptual level; that seemed to be abolitionism's only chance.

✎ THE FIRST MONOGENIST RACE THEORY

Easton's *Treatise* brought race out of the paralytic Jeffersonian natural historical field and fully into the evangelical Christian moral one. Easton did so more sweepingly, originally, and effectively than any white Garrisonian writer. The *Treatise* began with a long introduction on race theory and ancient Egypt, followed by a first chapter discussing African Americans' "intellectual character" and its relationship to reproduction and nature. The next chapter dealt with blacks' political position in the United States and the state of American republicanism under slavery, and the following one tried to pin down the "nature of prejudice" in what Easton regarded as the core justification of slavery—the idea that blacks were best suited to labor in the heat. The final chapter further developed his refutation of this idea, arguing that African Americans were American "in both birth and blood" and deserved "all the Civil, Religious, and Social Privileges of this Country."

Easton began with nature, but in a new way, by asserting that mono-genism could be taken for granted: "I conclude that, by this time, one great truth is acknowledged by all Christendom, *viz.*—God hath made of one blood all nations of men for to dwell on all the face of the earth. Or, in other words, I conclude it is a settled point with the wisest of the age, that no constitutional difference exists in the children of men, which can be said to be established by hereditary laws." Accept that, and it fol-lowed that any differences had to be arbitrary, "casual or accidental." "The same species of flowers is variegated with innumerable colors; and yet the species is the same, possessing the same general qualities, under-going no intrinsic change, from these accidental causes. So it is with the human species."[15]

Monogenism, then, need not be proved. It could be absolutely as-sumed. No other important monogenist of the day had begun simply by assuming monogenism as he did, then launching into a discussion of monogenism's implications for variety, race, slavery, and American re-publicanism and Christianity, and with no extended proofs of human unity to follow. Driven by anger and exasperation, the *Treatise* was the first instance of a truly, confidently monogenist American race the-ory. It is unlikely that any white writer, not even the most radical Gar-risonian, would have attempted something like Easton's audacious re-casting of the whole natural history of man. Easton so dramatically reconfigured race and nature that on first reading the *Treatise* may seem wild, wilder and less well-conceived than Walker's *Appeal*. Upon ex-amination, though, the *Treatise* is revealed as a remarkably careful and self-conscious text, an intellectual achievement rivaling or surpassing Walker's.

Easton unsentimentally analyzed the deep and baleful effects of slav-ery and prejudice on black people, slave and free. This did not mean that he was by implication repudiating the idea of redemptive suffering. African Americans derived from their experiences, he believed, a realis-tic view of the world. However damaged he was himself as a black man, however much nature had in him not been permitted to "finish her work," Easton, as a black man, could perceive the truth about race and nature better than whites, who were blinded by sin and power. He could show how much blacks' perspective truly differed from whites,' how pointless had been his father's, the black conventions,' and even Garrison's or Walker's previous efforts at convincing whites to repent through a supposedly shared national language of Christianity, history, respectability, and republicanism. All that took place in a chasm of irrelevance. On one side stood the grand inscrutability of God and nature, on the other cowered the unspeakable, unnatural evils of men, evils so terrible that they destroyed thought and surpassed the strongest words. Abolitionism could not stand in the middle.

Easton's perspective also did away with the notion of a "chain of beings," with humans halfway between animal bestiality and perfect angelic reason. For Easton, nature harbored no threat, only sin did, and sin was not of the body. He did not anathematize sexuality as animalistic. For him, God and nature existed together, consorted almost as man and wife, in a realm of blamelessness and blessedness. The realm of human minds and societies, on the other hand, was entirely different, fallen, yielding monstrous abortions of nature's powers of reproduction. Combining "biblical science"—the then popular genre of works attempting to establish the literal accuracy of the Bible on matters such as chronology or human unity—with eighteenth and early nineteenth-century natural history environmentalism, Easton preached a philosophically idealist vision of race and the immediate perfection not just of whites but of blacks as well.[16]

⎰ BIBLICAL SCIENCE

Easton's reconfiguration of the relationships among God, nature, and man extended the Christian humility before nature and God of a writer like Clement Clark Moore or of certain Christian natural historical thinkers of Easton's day. Like many intellectuals and naturalists of his time, especially the devout ones, Easton realized that the problems of heredity and variation were the biggest chink in monogenism's armor, that they cast doubt on the biblical view of creation. In Easton's *Treatise*, this realization combined with an insight not unlike Young's in the *Ethiopian Manifesto* that in human reproduction under atrocious conditions lay the core of the construction and perpetuation of blackness and slavery in the New World as they now existed.

The Bible said that of one blood God had made all humans. But it didn't look like that, as exploration and natural history continually pointed out fresh differences among peoples. So, as we have seen, many defenders, white and black, of the unity of man embraced the notion of heritable variation in response to environment. Yet as we have already seen, the more sophisticated naturalists like Buffon and Blumenbach had come to question not only the sufficiency of the inheritance of acquired characteristics as an explanation of human or natural diversity but the validity of the idea of the inheritance of acquired characteristics itself. It had become evident, as Easton seemed to know, that certain, and perhaps all, acquired characteristics were not heritable. And many naturalists now worried that the theory, if taken to its logical conclusion, could lead to cosmic anarchy or evolution, as first proposed in 1801 by the French arch-materialist, Buffon's student, and inventor of the term "biology"—Jean Baptiste Lamarck. Thus, Blumenbach's notion of an inborn generative force carrying innate potentials for variation that could be brought out or atrophied by the environment. But there was a limit to the process. Species would never transform. Blumenbach's hypothesis was more or less arbitrary; no concrete evidence existed either for or against it. Stanhope Smith combined the inheritance of acquired characteristics with state of society, to attribute to sin and climate all the vagaries of human diversity. His scheme could not logically allow blacks to be both different from and equal to whites, although he seems to have believed that both the ancient Egyptians and Haitian soldiers were both different and equal.

Over the next fifty years defenders of the unity of human origin would constantly flirt with developmentalism, the concept that nature develops in one direction over time, as compared with the traditional eighteenth-century view of change as deviation from a norm. Lacking evidence and fearing the religious implications, however, they would abruptly break off the acquaintance. An alternative to both Blumenbach and Stanhope Smith would be the idea, put forth by Georges Cuvier, Lamarck's great antagonist, that study of organic form revealed that nature changed and developed step-wise but without accident or mess. God miraculously introduced new, more advanced forms after great, miraculous catastrophes instantly wiped out all the old ones. A conventional Christian like Easton, had he known of Cuvier (there is no evidence he did), would not want to posit, as Cuvier's theory did, an extreme age for the earth. Cuvier's theory also tended toward racial innatism; the American School of Ethnology would use it to argue for polygenism.

Traditional Christians, left with the inexplicable facts of variation and heredity, resorted to inscrutability: variation occurred, they said; nobody understood why; species somehow remained constant nonetheless; it was obviously God's work. Historians of science once argued that in taking such an approach, monogenism almost verged on the theory of evolution by natural (that is, environmental) selection of random, heritable variations, but intolerant orthodoxy drove defenders of human unity of origin into confusion and the worship of imponderables. Following this reasoning, William Stanton, in his classic history of the polygenist American School of Ethnology, saw ethnological polygenism, for all its racism, as ultimately progressive, if only because it swept away monogenist confusion about variation and paved the way for the acceptance of Darwin's far more radical and secular challenge to the biblical worldview.[17] Although Stanton's account of the school's doings remains definitive, more recent historical work makes clear that the assumptions of his day about the history of biology were teleological and that until almost the mid-twentieth century, Darwinian natural selection itself was rarely understood or accepted even by supposed "Darwinists."[18] Today, forty years after Stanton's book came out, the line between the "new" biology of the nineteenth century and the "old" environmentalist natural history of the eighteenth has become tenuous to historians of science and to biologists themselves. Furthermore, as we will see, not only did American polygenism react to natural history, it did not really attempt to break with it. Its attempt to "purify" the Enlightenment of monogenism and environmentalism was disingenuous, and far more absurd and forced than what may appear in hindsight to be Easton's most fanciful conceits.

Easton's interest to us lies precisely in how his work seems to be familiarly "full" and "alive" and not part of the arid, flat sensibility of Linnaean natural history but also not innatist yet also not biological in any way. Easton was very clear in dissociating heredity from what Americans understood by race. This dissociation allowed Easton to dismiss assertions that blacks were mentally inferior on a hereditary biological basis (we would say genetically), and he preserved the literal accuracy of the Bible, avoiding too intimate association with Enlightenment arch-rationalism. He declared at the outset that it would be foolish to conclude from the wonders of nature, as some people naively did, that Nature herself was God. It is evident from the *Treatise* that Easton had been exposed to some of the Christian natural historians of his time and understood that the problem of variation and heredity was a morass in which abolitionism and faith could founder and sink.

He distinguished the realms of God and nature on the one hand, and mind and human society on the other, in terms of unfallen beauty and play, even sexual play (leading to the mysteries of heredity and variation), as opposed to fallen human sin. Within species, nature "possesses a mysterious power to produce variety," based on laws unknown and unknowable to man, "for it is impossible for man to comprehend nature or her works." Reproduction in nature was glorious. It was a pleasure to observe the varieties among a single species of flowers, or even the differently colored kernels on a single ear of corn, "and what makes the observation more delightful, they are never found quarreling about their color, though some have shades of extreme beauty." And among humans climate and geography did not cause color varieties.[19]

Differences in intellect or character among humans were another matter. Such differences could have nothing to do with either nature or God: "Mind can act on matter, but matter cannot act upon mind; hence it fills an entirely different sphere; therefore we must look for a cause of difference of intellect elsewhere, for it cannot be found in nature. Nature never goes out of her own limits to produce her works; all of which are perfect so far as she is concerned, and most assuredly God's works are perfect; hence, whatever imperfections there are in the mind, must have originated within its own sphere." The mind was warped by something in its own realm, namely sin, not nature, certainly not God. If in Eden "man was perfect," after the fall "a difference of mind emerged." Abel had a noble mind, "but in Cain we find quite the reverse." Europe was to Africa as Cain was to Abel.[20]

Bad circumstances, a dearth of complex stimuli, and lack of opportunity for learning and self-expression inevitably yielded mental degradation. Patterns of historical and cultural differences represented the human response—the reaction of the immaterial mind—to the experience of environment, social and physical. "It is manifest, therefore, that the more varying or complex the state of a people is incidentally rendered, the more power there is extant to call up renewed energies of the mind, the direct tendency of which is to confirm and strengthen it."[21] A survey of behavior, manners, and customs throughout history would prove this—and much more. The *Treatise* presented a moral and historical racial classification—one laid out through an inversion of the language of environmentalist natural classification, a language that had acquired characteristics accumulating over time as groups with common experience and recent ancestry diverged from a common original set of parents. For Easton, manners and customs took on inertia and shaped bodies, but the influence was not hereditary and ran only one way, from mind to body. Since mental patterns acquired staying and shaping power over time, the realm of mind could therefore be studied through history, yielding portraits of national intellect and character, and finally an explanation for the course of human world history, including slavery and prejudice, and even for the often physical degradation of slaves and victims of prejudice.

This mind-over-matter fusion of the Bible and environmentalist classification allowed Easton to praise Egypt more highly and to attack whiteness and condemn blacks' present debilities with more vitriol than any previous antislavery writer, white or black—including Walker—and to do so without seeing black degradation as in any way a hereditary, natural reality. At the same time, Easton did not have to posit even for argument's sake some natural "blackness" or ineffable connection between ancient Egyptians and African Americans.

Basically unfallen virtue and intellectual ability had been preserved in ancient Egypt, Easton said, while sin reigned in Northern Europe. For ten pages Easton catalogued three millennia of Egyptian prosperity and original genius, as compared to fifteen hundred years of barbarism wrought by Europeans. Noah's son Ham, patriarch of the black family of mankind, wandered into salubrious Africa, where his virtuous descendants built magnificent civilizations, raised the pyramids, invented painting, sculpture, architecture, mathematics, and astronomy, and spread their knowledge across the world. They sailed the Mediterranean to bring peace and enlightenment to the warring Greeks. Leaving colonies in Attica and the Pelopponesus, they established the institutions that "gave rise to the spread of the morals, arts and sciences in Greece, which have since shed their lustre upon Rome, Europe, and America."[22]

Noah's son Japheth, the patriarch of the white family of mankind, wandered into Asia Minor, and the descendants of his son Javan peopled Greece; a few strayed into harsh and cold northern Europe, where they seemingly became completely debased. Easton did not attempt to explain the rapacity of the Northern Europeans and indeed all the children of Javan, except those in Greece and Rome, whose character was partly shaped by Egyptian learning and benevolence. It was just a fact of history that "the Goths and Vandals, and other fierce tribes, who were scattered over the vast countries of the North of Europe and Northwest of Asia, were drawn from their homes by a thirst for blood and plunder." The entrance of the German tribes on the stage of world history spelled the destruction of classical civilization: "From the fourth up to the sixteenth century, they were in the deepest state of heathenish barbarity. A continual scene of bloodshed and robbery was attendant on the increase of their numbers . . . And since that period, all Europe and America have been little else than one great universal battlefield."[23]

Easton did not condemn all Europeans. "Many great and good men have lived and died" in Europe. Yet whether European accomplishments could rival those of the Egyptians of old remained doubtful. "Any one who has the least conception of true greatness, on comparing the two races by means of what history we have, must decide in favor of the descendants of Ham. The Egyptians alone have done more to cultivate such improvements as comports to the happiness of mankind, than all the descendants of Japhet put together." Had the Egyptians been disposed to stay at home and hoard their knowledge of civilization, the world might still be sunk in barbarism. Had the Egyptians been warlike, they could have readily defended themselves against European depredations or destroyed Europe. "But it is not the genius of the race. Nothing but liberal, generous principles, can call the energies of an African mind into action. And when these principles are overruled by a foreign cause, they are left without any thing to inspire them to action, other than the cravings of their animal wants." Africans born and bred under slavery and prejudice could have no volition or moral responsibility. They were hardly men at all. By the present time, "circumstances have established as much difference between contemporary American blacks and their ancestry, as exists between them and any other race or nation."[24] Their degradation by slavery and prejudice began in the womb itself.

☉ AFRICAN AMERICANS' EDUCATION IN PREJUDICE

Sin interfered with natural processes of growth, especially gestation. Mothers had to live clean, healthy, and happy lives to carry to term healthy, strong, intelligent children. African American women in slavery were not only beaten and abused but witnessed unspeakable horrors, so that their minds were not clear: "see her weeping eyes fixed alternately upon the object of her affections and him who accounts her a brute— think how she feels on beholding the gore streaming from the back, the naked back, of the former, while the latter wields the accursed lash, until the back of a husband, indeed the whole frame, has become like a loathsome heap of mangled flesh." Since "mind acts on mind" and "like causes produce like effects," witnessing "the distended muscles on the face of whipped slaves" would fix the same expression, and all slaves' other debilities, in an African American slave mother's unborn children. Or she herself might be abused and pass the effects on.[25]

Easton derived this notion of "maternal impression" from natural history and common lore, the latter as found in *Hunter's Sacred Biography,* a standard biblical exegesis. Easton cited Hunter's gloss on maternal impression's classic example, in Genesis, where Jacob placed striped reeds in front of Laban's flocks as they mated, and all the new lambs were born with striped coats. According to Easton, what the slave mother saw and suffered, her emotions and also her perceptions, imprinted the child in her womb.

This imprinting was not inherited beyond one generation but imposed upon offspring one by one as their mothers experienced the iniquities of slavery. Most people of Easton's day saw in maternal impression a way to explain permanent hereditary variations by bridging the gap between mind and nature. If they only bred with one another, all lambs descended from Jacob's striped ewes would have striped coats for all time, without ever having to repeat the exercise of the reeds. Such hereditary maternal impression was applied to race in the American Philosophical Society *Transactions* of the 1780s and 1790s; it was also a minor argument in Stanhope Smith, especially the 1810 *Essay*. In 1819 the British physician William Wells reported to the Royal Society of London that popular opinion attributed to maternal impression a case of a child with black and red spots born to a white woman in England: the mother had been startled by a lobster during pregnancy.

Wells thought little of the lobster theory, but he did not in principle reject maternal impression. Further, the story suggested to him that random heritable variations might possibly have led to racial difference: cases similar to that of the spotted child must have occurred in Africa long ago. Since their new darker skin would have been well protected from the sun, these children would have prospered, had many offspring themselves, and thus spread blackness across Africa.[26] Darwin himself relied on maternal impression in *The Expression of the Emotions in Man and Animal* (1872) as a mechanism for emotions to shape heredity over the generations.

Easton ran it the other way: maternal impression as applied to blacks had nothing to do with the workings of an uncorrupted nature. It was the means by which slavery and prejudice violated nature, preventing nature from proclaiming God's glory. Mind corrupted the organization of matter. Human abuse, not nature, made the slaves display all the characteristics disgracefully enumerated by those hypocritical, deistical "moderns," as Easton put it in an implicit attack on Jefferson, wont to "philosophize, upon the negro character": "contracted and sloped foreheads; prominent eye-balls; projecting under-jaw; certain distended muscles about the mouth, or lower parts of the face; thick lips and flat nose; hips and rump projecting; crooked shins; flat feet, with large projecting heels." Regarding their minds, "it is said that their intellectual brain is not fully developed; malicious disposition; no taste for high and honorable attainments; implacable enemies one to another; and that they sustain the same relation to the orang outang [sic], that the whites do to them."[27] Most free blacks, subject to prejudice their whole lives, were little better off. It was all the fault of slavery and prejudice, not nature. A vicious cycle of horror and witness operated.

Easton's use of the notion of maternal impression to support the notion of nature's inscrutability and perfection suggests in some respects the use of epigenesis by the leading theoretician of late Enlightenment German Romanticism, Johann Gottfried von Herder, whose ideas profoundly shaped nineteenth-century European racial thought. Herder applied epigenesis to human history in a thoroughgoing way in his final work, the famous *Ideen zur Philosophie der Geschichte der Menschheit* (1784–1791; translated as *Outlines of a Philosophy of History*), which historians have sometimes, questionably, made into a precursor both to an organicist view of race and to cultural relativism. Herder suggested that different peoples or races embody different "thoughts" in the mind of God. This vision partly derived from Herder's study of epigenesist embryology, which led him to draw an analogy between the growth and development of an embryo and the growth and development of an idea. He had debts to Buffon's and especially Blumenbach's epigenesist physiology. Herder's approach was not a nineteenth-century biological one; rather, it was, like Buffon's or Blumenbach's vitalism, a form of quasi-teleology. The vital force of a given species never changes; variety results from the interaction of that force with the environment.[28]

In Herder's view, civilizations, like human embryos, developed epigenetically; cultural changes occurred only in response to the environment, as the vital force of groups of humans collectively interacted with any given environment. Thus, the "idea" of a race or civilization emerged out of this relationship. To grasp other races and other civilizations, Herder said, one had therefore to try to understand their experiences, how they lived and thought in response to their circumstances, an understanding that was probably impossible without actually living and thinking as the other did. The Negro, Herder declared, had more justification in experience "to term his savage robbers [meaning Europeans] albinoes and white devils" than Europeans had "to deem him the emblem of evil, and a descendant of Ham, branded by his father's curse." Europeans should not scorn Negroes, because Europeans had never lived in Africa as Negroes and could not grasp the unique and worthwhile idea that God intended the African to express in Africa. Herder could judge ethnocentrically, as shown by his further discussion of Negroes: "That finer intellect, which the creature, whose breast swells with boiling passions beneath this burning sun, must necessarily be refused, was countervailed by a structure altogether incompatible with it.

Since then a nobler boon could not be conferred on the negro in such a climate, let us pity, but not despise him; and honour that parent, who knows how to compensate, while she deprives."[29] That is, to accommodate the sweltering African climate, Negroes were better off being stupid and insensible. This was very different from Blumenbach's aesthetic relativism. While all races and civilizations exemplified different parts of God's mind, Herder plainly thought, some environments, some divine "thoughts," some races and civilizations were better than others, though all had something distinct and worthwhile to contribute. Man had to avoid arrogance in face of the unfolding of God's ineffable thoughts.

Easton's position may be understood as in a sense an inversion of Herder's. For Easton, nature was utterly incomprehensible and had nothing to do with God's plan for the world. Character, morals, and intelligence, on the contrary, were simple to understand as being directly related to God's scheme for salvation. Inscrutable variety equaled "Nature" equaled the idea that Nature, per se, was as yet unknowable or perhaps permanently so, while national differences in intellect were easily explained in Christian terms. In other words, Easton saw minds or souls, plastic in a fallen world, shaping bodies almost epigenetically.

Sin was involved for Easton in a way it apparently was not for Herder or Blumenbach. For him, correspondences between circumstance, body, and mind demonstrated individual moral responsibility before God. Blacks' characteristics showed how whites' sins had interfered with nature and God in the most terribly intimate manner imaginable. Yet the natural process of reproduction was somewhat resilient, even when twisted by such horrors, and whites could change their behavior tomorrow. The effects of slavery and prejudice could be immediately reversed. As an immediatist, Easton cast the effects of slavery and prejudice as not genetically heritable but rather like a disease that could attack the unborn child as well as the mother, but it was a disease of the mind that could be cured in one generation. Immediatism had been applied to blacks.

☙ SLAVERY AS A DISEASE

Concluding his first chapter, Easton considered the not uncommon case of African American children of mixed slave and free parentage, whether between free white masters and slaves or free blacks and slaves. Sometimes the child inherited the free parent's—white or black—usually superior intellect, sometimes not; sometimes the child averaged, so to speak, the capacities of the parents. But sometimes intelligence would appear seemingly spontaneously: if nobody understood nature's laws of heredity, those laws plainly were not "scrupulously rigid." Hence nature's inscrutability offered a modicum of redemption. Flukes in the process of heredity might work to blacks' advantage in the end: "when nature has been robbed, give her a fair chance and she will repair her loss by her own operations, one of which is to produce variety."[30]

Slavery and prejudice interfered with nature's normal workings like a disease, and nature tried to resist. "Slavery, in its effects, is like that of a complicated disease, typifying evil in all its variety—in its operations, omnipotent to destroy—in effect, fatal as death and hell." Language could never express the poisonous consequences: even with all the excitement generated by Garrison, "the story is not yet half told, neither can it be. We, who are subject to its fatal effects, cannot fully realize the disease under which we labor." The next, dense sentence figured the African American community as by now dead, dead and half rotted. A corpse could not be expected to act as if it was alive, yet prejudice "comes up in the character of an accuser, and charges our half destroyed, discordant minds, with hatred one towards the other, as though a body composed of parts, and systematized by the laws of nature, were capable of continuing its regular configurative movements after it has been decomposed."[31]

In the most important passage in the *Treatise,* Easton pulled together the interrelationships of nature, God, and the outrages wrought by slavery and prejudice. Prejudice and slavery usurped divinity by raping a feminine Nature whose proper task was to proclaim God the father's (and husband's) glory by giving birth to diversity:

> When I think of nature's laws, that with scrupulous exactness they are to be obeyed by all things over which they are intended to bear rule, in order that she may be able to declare, in all her variety, that the hand that made her is divine, and when, in this case, I see and feel how she has been robbed of her means to perform her delightful task—her laws trampled under feet with all their divine authority, de-

spoiling her works even in her most sacred temples—I wonder that I am a man; for though of the third generation from slave parents, yet in body and mind nature has never been permitted to half finish her work. Let all judge who is in the fault, God, or slavery, or its sustainers?[32]

Easton possibly meant to imply that slavery and prejudice worked like a venereal disease attacking the child in the womb, blighting every process of growth and formation.

❧ WHITES' EDUCATION IN PREJUDICE

The rest of the *Treatise* exposed color prejudice as the lynchpin of the slave system. Blacks were entitled to every right and privilege of American citizenship. Nothing upheld slavery but the inane idea that black people had been made by God to labor in hot climates for the gain of whites.

Slavery had no justification in law and property rights, no justification that anybody actually believed anyway, as could be seen in the actions of American courts regarding fugitives from slavery. "If a white person is arraigned before a justice, as a fugitive slave, it would not be all the evidence that could be collected to prove him a slave, however true, that would induce a justice at the North to give him up, if he were able to prove that he was of white parentage."[33] A white person ipso facto could not be a slave, meaning that law and property rights had nothing essential to do with maintaining slavery. Perhaps black skin itself caused both slavery and prejudice; but then dark-skinned blacks would be hated more than light-skinned ones, in proportion to the difference in hue. Such was not the case.

Easton's third chapter tried to prove definitively that slavery, not black skin, caused prejudice. Skin color could not be regarded as a thing or a part of the body that somehow made black people really different from whites. It had no "body and parts"; it could not truly cause anything. "It serves only as a trait by which a principle is identified."[34] That principle, that true cause of prejudice, was the concept of slavery itself, the idea of the slave's inferior status and lack of rights. Slavery was terribly real, a European sin of avarice that ruined African Americans and debased every aspect of American life. Prejudice was a sin born of the mere accident that vulnerable Africans happened to have dark skin and powerful and greedy Europeans, white.

Slavery and prejudice worked together in a diabolical system revolving around the idea that black skin suited blacks to hard labor in the heat. If blacks could endure the heat better than whites, proslavery's reasoning went, then God must have made the black man for southern slavery: hence, white Americans argued, there could be no harm in acting in accordance with God's purposes and making the Negro work. Indigo, tobacco, and sugar were great boons to the world, and blacks might as well be forced to produce them, for Negroes, whites thought, "are a lazy crew at best" and, left to themselves, would not work at all. Easton maintained that it was no coincidence that the idea that blacks worked better in the heat—"the production of modern philosophy"—arose exactly when Negro chattel slavery appeared in the New World. That idea, he insisted, "has been the almost sole cause of the present prevailing public sentiment in regard to the colored population." It was only an idea, sustained by custom and education, and had nothing to do with nature: the truth was that "the whole system is founded in avarice."[35]

Not even Walker expressed such rancor at the "universality" of whites' pervasive "education" in prejudice. "Children in infancy receive oral instruction from the nurse," Easton wrote. "The first lessons given are, Johnny, Billy, Mary, Sally, (or whatever the name may be,) go to sleep, if you don't the old *nigger* will carry you off; don't you cry—Hark; the old *nigger's* coming—how ugly you are, you are worse than a little *nigger.*" Older children are exhorted to behave and study or they will "be poor or ignorant as a *nigger;* or that they will be black as a *nigger;* or have no more credit than a *nigger;* that they will have hair, lips, feet or something of the kind, like a *nigger.*" White children in classrooms are sent "to the nigger-seat, and are sometimes threatened with being made to sit with the niggers, if they do not behave." If readers doubted anything he said, Easton told them to "travel twenty miles in any direction in this country, especially in the free States," and their own eyes and ears would convince them. Well dressed and respectable, Easton had traversed the North for years: "See nigger's thick lips—see his flat nose— nigger eye shine—that slick looking nigger—nigger, where you get so much coat?—that's a nigger priest—are sounds emanating from little urchins of Christian villagers, which continually infest the feelings of colored travellers." Colored travelers were besieged with hate. Blacks had to sit in "nigger pews" in church.[36] Taverns, inns, and bookstores throughout the nation displayed caricatured Negro heads everywhere. Prejudice was protean. It made the free black man seem a prodigious monster but the slave no man at all, rather a diminutive, sexless, unrepellent thing. "Mechanical shops, stores, and school rooms, are all too small for his entrance as a man; if he be a slave, his corporeality becomes so diminished as to admit him into ladies' parlors, and into small private carriages, and elsewhere, without being disgustful on account of his deformity, or without producing any other discomfiture."[37] Easton did not openly discuss what happened to slave women.

Easton's final chapter tried to prove conclusively the irrelevance of skin color. African Americans were American in birth and blood, language and religion. What was blackness anyway? If black iron absorbed heat and brass reflected it, that was because reflective particles were in the brass and absorptive ones in the iron. Analyze iron or brass, and such particles would be found, but cut into a black man and "before the dissecting knife passes half through the outer layer of the skin, it meets with the same solids and fluids, and from thence, all the way through the body" as in a white man. Except for the outermost layer of skin, the two bodies, white and black, were identical. How could one reflect heat and the other retain it? Animal color "has neither the power of retaining nor emiting [sic] heat—and for the very good reason it possesses no properties."[38]

This was rather weak reasoning. In the eighteenth century and before, in sources a person like himself would have known well, the skin had been dissected and examined, and material differences found in what seemed the middle layer—Stanhope Smith's "rete mucosem." Several mechanisms had been proposed to explain the emergence of black skin as an adaptation to heat, with the corollary, accepted by most monogenists and polygenists alike, that blacks really were better adapted or suited to hot climates and strong sun. It was also recognized that Africans had better resistance to tropical disease but could prosper also in temperate or mildly hot climes, whereas European colonies had never succeeded on the West African coast. Easton saw how these facts contributed to the defense of slavery, and he never argued for black physical superiority or superior adaptability as Walker did. Stanhope Smith, other monogenists, and many African Americans thought that the idea of blackness as adaptation would be able to answer prejudice. They believed that polygenism per se was blacks' main enemy, or rather that polygenism lay at prejudice's heart. Easton knew better, saw how dangerous invoking an adaptive African physical nature would be for African Americans. Because it could confirm the fundamental premise of prejudice and the slave system, the idea of black "warmth" would be a disaster for African Americans.

While deeply aware of African Americans' plight, and notwithstanding his praise for a black Egypt, Easton romanticized their sufferings less than any other surviving major nineteenth-century American antiracist writer, white or black. His own experience no doubt contributed to his view of the pervasive effects of American slavery. He wore good clothes, had respectable manners, and grew up expecting to be a truly free, prosperous man like his father—a leader, minister, and teacher. He heard the racist jeers in the streets as he walked by, spoke to fugitive slaves and listened to their sorrowful tales, and in vain tried to uplift free black communities throughout the North. He knew hateful white children and the kind of men who forced him and his father to abandon uplift projects, who had assaulted Garrison, threatened Walker, murdered blacks across the North, and may have burned his own church. He also knew Walker, Cornish, Garrison, and other decent white people and accomplished, proud, yet desperate African Americans. The distance between his father's life and his own, between his upbringing and other blacks', between himself and men like Garrison, may well have yielded an unusually strong and concrete sense of alternatives, a sense that life did not have to be the way it was for African Americans. Suffering was no boon and poverty no blessing. Life could and should be better.

The *Treatise* attempted to recreate in its (white) readers' minds what being black in the United States was like, how different and unspeakably worse blacks' experience was than other people's. "A slave is metamorphosed into a machine, adapted to a specific operation, and propelled by the despotic power of the slave system, without any motive to attract

. . . A slave, as such, in undergoing the change from a moral, intelligent, being, to a mere machine, lost all the innate principles of a freeman."[39] Most free blacks, slaves to prejudice, were little better off.

⁊ BLACK IMMEDIATISM

Easton gave his white readers no possibility of release from their guilt except emancipation and restitution. They could not have the catharsis of imagining some horrible moment of impending apocalyptic doom or a jubilee of deliverance, as furnished by Jefferson's impassioned lament in "Query XVIII" in *Notes* and reprised by colonization, by Lundy and Niles, even to a degree by *Freedom's Journal* contributors, Walker, and Garrison. Easton did not invoke St. Domingue or Exodus imagery. In his view, blacks would be too outnumbered and degraded by the slavery system to fight, much less win, an insurrectionary war. Nor could a great Egypt somehow be restored by African Americans themselves. For all his celebrations of Egyptian black grandeur, Easton tried to ensure that Egypt could not be used as a promise of redemption for whites or deliverance for blacks.

Instead of pointing to Egypt or to St. Domingue, Easton's concluding paragraphs compared the antebellum United States to heaven at the moment before the defeat and expulsion of Lucifer. Earlier in his second chapter Easton had argued that as the fallen angels living in heaven had twisted God's perfect laws, making perfect hell out of that ideal, white Americans had perverted and betrayed the laws and institutions of republicanism. Now he tried to show that, like Lucifer before the expulsion, they still had the chance to turn back. They could appeal to God and be saved. They could show their repentance by assuming the morality of the Good Samaritan and Jesus Christ toward blacks, whose minds and bodies, expressions of whites' own sins, whites now had the almost godlike power to cure. Sin could be erased. Then blacks' foreheads would broaden, eyeballs recede, and eye muscles "become contracted to an acuteness, corresponding to that acuteness of perception with which businessmen are blessed." Their souls would fire with gratitude "towards their benefactors on earth, and to their great Benefactor above."[40] As nature began to finish her work, paradise, or rather heaven itself, might be regained. Easton here can be seen as making a Miltonic appeal to whites' egotism by casting them in his final paragraph as the protagonists in the fundamental cosmic story.

Blacks' fate was a great instance of undeserved suffering. But in witnessing it, wringing their hands over it, even fearing its consequences, whites would find no release from their sins. Only immediate emancipation would help them. Blacks did not need somehow to be "trained" in the responsibilities of freedom. They did not have to be "prepared" somehow for freedom, as many Garrisonians believed. They needed aid; whites had to act like the Good Samaritan. Everything that slavery had taken away had to be restored. "Merely to cease beating the colored people, and leave them in their gore, and call it emancipation, is nonsense."[41] Garrisonians saw conversion immediately transfiguring whites and bringing immediate emancipation. For the ex-slaves there would be the slow process, in effect, of social engineering, of remaking them after emancipation into properly moral members of society. Going beyond Garrisonian liberal environmentalism, Easton's environmentalism was truly radical and immediatist, a formula for instantly reversing slavery's effects.

Converting the previously inchoate cultural elements of an earlier environmentalism like that found in Stanhope Smith's 1810 *Essay* into an explicit mechanism, Easton achieved something that, so far as I know, no other previous American had done and that few have managed since: concretely to imagine an immediate end to all the ravages of prejudice and to the long history of white venality. The *Treatise*, then, was brilliantly conceived, in essence an anti-cathartic work aimed mainly at whites. Easton attempted to make radical action, not guilt, witness or sympathy, not fear, loathing, and the drama of internal conversion, the reader's only release.

7

The New Ethnology

*Nothing so humbles, so crushes my spirit, as to look into a mad-house,
and behold the driveling, brutal idiocy so conspicuous in such places; it
conveys a terrific idea of the disparity of human intelligences. But there is
the unyielding, insuperable reality. It is désolante indeed to think, to
know, that many of these poor mortals were born, were created so!*

Samuel George Morton, letter to George R. Gliddon, May 30, 1846

For quite some time before the late 1830s, some naturalists apparently
believed that brain size correlated with intelligence and that Negroes
had smaller brains and hence lesser intellect than whites. "Mutability" in
Freedom's Journal denounced such "craniologists"; William Goodell in
the *Emancipator* agreed with the craniologists but saw the Negro's
moral nature as equal and concluded that monogenism and the rightness of immediate abolition was proven. Craniology as then understood
was supposed to demonstrate the status of racial characteristics in the
present; it had begun with Blumenbach as a matter of determining race
based on skull shape, not size; it was a measure of environmental effects,
not innate qualities; and it was emphatically not employed as a criterion
for species classification.

In the late 1830s and the 1840s, craniology became dramatically
more important, with skull size and capacity seen to determine species
or at least very long-term racial entities. The leading American "ethnologists," the Philadelphia physician Samuel George Morton and his cohorts, examined skulls and reported that on average, Caucasians had always had, even since Egyptian times, significantly larger brains than
nonwhites. Morton's *Crania Americana,* published in 1839, and particularly *Crania Aegyptiaca,* published in 1844, were the foundational
texts of an American scientific movement arising around Morton in the

late 1840s.[1] Its leading members, besides Morton, were the self-proclaimed Egyptologist, huckster, and irreligionist George R. Gliddon, the Alabama physician Josiah C. Nott, and the world-famous Swiss botanist and icthyologist Louis Agassiz, who had joined the Harvard University faculty in 1846. European naturalists named this movement the "American School" of ethnology in recognition of its obvious connection to what by the 1850s had become the great American issues of the day—race and slavery.

Historical interest has gone less to the modest and seemingly sincere scientist Morton than to his frankly polemical, colorful, extremely racist successors, especially Nott, who after Morton's death in 1851 made the school into a major element of the proslavery argument. Morton is actually the more significant figure. He fathered the movement: the "scientific" racism that his work upholds was not exactly already "in the air," as historians have been wont to believe. Morton invented an apparently legitimate scientific language, as it were, for the idea that human diversity had a biological basis and could not be altered in any foreseeable time span and that racial groups stood in a hierarchy of value, with black people on the lowest rung. In other words, race was a fixed entity and racial inferiority a fact. In real fact, Morton's evidence—simple measurement of cranial capacity—not only was flawed but by the standards of its own day it was unsophisticated, simplistically one-sided quasi-biology. And if we look carefully at his most important work, it becomes plain that his scientific conclusions required disingenuousness and a complex exercise in self-presentation.

There was little simple or ingenuous about Morton's self-presentation as an honest man seeking the truth in the most concrete possible way, with no concern for theory or abstraction. He did not come out openly for polygenism until late in his career, in 1849, several years after his self-proclaimed untheoretical, concrete work had already seemingly discredited the idea that blacks were only superficially distinct from whites. He was probably not a closet polygenist when he did that earlier work. His studied public indecision on the unity question in 1839 or especially 1844 (when it is more plausible that he privately tended to polygenism) contributed to his persuasiveness. So did his constantly reiterated concreteness, his careful avoidance of larger questions in favor of supposedly objective investigations of anatomy. And internal evidence in his texts shows that he deliberately distanced himself personally from sympathy for black people and from the cruel "scientific" truth of permanent black inferiority.

This so-called truth, in which Morton dissolved individuals into immutable racial types, was connected to and legitimated by how he and most Americans understood biology. Even African Americans writing on science and race in the antebellum years, if rejecting polygenism, subsumed individuals into biological group categories. Easton, it turns out, had been on point in focusing on the problem of variation as being at the heart of American perceptions and justifications of race. Contemporary science could not handle individuality and repressed it; such repression was the conceptual knot holding together American prejudices and race thinking in general.

⋑ DEVALUING MORAL PERCEPTION

Morton, born in 1799, early in life displayed interest in natural history and had as mentors several prominent local scientists, including an anatomist who might have stimulated his passion for comparative anatomy and specifically craniology. Morton began to collect skulls in 1820, the year he received his M.D. degree from the University of Pennsylvania. After studying at the University of Edinburgh and making his grand European tour, he returned to the United States in 1824 to start medical practice but still found time to produce a classic tract classifying the fossils from Lewis and Clark's expedition. In 1820 he was elected a member of the Academy of Natural Sciences of Philadelphia and in 1831 became the academy's corresponding secretary, which gave him the opportunity to correspond with distinguished European scholars and naturalists. Morton became the center of a circle of local naturalists and intellectuals and hosted weekly "soirees" in Philadelphia for visiting men of science, all of which, along with his growing prominence as a naturalist, enabled him to get crania for his collection.[2]

In 1837 Morton issued a prospectus asking for skulls for a book on Native American ethnology. One of his friends showed his devotion by robbing an Indian grave and carrying "his spoils for two weeks in his pack, in a highly unsavory condition, and when discovery would have involved danger, and probably death."[3] Soon Morton had enough skulls to form a sample satisfactory to him for study and comparison. The results appeared in 1839 in *Crania Americana,* complete with beautiful life-sized engravings of important skulls. Study of American Indian, "white," and Negro crania led him to posit that whites had significantly bigger brains than nonwhites, connoting, he thought, higher intelligence, and that skulls of nonwhites could be arranged in a hierarchy of size and mind, with Negroes at the bottom by far. He did not speculate on the origins of these different groups, that is, the possibility of polygenism.[4]

Crania Americana also endorsed a quintessentially eighteenth-century doctrine about the effects of circumstance on individual bodies and minds: phrenology, the study of brain localization originated by the Austrian anatomist Franz Joseph Gall, which attempted to fix distinct places in the skull, or "bumps," that signified mental characteristics. Even mid-nineteenth-century antislavery whites like the writer Lydia Maria Child accepted phrenology but believed also that environment and behavior could enhance or depress mental characteristics by stimulus or disuse: were blacks or Indians given the chance to exercise their "moral and intellectual faculties," Child wrote, their skulls and brains would come to resemble whites'. Harriet Beecher Stowe, in her great antislavery novel *Uncle Tom's Cabin* apparently relied on phrenology in categorizing the mental organization and consequent outward appearances of Negroes, whose "benevolence" and "veneration" she contrasted to white "abstract ideality" and "pride and courage"—all phrenological properties.[5] Morton was explicit about phrenology in *Crania Americana,* which contained an appendix written expressly for the book by the famous Scottish phrenologist and monogenist George Combe, an acquaintance of Morton's. Morton himself wrote at the beginning of his main text that if some specifics of Gall's system might be doubtful, he did recognize "a singular harmony between the mental character of the Indian, and his cranial developments as explained by Phrenology."[6]

Crania Americana contained an extended "Note" on Egypt that indicates Morton's unease about the idea of a black Egyptian deity. He rebutted Volney's "hasty" observation that the Sphinx had flat features and bushy hair: that could not be taken as testimony that the Egyptians were "real Negroes." White Egyptians might have made a Negroid Sphinx: there were precedents for nonblack peoples venerating Negro idols. The Buddhists of Asia, Morton explained, "represent their principal god with Negro features and hair, and often sculptured in black marble; yet among the three hundred millions who worship Budha [sic], there is not, perhaps, a solitary Negro nation." Or perhaps the Sphinx was not an Egyptian deity at all but one worshipped by Egypt's Negro population, "who, as traffickers, servants, and slaves, were a very numerous body."[7]

Antebellum European American attitudes toward Egypt were ambivalent. Egypt might have been grand but it was not necessarily benign: it could be gloomy, death-like, oppressive, and maddeningly obscure. Egypt seemed to lie at the very edge of chronological and historical knowledge and of the Judeo-Christian tradition itself, against which Egyptian mysteries might be pitted as dreary and disgusting as well as fascinating, or merely as terrifyingly enormous and inscrutable.[8] Melville for instance equated the brow of Moby Dick with Egyptian hieroglyphs, an association he used to mock phrenology, which could never read that brow. During the Egyptian Revival in American architecture starting in the 1820s, Egyptian motifs at first appeared in prisons and courthouses, places of state power and possible awful punishment and social death. It was hardly accidental that the key proof of polygenism and the natural rightness of white supremacy and even slavery would derive from archaeological work in Egypt.

Morton's ethnology was a form of archaeology, with the body's remains unearthed and examined to reveal perceived hidden realities of race. Such investigation was seen to have been most tellingly performed on skulls from mummies dug out of the oppressive darkness of Egyptian catacombs, which brought to light white superiority. Morton and his followers did not present slavery and white supremacy in Egypt as happy realities; they were harsh ones, but necessary for the functioning of society. Moral perception and sympathy with suffering were too easy and blind to reality: nonwhite inferiority was a natural truth, albeit hard to confront.

Despite his aversion to the idea of great black Egyptians, Morton may have been at the outset torn between adaptationism and innatism and between seeing nonwhites as individual people and seeing them as inferior races. In 1837, trying to improve his health, he had sailed to Jamaica and the other British West Indian islands. In his journal he wrote of his encounter with this overwhelmingly black slave society that was in transition to "apprenticeship" and freedom. His first impression was of the slaves' contentment: "The streets of Bridgetown were thronged with slaves of every hue, who appeared to have fewer cares and less occupation than any *free* people I ever [beheld?]. Their shrill voices rang continually on the ear, singing, talking, laughing, whistling, every sound but that of lamentation." He also wrote more sympathetically about blacks as individuals. The sounds of a slave chain gang woke him one night, and: "Alas, thought I, if each of these bondsmen of Africa was to be interrogated on the subject of his private history, what a tale of suffering and outrage would be unfolded."[9]

If Morton found the plantation Negroes in the West Indies ugly, lazy, and degraded, he did believe in emancipation, but with some reservations. Wondering whether, "notwithstanding the restraint and coercion" of the British West Indian apprenticeship laws, "this fine island will be infested with needy vagabonds," he thought that sufficient training in freedom, as provided by Pennsylvania's much more gradual emancipation legislation, would turn black ex-slaves into capable workers. Implicit was a Revolutionary-era style environmentalism plus perhaps some respect for the accomplishments of Pennsylvania's post-emancipation free black community. "The blacks of this island," he wrote of Jamaica, "have in my eyes a very repulsive appearance, they have the genuine African face, are listless and stupid in their manner, and singularly uncouth in their deportment. The women, in particular, are thin and squalid, and I suppose degenerate to the last degree; to which the philanthropist will justly reply, that these are the unavoidable attributes of slavery; and that to improve the condition of them we must first remove their bonds." More than once in his journal Morton exclaimed against the evil and hypocrisy of laws at home forbidding free blacks education, which was encouraged in Jamaica: "How different from the laws of the United States and what a humiliating comment on the statutes of Connecticut, where a few psalm singing hypocrites can be found to enforce a diabolical law against the education of *free* coloured people."[10]

Although he would begin *Crania Americana* the following year, not once in his Jamaica journal did Morton say a word about comparative anatomy, much less skull size or shape. His Jamaica journal was significantly less prejudiced than Jefferson's *Notes on Virginia,* and Morton was notably more able than Jefferson to see blacks as individuals with worthwhile human histories. Morton's journal, however, was a journal, not a scientific work. Perhaps the distinction he would later make between science and sentiment was already axiomatic for him, the sympathetic, humanistic role of the observer sharply distinguished from the objectivity required of the naturalist.

Urbane, retiring, and unconfrontational, Morton, as William Stanton wrote in his study of the American School, *The Leopard's Spots,* "was an altogether improbable person to foment revolution in American science, to provide the boots and saddles and spurs with which to ride the mass of mankind."[11] Perhaps not. Perhaps the spurs and saddles, to be accepted, had to be made by such a moderate, knowledgeable, even liberal scientist who could separate "science" from humanism, the group from the individual. These distinctions were how he legitimated craniology, which he presented as a kind of deliberately removed and even partly distasteful scientific exercise. One's feelings had to be repressed; they might do one credit as a human being, but they had no place in impersonal and objective scientific discourse. For Morton, if the inferiority of Negroes was regrettable, it did no good to deny that truth—God had seen fit to make lunatics and fools; He had also made Negroes.

Jefferson or Stanhope Smith or others within the natural republican vision would not have accepted Morton's approach. Science, nature, and moral perception had to be one. But by the late 1830s even African Americans like Easton or white abolitionists like Garrison admitted that no such unity existed, that to argue for immediate emancipation, nature and morality had to be effectively divorced, and they came down on the side of morality. The divorce may largely be what made mid-nineteenth-century perceptions of race different from what came before. Empathy for blacks as individual humans can be found in quite racist sources in the mid-nineteenth century, including, as African American critics would observe, writings of members of the American School.[12] The physician Josiah Nott ministered to slaves, apparently sympathetically and well. It was by then possible in scientific and political public discourse fully to dissociate such person-to-person human contact from one's presentation of race as a fixed hierarchy, and to do so with no sense of hypocrisy or profession of guilt.

❦ THE POLITICS OF ADAPTATION

The politics of the study of nature was shifting. In the wake of the tumults of the French Revolution and then the European upheavals of 1830 and 1848, the idea of change in nature, especially the idea of evolution, seemed to European conservatives and even liberals to threaten not just the possibility of a stable natural order but the possibility of a stable social order based on natural distinctions among humans or on a natural human need for social hierarchy. Morton and the American School's approach rested on a distinctly American gloss on the most important early European attempt to deny evolution, the complex biology of Cuvier, "the Napoleon of French science." The American School, though, argued not against Cuvier's nemesis, and Buffon's student, the early evolutionist Lamarck, but against a monogenism that had itself become so conservative that its greatest champion, the British ethnologist and Quaker physician James Cowles Prichard, ultimately commended Morton's work.

The aims of the Americans were rather different from those of European scientific defenders of order and gradual progress. In Europe before the French Revolution and for some time afterward, the idea of change over time in nature had not seemed dangerous because change was primarily conceived as being in some sense degeneration from a given standard or at least deviation from a norm. Adaptation therefore did not imply major qualitative change in one direction over time—the transformation of entire species (later called evolution). This presupposition made it easy to devise essentially hypothetical mechanisms, like Blumenbach's "formative force," that precluded qualitative change.

Notions of nature as a self-sustaining dynamic economy that could change significantly but not fundamentally owed much to medieval conceptions of a designed but fallen world where sin and virtue did battle. That kind of conception was all very well when real hope still existed that reason, virtue, and godliness might prevail over the entire globe.

Once that faith was undermined, in part by political upheavals in Europe, adaptation could much more easily be conceived as qualitative change, even as the transformation of species. Change might then be understood as so pervasive that nature had no God-given order at all. Or perhaps the order was radically progressive, with no stable balanced hierarchies but rather with constant "upward" movement toward increasing complexity and better adaptedness. At the same time, everyone except those wholly repudiating the Enlightenment wanted to be able to say that human beings were progressing, however slowly, and not constantly fighting a losing battle against degradation and sin in this fallen world. The problem was how to conceive and show gradual, meliorated progress rather than thoroughgoing, sudden change; or perhaps sudden change could be tamed.

In the United States the vision of natural economies that could deviate or degrade but not transform in response to circumstance was part and parcel of the vision of America as a natural republic, a vision that took a long time to dim, since there was no single moment of sharp disillusionment like the Reign of Terror and Napoleonic imperialism. In the United States, revolution and republican ideology in themselves were not so threatening (as applied to white people anyway), and there was no *ancien regime* to protect. Little danger existed in recognizing the self-evident complexity of the circumstances going into the myriad individual differences that made up human diversity. Such recognition would not undermine the possibility of social order, and it was easy enough to use conservative versions of social environmentalism to argue that nothing could be quickly done about slavery. The laws of nature did not have to dictate innate black inferiority, only that social facts like prejudice and slavery were so deeply embedded in the harmonious if not perfect social fabric that they could not be disturbed with impunity. Always the ostensible question was more the social status of slavery and prejudice than whether blacks were created innately inferior. The natural republic, then, remained available as a radically egalitarian ideal until the backlash against *Freedom's Journal,* Walker's *Appeal,* Nat Turner's rebellion, and Garrisonianism's advent combined to kill it. But the death throes lasted for a while. Easton wrote his prophetic *Treatise,* radically dissociating nature from human minds and morals, during that time.

Ethnological racism tried to cement human diversity to a grimmer vision of nature's balance. Its supposed concreteness and objectivity claimed to discover natural truth, in an attempt not to make progress compatible with social hierarchy, as so much of nineteenth-century European naturalist politics tried to do, but to segregate progress and restrict it to whites. Morton and other Americans read conservative European biology through an antebellum American white supremacist's lens, a lens that did not block out eighteenth-century republican ideals and so did not loathe the Enlightenment or see a radical break with it but merely restricted its application to whites. Morton did not find eighteenth-century natural history and nineteenth-century biology intrinsically incompatible. Rather, he saw natural history as having been hobbled by sentimental egalitarianism from recognizing the fundamental truth that God had designed the Negro to be inferior and servile. Morton did not reject a harmonious nature; he only said that nature's truths were sometimes hidden to human eyes and "desolanté" to human sympathies.

In Europe, by comparison, serious threat to social stability from science had first come from radical transformationist doctrines, which were usually staunchly monogenist and which, if seeing "savages" as desperately inferior, proclaimed the equality in Europe of rich and poor, aristocrat and commoner, and the potential equality even of savages. According to Lamarck's scheme of evolution of species via the inheritance of acquired characteristics, no innate template guided adaptation and prevented transformation. All matter had an inherent tendency to organize itself into higher, more complex forms. Distinction between "dead" and living matter did not exist: inanimate matter was always progressing toward life, which arose through a kind of spontaneous generation. Lamarck replaced Buffon's vitalism or Blumenbach's formative force with an outright, radically progressive materialism. His position challenged ideas of social hierarchy ordained by nature, and social radicals often espoused it. In their attempts to create a meritocratic society, so did many members of the growing British middle and upper-middle classes, including Charles Darwin's grandfather, Erasmus Darwin, whose 1791 *Zoonomia* anticipated Lamarck.[13]

Soon, though, as the Napoleonic wars drove British liberals and free-thinkers underground, talk of evolutionism became taboo, and Erasmus Darwin and his colleagues moderated their views.[14] Lamarck's theory so worried some naturalists that a few of them entirely rejected the notion of adaptation to environment, sometimes in the form of teleologies of directed progress. In his 1813 *Researches into the Physical History of Man,* a revised and expanded version of his 1808 doctoral dissertation, Prichard proposed that human beings were developing from black to white in a kind of God-given progressive scheme, in which environmental adaptation had no place. God meant human beings to develop toward civilization and whiteness, with no exceptions. Environmentalist racial theory had to be wrong because it could not explain variation and heredity. To Blumenbach's argument that the ancient Egyptian population was not uniformly Negroid, Prichard replied: Of course not, Egypt was civilized, so the Egyptian upper class must have been turning white or partly white.[15]

In Prichard's formulation, modern, white, civilized Britons were remarkably developed, far beyond mankind's original state, through a process so long and gradual that all the French heresies about quick and easy revolution and progress stood revealed as the purest fantasy, as also were the eighteenth century's morbid speculations about degeneration. But for Prichard's contemporaries the implication that Adam had been black was seemingly too high a price to pay for conservatism. And, as Stanhope Smith's move from simple degeneration in the 1787 *Essay* to complexity in the 1810 version attests, there seemed to be just too many exceptions for any single rule to explain human variation and the degrees of civilization around the globe. Most naturalists in 1813 would not accept a reductionist scheme like Prichard's.

They also remained willing to see processes of heredity and all matters of internal organic structure as inscrutable. They did not have to understand the mechanisms fully, only to propose something roughly plausible. What had to be shown was not exactly how variation and heredity worked, only the likelihood of common descent among varieties within species. Recall Blumenbach's definition of species (also used by Stanhope Smith): "Animals ought to be ranked in the same species when their general form and properties resemble one another, and the differences which subsist among them may be derived from some degenerating cause." This approach allowed for much complexity and individuality, especially if "degeneration" was seen more as neutral variation than debasement. Thus Stanhope Smith in 1810 posited a complex interaction between climate and state of society that produced a vastly intricate continuum of human variation: there were whites with full features, blacks with "Grecian" features, blacks with straight hair, blacks with fine minds (as in Egypt), and so forth. Human variety resulted from an interplay of two adaptive forces, physical environment and state of society. Blumenbach's "esthetic" approach was a more sophisticated and secular version of this late natural historical forces-acting-on-individuals reasoning.

Prichard himself soon went back to a climatic monogenism in the second edition of the *Researches into the Physical History of Man,* issued in 1826, the most comprehensive survey of the subject ever written up to then. He did break new ground in one way that added to complexity. The pattern of civilization across the globe, he said, could never be mapped in any broad and simple scheme of development. Civilization was passed from group to group in a complicated and haphazard historical process more or less unrelated to humankind's varied skin color or features, a process, George W. Stocking observes, resembling what anthropologists later called the theory of "diffusion."[16]

That haphazardness always seems to have disturbed Prichard, and in the third, final, and even more extensive edition of his *Researches* (1838–1847), he tried to return to teleological developmentalism and progress. Instead of diffusionism, he proposed schemes more and more resembling what anthropologists later termed the theory of "independent invention" or "parallel cultural evolution." Each individual civilization moved along a similar path, but at different rates which might be influenced by environment. Civilization would not easily spread in bad circumstances. In the final volume Prichard compared the ancient "aborigines of Europe" to the "most destitute of tribes of Southern or central Africa" of his own day.[17] In his thinking here, the two groups occupied analogous positions on a scale of biological and cultural development, whose steps could not easily be skipped or accelerated. Prichard was unclear on all this, however, and sometimes seemed to advance degenerationist arguments as well.

What he did do in no uncertain terms was to show that social radicalism and Lamarck scared him more than did rejecting the literal truth of the Bible. Prichard willingly abandoned the biblical time scale in order to defend monogenism and the idea of non-transformational change. If human beings were only five or six thousand years old as the Bible said, then the races could not have derived from a single "original stock," but to him they plainly did, so the time scale had to be amended. Egyptology, he said, confirmed this conclusion: recent expeditions revealed that the Egyptian monuments, carved no less than three thousand years ago, showed the same racial distinctions as were apparent in the mid-nineteenth century. Blacks and whites could not have diverged from a common ancestor in a mere five or six thousand years.[18] That would be Morton's and the American School's argument against adaptationism exactly. But they went further, conceding neither one "original stock" nor an original starting gate for all peoples.

℘ REJECTING ADAPTATION: CUVIER

For Morton, the idea of adaptation had to be wrong because the evidence was in his view overwhelming for a relatively short time span for the existence of human beings as they now appeared. Here Cuvier and organicism came in. Cuvier loathed eighteenth-century adaptationism for its claim that the great variety of visible life resulted from an almost random interaction between organisms and a shifting, often "degraded" environment. Instead, if naturalists considered only what they could know for certain—organic structure in the here and now—it became clear that there was a fixed, divine order of living beings.

Cuvier therefore redid natural classification, on the basis of fixed, internal organic form rather than function or external appearance. For instance, the skeletal structure of a man's arm, a bat's wing, and a horse's front leg are all quite similar, even though arm, wing, and leg look very different on the outside and perform different functions. The naturalist's task was to recognize structural homologies and figure out the core structural plan beneath each great branch of creation. Human beings, bats, and horses all became part of the same broad "vertebrate" (actually Lamarck's term) type, or "embranchement," because the internal structure of all three species was homologous and based on the backbone.

Once naturalists realized that the backbone was the core feature, organic structural homologies appeared everywhere in the vertebrate group. It became possible to map the vertebrates from simple to complex, from those that were little more than just a backbone—such as a certain simple type of fish, which Cuvier selected as the basic "type" for the vertebrate group—to highly complex forms like man.[19]

This was not an ahistorical scheme, only a non-adaptive one. Cuvier's structural map could properly be broken down historically, into stages of stepwise development and diversification. There were, so to speak, expanding concentric circles of forms of new complexity radiating outward from the core species within each of the *embranchements* (he counted four). There was nothing random here, though: individual variation and adaptation to environment played no role. For Cuvier, organicism meant that significant gradual adaptation to environment was *ipso facto* impossible. Organisms were functional wholes, so complex that even small adaptive changes in any one part could wreck the delicate balance of the whole. Thus if each of the *embranchements* was a flexible type that could systematically be varied over time to meet a great range of shifting conditions, the action of God, not adaptation to environment or mere randomness, was the mechanism. God had to be directly responsible for the variation, since active adaptation by living beings themselves was impossible.

Cuvier's God intervened in nature in discrete acts of destruction and new creation—the theory of "catastrophism." The natural history of the world was divided into distinct epochs, punctuated by divinely ordained disasters. Cuvier posited eight such ages, the first seven, he implied, corresponding to the seven "days" of biblical creation and the eighth to the biblical Flood. At the start of each epoch, God introduced a series of new, higher species and recreated many but not all of the old ones, thus advancing the development of each of the great "types" to a new stage of complexity and diversification. Hence Cuvier explained the fossil record of extinct forms. Within each epoch, species remained absolutely fixed. For proof Cuvier called upon evidence gathered by Napoleon's Egyptian Expedition: mummified cats and ibises that were physiologically exactly the same as their modern counterparts.

The same was true for human races, which Cuvier refused to say were distinct species. In his view the monogenism/polygenism debate was moot. In the current epoch, there were three "great races" exemplified by three "types"—the Caucasian, the Mongolian, and the Ethiopian. These three "great races," separately created, had been allowed to survive the Flood and had wandered into different parts of the world, where they had not adapted to environment in any major way. But since the "types" doctrine tried to avoid speculation in lieu of evidence, and catastrophism taught that we cannot know for sure what a previous epoch was like, there was no way to say for sure if blacks, whites, and Asians shared a common ancestor in previous eras. No matter. Whatever their Providential origin, since the Flood the races had been distinct and unchanging and would remain so for the foreseeable future.

Cuvier's system was arithmetical, accretion by discrete acts of miraculous addition, but with the benefit of more clearly perceiving a new kind of complexity—internal, organic form. Buffon's or Blumenbach's approach to natural history had been process-oriented, a calculus, dealing in curves produced by complex forces interacting over time. The process acted on a reflective surface, not within an organism; if there was internal variation, it was intrinsically limited by the template of something like Blumenbach's formative force. There would be no transformation. Stanhope Smith, for his part, had tried to frame a moral calculus of a uniquely human diversity.

ᕫ LET US SEARCH OUT THE TRUTH, AND RECONCILE IT AFTERWARDS

In terms of its impact on serious science, Morton's work was a provincial footnote to Cuvier. Except for its political implications, Morton had nothing new or interesting to say about organic structure. Instead of mummified ibises and cats, his most important book, *Crania Aegyptiaca; or, Observations on Egyptian Ethnography, derived from Anatomy, History, and the Monuments* presented the results of his examination of Egyptian skulls. (They had been dug up or robbed from tombs by Gliddon when he was American consul-general in Cairo.) Using Blumenbach's schema, Morton classified by race every skull he received. Then, following the method he developed in *Crania Americana,* he measured cranial capacity with lead shot and came up with statistical averages of brain size for each race.

Unlike *Crania Americana,* the new book ignored phrenology, which was coming under increasing criticism from naturalists as more like palm-reading than science. Now Morton would deal only in hard facts. In a Cuvierian way, he argued that the ancient Egyptian slaves had been black and small-brained and their masters white and large-brained, and that the difference in cranial capacity that he found (nine cubic inches) had not changed since Egyptian times. In all recorded human history, races were frozen in place, with whites at the top and blacks at the bottom.

Morton did not mention Cuvier's types doctrine or catastrophism, nor did Morton give any indication of what he must have known, that Cuvier's theory was not the only nineteenth-century approach to internal organic structure and could not be taken as definitive by the 1840s. New forms of vitalism, often carrying radical social implications, were strong, especially in Germany; in France, the vitalist biologist Isidore Geoffroy Saint Hilaire held his own in a celebrated debate with Cuvier.[20] The idea of change in nature over time was hardly dead. Morton ignored that. Instead of directly referring to Cuvier's types doctrine or to catastrophism—which anyone at the time with a good scientific background would have recognized as his model—Morton presented himself as a humble comparative anatomist with no theoretical assumptions or commitments. He stayed with what he saw as the undeniable facts taught by Egyptian cranial capacity. In all recorded history, whites had significantly bigger brains than nonwhites. Morton took such "realism" to the point of disingenuousness when he claimed that *Crania Aegyptiaca* followed in Blumenbach's footsteps, that it answered Blumenbach's call for "a very careful, technical examination of the skulls of mummies hitherto met with, together with an accurate comparison of these skulls with the monuments." That, Morton said, "is precisely the design I have in view in the following memoir."[21]

Morton did not or would not grasp how different Blumenbach's esthetic approach was from his own, or how much Blumenbach and the phrenologists, all of whom cared primarily about individual idiosyncrasies and skull shape, not size, had in common. Blumenbach, who lived to 1840, proclaimed to the end the virtues of environmentalism and monogenism; he had no interest in cranial capacity. Although he judged Caucasians, with their long, narrow, harmoniously shaped ("doliocephalic") skulls the most beautiful and representing the original human type, the round ("brachiocephalic") skulls of dark skinned, full featured people could be harmonious too. What counted was not size but harmony, best judged in terms of individuals, not aggregate types.

In the third and most influential edition of his *Natural Variety of Man* (1795), Blumenbach had distinguished three main facial types in ancient Egypt, in a passage that obsessed Morton, Prichard, and other mid-nineteenth-century ethnologists: "The first like the Ethiopian; the second the Indian; and the third, into which both of the others have by the progress of time and the effect of the specific and peculiar climate of Egypt degenerated, spongy and flaccid in appearance, with short chin, and somewhat prominent eyes." The Ethiopian face, albeit degenerated from the white human prototype, could often be harmonious and beautiful and Ethiopians could have intelligent minds. Black skin did not necessarily connote inferiority. Blumenbach did harbor prejudice in favor of European skulls, minds, bodies, and culture, but his distinctively eighteenth-century approach to race—pictorial, aesthetic, individualistic, and flexible—was not concerned with discovering internal organic realities. And as we have seen, his 1805 *Contributions to Natural History*, with its considerable material on Egypt, contained a chapter on the humanity and high intellectual accomplishments of full Negroes.[22]

In *Crania Aegyptiaca* Morton ignored all this and did not mention once that Blumenbach thought that one third of the ancient Egyptians resembled Negroes. Morton's only discussion of Blumenbach's Egyptology in *Crania Aegyptiaca* came in a "Note" at the end of the text. Here Morton gave the reader to understand that he had had access only to a summary of the 1810 and 1811 *Contributions* written by another Egyptologist, August Wiseman, who reported that Blumenbach had posited three distinct Egyptian physiognomies, the first like Negroes, the second like Hindus, and the third like the Berbers, the standard Egyptian type. "But," Wiseman continued, as quoted by Morton, "I think an unprejudiced observer will not easily follow him so far. The first head has nothing in common with the *Black race,* but is only a coarser representation of the Egyptian type; the second is only a mythological or ideal purification."[23] Blumenbach's Berber type—to him a hybrid of the Ethiopian and Hindu (both themselves, especially the Ethiopian, divergent from the original Caucasian form) that had degenerated over time—became Morton's Egyptian Caucasian, the supposed ancient Egyptian standard.

According to Morton, Blumenbach could not be blamed for the mistake because he had had to rely on inadequate sources—only a few skulls and Enlightenment travel accounts and inaccurate if grand reproductions of Egyptian monuments from Napoleon's Egyptian Expedition. (As we will see, Prichard also made this critique.) Now, Morton said, not only had Gliddon provided a large sample of crania, but new French and Italian expeditions had published facsimile copies of the Egyptian inscriptions. If Blumenbach had seen them, "he would at once have detected an *all-pervading physiognomy which is peculiarly and essentially* EGYPTIAN; and in respect to which all the other forms,— Pelasgic, Semitic, Hindu and Negro are incidental and subordinate; sometimes, it is true, represented with the attributes of royalty, but for the most part depicted as foreigners, enemies, and bondsmen."[24]

Morton, then, maintained his respect for Blumenbach selectively. He presented Blumenbach simply as having had the genius to bypass eighteenth-century egalitarian assumptions and recognize the biological truth that skull shape and race corresponded, the insight that supposedly made the hard, objective findings of craniology possible. In his scientific writing, Morton always presented himself as above all a realist anatomist with no interest in theoretical pronouncements. If Blumenbach, the best of the eighteenth-century environmentalists, Morton said, had had good evidence to work from, he would have abandoned his environmentalism and sentimental egalitarianism to face the truth.

Morton did not openly challenge the idea of race as adaptation until the last sentence of *Crania Aegyptiaca,* and only implicitly: "The physical or organic characters which distinguish the several races of men are as old as the oldest records of our species." He argued in the text that environmentalist assumptions sometimes marred naturalists' observations of race, but he also said that monogenism led Prichard rightly to assert a common ancestor for Egyptians and Hindus. According to Morton, what mattered was the evidence: the concrete measurements of specific skulls. Egyptians, Morton declared, were "the Misraimites of Scripture, the posterity of Ham, and directly affiliated with the Libyan family of nations." This "Egyptian race" was "at different periods modified by the influx of the Caucasian nations of Europe—Pelasgi, or Hellenes, Scythians and Phoenicians" and the Egyptian kings came from these Caucasian "nations." As for Negroes, they had drawn water and hewed wood in Egypt of old: "Negroes were numerous in Egypt, but their social position in ancient times was the same that it now is, that of servants and slaves."[25]

Morton plainly believed that a natural hierarchy existed among Caucasians themselves. He distinguished from among his skulls six types of Caucasians, situated in various geographic areas, the least Caucasian in the hottest climates or furthest from Egypt and Western Europe. At the top of the list stood the "Pelasgic" branch, the same as the ancient Greeks. These people had the most beautiful, delicate, and also biggest skulls (with a mean cranial capacity of 88 cubic inches), the largest facial angle (with a mean of 80°), and evidence from both tombs and inscriptions, Morton said, showed that Pelasgic Caucasians dominated the Egyptian ruling classes. Next was the indigenous Egyptian type itself, a split-off of the "Libyan" branch of the Caucasian race, with somewhat smaller brains and features than the Pelasgics and a lower facial angle but still definitely Caucasian. Then there was a series of different "Caucasian" peoples, in descending order. After these came those with "Negroid" skulls (mean cranial capacity, 79 cubic inches; mean facial angle, 75°), a debased mixture of Egyptian Caucasians and Negroes, and then a few Asians (or "Mongols"). Finally there were Negroes themselves, small-brained, coarse-featured, low-browed, with thick, ungainly skulls (mean cranial capacity 73 cubic inches, facial angle 75°).

How could there be such different kinds, effectively varieties, of Caucasians if race was absolutely fixed? Why would Caucasians have markedly darker skin, darker hair, and slightly coarse features in hot climates if all Caucasians were created equal and stayed that way? So Morton could not dismiss environmentalism entirely: it was an implicit explanation for diversity within the Caucasian group. Later, he and his followers would argue that there had been many separate creations of distinct "local races" within each "species" (the Cuvierian "great race"), so each Caucasian variety was naturally distinct, but there is no evidence that Morton thought that way in 1844. His correspondence with Nott suggests that he rejected the idea of local creations within species until perhaps 1850.

Furthermore, his proclaimed reliance only on "scientific" evidence notwithstanding, Morton could not have done without proportions and esthetic judgments, on which he relied heavily in individual cases where cranial capacity alone could not firmly establish Caucasian superiority. Constantly he remarked on the beauty of some Caucasian skull—especially when that skull was small or narrow or had a low facial angle. The individual, harmony, beauty, proportion, did matter—if that individual was white. The few big "Negroid" crania in his collection he denigrated as ill-proportioned. There was only one fully Negro skull in his Egyptian sample, testifying, he thought, to the low station of Negroes in Egypt. Few would have made it into the tombs.

Morton filled *Crania Aegyptiaca* with facsimile reproductions of Egyptian inscriptions supposedly showing Negroes as slaves and servants. He constantly pointed to the coarseness of these Negroes' expressions and the ugliness of their faces, as contrasted to the supposedly noble "Caucasian" countenances of the major Pharaohs. He called attention to a representation of the noble, and to him obviously Caucasian Ramses commanding a group of lowly, disfigured, and frightened Negro troops. Morton even tried to make the ancient Ethiopians, or at least the Ethiopian ruling class, white, a branch of the Egyptian Caucasians, and a people with "no affinity, even in the remotest times, to the Negro race."[26]

Again, the supposedly stand alone, unvarnished facts of craniology could not prove Morton's point. For instance, arguing against the idea of a black Egyptian ruling class, he said that the Egyptian rulers as represented in the inscriptions were no darker or lighter than any other Caucasians living at similar latitude. What, other than environment, could explain latitudinal differences among Caucasians he did not say. He argued that Herodotus's conviction that the Ethiopians were jet black with tightly curled hair came from mistakenly thinking that an army of Negroes employed by Ethiopian kings was actually comprised of Ethiopians themselves. As for the few Negroid crania buried in Egyptian catacombs, Morton attributed their presence to the way that "persons of this race have been capable, in all ages, of elevating themselves to posts of distinction in the east, and especially and proverbially those who have belonged to the class of eunuchs." Why the lordly Caucasians should have mixed with Negroes to produce Negroid people Morton also did not say, though he implied that the sheer numbers of blacks in Egypt made such mixture inevitable. In his view, the slave trade between Egypt and lower Africa had been vast: "upwards of ten millions of Negroes" were brought as slaves into Pharaonic Egypt. Truly Egypt was Morton's model for the New World, horrors and all.[27]

Crania Aegyptiaca was nothing if not a case of a white supremacist protesting too much that Pharaoh was not black and that race had nothing to do with circumstance. The book was not biology in any productive sense: Morton used organicism, that is, an internal perspective, in a highly simplistic way: measurement of assumed brain capacity. And despite his insistence that skull size was what really mattered, he still required history, representations on the monuments, aesthetics, proportion, and environmentalism to make his case.

Even on grounds of skull size alone, Morton's measurements and conclusions were faulty. The paleontologist and historian of biology Steven Jay Gould repeated Morton's experiments on skulls from Morton's extant collection and found that the "black" skulls were not smaller than the "white" ones. Confronted with a distressingly large Negro skull, Morton unconsciously would have poured in a small quantity of lead shot to measure volume and then failed to pack the shot down, Gould speculates. Faced with a disturbingly small Caucasian skull, he would have crammed in as much shot as he could, then forcefully tamped it down. Gould also shows that Morton made several serious but again probably unconscious statistical errors that prejudiced his findings in favor of Europeans. Gould stresses Morton's unawareness in all this because, according to Gould, Morton was an honest man and a northerner who disliked slavery and avoided open proclamations of polygenism until 1849.[28]

More important, it seems to me, especially since Morton's antislavery was questionable at best by the mid-1840s (as Stanton showed, Morton would invite John Calhoun to use his work as an argument for the annexation of Texas as a slave state), Morton's disclosure of his measurements and calculations meant that his findings could be easily checked.[29]

He no doubt would not have been so forthcoming if he had deliberately fudged his work. *Crania Aegyptiaca* discussed, and accurately reproduced, every single Egyptian skull in Morton's collection, so that Morton in effect openly invited confirmation by others. None of Morton's contemporaries took up the invitation; none verified or replicated his work. Assuming that whites were smarter than yellows, reds, browns, and blacks, his white readers seem to have accepted without question both his supposed demonstration that whites had bigger brains and his assumption that brain size correlated with intelligence.

According to today's physical anthropology, skulls can indeed be calibrated for race, but by shape alone, not size, which had been Blumenbach's insight, not Morton's. Individual brain size seems to bear no relation to intelligence. Brain size as a proportion of total body weight may give an indication of the intelligence of a population as a whole; yet important exceptions exist, such as species of birds that display considerable intelligence despite proportionally small brains relative to body weight. And although women, in comparison with men, have slightly smaller brains proportional to body weight, in the aggregate and on average they score on intelligence texts exactly the same as men.

Taking Morton's findings at face value, Prichard was impressed by the work leading up to *Crania Aegyptiaca.* When Prichard in his 1845 *Natural History of Man,* a popular survey of the field, said of Morton's work on Egypt that "a most interesting and really important addition has lately been made to our knowledge of the physical character of the Ancient Egyptians." Morton knew that his reputation had been made. Prichard had already written privately to Morton to praise his work on *Crania Americana.*[30]

If Morton's research seemed valid, Prichard did question the logic of craniology as the basis for polygenism (which Morton had not yet argued). In *Natural History of Man* Prichard observed that what could seem the same trait, including skull shape, among peoples in very different climates or geographies did not necessarily mean that those two peoples were related or the same. They would have to be seen as the same if it was already established that "all the organic differences observed in mankind" were the marks of separate, fixed species. "But while it is still allowed that they may be merely varieties, which, for aught that has been proved to the contrary, may have been produced by external agencies on the different branches of one original stock, it must be considered probable that similar causes may have produced on many different tribes similar effects; and the inference is, that a mere resemblance in some particular anatomical characters affords no infallible proof of near relationship."[31] Hence the polygenists reasoned in circles: they had craniology as proof of polygenism, when logically innate racial differences had to be assumed if craniology was to work as a basis for species classification. Prichard, lacking a physiological theory of adaptation, could only speak of possibility—"it is still allowed," "they may be," "for aught that is proved to the contrary," "it must be considered probable," "no infallible proof." He could propose nothing definite or material of his own.

The idea that the founders of civilization, the Egyptians, could have been black, had always so disturbed Prichard that he would forget his logical critique of craniology and broach a confident organicism. Prichard wrote the body of *Natural History of Man,* including the attack on craniology and innatism as applied to mankind, before encountering Morton's work on Egypt, but he added an epilogue, "Recent Additions to Ethnography," containing a ten-page laudatory account of a preliminary paper on Egypt delivered by Morton to the American Philosophical Society. To Prichard, Morton rightly concluded that all the ancient Egyptians or at least the ruling class had had white skin. According to Prichard, Blumenbach's work on the subject had been corrupted by reliance on unscientific and prejudiced eighteenth-century accounts (for example, Volney and Napoleon's Egyptian Expedition). Now there were Morton's objective skull measurements, which Prichard found superior not just to Volney's but to others' anecdotal accounts.

Like Morton, Prichard presented himself as rescuing the good in Blumenbach from the idealistic prejudices of the eighteenth century. Morton saw adaptationism itself as a product of such prejudices. Where Prichard on balance should be seen as an adaptationist, if a highly conservative and convoluted one, all Morton really preserved from Blumenbach was the idea of calibrating skull shape for race. Morton treated Blumenbach disingenuously, used Blumenbach's and the eighteenth-century's supposed blind egalitarianism as a straw man that could be knocked down in lieu of direct assaults on Prichard and nineteenth-century monogenism. Blumenbach's great insight, craniology, would be purified of sentimentalism.

More modern naturalists, even Alexander von Humboldt, the most famous naturalist and explorer of the time, remained blind regarding race, Morton thought. In an 1846 letter to Gliddon, Morton quoted Humboldt's famous statement on the monogenism/polygenism debate: "And now regarding the unity of the human species, we reject, by necessary consequence, the sad [désolante] distinction of superior and inferior races." In a passage revealing his idea of the politics and morals of the scientific study of race, Morton reproved Humboldt for taking a thoroughly unscientific attitude, however much his feelings did Humboldt credit as a man:

> Humboldt's word désolante is true in sentiment and in morals—but, as you observe it, it is wholly inapplicable to the physical reality. Nothing so humbles, so crushes my spirit, as to look into a madhouse, and behold the driveling, brutal idiocy so conspicuous in such places; it conveys a terrific idea of the disparity of human intelligences. But there is the unyielding, insuperable reality. It is désolante indeed to think, to know, that many of these poor mortals were born, were created so! But it appears to me to make little difference in the sentiment of the question whether they came into the world without their wits, or whether they lost them afterwards. And so, I would add, it makes little difference whether the mental inferiority of the Negro, the Samoiyede, or the Indian, is natural or acquired; for, if they ever possessed equal intelligence with the Caucasian, they have lost it; and if they never had it, they had nothing to lose. One party would arraign Providence for creating them originally different, another for placing them in circumstances by which they inevitably became so. Let us search out the truth, and reconcile it afterwards.[32]

☙ NOTT: CHRISTIANITY AS STRAW MAN

Morton's friend, the Philadelphia physician Henry S. Patterson, reprinted Morton's letter to Gliddon on von Humboldt in a biographical sketch of Morton that appeared as the prologue to the prodigious and explicitly Cuvierian *Types of Mankind* by Nott and Gliddon. Published in 1854 and including an important article by Agassiz, *Types* was the American School's major document after *Crania Aegyptiaca* and a frankly anti-clerical work. (Gliddon had already written in 1850 of the works leading up to *Types:* "the parson-skinning goes on bravely."[33]) Nott in the Introduction to *Types* deemed the controversy over polygenesis the "last great battle between science and dogmatism," and he said of Prichard: "We behold him, year after year, like a bound giant, struggling with increasing strength against the cords which cramp him, and we are involuntarily looking with anxiety to see him burst them asunder. But how few possess the moral power to break through a deeprooted prejudice!" Nott dramatized the American School's efforts and in the process reversed the logic of radical abolitionism. For him, rejecting racial equality, not upholding it, was what took moral courage.[34]

Perhaps it was also ordained by God, and Acts 17:26 (God "hath made of one blood all nations of men for to dwell on all the face of the earth") could finally be supplanted by a new and higher scientific revelation. Morton himself, in a letter of 1851, told Gliddon: "The doctrine of the original diversity of mankind unfolds itself to me more and more with the distinctness of revelation." Glossing this letter, Patterson cast Morton as a kind of John the Baptist of innatism: "As the mountain summits are gilded with the early dawn, while the plain below still sleeps in darkness, so it is the loftiest spirit among men that first receives and reflects the radiance of the coming truth."[35]

Despite this hyperbole, *Types,* like Morton and Cuvier, challenged the Bible less seriously than most natural historical environmentalists did. Instead of positing, as Buffon or Prichard and other naturalists did, a vastly ancient, constantly changing world which God had created but in which He did not subsequently intervene, Nott and Gliddon were defying the most conservative biblical chronology. If some passages of *Types* did proclaim a vast age for the earth, these were mere anticlerical provocations with no attempts at scientific justification. Yet Nott and Gliddon proclaimed themselves as intrepid scientists and secularists simply because they cited authorities providing concrete reasons to expand that chronology by one or two thousand years. Drawing on the Prussian Egyptologist Karl Richard Lepsius's monumental 1849 *Chronologie der Aegypter,* they argued that, as Nott had already written in his 1849 *Two*

Lectures on the Connexion between the Biblical and Physical History of Man, "the chronology of Egypt, even for some centuries beyond Abraham, is no longer a matter of speculation, while that of Genesis vanishes before it." Lepsius's work put the earliest Egyptian records at 3900 B.C., only a hundred years after Bishop Ussher's date for the creation. But as Lepsius, a religious man and a monogenist, well knew, almost nobody with a decent education believed any longer in Ussher's chronology. Lepsius himself did not think that his own work undermined the basic biblical account of time and creation. Nott and Gliddon saw fit to ignore this. As Herbert Hovenkamp has shown, their critics did not.[36]

For example, an article by the southern botanist and Episcopal minister Moses Ashley Curtis in the important *Southern Quarterly Review* gave extensive coverage to the monogenesis/polygenesis debate stimulated by the American School. Curtis lit into Nott's treatment of biblical chronology in *Two Lectures.* Nott, Curtis charged, had made Ussher into a straw man. Curtis asked why Nott had focused only on Ussher's chronology and ignored the Septuagint chronology, which was considered "just as authoritative" as Ussher's (and on which, although Curtis apparently did not know it and Nott and Gliddon did not admit it, the devout Morton had relied in *Crania Aegyptiaca*). "Why," Curtis wrote, did Nott "assume the year 2348 [B.C.] as 'our date' of the Deluge, as if we were necessarily committed to it, and thus leave the unlearned to infer that Menes, whose era he puts at 2750 [B.C.] must have reigned in Egypt 400 years before the Deluge, when by the Septuagint chronology, his time would be 500 years *after* the Deluge?"[37] Curtis must have realized himself that even the Septuagint chronology put the Deluge at circa 3300 B.C., still six hundred years after Lepsius's date for the earliest Egyptian records. But note that Curtis called the Septuagint "as authoritative" as Ussher, implying that no time scheme as yet had definitive claims: a few centuries could presumably be found somewhere.

There was one argument, however, for which probably no one but African Americans and a few of the most radical white abolitionists would criticize the later American School. As read by Nott and Gliddon in *Types,* Lepsius had seemingly given the *coup de grâce* to the idea that Negroes had anything to do with founding Western civilization. Lepsius's 1843 expedition to the Nile Valley had supposedly proved that Meröe, capital of ancient Ethiopia, had been founded as much as a thousand years *after* the founding of the first great Egyptian cities. That mattered because before Lepsius's expedition, many natural historians and even biblical scholars and "biblical scientists" generally thought that civilization first appeared in the Upper Nile in what became ancient Ethiopia, then quickly spread down river into what became the greater and more advanced civilization of Egypt. In popular parlance, and in the Bible too, "Ethiopian" meant "black"—as in "Can the Ethiopian change his skin, or the leopard his spots?"—and Herodotus said that the Egyptians were less black-skinned and curly-haired than the Ethiopians. Volney's *Ruins* was set not in Egypt but in Ethiopia, where, Volney said, the arts and sciences were founded. The issue of the Ethiopians had been a problem for the American School, which had to try to confront the existence of Ethiopian civilization; and Morton's claim that the Ethiopian ruling class had been Caucasian had no skulls to support it. Now, based on Lepsius, Nott and Gliddon could say that Ethiopian civilization was a partly Negro-ized parody of absolutely original, white supremacist Egyptian civilization. Egypt came first and it was white; Ethiopian civilization was black, or rather probably mulatto—an apish imitation in any case.

Thus, in *Types of Mankind,* Lepsius, a devout Christian (and seemingly a follower of Blumenbach's racial theories), became the hero of polygenists and supposed parson-skinners Nott and Gliddon. *Types* cast Lepsius's discovery that Egypt preceded Ethiopia as polygenism's clinching argument. In a passage recalling Morton's comments on Blumenbach's errors in *Crania Aegyptiaca,* Nott declared that had Prichard "lived but two years longer, until the mighty discoveries of LEPSIUS were unfolded to the world, he would have realized that the honorable occupation of his long life had been only to accumulate facts, which, properly interpreted, shatter everything he had built upon them."[38] Morton and Lepsius, Nott said, knew how modern science had to build. Patterson presented Morton as combining the best of modern scientific method with the spirit of traditional scholarship.

Morton, like an old-fashioned gentleman-scholar, Patterson wrote, relied on authorities rather than current fads and prejudices; he consulted the dead from his study. And, like the contemporary "higher criticism" (source analysis and critical reading of the Bible) coming into vogue as a model of scientific scholarship, Morton did so in a newly objective way. He recognized the biases and limitations of histories and travel accounts and also of artistic reproductions of ruins. Reasoning on scientific principles, he used an objective method as a check: the measurement of skulls. Then, Patterson said, Morton's armchair conclusions received confirmation in the field from Lepsius. Now, finally, because of Morton and Lepsius, ethnology's last vestige of absurd superstition, the attempt to trace all humanity back to a single pair, could be dispensed with. Morton's craniology, confirmed by Lepsius's modern field work, brought the natural history of man into the field of objective science. "Ethical principles require a different order of evidence from material phenomena, and are to be regarded from another point of view," Patterson pronounced. "If, then, the doctrine of unity gives no essential guarantee of universal liberty and equality, why reproach the opposite doctrine with destroying what never existed?" The logic of abolitionism had been inverted. The ideal of equality, Patterson said, not the natural fact of white supremacy, rested on false premises and prejudice against science. Giving up "prejudices" like "all men are created equal" did not mean giving up white grandeur, mystery, or supremacy, or denying gloom and oppression. It meant turning the horrors they involved, and that had been exposed and denounced by abolitionists, white and black, into natural imperatives.

Morton won international fame, and the American School rose to prominence both in America and Europe. As far as the imagery surrounding ancient Egypt goes, it is unclear what effect *Crania Aegyptiaca* or *Types of Mankind* exerted on racial themes already in popular American consciousness about Egypt. The notion of a white supremacist ancient Egypt had for some time held attractions for proslavery writers in the common argument that only slavery could sustain civilization in a warm climate (recall Dew's *Vindication of Personal Slavery*). As William Harper in his 1852 *Memoir on Slavery,* a major proslavery tract, declared, "Let it be remembered that all the great and enduring monuments of human art and industry—the wonders of Egypt—the everlasting works of Rome—were created by the labor of slaves. There will come a stage in our progress when we shall have facilities for executing works as great as any of these—more useful than the pyramids—not less magnificent than the Sea of Moeris." Furthermore, "In our own country, look at the lower valley of the Mississippi, which is capable of being made a far greater Egypt." And indeed, a major city on the lower Mississippi was Memphis, Tennessee, founded in 1819 by Judge John Overton and General Andrew Jackson. Memphis was the first capital of Egypt, and Overton and Jackson hoped that their new version would become the center of a slave empire surrounding the Mississippi the way that ancient Egypt had embraced the Nile.[39]

The craniology of the careful and devout Morton might have been easily absorbed, but "Niggerology" or "the nigger business," as Josiah Nott called the American School's later work in a private letter, might seem to jibe badly with attempts to present a coherent, Christian patriarchal southern proslavery worldview. The American School baited the parsons and railed against biblical chronology. It did not seriously challenge the (white) biblical worldview, the belief, in brief, that human history was only a few thousand years old and that human beings were meant to be masters of beast, bird, and tree (and Negro). Morton had explicitly invoked biblical chronology in *Crania Aegyptiaca,* which did not openly espouse polygenism. As Fredrickson shows, open polygenism could easily be reconciled with Scripture, for instance in the popular idea that Genesis only applied to whites and that Negroes were a distinct "pre-Adamite" creation; Jefferson Davis preached pre-Adamitism on the floor of the United States Senate.[40] The American School offered much in refuting Volney, Denon, Grégoire, and African Americans: "scientific" proof of Negro inferiority and an image of a white supremacist Egypt, the original, God-given slave society.

Although a large and expensive book, *Types* sold out a run of 3,500 copies in four months. The pre-publication subscription list for *Types* (some five hundred names) read like a Who's Who of the political and intellectual lights of the day; Edward Everett, by then the United States Secretary of State, ordered a copy for his department and for himself, as did the Secretary of the Navy. Nott and Gliddon's arguments would appear in books, newspapers, tracts, and stump speeches, North and South, throughout the Civil War era. The appearance of Darwin's *Origin of Species* in 1859, which destroyed all the American School's major arguments, did not stop sales; by 1870 *Types* had gone through ten editions.[41]

Not only did *Types* sell, but Nott suffered little if at all in the South for his superficial irreligion. A success in the highest southern circles, he associated with men like James Henry Hammond, firebrand, senator, one-time governor of South Carolina, and author of the famous 1858 "mud-sill" speech to Congress defending slavery with the argument that every society had to have a "mud-sill" class to do the dirty work. At least southern mud-sills were well cared for, Hammond said, while northern workers had to fend for themselves. It was to Hammond that Nott described the American School's work as "niggerology" and in the same letter admitted that his own major aim was proving practical, de facto permanent black inferiority rather than polygenism as an abstract theory.

A wry man who took a conservative and jaded view of life and society, Nott ministered to all and sundry in his medical office and in the plantation fields and made important contributions to our knowledge of yellow fever, as well as serving as a medical examiner in the Confederate army. Hammond was a parvenu who clawed his way into South Carolina aristocracy through sheer ambition, ability, and a strategic marriage. Then sexual indiscretions with his nieces blighted his career, and in the end he became embittered by southern life and rash sectional adventurism regarding slavery. Eugene D. Genovese sees Hammond's career as the emblem of the "slaveholders' dilemma," the movement from confidence to the final realization that, confronted with free labor's superior productivity, the supposed gradual, meliorated progress of slave society would have to fail. Slave society would destroy itself or be absorbed, its distinctiveness annihilated either way.[42]

Nott's pessimism was more thoroughgoing, an advance over Morton's "désolante" realism or even Hammond's proslavery desperation. Nonwhite inferiority never desolated Nott; he championed white supremacy with relish and feared that free labor would lead to racial amalgamation and thus ultimately to human extinction, since in his view mulattos were a less fertile hybrid. For him the problem of modernity was more a racial (and sexual) than a class dilemma. He preached the evils of amalgamation and the inferiority of Negroes partly to convince ordinary white people in the North to let the South be. Although the School's doctrines won a huge following in the North, when it turned out that most northerners hated both Negroes and slavery, Nott despaired. So would African Americans.

8

Effacing the Individual

To the untrue man, the whole universe is false,—it is impalpable,—it shrinks to nothing within his grasp. And he himself, in so far as he shows himself in a false light, becomes a shadow, or, indeed, ceases to exist. The only truth that continued to give Mr. Dimmesdale a real existence on this earth was the anguish in his inmost soul, and the undissembled expression of it in his aspect. Had he once found power to smile, and wear a face of gayety, there would have been no such man!

Nathaniel Hawthorne, *The Scarlet Letter* (1850)

As the slavery controversy escalated with the Mexican American War and the political confrontations of the 1850s, race thinking intensified. The American School, abolitionists of all kinds, and free blacks themselves ultimately came to see questions of progress and change, stability, anarchy, and decline, in terms of supposed laws of racial entities, especially supposed laws of the benefits or perils of race mixing. Races, not individuals or nations, changed over time, and not in terms of conformation to or degradation from an ideal norm. African American ideas and ethnological racial concepts intertwined. The obsession with amalgamation that we see in public writing suggests that on some level it was recognized how far such blending had gone in actuality, so that neither group could claim to be the norm. Morton had presented all sorts of convoluted arguments to ensure that nobody could see Pharaoh as black. Abolitionism and the prospect of a nation of millions of free blacks could not be countenanced.

In the 1850s Nott fixated on the fixity of racial type. Westward expansion and industrialization transformed the United States, yielding sectionalism, disunion, and war. It was becoming incontrovertible to virtually everyone, American School members included, that change was becoming a fact of life, one that could involve the relations between the races. Settling the New World could not be cast as a simple story of discarding European corruption and establishing natural harmony. To almost everyone a certain amount of freedom, dynamism, even mixture of different peoples seemed good—progress could come from diversity—but ethnology cast blacks as too different to mate successfully with whites (although in reality it was happening all the time).

In his ethnological researches Nott claimed to prove that blacks and whites were distinct, if closely related, species. Based on population statistics, he maintained that mulattos were weaker and less fertile than pure blacks or whites. Amalgamation, carried on for many generations, fatally weakened both parent races. At the same time, Nott conceded that amalgamation among what he considered separately created European "local races" had made the Anglo-Saxon race—or "hybrid," as he put it—great. Ruefully and despairingly, he recognized the problem of arguing for racial hierarchy in the midst of an industrializing world that was leaving behind old notions of order. Constantly driving men to overreach themselves, desire for profit and progress moved races from the original environments where God had meant them to live and brought them into close contact with each other. The results, Nott predicted, would be racial equality, amalgamation, and, finally, extinction of the white race or all races. The prospect of black freedom had set his agenda too. He condemned amalgamation and a free society, while upholding slave cotton culture as a check on the free market (to which cotton culture was tied) and slavery as a check on race mixing (which slavery abetted); this put him in an impossible position. He devised disingenuous arguments, based on a great fear that freedom was getting more and more dangerous, verging on anarchy. Nott's writings were nonetheless clever and popular, posing a new set of paradoxes that appealed to white, especially southern, anxieties about black freedom and amalgamation.

Whites, like Harriet Beecher Stowe, who were making blacks redemptive and calling for immediate emancipation also abhorred biological mixture between the races. These advocates of what Fredrickson termed "romantic racialism" presented blacks as Christ-figures, gentle, "feminine," long-suffering, and virtuous, as opposed to the aggressive, sinful, masterful, and "masculine" Anglo-Saxons. One would think that such a view would make it natural for male and female to mate—but no, romantic racialists wanted only a cultural marriage, not a real one; blacks and whites would improve one another at a distance. It might even be in blacks' innate nature to sacrifice themselves to redeem white sin.[1]

Some African Americans, like Frederick Douglass or Henry Highland Garnet, now openly championed amalgamation. Douglass himself had a European American father. By the 1850s, dissatisfied with Garrison's disdain for politics and black racial activism, and insistence that moral suasion was the only way to end slavery, Douglass broke with Garrisonianism. He would say that America's strength flowed from its diversity and hybridity, its "composite nationality," which his own life story triumphantly represented. But his use of representative identity was less successful and more complex as a response to ethnology than historians have recognized.

Arguably the greatest intellectual and literary accomplishment of the period's writing about race was the querulous, often bitter voice of the black physician James McCune Smith. The "most educated Negro of his day," according to the black divine Alexander Crummell, McCune Smith was one of the few people in the antislavery camp qualified to tackle the American School on scientific grounds.[2] In mocking and inverting Nott, McCune Smith's writing approached the complex, sympathetic pessimism of the best American prose of the time. He saw—and, crucially, thought it important to try to make others see—the price that Americans of African descent paid when they gave of themselves to try to uplift the nation, when they had to think and act in terms of race at all. He believed the sacrifice was probably necessary but terrible and inane. Trying to do Nott one better and himself come up with a race theory, McCune Smith wound up recreating a "black" version of Nott's self-pitying, twisted racial pessimism. As a physician and statistician, he theorized race scientifically. In doing so he followed the American School and the social science of his day in effacing individuals into races, but resented it bitterly.

☞ SEGREGATING DIVERSITY

Nott extended the white supremacist domain to history, mutability, the rise and fall of empires and peoples, even to what environmentalists had seen as individual variety. He explained it all in terms of the blending of original racial Cuvierian "types" and managed to make diversity and complexity virtues within the white race but anathema if extended beyond it. Like Morton's work, however, his arguments were throughout so artful, so reliant on environmentalist ways of thinking, and so dependent on hidebound biblical assumptions long abandoned by the better monogenists that it is absurd to say that his theory constituted an internally consistent, coherent original innatism or scientific "racism." Rather, he had crafted a powerful, self-conscious set of contradictions and paradoxes derived from engagement in a larger debate.

Nott's position required a theory of nature that put each original people in their own appointed primordial region. Polygenism had typically argued that there had been several distinct acts of creation of the races, each of which then spread out, varying slightly in the process of settling in its great portion of the world. Nott rejected even that small degree of variation and adaptation. In his view, there had been no diffusion of peoples to populate the globe at all, and no environmental variation whatever: instead, each of hundreds or thousands of local regions inhabited by man had had its own, separately created indigenous group. As Agassiz argued, God created hundreds or even thousands of local habitats in their entirety around the globe, people included. Even small regional differences among humans were originally given.

To the American School, Celts or Saxons or Franks, although distinct "local races" separately created by God for specific zones, were not necessarily distinct species. The School reserved species distinction only for differences among "great races." By this was meant broad regional groups—Europeans, Ethiopians, American Indians, Malaysians, and Mongoloids (Blumenbach's categories)—which Nott believed were comprised of many distinct, separately created yet closely similar "local races." Although the American School took the concepts of "great races" and "types" from Cuvier, it still followed Blumenbach's racial categories, which, based on skull shape, correlated roughly to geography; these racial categories underlay Morton's craniology, always the School's bulwark. The School under Nott read the Cuvierian "great race" notion backward into Blumenbach's categories, so that the "Caucasian" became the representative "type" for the European "great race" (Cuvier's concept), with its hundreds or thousands of "local races." The "Ethiopian" became the representative "type" for the African "great race," itself made up of numerous "local races," and so forth.

Nott presented all this as certain scientific truth, buttressed by Agassiz. In the scientific world Agassiz was an implacable enemy of the idea of transformation of species that saw common descent in each great branch of creation or even among all living things. He insisted that the fine interrelationships within what in the twentieth century would be called ecosystems demonstrated that there could have been no common descent, nor indeed much spreading of living things into new environments nor environment altering living beings. This was the "correlation of parts" applied not just to individual organisms (as Cuvier had done) but to the interrelations of all living things in an entire region. But here Agassiz was intellectually very conservative. The scientific climate had changed. Although evolution may not yet have been widely accepted in the 1850s (and was not systematically presented by Darwin until 1859), the ideas of gradual change of some sort in nature and of the constant spreading of species into new zones with attendant patterns of diversification were now widespread.[3] So Nott's ideas were hardly up-to-date science, much less certain scientific truth.

His strict creationist version of polygenism, however, would appeal to white supremacists and proslavery men in the United States. They required an anchor against the sea changes sweeping the nation, a way to say that black inferiority and subordination would remain God-given truth. Retrograde creationism was essential to Nott's racial histories, which provided that anchor but would become unmoored if it were granted that human diversity had a complex past going back much farther than a few thousand years. If such a past existed, how could one prove innatism, much less determine what the original local races were? Nott had to take it as given that humans as they now existed only went back a few thousand years—that is, for all his rejection of biblical chronology and parson-baiting, to about the time of the biblical Flood. One can hardly conceive of a more biblical argument for the idea that only amalgamation could change racial type than what Nott said at the 1850 annual meeting, held in Charleston, of the newly formed American Association for the Advancement of Science. He presented a paper, "The

Physical History of the Jews, in Its bearings on the Question of the Unity of the Races," that aimed to show that the Jews, whose religion forbade exogamy, had not changed physiologically since Old Testament times despite differing environments.[4]

Nott used this Old Testament evidence to dismiss Prichard for being hidebound, and after hearing Nott's paper, Agassiz stood up and openly proclaimed polygenism for the first time. Thus fortified, Nott felt confident enough to tell Morton, who had himself come out openly for polygenism the previous year, that it was dubious at best to treat as the same primordial creation peoples as obviously distinct as the Germanic, the Hindu, the Egyptian, and the Hebrew.[5] More precise terms than "Caucasian" were needed, terms tracing back to the great original diversity of creation. *Indigenous Races of the Earth* (1857), the successor to *Types,* but mostly written by Gliddon, would count thirty separate such distinct, originally created subspecies of the Caucasian "great race" depicted on the ancient Egyptian monuments alone.[6]

Nott's contradictions and insidious use of sources surpassed Morton's. In working out his position Nott drew on Blumenbach's categories, Morton's craniology, and his own research into fertility—although, as he well knew, Blumenbach was an environmentalist and Morton had refused to take a stand on the unity question in his most important studies. Nott's own fertility research took its very definition of species from the arch-environmentalist and monogenist Buffon. Nott's first ethnological tract, published in 1843, was a paper on the infertility of mulattos: "The Mulatto a Hybrid—Probable Extermination of the Two Races If the Whites and Blacks are Allowed to Intermarry."[7] Mulattos, Nott conceded, were obviously fertile to some degree. Still, population statistics revealed that they were less fertile than their parents and if not absorbed into one of the parent races would finally disappear, even if such absorption would damage the parent races. Buffon, as Nott realized, had adopted a relative fertility definition of species in answer to critics like Lord Kames who pointed to distinct species that could breed fertile offspring. Buffon, however, remained a monogenist who always despised the very term race, and he never thought that human diversity affected human fertility. For Nott, his assumed relative infertility of the mulatto proved that Negro and Caucasian were distinct species although they could breed offspring capable for a few generations of having children.

Nott had turned the most historicist eighteenth-century approach to natural history—Buffon's defining species not just in terms of reproduction, that is, fertility versus infertility of the first crosses between two groups, but in the very gradualist terms of classifying closely related species by determining relative fertility over many generations—in innatism's favor. If the statistics and supposed medical findings and the sources Nott enlisted to do it were as dubious as Morton's craniological measurements, calculations, and use of Blumenbach, if there was no good evidence for mulatto infertility, and there was not, nobody checked Nott's work either.

His statistics were of course not the issue. If anything, slavery showed that mulattos were fertile, but Nott knew that most whites would not discuss it. His position depended on his knowing what would not be said. The case for polygenism could only really be opposed by arguing that amalgamation did no harm to human biology or to society, which almost no white Americans would say and blacks would be reviled for saying. Nott offered abolitionists what would be for them a difficult choice: accept segregation (and slavery) or champion amalgamation.

Nott's advocacy of mixture of local races within species was a way to steal both abolitionism's and free labor's thunder and segregate any possible virtues of universal freedom and progress. In his presentation, diversity was salutary among whites, indeed it was the very engine of progress. The Caucasian "great race" or "species" was superior precisely because of its relative "impurity." The Caucasian race as it now existed was hybridized, the product of sexual amalgamation among different primordial European peoples, a blend of the products of all the varied but relatively similar ecosystems in Europe. This "hybrid," as Nott called it, proved so successful that it went on to conquer the globe. In two articles of 1853, with *Uncle Tom's Cabin* already out and controversy over the Compromise of 1850 and the Fugitive Slave Law making disunion a real possibility, Nott championed the progressiveness of intra-species ("local race") "hybridity." The Caucasian was a true "cosmopolite," a super-progressive blend of the primeval races of Europe, combining the virtues of all. Whites had to forget their own divisions and stick together to keep the Negroes down and distinct.[8]

Nott's praise of diversity within the white great race had predictable limits, especially for a white southerner disdaining the free labor society in the North that was beginning to include any and all European immigrants in the "white" fold. When he first began to argue for distinctions among the Caucasian branch of humanity in his *Two Lectures* of 1848, written under the influence of Agassiz's multiple creations theory, Nott said that the Germanic variety's superiority would soon cause the extinction of the supposedly dark-skinned Celt, the lowliest subspecies within the Caucasian family.[9] Not only did he despise the Irish, he never had much good to say about Slavs or even most southern Mediterranean peoples, who were sufficiently different from Anglo-Saxons that Anglo-Saxon/Mediterranean crosses would be somewhat weak and unprolific if still perpetually fertile. By the Caucasian "hybrid," then, he really meant not a fusion of all European peoples, but just the Anglo-Saxon narrowly construed, a mixture of the local races produced in Germany, France, and Britain (excluding Ireland). This lordly Anglo-Saxon, supposed bastion of southern civilization, was allegedly besieged in America by inferior European stocks, not to speak of free blacks.

Nott brought to the United States the work of a major European proponent of Nordic supremacy. In 1855 Nott arranged for a translation into English of the just recently published *Essai sur l'inégalite des races humaines* by the anti-democratic and anti-Semitic Count Arthur de Gobineau. Gobineau, however, had no interest in challenging Genesis and monogenism: his *Essai* recognized that mulattos were fertile and pointed out the seriousness of this objection to the polygenist case. The American translation sponsored by Nott omitted these sections, about which omission Gobineau complained.[10] Nobody in America seemed to notice or care: after perusing Nott's edition of Gobineau, the Mobile, Alabama, *Register* proclaimed that Gobineau's work would take deep hold in the South and perhaps the North as well. Because the work came "from a French Savan [sic], it will not be charged with sectional prejudice as many of our Southern books are."[11]

Nott's whole approach, and the American School's open polygenism that he was largely responsible for, depended on the unspoken sexual hypocrisy of the primarily Anglo-Saxon men who had settled the American South. In the late seventeenth century slave states had begun to outlaw sexual intercourse between white women and black men, but not between black women and white men. Ignoring children of white men born to black women, such laws were a blatant attempt to bolster Negro chattel slavery. Because children followed the legal status of the mother (meaning that the child of a slave woman was a slave), mulattos with white fathers were slaves and posed no danger to the slave system. White men did not outlaw that kind of mixture; they profited from it but did not speak of it. Only "mixed" children born to white women were anathematized.

A psychosexual economy of repression and projection seems to have emerged that exonerated lust and greed among white men. Black women came to be seen as hypersexual, so lustful that sexual intercourse with them was always voluntary, never coerced. The black woman could not be raped. The white woman, by contrast, became a flower of chastity to be chivalrously protected and defended from the black male beast, a natural rapist. Nott made black/white amalgamation into not just the very essence of social anarchy (there was nothing new in that perception for an elite white male American) but of racial apocalypse, extinction of all races. Yet Nott also could echo, with his own Anglo-Saxon slant, people like Hector St. John de Crèvecoeur, who had predicted in the late eighteenth century that America would produce a "new man" through blending of different European immigrants, a view expressed by Emerson more than half a century later.

Nott ingeniously combined these two longstanding ideas of amalgamation. The result was a theory that intraspecies mixture among the best Europeans meant progress, but between any Europeans and any Africans (because they were distinct species) it led to decline and death. And all the great races might be destroyed by the fruit of modern science and technology, namely, world imperialism and expansion and its attendant mixtures of peoples, as the Anglo-Saxon's very success inevitably bred disastrous hybridity across great race lines. Nott had crafted an ethnological version of the slaveholders' dilemma.

⊙ EGYPT AND A PROSLAVERY ENLIGHTENMENT

He also married the Enlightenment and slavery, contradictions be damned. Nott's biographer Reginald Horsman writes that Nott "had two powerful beliefs—one was a conviction of racial inequality and the necessity of white supremacy, and the other was opposition to religious interference with the course of scientific inquiry."[12] Horsman's conclusion, however, that Nott would have made a better advocate for white supremacy had he not provoked the clergy at every turn is questionable. The contradiction was likely what made him persuasive. Nott did, as Horsman observes, resemble a crusty eighteenth-century rationalist bewailing human unreason and religious superstition in the style of Voltaire, who had himself espoused polygenism because the Church and blind optimists about human nature opposed it. I would say that Nott's eighteenth-century quality, his bitter disappointment at the failure of eighteenth-century rationalism, was the cornerstone of his appeal and his racism. He offered readers a proslavery enlightenment—both in the small "e" sense of an intellectual epiphany about the nature of race and in the large "E" sense of eighteenth-century rationalism and Voltairean skepticism. His polemics were effective because they were couched in the eighteenth-century language of reason as opposed to superstition, of truth as opposed to obscurity and blind faith, only his truths were nineteenth-century American and racist. They were not self-evident and uplifting but hidden, ugly, and mocking.

Reconsider the comments to Hammond that Nott's ethnological work was "niggerology" or "the nigger business," lines usually read as testimony to his hateful, confident white supremacism. Hateful, yes; confident, no. As Nott himself no doubt knew, calling ethnology "niggerology" or "the nigger business" turned ethnology from Morton's purportedly high-minded, objective search for truth into a contemptibly low calling, no better than slave trading, a profession urbane southern gentleman commonly described in such degrading terms.

The sectional conflict, as Horsman shows, turned Nott into a diehard pessimist who would write, several years before war destroyed his beloved slave South, that man was the most irrational of animals. The vices of civilization balanced or overbalanced its virtues. Mankind did not progress except in the realm of scientific knowledge, which caused as many problems as it solved. He tried to stand firmly fixed to the image of ancient Egypt as the great archetype of a thriving white supremacist civilization, an ideal that the American South, he realized, might not be able to recreate for long. Hence his abiding worship of Morton's work on Egypt. Nott saw that the course of modern history might be against the slave South, and he bemoaned human error and the over-reaching modern drive for freedom and progress.

☞ FREE BLACKS AND THE PROBLEM OF ANONYMITY

McCune Smith, on the opposite end of the ideological spectrum, also despaired. He did not abhor progress or much enjoy perversely painting himself into a corner, as Nott did. He was extremely annoyed and angry his whole life at being put into the position wherein he could not evaluate black people or himself as individuals. The effacement of individual African Americans into blackness, and of progress into iron laws of race, seemed to make his life as a physician and intellectual worthless.

In a series of letters exchanged with the white abolitionist and philanthropist Gerrit Smith, McCune Smith confessed his doubts, justified his positions, dispensed medical and philosophical advice, and railed against obdurate prejudice and sin. In one 1846 scrawl, he despaired that prejudice was so awful that he wanted to give up: "each succeeding day, that terrible majority [of whites who hate black people] fall sadder, heavier, more crushingly on my soul. At times I am so weaned from life, that I could lay me down to die." In 1848 he declared, "In the series of metamorphoses I must have had a coral insect for a millio-millio-grand-father, loving to work beneath the tide in a superstructure that someday, when the labourer is long dead and forgotten, may rear itself above the waves and afford rest and habitation for the creatures of this Good, Good Father and All."[13] McCune Smith tried to make the best of it and accept the transformation of species and a vast age for the Earth, but he hated putting himself and his fellow African Americans in the anonymous, self-sacrificing role.

He had spent his life trying to rise above the waves. Born in New York City in 1813, the son of a slave woman and a merchant, he was a prize student at the New York African Free Schools run by white philanthropists. Refused entry to American medical schools on account of his color, he sailed in 1832 for the University of Glasgow, where he earned his M.D. in 1837, and then returned to New York to set up an interracial medical practice and pharmacy on respectable West Broadway. Precocious and self-confident in public, he argued all his life that blacks had to cultivate self-discipline, sobriety, and, as he put it in his introduction to Douglass's great 1855 autobiography, *My Bondage and My Freedom,* "a sacred thirst for liberty and for learning, first as a means of attaining liberty, then as an end in itself; a will; an unfaltering energy and self determination to obtain what his soul pronounced desirable; a majestic self-hood."[14] African American community meetings honored him; white groups invited him to speak for abolition or to debate white polygenists. He quickly became co-editor, along with Cornish, of a new African American newspaper, *The Colored American,* where in his brief editorial tenure he expressed his growing frustration with Garrisonian disdain for black political agitation and racial activism. In the 1840s, McCune Smith would be perhaps Garrisonianism's most outspoken African American critic. He lambasted the whites' refusal to identify with blacks or admit their debts to black activism and support.

He would also help direct Gerrit Smith's attempt to settle African Americans on several thousand acres of farmland (where John Brown would live after 1854 in upstate New York and where the plan for the raid on Harper's Ferry was first hatched, with Gerrit Smith's aid and financial backing), and he participated in most of the major black conventions and abolitionist and anti-colonization initiatives of his day. He wrote the first medical case history by an African American to appear in a major medical journal, the *New York Journal of Medicine.* In 1837 he delivered a lecture, "The Fallacy of Phrenology," later published in *The Colored American,* powerfully refuting phrenology as contradictory and unproveable. The whole idea of materializing mind McCune Smith denounced as impious, a challenge to faith and a denial of the reality of the unseen. Society was not made up of brains but sovereign, striving individuals with souls. That struggling humanity, he always insisted, was what deserved study, empathy, and aid.

A co-founder of the Statistical Institute, a New York City–based group dedicated to the statistical analysis of society, he campaigned to correct the 1840 census's flagrant overrepresentation of free black insane persons in the North. The *New York Tribune* published his statistical analysis of the African American population in which he tried to prove that freedom did not make blacks sick, drive them crazy, or kill them.[15]

⌒ INDIRECTION AND CRITIQUE: SOCIAL HISTORY

During most of his career McCune Smith did not publicly target the American School's specific ethnological arguments. He went after ethnology only indirectly, by implication, and he resisted discussing blacks as a race or as victims. The sympathetic identification with ordinary black people that McCune Smith at his best tried to evoke in his readers, most of whom had some white ancestry and could not be seen as purely "black," was not the pathos that Garrisonians or Easton saw in the slave's fate. Nor was it the Christian sympathy of the new breed of non-Garrisonian antislavery reformer searching for self-sacrificial black Christ-figures who would help to convert proslavery sinners. Although in the end McCune Smith's attempt to escape race failed, his efforts to show black people as individuals were virtuosic; they might be seen as pioneering the social history of African American life.

In a regular column he wrote between 1852 and 1854 in *Frederick Douglass's Paper* under the pseudonym "Communipaw" (a name taken from a colonial-era interracial community of Native Americans, blacks, and Dutch settlers located in what is now Jersey City and famous for having resisted an invasion of Virginians demanding submission to the British Crown), McCune Smith produced a ten-part series, "The Heads of the Colored People, Done with a Whitewash Brush." Although the series title implicitly ridiculed phrenology and craniology, McCune Smith did not mention Morton or Nott in the installments. He illustrated the lives and thoughts of free blacks in portraits that harped on whites' sexual hypocrisy and offered a living refutation of the American School's nonsense of differentiating among dead skulls and hard and fast "races." Better, he was saying, to scrutinize the living heads of purportedly "black" people, both slave and free, actually of combined African and European ancestry and complex pasts, trying to make their way under awfully demoralizing circumstances.

The first "Heads" installment described a legless black newspaper vendor—his noble aspirations, hard work, degraded status, greasy hair and clothes, and withal dignified bearing. "Our colored news vendor *kneels* about four feet ten; black transparent skin, broad and swelling chest, whose symmetry proclaims Virginia birth, fine long hooked nose, evidently from the first families, wide loose mouth, sharpish face, clean cut hazel eyes, buried beneath luxuriously folded lids, and prominent perceptive faculties. I did not ask him to pull off cloth cap with long greasy ears, lest his brow should prove him the incontestable descendent of Thomas Jefferson and Black Sal." Next came a tirade against Jefferson's and the whole southern master class's hypocrisy and sin in producing "these crocus colored products of unphilosophical lust."[16]

McCune Smith's main point in beginning the "Heads" series with the crippled news vendor was to show that the worst white bigots could perfectly well see blacks' individual humanity, at least in a black man as an object of pity. Sympathy led the whole spectrum of New York's whites to go out of their way to buy their papers from this man: "many a b'hoy ["Bowery b'hoy," slang for New York's working class street toughs], half recovered from last night's debauch, staggers a square out of the way to deal with him . . . many a dandy, who thinks in a political sense, the negro almost a dog, snatches up a paper, and with half-averted face, throws down four times its worth, and rushes away from the *human sympathy* that has stolen away into his heart."[17]

The best of the "Heads" series was probably a portrayal of the stupor, squalor, and beleaguered nobility of a black washerwoman: "*Dunk! dunk!* [goes the smoothing iron] and that small and delicately formed hand and wrist swell up with knotted muscles and bursting veins! And the eye and brow, chiseled out for stern resolve and high thought, the one now dull and haggard, and the other, seamed and blistered with deep furrows and great drops of sweat wrung out by over toil [sic]." This woman has two sisters who had been brought North as servants to white families, thereby escaping slavery, but who then returned to bondage for the sake of their children left down South. This washerwoman, an ex-slave who had been seduced or raped by her white master, would stay in New York, and she had a child with her:

Yes! well, I had forgotten to say, that, alongside the ironing table, was a good-for-nothing looking quarter grown, bush-headed boy, a shade or two lighter than his mother, so intent upon "Alladin; or, the Wonderful Lamp," that he had to be called three or four times before he sprang to put fresh wood on the fire, or light another candle, or bring a pail of water. A boy of three, but no evidence around the room, that he called any one father, nor had he, ever, except the unseen, universal "our Father, which art in Heaven!" A sort of social Pariah, he had come into the world, after the fashion which so stirs up Ethiop's pious honor. And yet, genial, forgiving nature, with a healthy forgetfulness of priests and the rituals, had stamped upon this boy's face with no lineament particularly hideous, nor yet remarkable, except a "laughing devil" in his eye that seemed ready to "face the devil" without Bern's prophylactic.[18]

How different this picture from what can only be called abolitionist pornography about the rape of slave girls that was churned out by the late antebellum white antislavery press and sometimes by black writers. How different also from the moralizing of free black writers like "Ethiop," William G. Wilson, a rival black columnist who had self-righteously condemned slave girls' supposed lasciviousness. In the piece on the laundress, McCune Smith mocked Ethiop's unfeeling, foolish attack and evoked the mulatto child's cheerfulness in the midst of misery, as well as the mother's perseverance despite her lonely predicament. Frederick Douglass warned McCune Smith that his "faithful pictures of contented degradation" would get hot suds dropped on McCune Smith's own head by black washerwomen.[19] Still wrapped up in the Manichean abolitionist imperatives of denouncing slaveholders as utter wretches and calling for free blacks to uplift themselves through the same manful individual effort that had pulled him out of slavery by his bootstraps, Douglass missed McCune Smith's subtlety.

McCune Smith's style was both sympathetic and critical, as he portrayed African Americans' corruption and nobility, squalor and striving, and asked why black people should not be allowed to have faults if they were human too. He could produce in another of the "Heads" series a gothic fantasy about a ghoulish black sexton accused of eating corpses, a fantasy that at once mocked the sexton's greed in stacking corpses into plots by the dozen so that people wondered where the bodies went, and superstitious blacks' and prejudiced whites' fears that the man was some kind of vampire or cannibal.

If something of a "haughty intellectual," as David W. Blight observes, McCune Smith was not detached.[20] As a practicing physician who turned no one away—his case study for the *New York Journal of Medicine* described the effects of opium addiction on black prostitutes he had treated—he knew free blacks' lives intimately and his writing reflected his experiences in treating abolitionists and bootblacks, school mistresses and street walkers. He had learned that the American obsession with wealth and power upheld racism and contempt for the unfortunate. As John Stauffer shows, McCune Smith, partly through his relationship with Gerrit Smith, Frederick Douglass, and John Brown, came to believe that God dwelled within each individual. By trusting and following the promptings of the true heart, through a mixture of empathy and self-reliance, Americans could remake the world, "realize a sacred and integrated society." Yet the passionate heart and the rational head had always to be kept in balance. It would take thinking and feeling, analysis and action, even great violence, to recreate society.[21]

McCune Smith showed no patience with romanticizations of blacks' sufferings or visions of black people as somehow redemptive because emotional and nonintellectual. The standard nineteenth-century dichotomies of race—normal versus degenerate, smart versus stupid, masterly versus servile, human versus animal—rarely appeared in his work. Nor did the romanticized antislavery divisions—man versus woman, reason versus faith, sinner versus saint—that were in some respects more favorable to African Americans.

McCune Smith's personal tension between his frustrated intellectual aspirations and his career as a doctor to the poor and despised seems to have made him clear-headed (if sometimes caustic), capable of writing about ordinary individuals with empathy and an ability to demonstrate the paradoxes of race. Most of the time he balanced heart and head. He lost control of his voice only when on the eve of Lincoln's election he finally proposed an alternative race theory to the American School's ethnology, which he detested but on some level understood he could not disprove without abandoning the best of himself and his fellow African Americans.

Until then, he stayed with implicit critique and produced an extraordinary body of writing. Thus when in 1849 chance brought a remarkable ethnological case before both him and Morton, McCune Smith ignored Morton and ethnology and made that case into an individual portrait of a life affirming universal human potential. In the process he gently rebuked white philanthropists for typecasting blacks as helpless self-sacrificial sufferers.

Some years before, a merchant traveling to Cape Town in southern Africa happened upon a boy, half alive, amidst a field of carnage left by one of the affrays that pitted tribes of "Bushmen" (regarded by whites as the most degraded of humans) against marauding "Caffres" (renegade Negroes). Upon reaching Cape Town, the merchant left the boy, whom he named Henry, with Isaac P. Chase, United States Consul to the Cape of Good Hope. On his return home to the United States in 1848, Chase visited friends and associates along the Eastern seaboard and brought Henry along. Later, having to return abroad, Chase left the boy in New York at the Colored Orphan Asylum. As the Orphan Asylum's staff physician, McCune Smith had contact with Chase in dealing with Henry and would surely have known that Chase had taken Henry to the Academy of Natural Sciences of Philadelphia, where Morton and several other Philadelphia naturalists spent an afternoon examining the boy. Henry, Morton reported to a meeting of the whole membership of the Academy, displayed the "upswept buttocks" and the "osseous framework" of the famous statuette the "Hottentot Venus," although Morton conceded that a thorough manual examination of Henry's anatomy would be needed to confirm the resemblance. Henry's skull, Morton said, was "flattened in the coronal region, full behind, and rather broad between the parietal bones." That had implications according to the phrenology Morton now claimed to disdain but actually still followed: nether regions of the brain supposedly harbored animal passions, while the coronal region housed the intellect.[22]

Henry next turns up in January 1849 at the Orphan Asylum's annual meeting. The *National Anti-Slavery Standard,* influential organ of the American Anti-Slavery Society, carried a report of the meeting: "The most interesting incident of the evening was the appearance, in a dialogue, of a young Bushman not long since captured and brought to this country. Probably a lower specimen of the African race could not be procured, or one whose circumstances had been more unfavorable to the development of his mere human faculties. Nevertheless the boy spoke English with considerable fluency, and behaved himself altogether like a reasonable creature."[23] After listening to the students' recitations and a presentation of the yearly "Appeal" for contributions, and then visiting dormitories and classrooms, the audience at the Orphan Asylum heard McCune Smith give an address on the subject of Henry the African savage turned student and apprentice. In observing Henry, McCune Smith examined his skull and used the occasion implicitly to mock Morton and the American School: "his head is well formed, and the facial angle not only excels that of the Caucasian (in what is called the Intellectual grade) but equals that which the Greeks gave Jupiter, that is 90 degrees."[24] Making no open pronouncements about ethnology or skull size, McCune Smith said that despite Henry's awful upbringing among pagans who ate lizards and snakes, did not believe in God, practiced polygamy, and left their children to fend for themselves from the age of four, and regardless of his color or features, Henry had learned English, absorbed Christianity, and begun to master a trade.

McCune Smith used Henry to blunt the prejudices of his white philanthropic audience. The Orphan Asylum "Appeal" had proclaimed "the difference of colour" to be "created by God" and deemed the orphans—most of whom in reality had parents too poor to support them—"almost as strangers in a strange land among us." Although the "orphans'" well-being and accomplishments could be seen in the asylum's dormitories and classrooms, "the pure morality and happy religious influence are better learned from the history of individuals. The last report gives a description of some of the parting hours of a few of the children, who during the past year have been removed to a better world, which must touch the heart of every Christian philanthropist."[25]

In his speech McCune Smith transformed this sentimental image of the dying, redemptive black child. Henry's case had pathos, to be sure, but what Henry had lost was not worth lamenting. That he could only remember of his native language "a few clicks of the tongue, such as we would express pity with" made McCune Smith realize how "utterly an orphan he is." It also showed that Henry had been civilized and Christianized—"living proof that the most barbarous mode of life has not been able to erase from one of God's creatures the stamp of humanity; that nature at the most can never make man and his offspring so hideous as can slavery." McCune Smith had read of one "Mr. Ledyard," a British traveler in the East, who became obsessed with exploring several enormous mounds on the banks of the Tigris: "He finally penetrates deeply into the earth, and Nineveh is disclosed before him!" McCune Smith declared that the founders of the asylum "literally made excavations in the mud and mire of murky cellars, and brought to the light of day the living images you see before you; full of life, full of hope, full of energies, which are being rightly directed to help roll on the flood of light and life, liberty and civilization which God had entrusted to the hands of the American people."[26]

McCune Smith spoke of life, hope, and energy being restored and properly directed in American liberty's name, not of sick children breathing their last with Jesus's name on their lips. The "orphans" were "living images" of humanity and energy to be properly directed. There was nothing to "race."

McCune Smith was at his very best at breaking race down in individualistic terms when he exposed the hypocrisy of the work of a junior member of the American School of Ethnology, the traveler and archaeologist Ephraim George Squier, friend to Gliddon and sort of protégé of Morton's. At one time United States Chargé d'Affaires in Nicaragua, Squier wrote a book about Nicaragua which McCune Smith, as "Communipaw," reviewed in *Frederick Douglass's Paper* in January 1852. Yet even here McCune Smith did not directly refer to the American School: instead of engaging ethnological arguments, the review made Squier into the archetypical white American blinded by greed and hate yet able to see blacks' humanity in an exceptional situation but driven by lust, to see it only with half-averted eyes.[27]

Horace Greeley, antislavery editor of the *New York Tribune*, who had published McCune Smith's writing on the census controversy, had recently betrayed free blacks' cause by repeating the old Jeffersonian and colonizationist saw that after emancipation blacks and whites could not live together in the United States as equals. McCune Smith used Squier to show that even the most prejudiced white Americans knew in their hearts that race was artificial, not innate, and that nothing but the whites' own blind greed prevented American racial equality and social integration. "Mr. Squier, brought up in Albany, as full as any man of filthy American prejudices, of nasty negro hate, a witness from the other side, says, that caste has been artfully excited, created between the races in Central America." The "other side" obviously referred to Squier's place in the American School. Squier went on to say, and McCune Smith quoted him: "In respect to *physique,* leaving color out of the question, there are probably no handsomer men in the world than some of the sambos or offspring of Indian and negro parents." But the Negroes in Nicaragua were not the same as those in the United States; they must have come from a different place in Africa. They had "aquiline noses, small mouths and thin lips."[28]

McCune Smith retorted by using Squier's lecherous descriptions of Nicaraguan Negro women and especially mulatto young women as the pretext for a biting, explicitly psychosexual, political, and economic analysis of white American blindness to blacks as people:

> One does not know which most to admire in the above [Squier's descriptions of black and mulatto girls], the *"couleur de rose,"* which the necessity of eating, drinking, dancing, sleeping and negociating with these negroes throws around their features, in the vision of our *Charge d'Affaires;* or the intoxicating influence which the gorgeous scenery, or large black eyes, and "peach complexioned damsels" have thrown over his brain; for be it known he "admits the corn" of his having been smitten in Nicaragua by damsels of each several race, or the asinine stupidity which assumes that an American with the seven fold gauze of prejudice before his eyes, *when in the United States,* can even *see* the physique of the black men whom they so eternally wrong and at the expense of a thousand hells within their seared and still burning consciences, still persist in wronging, or the miraculous ignorance of the ethnography of Africa which our author exhibits. Mr. Squier professes to be an Ethnographist. He is a member of the New York Ethnological Society; he should know, therefore, that the Joloffs, on the Guinea coast, are just such looking Negroes as those of Nicaragua; that throughout that coast travelers are struck with the European fea-

tures of the natives; that just such looking negroes abound in the United States; and that the *negro* "with us" is not an actual physical being of flesh and bones and blood, but a hideous monster of the mind, ugly beyond all physical portraying, so utterly and ineffably monstrous as to frighten reason from its throne, and justice from its balance, and mercy from its hallowed temple, and to blot out shame and probity, and the eternal sympathies of nature, so far as these things have presence in the breasts or being of American republicans! No sir! It is a constructive negro—a John Roe and Richard Doe negro, that haunts with grim presence the precincts of this republic, shaking his gory locks over legislative halls and family prayers.[29]

This was arguably the most concentrated, astute antiracist statement of the entire antebellum era. It was also limited. There remains something self-consuming, even morbid, about his style dealing with Squier, a sense perhaps of what he had not confronted. Scientifically educated, up to date on ethnology, McCune Smith was fully capable of using statistics and citing anatomy in his own right. The critique of Squier, if brilliant, had the weakness of most attacks on prejudice: defensiveness regarding science. McCune Smith writes of the New York Ethnological Society, not the American School; of Squier, not Morton, Nott, Gliddon, or Agassiz; of Squier's Nicaragua book, not *Crania Americana* or *Crania Aegyptiaca* (*Types of Mankind* had yet to appear). McCune Smith does not discuss polygenist theories; nor does he cite Prichard or other monogenist authorities, although his writing on the 1840 census's supposed findings of extremely high Negro insanity rates in the North testified that he had already read Prichard and the rest carefully.

During the census controversy—which involved leading physicians like the medical statistician Edward Jarvis and major politicians like John C. Calhoun and John Quincy Adams, McCune Smith, with Jarvis's endorsement—wrote a long petition to Congress, printed by Greeley in three parts in February 1844 in the *New York Tribune,* that refuted the census figures and the claims of the South's leading journal, the *Southern Literary Messenger,* that freedom drove blacks mad. In New York City, McCune Smith noted, black insanity (and criminality) rates were considerably lower than white ones: "Freedom has not made us mad; it has strengthened our minds by throwing us upon our own resources, and has bound us to American Institutions with a tenacity which nothing but death can overcome."[30]

Earlier, McCune Smith had speculated that, since the 1840 census seemed to show that African American birth rates were declining relative to white rates, perhaps blackness had no future as a distinct entity in the United States. He addressed the issue in an 1841 lecture, "The Destiny of the People of Colour," before the New York Philomathean Society and the Hamilton Lyceum (educational societies established by New York free blacks): "It has been asserted by intelligent men, that the day will come when the colored population of these United States, shall have entirely disappeared." Inevitable amalgamation with ever growing numbers of whites would mean that African Americans' descendants would lose the mark of black skin. There was nothing to fear in that. If blacks would not, as blacks, enter the promised land of equality, their no longer "black" descendants would: "Harmodius and Aristogiton lived not to see Athens free, those who fell at Marathon beheld not from mortal eyes their country safe from the relentless clutches of a foreign foe, Toussaint L'Ouverture saw not his own Haiti free from foreign rule."[31]

McCune Smith also tried to prove that nothing in the American climate or free society was unhealthy for blacks. The proof was the culmination of his statistical work, a long article entitled "A Dissertation on The Influence of Climate on Longevity," written in 1844 and published by the influential *Hunt's Merchant's Magazine* in 1846.[32] McCune Smith had previously submitted the piece for a prize at Harvard University (he lost). Using the methods of the pioneering Belgian statistician Adolphe Lambert Quetelet and also a few arguments from Prichard and others, McCune Smith rigorously showed that black mortality rates were lower in the North than in the South, and in the North no worse than white rates. All peoples best prospered in moderate climates, although blacks survived extreme heat better than whites.

In the *Hunt's* piece he was obviously trying to find a way to tackle not just Calhoun but the American School, to formulate a population statistics version of environmentalism to refute Morton and Nott's supposed statistical averages of racial brain size. He did not come out and say so, however: for more than a decade thereafter, he proposed no alternative to the American School's explanation for race. That alternative, which first appeared in print only in 1859, had been gestating for a number of years and was known by 1854 at least to Frederick Douglass.

☙ THE CLAIMS OF THE MULATTO: DOUGLASS

The two were well acquainted and mutually admiring, especially once Douglass began to break with Garrison. Douglass would eventually say that McCune Smith had influenced him more than any other black man. McCune Smith told Douglass in a letter, "You are a living embodiment of all the philosophy of our side." Douglass replied to McCune Smith, "You are the first thoroughly educated man among us."[33] As the "living embodiment" of the philosophy of abolition and black civil rights, Douglass could stand as a symbol of black intellectual capacity, a living refutation of the American School. On July 12, 1854 Douglass tackled ethnology in a major lecture, "On the Claims of the Negro Ethnologically Considered," which among other ideas, made use of McCune Smith's new concept of race. The first commencement address by an African American at an American college, it was delivered to the Literary Societies of Western Reserve College in Hudson, Ohio.[34]

"Claims" was more a moral than a scientific tract. Aided by materials provided by Archibald Alexander, an amateur ethnologist and president of the University of Rochester (Douglass lived in Rochester), and another University of Rochester professor, Douglass produced twenty-five tightly argued pages mirroring what he elsewhere called the "marvelously calm philosophical discussion of the origin of races" in Prichard's *Natural History of Man,* his main source for most of the speech. Historians see Douglass as ethnology's most perceptive antebellum critic: in Waldo E. Martin's words, "Claims" exposed Morton's arguments as "logically and methodologically fatuous."[35]

Douglass did so up to a point. Close reading reveals a basic concession, in a sense, to the new ethnology, but in a turnabout that converted the pessimism and bitter racism of a Nott into something positive. In the end Douglass acknowledged the existence of two very real, possibly innate black and white racial entities that he said should be blended to produce a vital new entity. And environment for him explained only blacks' bad traits born of suffering and abuse. The effects of the sun or of what, drawing on the old degenerationist environmentalism, Douglass termed rank African "miasmas" did not account for the Negro's gifts and fortitude, which Douglass said America desperately needed to ensure progress. He finally conceded that that polygenism might be true and wrote as if blackness was in some major sense innate.

For Douglass, the American School's polygenism, however, was self-evidently not scientifically objective but a perverse brand of proslavery: "The evils most fostered by slavery and oppression are precisely those which slaveholders and oppressors would transfer from their system to the inherent character of their victims. Thus the very crimes of slavery become slavery's best defense." Polygenists always compared the noblest Caucasians to the most degraded Negroes and never to the many black men whose heads and countenances furnished fit counterparts to the most accomplished whites. Whites were so hypocritical that they would not accept these individuals as instances of black intelligence, for in America "to be intelligent, is to have one's Negro blood ignored." But everybody knew, Douglass said, that intelligence came from the mother, and like himself, most mixed African Americans had black mothers.[36] He probably took this quite unusual idea of matrilineal intelligence from Prichard: although most naturalists since Aristotle traced intelligence to the father, Prichard traced it to the mother.

The core of "Claims" was the idea of a black ancient Egypt, yet Douglass did not mention *Crania Aegyptiaca,* which had been out for eight years by 1854. Douglass merely assailed Morton's few, cursory, and *ad hominem,* if quite prejudiced, statements on Egypt in *Crania Americana;* nor did he deal directly with the tenets of Morton's craniology. In *Crania Americana,* Morton had described the Copts and Fellahs, who, Douglass said, "every body [sic] knows are descendants of the Egyptians," as having round, wide noses, thick lips, brown skin, and black, curly hair. Then, Douglass said, Morton had the gall to say that the Copts and Fellahs "derive from their remote ancestors some mixture of Greek, Arabian, and perhaps even negro blood." Morton had also observed that the black-skinned and curly-haired Nubians "generally show traces of their social intercourse with the Arabs, and *even* with the negroes." Douglass commented, "The repetition of the adverb here 'even,' is important as showing the spirit in which our great American Ethnologist pursues his work, and what deductions may be justly made from the value of his researches on that account."[37]

Morton would have seen Douglass's critique as unscientific because it was not backed by extensive and supposedly objective measurement of Egyptian skulls. To make a serious scientific case, Douglass would have had to tackle *Crania Aegyptiaca*. Had he read it? It seems hard to believe that Alexander would not have lent Douglass a copy of the book or at least made him aware of Morton's research into Egyptian skulls, work that Prichard himself accepted and praised in the epilogue of *Natural History of Man*. As for the American School's major production, *Types of Mankind*, Douglass merely dismissed it as hopelessly prejudiced. In ignoring craniology, Douglass ignored the links among Prichard's retreats, Morton's equivocations, and Douglass's true adversary, Nott's frank polygenism.

Douglass did say in general terms that since environmentalism had not been definitely disproved, physiological differences (which might result from environment) could not be a sure basis for racial classification. This was Prichard's argument in *Natural History of Man*. Perhaps language was a better way to classify humans, Douglass suggested. Since most linguists agreed that all African tongues, including ancient Egyptian, made up a single family, all Africans, including ancient Egyptians, were racially one. (Morton paid little attention to philology. Nott and Gliddon knew that linguists' claims for monogenism and African unity had influence among scientists and had to be dealt with if the American School were to carry the day: *Types* made a weak stab at the problem, and the 1857 *Indigenous Races* would try more substantially but ineffectively to refute the linguistic argument for monogenism.) Douglass further cited at some length "authorities as to the resemblance of the Egyptians to negroes": Denon, Prichard, Volney, Herodotus, Aeschylus, and a few nineteenth-century British writers.[38] Again, Morton's contrary "evidence" in *Crania Aegyptiaca* was not mentioned.

Not only did Douglass ignore Morton's most important work, he himself more than flirted with an innatist view of racial character. In a pro-"black" way, "Claims" revised the double standard followed by most racist whites at this time. European Americans increasingly attributed black inferiority to a God-given nature, not to slavery or African conditions, while tracing white poverty or degradation to circumstance (and black and abolitionist scheming). In "Claims" Douglass was more consistent: he had each people's degradation as circumstantial but their good qualities as somehow innate.

Douglass's environmentalism was negative and defensive. He reported that on a trip to Britain he had seen a crowd of Irish peasants with the same degraded characteristics, physical and social, as plantation slaves: vacant stares, gaping mouths, badly formed ankles, retreating foreheads, and petty, small minds. "Yet . . . there are no more really handsome people in the world than the educated Irish people." He seems to have seen West Africans as a degenerate versions of what was probably an innately distinct and redemptive Negro type. Douglass said:

> But what does it all prove? Why, nothing positively, as to the main point; still, it raises the enquiry—May not the condition of men explain their various appearances? Need we go behind the vicissitudes of barbarism for an explanation of the gaunt, wiry, ape like [sic] appearance of some of the genuine negroes? Need we look higher than a vertical sun, or lower than the damp, black soil of the Niger, the Gambia, the Senegal, with their heavy and enervating miasma, rising ever from the rank growing and decaying vegetation, for an explanation of the negro's color? If a cause, full and adequate, can be found, *why seek further?*[89]

Douglass himself had to go further. The Negro had to be needed in the United States. Now he invoked McCune Smith. According to "Claims," knowledge of history and McCune Smith's statistical work both proved that "ethnographically isolated" peoples degenerated, while mixture and dynamism built great civilizations and nations. Douglass did not note that McCune Smith never had racial differences as innate and always remained a thoroughgoing environmentalist. According to Douglass, the United States had so far prospered because of its "composite character" (Douglass's term), just as invasions, alliances, and mixture with other peoples had brought Britain from barbarism to preeminence. Now slavery and racial caste threatened to cast down the United States. America needed to embrace the gifted Negro as a free man. Maybe polygenism was true; perhaps the case for monogenism was not definitive. No matter: "A diverse origin does not disprove a common nature, nor does it disprove a united destiny."[40]

At the speech's end, Douglass went beyond scientific proof. If science and reason could say nothing certain about race, American experience could. In America blacks had shown their adaptability and tenacity. Their concrete individual stories showed that blacks would never be moved or destroyed. The Indian had died out "under the flashing glance of the Anglo-Saxon. Not so the negro; civilization cannot kill him. He accepts it—becomes a part of it. In the Church, he is an Uncle Tom; in the State he is the most abused and least offensive." (McCune Smith shared this view of Indians as weaker and less adaptable than blacks.)[41] Blackness existed here for Douglass as a positive entity both in the sense of being distinctly real and in the sense of being good.

"Claims" thus may be seen to parallel in this respect romantic racialism.[42] Uncle Tom nobly but passively endures life's suffering, allowing himself to be whipped to death by his master; this Christ-like act of self-sacrifice converts his master to Christ and antislavery. Passive, redemptive, morally superior—indeed, even Christ-like—Negroes like Tom redeemed the Anglo-Saxon, whose gifts were inventiveness and progressiveness but whose faults were avarice and wrath.

Douglass, though, was not a romantic racialist in Stowe's mode. We might read his "Claims" as presenting feeling and experience as the true basis for race, but that was only by default because of the failings of contemporary science. Douglass never repudiated reason or science, he never advocated a feminized, irrationalist racialism, and he did not take on the mantle of meek victimhood. Neither did other major antebellum black writers, including McCune Smith, who opposed the patronizing thinking of romantic racialism that could ultimately justify white supremacy. McCune Smith seemed to have realized that if for whatever reasons blacks were somehow morally better than whites, less corrupted by power, less aggressive and masculine, less greedy, more human and loving, then in a world still governed by power and wealth, whites would naturally own all the property and run the government. A romanticized black race was no match for power.[43]

Douglass himself was a repudiation of the black man as "feminine" and passive. After all, he had escaped from slavery and educated himself within the race-blind liberal environmentalist Garrisonian camp, which saw prejudice as entirely a result of caste and the consequent degradation of despised people. In the late 1840s Douglass began to pull away from Garrison in favor of black political action and violent resistance to slavery; the breach was complete in 1851. As William L. Andrews has shown, Douglass broke with Garrison in large part by coming to see himself as a representative American man, whose struggles and mixed racial heritage of both blackness and whiteness embodied the larger meaning and potential of America.[44] For Douglass, seeing depth and worth to blackness was part of the liberation from Garrison and from subservience to white paternalism in all forms. He was claiming his own life and history as representative of the meaning of blackness and America.

McCune Smith presented Douglass in such terms in his introduction to *My Bondage and My Freedom,* where he dissected Douglass's genius. Characteristically McCune Smith used a scientific idea, that ontogeny recapitulates phylogeny, to capture "the secret of his [Douglass's] power." "Naturalists tell us that a full grown man is a resultant or representative of all animated nature on this globe." In its development the human embryo seems to go through the whole series of living things from simple to complex, ending finally at the highest stage, the human adult. "In like manner, and to the fullest extent, has Frederick Douglass passed through every gradation of rank comprised in our national make-up, and bears upon his person and upon his soul every thing that is American." Douglass's remarkable abilities traced not just to his varied experiences but to his mixture of black and white: "The versatility of talent which he wields, in common with Dumas, Ira Aldridge, and Miss Greenfield, would seem to be the result of the grafting of the Anglo-saxon on good, original, negro stock." Alexandre Dumas, the great British actor Ira Aldridge, and the concert singer Elizabeth Taylor Greenfield, "the Black Swan," were, like Douglass, all mulattos. So, McCune Smith continued, were the ancient Egyptians. "The Egyptians, like the Americans, were a *mixed race,* with some negro blood circling around the throne, as well as in the mud hovels." Thus the very paternity of supposedly "white" civilization lay in European/African mixture.[45]

Stowe and fellow white romantic racialists abhorred race mixing. Douglass, McCune Smith, and other like-minded antebellum African

Americans did not. Their amalgamationism was for the most part a proclamation of the reality and equality of race in the present and of the need for white America to embrace blackness at once. Then the nation would progress by conforming to the laws of history and God's plan for universal salvation. Paradoxically, race would make the promise of the American Revolution and the integrity of African American individuals real. Analogous to Nott in his "white" way, African Americans probably believed that they were, in the process, reconceiving the promise of "all men are created equal" in a distinctively nineteenth-century and "black" way.

The sardonic, provocative racialism of previous African Americans' "blackness" had come to seem inappropriate, and a sincere, straight view of a "black" enlightenment (small e and large E) the proper stance. The language McCune Smith used in his introduction to *My Bondage* to describe Douglass's break with Garrison suggests why. The Garrisonians, McCune Smith wrote, "failed to fathom the highest qualities of Douglass's mind." They would not "delve into the mind of a colored man for capacities which the pride of race led them to believe to be restricted to their own Saxon blood. Bitter and vindictive sarcasm, irresistible mimicry, and a pathetic narrative of his own experiences of slavery, were the intellectual manifestations which they encouraged him to exhibit on the platform or in the lecture desk."[46] Many African Americans now espoused a "black" point of view with a racial "stock" behind it. They argued that including that perspective, and even that blood, was the only way to build a healthy America and balanced and virtuous Americans. David Walker's messianic, questioning vagueness regarding race or Easton's irrationalism toward nature and outrage at the idea of naturalizing mind and morality would not do. Not after Garrisonians and romantic racialists tried to confine blacks to the role of outraged victims, and not after the intensification of racism, scientific and otherwise, that was the national backlash against immediatism.

One might expect that some African Americans would have gone in for something like Herder's idealism, for seeing a blackness developing in connection with African warmth and distinctive civilization. Not so. To deal with ethnology and create space for "black" voices, good traits either had to be universally human and race irrelevant, or if racial, such traits had to be more than mere reflections of circumstance. Without a scientific theory of heredity and mutation, there could be no explanation for neutral, irrelevant difference except irrationalism, and for positive difference, no explanation except typological thinking. Without recourse to random variation, rationalized attempts to combine biology and environmentalism would now almost inevitably have to address and celebrate American diversity in terms of the mixture of very real racial entities, types. Even if one could find a way to argue that the environment produced such entities, the individual would still be effaced and racial categories validated as much more than mere names. If individuals had complex histories and heritage beyond "race," that would be because of their mixed lineages.

Some African Americans went so far as to say that slavery's very expansion made the marriage of sinful white and redemptive black inevitable. One case in point is Henry Highland Garnet, McCune Smith's schoolmate and lifelong friend and Douglass's sometime adversary, a major African American abolitionist, early proponent of militant black political action and opponent of Garrisonian moral suasion, and eventual advocate of selective African American emigration to Africa. In an 1848 address, "The Past and Present Condition, and the Destiny, of the Colored Race," Garnet predicted: "the Western World is destined to be filled with a mixed race." In the wake of the Mexican-American War, Garnet was telling the slave South and racist whites everywhere, in effect, that American notions of Manifest Destiny would lead to melding into the American population people of color in Mexico, blending away historic white rapacity. While black ancient Egyptians and Ethiopians built the pyramids and founded the arts and sciences, the ancestors of the Anglo-Saxons had "made night hideous by their wild shouts, and day was darkened by the smoke which arose from bloody altars, upon which they offered human sacrifice."[47] Mixture with Negroes would only help such people. Amalgamation and true democracy, not empire, were America's full Manifest Destiny.

⑨ JAMES MCCUNE SMITH'S FINAL THEORY: ENVIRONMENTALIST TYPOLOGY

After writing his "Dissertation on The Influence of Climate on Longevity," in 1844, McCune Smith put his knowledge of medicine and population statistics together to craft a sequel, one that asserted a theory of race and history that fully enlisted nature's hidden truths on blacks' side. That he did not publish his idea, which combined environmentalism and the types doctrine, until 1859 was not for lack of opportunity. Given how much he drew on McCune Smith's thinking in "Claims," Douglass would surely have printed the new work, which was entitled "Civilization: Its Dependence on Physical Circumstance," when it finally did appear, in a new African American paper, the New York City *Anglo-African Magazine*. Less known and less widely read than any of Douglass's several newspapers, the *Anglo-African* was intended to be intellectual and bridge the gap between antislavery and the larger thinking and reading man's world. The first issue, hastily thrown together, needed material. McCune Smith knew the prominent African American publishers Thomas and Robert Hamilton, and he seemingly had "Civilization" on hand. It appeared as the leading article in the *Anglo-African*'s first issue in January 1859.[48]

As the *Anglo-African*'s title attests, the Hamilton brothers were trying to sell the idea that African Americans had already absorbed, physically as well as mentally, the virtues of Anglo-Saxon civilization and could become the forebears of a new, progressive "Anglo-African" future for the United States. Thomas Hamilton's "Apologia," in first issue, proclaimed that blacks, "tough, wiry, and malleable," had in America survived the ordeal of slavery to become an "Anglo-African race," capable of high civilization, and fresh, strong, and vital. The white race had become stagnant, but "the negro is something more than mere endurance; he is a force." Hamilton directly mocked Nott's statistics, and other Anglo-African material lampooned the craze for Egypt, black and white.[49]

McCune Smith's "Civilization," like the earlier "Dissertation," relied primarily on Quetelet, but here not just on Quetelet's statistical methods but on his boldest, chanciest theories. Quetelet had audaciously argued that the statistical study of society might achieve predictive power equal to Newtonian physics' ability to foretell the movements of the planets: the laws of social development could be understood by measuring vast numbers of individuals and calculating the average. He realized that every different method of gathering population statistics yielded different results, and each set of environmental and social circumstances itself produced a different "average man." The goal was to use as large and varied a sample as possible: "The greater the number of individuals observed, the more do individual peculiarities, whether physical or moral, become effaced, and allow the general facts to predominate, by which society exists and is preserved," an approach that ignored the individual and always generated a simple curve with standard deviations and a mean almost exactly in the center. Quetelet's "social physics" enjoyed a vogue in European liberal circles.[50] By 1846 he had turned the average man into a "type," a standard of beauty and character for a given civilization, epoch, or race. When Quetelet tried to derive the "laws" of social development, he only analyzed the supposed "mean" generated by a set of circumstances or measurements and compared it to other such means. This position was narcissistic enough in its own right, for Quetelet made level of civilization into his fundamental yardstick: he assumed that the conditions producing the average man under high civilization (that is, Western European societies) were superior.

His method had a big advantage for McCune Smith: it effaced not just individuals but elites, and actually privileged the mass of ordinary people, who by sheer numbers mostly determined the average man. A liberal meritocrat, Quetelet attributed the progress of (European) civilization to ordinary people's struggles for life and improvement. That was what McCune Smith needed to reconceive races as populations best understood in terms of average types. Slaveholders had been saying for decades that blacks were magnificent physical specimens with the minds of children, a view that assumed some sort of idea of the conservation of energy, or at least a contrast between physicality and intellect, bestiality and humanity. As McCune Smith observed in "Civilization," the slaveholders' idea was that one could not be both a magnificent physical specimen and an intellectual giant. Quetelet's statistical approach had physical health and vigor going hand in hand with mental ability. If blacks were physically superior because of the laboring role they had been forced to play, McCune Smith reasoned, then they would also become intellectually great if given the opportunity to educate themselves. All the proslavery testimony that Negroes prospered in the slave South, never got sick or went mad, did the work of five white men, or would be terrifying warriors if ever roused, and all the northern racist fears that free blacks would take white jobs, could be transformed by Quetelet's statistical approach into testimony to potential black progressiveness and intellectual capacity. Blacks, the salt of the earth in America, were the most progressive Americans, and restricting them by slavery and caste would cripple then kill the society. American progress depended on removing racial caste.

This reasoning could be further extended to recast in environmental terms Agassiz's and Nott's multiple creations theory of "local races" and Nott's notion of salutary intra-species amalgamation. Each series of circumstances in the world created its own "average man"; each environmentally produced race, each environmentally shaped civilization yielded its own distinctive physiological "type." And if all such races were only "local," that is, if all were collective, and indeed environmental, variants of a single species ("great race," in the American School's Cuvierian terms) as Quetelet's approach assumed, and if amalgamation among "local races" was to the good, as Nott and the American School believed, then social and physical amalgamation between blacks and whites would yield a greater and more progressive mixture than the world-conquering Anglo-Saxon. Mirroring Nott's cleverness in appropriating the best of environmentalism, McCune Smith used Quetelet to turn Nott's argument for Anglo-Saxon hybrid superiority into an environmentalist brief for integration and black/white mixture. He transformed the whole white supremacist vision of blacks as animalistic into an argument for black intellectual capacity and progressiveness.

How then to explain Africa's supposed lack of progress and Africans' lack of intelligence? Quetelet served here too. According to his work, human resistance to cold was greatest at age seventeen and thereafter declined, while intellectual ability peaked at thirty-five; because inhabitants of very cold regions did not live long enough to reach their intellectual prime, cold regions never produced great civilizations. McCune Smith extended this reasoning with his own argument that in hot climates the torrid air retarded respiration, which prevented the discharge of wastes and stunted the mental development of inhabitants, precluding high civilizations there. Africa had much else going against it too. McCune Smith drew on Prichard's third edition of *Researches* and the first volume, published in 1857, of British historian Henry Thomas Buckle's *History of Civilization in England,* a work intended to be scientific in method that drew to some extent on Quetelet's ideas and traced the character of civilization to geography and climate.[51] Prichard and Buckle both basically saw modern Britain's great success as a function of the variety of its population, generated by Britain's varied internal environments and by its high level of contact with other nations. Africa, by contrast, was uniform, isolated, and difficult to traverse.

McCune Smith could now turn Nott's argument for Anglo-Saxon greatness to blacks' favor and craft a statistical and physiological but still adaptationist theory of amalgamation, history, and progress. Like Nott, McCune Smith said that the Anglo-Saxon was great precisely because it was not a singular "race" at all but rather a lucky physical admixture of many different environmentally produced groups living in "a fine climate and otherwise favorable geographic position." McCune Smith warned that even the Anglo-Saxon's achievements might crumble because of segregation, not amalgamation. Without the constant influx of foreign peoples, every civilization reached a "perfection of type" in its distinctive setting, then lapsed into conservatism, caste, and decline. Ancient Egyptian society could "originate and grow perfect" nowhere but in the Nile Valley or on the shores of some other river that overflowed "in periods synchronous with certain astronomical events." The floods had prompted the people there to mark the heavens, develop mathematics and record keeping, and practice organized agriculture. Civilization was born.[52]

Notwithstanding, Egyptian conditions were insufficiently varied, and Egyptian life consequently too stable and stagnant, to have produced "the more ideal and beautiful type of Greek civilization, nor yet the civilization of Great Britain." If slavery was ended and the Union preserved, still greater things could be achieved in the United States, blessed with a temperate climate and sufficiently diverse geography "constantly to reproduce variously endowed men," who would be brought together by the railroads: "all the elements of Progress lie within our grasp and must multiply with the duration of Christianity and of Union amongst us."[53] This was *Types of Mankind* crossed with Prichard's five-volume *Researches* and all McCune Smith's own meditations on population based upon his statistical work to refute the 1840 census.

"Civilization" ended by generalizing McCune Smith's most despairing individual outcry at the absurdity of self-sacrifice in blackness's name, the self-effacing "coral insect" metaphor from the 1848 letter to Gerrit Smith. "Civilization" concluded: "Higher, far higher than the labor of the coral, loftier than the toil of the monks, is the work allotted to the man of color in these United States; like them he is doomed to toil, but he toils with a reward constantly in his grasp, with the glorious result full in view; he knows that the progress of mankind is intrusted [sic] to his keeping, and he toils for the advent of that time of 'blissful tranquility' for the race, 'when the spiritual shall become regnant over the carnal.'"[54]

☙ RETURNING TO JEFFERSON

Later in 1859 *The Anglo-African* published, again as its lead article, McCune Smith's "On the Fourteenth Query of Jefferson's Notes on Virginia," which refuted Jefferson's claim that blacks and whites could never live together in freedom.[55] McCune Smith proclaimed that by enumerating the true principles of progress in "Civilization"—diversity and inclusion—he had already proved Jefferson wrong that blacks and whites could not coexist as free equals in the United States. Racism and ethnology were going out of date, as liberal-minded whites everywhere began to understand that progress depended on racial diversity and tolerance. One could see this realization, McCune Smith claimed, in the more respectful terms in which white newspapers now discussed free blacks—now called "coloured people," not "blacks," "Negroes," or worse.

And all Americans, including whites, were actually "coloured people." McCune Smith called upon a side argument from the third edition of Prichard's *Researches* holding that, physiologically speaking, there were only three skin color classifications for human beings and that all "Negroes" plus everyone but albinos and Nordic blondes occupied a single category. All Americans would soon come to agree with the great Prichard that physiologically most "whites" and all "blacks" were part of the same skin color classification: almost all were in truth "colored people." Albinos were diseased, Nordic blondes sickly and overly susceptible to the sun. The majority of African natives were not jet black, and many were not even curly-haired; African Americans' hair seemed to be straightening both as a consequence of "extreme culture" and the temperate American environment, and their skin might be lightening somewhat too. "The Ethiopian can change his skin." Morton himself, McCune Smith observed wryly, admitted that environment could change skin color: "'Although the Americans,'[meaning Native Americans] says Dr. Morton, 'possess a pervading and characteristic complexion, there are occasional and very remarkable deviations, including all the tints, from a decided white to an unequivocally black skin.'"⁵⁶ This was the only direct reference to Morton in the piece: as in Douglass's "Claims," Garnet's "Past and Present Condition," the "Heads" series, "Civilization," and other major African American attacks of the day on ethnology, craniology, and especially *Crania Aegyptiaca,* were essentially ignored.

Supposedly science now stood on blacks' side. Several of the most famous thinkers in the world, McCune Smith said, had independently discovered and promulgated the ideas he had himself thought up in writing the first draft of "Civilization" in 1844. The idea that civilization depended on variety and mixture had first been endorsed in public by Buckle, then by the "higher authority" of John Stuart Mill's *On Liberty,* which McCune Smith quoted at length in "Fourteenth Query." But McCune Smith claimed to owe nothing fundamental to Buckle or Mill— Quetelet was conspicuously absent from "Fourteenth Query"—because he (McCune Smith) had hit upon the diversity thesis on his own in 1844, before Buckle's or Mill's works had appeared. McCune Smith claimed first discovery of the "principles of progress."⁵⁷

Apparently he could not be just a "coral insect" sacrificing himself to obscurity for the future of the race. He had beaten Buckle and Mill to the discovery of the laws of progress: he, and his fellow laboring, suffering, thinking African Americans would have recognition now, as individuals who were both black and human; they would have a place. And they needed it now. After all, according to McCune Smith's theories, if the greatest mixture of diversity equaled the greatest civilization, the whitening of America, even if accomplished by the beneficent American environment, would prove retrogressive in the end. For as the African American type became swamped by the greater numbers of whites, it would disappear and could no longer contribute to the mix.

Here lay the danger in trying to engage with or invert Nott's arguments. Nott thought that type was fixed. When "local races" (varieties) or "great races" (species) mixed biologically, the results were immediate and permanent, for good or ill. Either way, the heritage of "blood" would remain forever. McCune Smith was an environmentalist. Once America absorbed the Negro, there would be no real mixture with lasting effects, so to speak, only a progression toward whiteness. The Negro would be gone for good as if he had never been there, since no place in America had the conditions to produce the Negro type. Thus environment plus amalgamation would ultimately reduce American diversity and put a brake on American progress. According to McCune Smith's logic, if diversity was to bring perfection in America, it had to be now or in the near future, when the Negro still existed and the intermingling had the greatest potential.

McCune Smith may have hoped against hope that such a millennium would come very soon or in a generation or two. He knew that it was more likely that progress, if it arrived at all, would be very slow, and he believed that it would through natural laws gradually shape a future with no place for blacks as black. In the only conceptual terms he had available, that would mean that in the end blacks would have to whiten up to count as Americans. As black individuals their lives had no meaning except self-sacrifice. Perhaps beneath all, he welcomed an end to blackness and the possibility of typological thinking and racial classification.

In 1864, on the verge of filling a new professorship in anthropology (the term "anthropology" came into use as a synonym for "ethnology" in the mid-1850s) created for him at Wilberforce College in Ohio, McCune Smith died at the age of fifty-one. He had lived just long enough to witness the Civil War, the Draft Riots that burned down the New York Colored Orphan Asylum, and the Emancipation Proclamation. He did not see the final victory of the Union and the constitutional abolition of slavery. He would certainly not have regarded the aftermath of Reconstruction as the progress of tolerance and inclusion. One wonders what he would have made of social Darwinism and the long persistence of race in America.

NOTES

1. THE FACE OF NATURE

1. "Thoughts on the Works of Providence," l. 74, in *Phillis Wheatley: Complete Writings,* ed. Vincent Caretta (New York: Penguin, 2001), p. 28.

2. Daniel Boorstin, *The Lost World of Thomas Jefferson* (New York: Holt, 1948).

3. Thomas Jefferson, *Notes on the State of Virginia,* ed. William Peden (Chapel Hill: Published for the Institute of Early American History and Culture, Williamsburg, VA, by the University of North Carolina Press, ©1955; 1982), p. 138.

4. Wheatley, "Thoughts on the Works of Providence," l. 114, in her *Complete Writings,* p. 29.

5. I am here developing David Grimsted's insight about Wheatley's use of "sable" for Africans' skin, as opposed to "black" for sin. See David Grimsted, "Anglo-American Racism and Phillis Wheatley's 'Sable Veil,' 'Lengthen'd Chain,' and 'Knitted Heart,'" in *Women in the Age of the American Revolution,* ed. Ronald Hoffman and Peter J. Albert (Charlottesville: University of Virginia Press, 1989), pp. 338–446; analysis of "sable" versus "black," p. 357, n. 41.

6. Wheatley, "On Being Brought from Africa to America," ll. 5–9, in her *Complete Writings,* p. 13; for her "benighted soul" in Africa, see l. 2.

7. Winthrop Jordan, *White over Black: American Attitudes toward the Negro, 1550–1812* (Baltimore: Penguin Books, 1969, ©1968).

8. Jefferson, *Notes,* p. 163. For an interesting if sometimes idiosyncratic presentation of the thesis that the slavery question was the worst nightmare of the American founding fathers, see Nwabueze Okoye, "Chattel Slavery as the Nightmare of the American Revolutionaries," *William and Mary Quarterly,* 37 (1980): 3–28.

9. This phrase is taken from Toni Morrison's influential and incisive *Playing in the Dark: Whiteness and the Literary Imagination* (New York: Vintage Books, 1993).

10. Wheatley, "Thoughts on the Works of Providence," ll. 91–94, in her *Complete Writings,* p. 28. I follow Grimsted's judgment that "Providence" is Wheatley's best poem (Grimsted, "Anglo-American Racism," p. 367).

11. These early Anglo-African writers are usefully collected in Vincent Caretta, ed., *Unchained Voices: An Anthology of Black Authors in the English-Speaking World of the Eighteenth Century* (Lexington: University of Kentucky Press, 1996).

12. Henry Louis Gates, Jr., *The Signifying Monkey: A Theory of African-American Literary Criticism* (New York: Oxford University Press, 1988), pp. 127–169; Henry Louis Gates, Jr., *Figures in Black: Words, Signs, and the "Racial" Self* (New York: Oxford University Press, 1987), pp. 61–79; William L. Andrews, *To Tell a Free Story: The First Century of Afro-American Autobiography, 1760–1865* (Urbana: University of Illinois Press, 1986), pp. 32–60.

13. Joseph J. Ellis, quoted in "DNA Test Finds Evidence of Jefferson Child by Slave," *New York Times*, November 1, 1998, pp. 1, 24; Joseph J. Ellis, *American Sphinx: The Character of Thomas Jefferson* (New York: Knopf, 1997). A recent but to my mind not wholly convincing (especially regarding race and slavery) attempt to argue that Jefferson's "contradictions and paradoxes are reasonable and understandable" is E. M. Halliday, *Understanding Thomas Jefferson* (New York: Harper Collins, 2001), quotation on p. xii. I strongly disagree with the interpretation of natural history advanced by Alexander O. Boulton, "The American Paradox: Jeffersonian Equality and Racial Science," *American Quarterly*, 47 (1995): 467–492. Ironically, the controversy over Jefferson's now apparently proven sexual relationship with Sally Hemings seems to have mitigated and humanized the current scholarly portrait of Jefferson as "a monster of self-deception" (Peter S. Onuf, "The Scholars' Jefferson," *William and Mary Quarterly*, 50 [October, 1993]: 671–699; quotation on p. 673). For an overview of the DNA tests and the implications of the Hemings controversy, see Jan Ellen Lewis and Peter S. Onuf, eds., *Sally Hemings and Thomas Jefferson: History, Memory, and Civic Culture* (Charlottesville: University of Virginia Press, 1999). The literature on Jefferson and race is large and growing, but the place to begin remains Jordan, *White over Black*, pp. 429–482; and also John Chester Miller, *The Wolf by the Ears: Thomas Jefferson and Slavery* (New York: Free Press, 1977); overviews of more recent work can be found in Lewis and Onuf, *Sally Hemings*, and Onuf, "The Scholars' Jefferson"; see also Lucia Stanton, "'Those Who Labor for My Happiness': Thomas Jefferson and His Slaves," and Paul Finkelman, "Jefferson and Slavery: 'Treason against the Hopes of the World,'" both in Peter S. Onuf, ed., *Jeffersonian Legacies* (Charlottesville: University of Virginia Press, 1993), pp. 147–180, 181–221.

14. On the long course of environmentalist thought, see Clarence J. Glacken, *Traces on the Rhodian Shore: Nature and Culture in Western Thought from Ancient Times to the End of the Eighteenth Century* (Berkeley: University of California Press, 1967).

15. The literature on the emergence of "race," both word and concept, in the West is too vast to be recapitulated here, but as with Jefferson, the place to start remains Jordan, *White over Black*. To begin acquaintance with recent scholarly think-

ing on the genealogy of race, consult the articles in "Constructing Race," a special issue of the *William and Mary Quarterly* (54 [1997]). A good introduction to scholarship on race theory is Les Back and John Solomos, eds., *Theories of Race and Racism: A Reader* (New York: Routledge, 2000). A good brief treatment of the course of racial thought in the period relevant to this study is Michael Banton, "The Classification of Race in Europe and North America: 1700–1850," *International Social Sciences Journal*, 39 (1987): 45–60. A useful broad survey of the historiography of race in North America is Audrey Smedley, *Race in North America: Origin and Evolution of a Worldview* (Boulder, CO: Westview, 1993).

16. Wheatley, "Thoughts on the Works of Providence," in *Complete Works*, p. 28, ll. 71–74.

17. Wheatley, "To the University of Cambridge, in New-England," in *Complete Works*, pp. 11, 12, ll. 7, 28–29.

18. For a sophisticated introduction to Linnaeus and the problem of classification, see Marc Ereshefsky, *The Poverty of the Linnaean Hierarchy: A Philosophical Study of Biological Taxonomy* (New York: Cambridge University Press, 2001); see esp. pp. 199–237.

19. An introduction to the protean qualities of eighteenth-century European Newtonianism can be found in Keith M. Baker, *Condorcet: fron Natural Philosophy to Social Mathematics* (Chicago: University of Chicago Press, 1975), esp. chaps. 2, 3.

20. Comprehensive discussions of the British compromise may be found in David J. Depew and Bruce H. Weber, *Darwinism Evolving: Systems Dynamics and the Genealogy of Natural Selection* (Cambridge: MIT Press, 1995); and Adrian Desmond and James Moore, *Darwin: The Career of a Tormented Evolutionist* (New York: W. W. Norton, 1994).

21. A good brief introduction to eighteenth-century French natural history is Jacques Roger, "Preface to the 1993 Edition," in Jacques Roger, *The Life Sciences in Eighteenth-Century French Thought* (Stanford: Stanford University Press, 1997), Keith R. Benson, ed., Robert Ellrich, trans., pp. xv–xxxvii.

22. Michel Foucault, *The Order of Things: An Archaeology of the Human Sciences* (New York: Vintage, 1973), p. 132; natural history is discussed in general on pp. 125–165. For a survey of major criticisms of this work, see J. G. Merquior, *Foucault* (London: Fontana, 1985), pp. 56–75. A good introduction to recent scholarly thinking on natural history may be gleaned from the articles in Nicholas Jardine, James A. Secord, and E. C. Spary, eds., *Cultures of Natural History* (New York: Cambridge University Press, 1996).

23. Foucault, *The Order of Things*, pp. 145, 150.

24. For an important evocation of the developing complexities of natural history's view of nature as a "dynamic and self-sustaining economy," see James L. Larson, *Interpreting Nature: The Science of Living Form from Linnaeus to Kant* (Baltimore: Johns Hopkins University Press, 1994), quotation on p. 8. For Buffon's sophistication, see Jacques Roger, *Buffon: A Life in Natural History*, Sarah Lucille Bonnefoi, trans., L. Pearce Williams, ed. (Ithaca: Cornell University Press, 1997).

25. This is essentially the view taken by many recent scholars such as Pamela Regis (*Describing Early America: Bartram, Jefferson, Crèvecoeur, and the Rhetoric of Natural History* [1992; rpt. Philadelphia: University of Pennsylvania Press, 1999]), Boulton ("Jeffersonian Equality and Racial Science"), and Alicia M. Gámez ("Making American Nature: Scientific Narratives of Origin and Order in Visual and Literary Conceptions of Race in the Early American Republic" [Ph.D. Diss., Stanford University, 1999]).

26. Lisbet Koerner, *Linnaeus: Nature and Nation* (Cambridge: Harvard University Press, 1999), p. 6.

27. Koerner, *Linnaeus,* pp. 87–88. Linnaeus went so far as to observe: "And the fact is that as a natural historian I have yet to find any characteristics which enable man to be distinguished on scientific principles from the ape" (Carolus Linnaeus, *Fauna Svecica* [1746], quoted in Gunnar Broberg, "*Homo Sapiens:* Linnaeus's Classification of Man," in Tore Frängsmyr, ed., *Linnaeus: The Man and His Work* [Berkeley: University of California Press, 1983], pp. 156–194; quotation on p. 170).

28. Linnaeus, undated autograph fragment, quoted in Koerner, *Linnaeus,* p. 91.

29. For Buffon's view of the economy of nature, see Roger, *Buffon,* pp. 228–231; Buffon quotation on p. 228. See also Peter Hans Reill, "Anti-Mechanism, Vitalism and Their Political Implications in Late Enlightened Scientific Thought," *Francia* 16 (1989): 195–212.

30. Buffon, "Initial Discourse," in John Lyon and Phillip R. Sloan, eds. and trans., *From Natural History to the History of Nature: Readings from Buffon and His Critics* (Notre Dame: University of Notre Dame Press, 1981), p. 123; for Buffon and physical and mathematical truth, see pp. 123–127. Lyon and Sloan revived Buffon's reputation as a scientist and precipitated a debate about eighteenth-century natural historical historicism; for a recent appraisal, see John H. Eddy, Jr., "Buffon's *Histoire naturelle:* History? A Critique of Recent Interpretations," *Isis,* 85 (1994): 644–661.

31. Buffon quoted in Roger, *Buffon,* p. 83.

32. The 1750 *Journal de Trévoux* review of Buffon is reprinted in Lyon and Sloan, *From Natural History to the History of Nature,* pp. 227–229. For Buffon

and Newton and the concept of force, see "Buffon on Newton's Law of Attraction" (1749), trans. and rpt. in Lyon and Sloan, pp. 77–88. Buffon develops his vitalism in his lengthy section on "The Generation of Animals," which is presented virtually entire in both major translations of Buffon into English: Georges Louis Leclerc, compte de Buffon, *Natural History, General and Particular*, 3d ed., trans. William Smellie, 9 vols. (London: A. Strahan et al., 1791); and *Barr's Buffon: Buffon's Natural History, Containing a Theory of the Earth, a General History of Man, of the Brute Creation, and of Vegetables, Minerals, &c. &c., from the French, with notes by the translator*, 10 vols. (London: H. D. Symonds, 1797–1807). In general, Smellie is better and more comprehensive for Buffon's view of particular animals or locations, while Barr was more interested in Buffon's theories of natural history and the problem of species. A broad philosophical evaluation of the implications of the vitalism/materialism divide for Enlightenment social thought is Fransesca Rigotti, "Biology and Society in the Age of Enlightenment," *Journal of the History of Ideas* 47 (1986): 215–233. The literature on these questions is large; in general, on the Continent especially, mid- and late-eighteenth-century naturalists were hostile to mechanism, although champions of mechanism existed, especially in Britain and particularly Scotland. See articles by P. B. Wood, cited below.

33. *Barr's Buffon*, vol. 5, pp. 187–188. See also Arthur O. Lovejoy, "Buffon and the Problem of Species," in Bentley Glass, Oswei Temkin, and William L. Straus, Jr., eds., *Forerunners of Darwin: 1745–1859* (Baltimore: Johns Hopkins Press, 1959), pp. 84–113.

34. Buffon's biographer (Roger, *Buffon*, p. 264) summarizes Buffon's view: "Man was not born man; he became it through a double labor on himself and on the world, and he must not slacken his effort. Man is an imperial animal: where he does not exercise his rule, he is not truly a man." In the end, Buffon basically grouped animals and plants in terms of their resemblance and usefulness to humans; as Leon Poliakov notes, his system of classification resembled a medieval bestiary, with the lion, lord of the beasts, parallel to man, lord of creation (Leon Poliakov, *The Aryan Myth: A History of Racist and Nationalist Ideas in Europe* [New York: Basic Books, 1974], trans. Edmund Howard, p. 165).

35. "In those climates alone, then, where circumstances combine to create a constant and incessant heat, do we meet with Negroes. This heat is necessary not only for the production, but even to the preservation of Negroes" (*Barr's Buffon*, vol. 4, p. 344).

36. This is Peden's translation, *Notes*, pp. 58–59.

37. As Antonello Gerbi observes: "So we come back to the point of departure, according to which nature in America is weak because man has not tamed it, and

man has not tamed it because he in his turn is cold in love and more similar to the cold-blooded animals, closer to the watery putrescent character of the continent. And the erotic-hydraulic explanation of the singularity of American nature goes round and round in this same vicious circle." (Antonello Gerbi, *The Dispute of the New World: The History of a Polemic, 1750–1900*, rev. and enl. ed., trans. Jeremy Moyle [Pittsburgh: University of Pittsburgh Press, 1973], p. 8.)

38. "Some centuries hence, when the lands are cultivated, the forests cut down, and course of the rivers properly directed, and the marshes drained, this same country will become the most fertile, the most wholesome, and the richest in the whole world, as it is already in all the parts which have experienced the industry and skill of man." (Buffon, quoted in Gilbert Chinard, "Eighteenth Century Theories on America as a Human Habitat," American Philosophical Society, *Proceedings*, 91 (1947): 25–57; Buffon's praise for cultivation of the New World quoted and discussed on pp. 28–30; Chindard does not provide a reference and I have not myself been able to locate this passage in Buffon's work.) Buffon may well have taken this favorable assessment of the powers of the New World's European colonizers from Montesquieu. On Buffon and Montesquieu, see Chinard, pp. 28–30; on Montesquieu in America, see Paul Merrill Spurlin, *Montesquieu in America, 1760–1801* (Baton Rouge: Louisiana State University Press, 1940).

39. William M. Smallwood, *Natural History and the American Mind,* in collaboration with Mabel Sarah Coon Smallwood (New York: AMS Press, 1967, ©1941), p. 315. Buffon's work was still being cited as a model for French prose in the 1820s: Jean Anthelme Brillat-Savarin, in his classic 1825 discourse upon the pleasures of the table, *The Physiology of Taste; or Meditations on Transcendental Gastronomy* (trans. M. K. Fisher [Washington, DC: Counterpoint, 1994]), declared: "By rights I should write wonderously well, for Voltaire, Jean-Jacques [Rousseau], Fénélon, Buffon, and later Cochin and d'Aquesseau have been my favorite authors; I know them by heart" (p. 29).

40. Until the past twenty years, Buffon's influence was seen by historians of science to have been mainly as a popularizer and stylist spurring interest in scientific subjects. For a recent and perceptive reiteration of this position, see Claude Blanckaert, "Buffon and the Natural History of Man: Writing History and the 'Foundational Myth' of Anthropology," *History of the Human Sciences*, 6 (1993): 13–50.

41. Peter Kalm, *Kalm's Travels in North America: The America of 1750*, ed. Adolph B. Benson (New York: Dover Publications, 1966, ©1937); Cornelius De Pauw, *Histoire philosophique et politique, des etablissments et commerce des Europeens dans les deux Indes*, 6 vols. (Amsterdam, 1770); Abbé Raynal, *Philosophical*

and Political History of the Settlements and Trade of the Europeans in the East and West Indies, trans. J. O. Justamond, 2d ed., 6 vols. (New York: Negro Universities Press, 1969). In his subtle and often profound study, *The Problem of Slavery in Western Culture* (Ithaca: Cornell University Press, 1966), David Brion Davis considered political and philosophical aspects of the relationship of slavery to perceptions of the meaning of America; see esp. pp. 3–28. He did not, however, deal with natural history and racial thought.

42. Antonello Gerbi, *The Dispute of the New World.* In 1788, Andrew Ellicott chronicled the climate at Lake Erie; Dr. William Barton produced a study of American longevity in 1791; in 1795, Dr. William Currie discoursed on the insalubrity of marshes and the means of removing them; Dr. William Dunbar reported a series of meteorological observations for Natchez, Mississippi in 1800. Barton's work was the most ambitious: deliberately using the same method of calculating population employed by Buffon, he concluded that mortality rates were significantly lower in the United States than in Europe, although Barton conceded that Paris was the most salubrious European city. Barton made one reference to race. Citing Franklin's estimate that the American population doubled every twenty years, he invoked a "Dr. Price" (probably Richard Price), who had observed that "in the black settlements, where the inhabitants apply themselves entirely to agriculture, and luxury is not known, they double their own numbers in fifteen years." Apparently slaves experienced the effects of agrarian American virtue even more than free whites. William Barton, "Observations of the Duration of Human Life, and the progress of Population in the United States of America," American Philosophical Society *Transactions,* 2 (1795): 25–61; quotation on p. 43.

43. William Peden, "Introduction" to Jefferson, *Notes,* p. xi. For the history of *Notes,* see also Douglas L. Wilson, "Jefferson and the Republic of Letters," in Onuf, ed., *Jeffersonian Legacies,* pp. 52–58.

44. Esmond Wright, *Franklin of Philadelphia* (Cambridge: Harvard University Press, 1986), pp. 8–9.

45. Jefferson, *Notes,* p. 138; Peter S. Onuf, "'To Declare Them a Free and Independent People: Race, Slavery, and National Identity in Jefferson's Thought," *Journal of the Early Republic,* 18 (1998): 1–46. For an interesting and related reappraisal of the importance of the rhetoric of slavery to Anglo-American collective identity and the American Revolution, see T. H. Breen, "Ideology and Nationalism on the Eve of the American Revoliution: Revisions Once More in Need of Revising," *Journal of American History,* 84 (1997): 13–39.

46. On the *Summary View,* see Stephen A. Conrad, "Putting Rights Talk in Its Place: The *Summary View* Revisited," in Onuf, *Jeffersonian Legacies,* pp. 154–

180; on the drafting of the Declaration, see Pauline Maier, *American Scripture: Making the Declaration of Independence* (New York, 1997), esp. pp. 146–147, on the excision of Jefferson's passage on the slave trade.

47. For Franklin and inoculation in context of American notions of nature, see Patricia Cline Cohen, *A Calculating People: The Spread of Numeracy in Early America* (1982; rpt. New York: Routledge, 1999), pp. 94–108.

48. Adams quoted in John C. Greene, *American Science in the Age of Jefferson* (Ames: University of Iowa Press, 1984), p. 37.

49. Hugh Williamson, paper read before the American Philosophical Society, August 17, 1770 (American Philosophical Society *Transactions* 1 [1770]: 272–280; quotation on p. 280).

50. Jefferson to M. Le Roy, November 13, 1786, in Boyd et al., eds., *Papers of Jefferson*, vol. 5, pp. 463–472.

51. When they employed naturalistic metaphors in relation to politics, eighteenth-century enlightened Americans tended to misconstrue Newtonian physics in terms of static equilibrium. See I. Bernard Cohen, *Science and the Founding Fathers: Science in the Political Thought of Thomas Jefferson, Benjamin Franklin, John Adams and James Madison* (New York: Norton, 1995).

52. Franklin to Richard Jackson, May 5, 1753, *Writings of Benjamin Franklin*, vol. 3, pp. 134–135.

53. Franklin, *Observations*, in *The Papers of Benjamin Franklin*, ed. Leonard W. Labaree (New Haven: Yale University Press, 1959–), vol. 4, p. 234.

54. On the relationship of the Scottish and American Enlightenments (a subject that has generated a large literature), begin with Henry F. May, *The Enlightenment in America* (New York: Oxford University Press, 1976); a recent reappraisal of this issue may be found in Daniel Walker Howe, *Making the American Self: Jonathan Edwards to Abraham Lincoln* (Cambridge: Harvard University Press, 1997), pp. 48–77.

55. P. B. Wood, "Buffon's Reception in Scotland: The Aberdeen Connection," *Annals of Science*, 44 (1987): 169–190; see also his "The Natural History of Man in the Scottish Enlightenment," *History of Science*, 27 (1989): 89–123.

56. On Rush's natural theology and debts to Hartley and Reid, see Eric T. Carlson, Jeffrey L. Wollock, and Patricia S. Noel, "Introduction," *Benjamin Rush's Lectures on the Mind*, eds. Carlson, Wollock, and Noel, (Philadelphia: American Philosophical Society, 1981), pp. 1–43, esp. pp. 27–36. To see how importantly Rush viewed the idea of not mixing with Negroes, consult a letter to Jefferson of February 4, 1797, in which Rush declares: "I am now preparing a paper for our Society in which I have attempted to prove that the black color (as it is called) of

the Negroes is the effect of a disease in the skin of the leprous kind. The inferences from it will be in favor of treating them with humanity and justice and of keeping up the existing prejudices against matrimonial connections with them." *The Letters of Benjamin Rush,* ed. Lyman H. Butterfield (Princeton: Princeton University Press, 1951), vol. 2, p. 786. A version of Rush's paper, "Observations Intended to Favour a Supposition that the Black Colour (as It is Called) of the Negroes Is Derived from the Leprosy" (American Philosophical Society *Transactions,* 4 [1799]: 289–297), was first delivered to the Philosophical Society in 1792. Rush had espoused a climatic explanation for Negro traits as early as 1773 (Benjamin Rush, *Address on Slavery of the Negroes* [Philadelphia, 1773]; see esp. pp. 24–26). See also John Mortimer, "Some Account of the Motley Coloured, or Pye Negro Girl and Mulatto Boy, . . . " American Philosophical Society *Transactions,* 3 (1787): 392–395. In any case, there was much discussion of Negro "whitening" in the early republic; such discussion is too well known to historians to be rehearsed at full length here. The best treatment of the subject remains Jordan, *White over Black,* pp. 512–541.

57. Charles Caldwell, *The Autobiography of Charles Caldwell, M.D.,* ed. Harriot W. Warner (Philadelphia, 1855), pp. 163–164, 268–289; the other major account of the Moss incident is Benjamin Smith Barton, "Facts Relative to Henry Moss, a White Negroe, Now in This City," *Early Proceedings of the American Philosophical Society . . . 1744–1838* (Philadelphia: American Philosophical Society, 1884), pp. 241–256. See also Jordan, *White over Black,* pp. 521–522.

58. Joanne Pope Melish, *Disowning Slavery: Gradual Emancipation and "Race" in New England, 1780–1860* (Ithaca: Cornell University Press, 1998); Melish discusses the "white Negro" question on pp. 137–150.

59. Like Melish, most historians have misread Stanhope Smith as at some point definitely predicting Negro whitening in America, when he had actually never done so, as he himself was quick to point out. Stanhope Smith to some degree lent himself to such misreading: on Stanhope Smith, see Chapter 2. Stanhope Smith discussed Henry Moss in Samuel Stanhope Smith, *Essay on the Causes of Variety of Complexion and Figure in the Human Species,* 2nd ed., ed. Winthrop Jordan (1810; rpt. Cambridge: Harvard University Press, 1965), pp. 58–59.

60. Jefferson, *Notes,* pp. 70–71.

61. Jefferson to John Adams, August 15, 1820, in *The Adams-Jefferson Letters: The Complete Correspondence between Thomas Jefferson and Abigail and John Adams,* ed. Lester J. Cappon (Chapel Hill: Published for the Institute of Early American History and Culture at Williamsburg, VA, by the University of North Carolina Press, 1959), vol. 2, p. 592. See also a comparison of Jefferson's statement to

Lucretius in Charles A. Miller, *Jefferson and Nature: An Interpretation* (Baltimore: Johns Hopkins University Press, 1988), p. 24.

62. For the most striking instance of Jefferson's materialist view of the mind, see Jefferson to Georges Cabanis, July 12, 1803, Lipscomb and Bergh, *Writings*, vol. 10, p. 404. See also Miller, *Jefferson and Nature*, p. 28.

63. Thomas Jefferson to John Manners, February 22, 1814, rpt. in Edwin Morris Betts, ed., *Thomas Jefferson's Garden Book, 1766-1824* (Philadelphia: The American Philosophical Society, 1985), pp. 528-531; quotation on p. 529.

64. Jefferson, *Notes*, p. 55.

65. Ibid., p. 33.

66. Ibid., pp. 62-64. For overviews of Jefferson, *Notes*, and Native Americans, see Jordan, *White over Black*, pp. 475-481; Anthony F. C. Wallace, *Jefferson and the Indians: The Tragic Fate of the First Americans* (Cambridge: Harvard University Press, 1999), pp. 75-129.

67. Jefferson, *Notes*, p. 47.

68. Ibid., p. 143.

69. Ibid., p. 138.

70. Ibid., p. 138. I have in this analysis been influenced by Jay Fliegelman (*Declaring Independence: Jefferson, Natural Language, and the Culture of Performance* [Stanford: Stanford University Press, 1993], pp. 189-195), although I disagree with Fliegelman's argument that there was a turn in Jefferson's discussion when Jefferson moved from discussing color to discussing beauty and sexual attractiveness; it seems to me that Jefferson's distaste focused on black skin itself.

71. Margaret Anne Doody, "Introduction" to Jane Austen, *Sense and Sensibility* (New York: Oxford University Press, 1990), pp. vii-xlvi.

72. Ibid., p. xx.

73. Jefferson, *Notes*, p. 64.

74. Ibid., p. 139.

75. Ibid., p. 140.

76. Ibid., pp. 140-141.

77. Ibid., p. 142.

78. Gary Wills's argument (in *Inventing America: Thomas Jefferson's Declaration of Independence* [Garden City, NY: Doubleday, 1978]), that Jefferson defined humanity based on the moral sense has been rejected. See especially Ronald Hamowy, "Jefferson and the Scottish Enlightenment: A Critique of Garry Wills's *Inventing America*," *William and Mary Quarterly*, 36 (1979): 503-523; and Howe, *Making the American Self*, pp. 48-50.

79. Jefferson, *Notes*, p. 143.

80. In his 1774 *Sketches of the History of Man,* which went through twelve editions between 1774 and 1825 and which Jefferson read, Kames forcefully rejected Buffon's intra-fertility approach to classification. But he also dismissed Linnaeus's scheme as totally arbitrary: "It resembles the classing of books in a library by size, or by binding, without regard to the contents: it may serve as a sort of dictionary, but to no other purpose." Jefferson would not have approved. (Henry Home, Lord Kames, *Sketches of the History of Man,* 2nd ed. [London: Strahan and Cadell, 1778], pp. 19, 11–14, 77–79. On Kames's aims and intellectual context, see Evan Radcliffe, "Revolutionary Writing, Moral Philosophy, and Universal Benevolence in the Eighteenth Century," *Journal of the History of Ideas,* 54 (1993): 221–240.)

81. Jefferson, *Notes,* pp. 162–163. Lewis P. Simpson argues that Jefferson saw slave rebellion as inevitable and that in "Query XVIII" he was abandoning the optimism of the Declaration of Independence (Lewis P. Simpson, "The Ferocity of Self: History and Consciousness in Southern Literature," *South Central Review,* 1 [1984]: 67–84).

82. Jefferson, *Notes,* p. 163.

83. Even after *Notes,* Jefferson continued to try to convince European naturalists that they were wrong about the New World and that they should abandon armchair theories in favor of hard facts. Gordon S. Wood presents an entertaining brief account of the absurdities of these efforts in "The Bigger the Beast the Better: Two Prominent Scientists Debate the Healthfulness of the New World Environment," *American History Illustrated,* 17 (1982): 30–37. Finding huge American animals would interest Jefferson throughout his life: on March 10, 1797, his paper, "A Memoir on the Discovery of Certain Bones of a Quadruped of the Clawed Kind in the Western Parts of Virginia," was read to the American Philosophical Society. This huge carnivore Jefferson named the "Megalonyx," or "Great Claw." Here at last was an American lion, lord of the beasts, even surpassing the great Old World lion, Buffon's paragon of the noblest animal species, akin to Old World man, lord of all nature. (Thomas Jefferson, "A Memoir on the Discovery of certain Bones of a Quadruped of the Clawed Kind in the Western Parts of Virginia," American Philosophical Society *Transactions,* 4 [1799]: 246–260.) Jefferson's vision of nature remained harmonious and rigid.

2. CULTURE AND THE PERSISTENCE OF RACE

1. Samuel Stanhope Smith, *An Essay on the Causes of the Variety of Complexion and Figure in the Human Species; to Which Are Added Strictures on Lord Kaims's Discourse, on the Original Diversity of Mankind* (Philadelphia: Robert Aitken,

1787); Samuel Stanhope Smith, *An Essay on the Causes of Variety of Complexion and Figure in the Human Species,* 2nd ed. (1810; rpt., ed. Winthrop Jordan, Cambridge: Belknap Press of Harvard University Press, 1965).

2. Mark A. Noll, *Princeton and the Republic, 1768–1822: The Search for a Christian Enlightenment in the Era of Samuel Stanhope Smith* (Princeton: Princeton University Press, 1989), p. 9; for an exegesis of the moral sense in Witherspoon's ethics-cum-theology, see pp. 28–59.

3. Ibid., p. 46. Both Witherspoon and Stanhope Smith cavalierly dismissed Edwards's belief that determinism refuted the notion of free will and that grace was absolutely necessary.

4. Samuel Stanhope Smith, *The Lectures, Corrected and Improved, Which Have Been Delivered for a Series of Years, in the College of New Jersey; on the Subjects of Moral and Political Philosophy* (Trenton, NJ: Daniel Fenton, 1812), vol. 1, p. 126. Bishop Berkeley's immaterialism, and David Hume's skepticism regarding even the existence of mind and soul, Stanhope Smith found clever but misguided in their assumption, following Locke, that "the direct object of the senses are not external things, but only the images, or ideas of those things." This claim was Jesuitical, Stanhope Smith said, needless, leading to endless barren speculations, but if "the common apprehensions of mankind be received as truth," if it was taken for granted that external objects really did exist, then the problem vanished. A science of morality became possible (p. 135). Such was the contribution of the Scottish Enlightenment, which Stanhope Smith exalted even above Locke.

5. Stanhope Smith, *Essay (*1787), pp. 109–110.

6. Noll, *Princeton and the Republic,* p. 116.

7. "Samuel Stanhope Smith's *An Essay on the Causes of the Variety of Complexion and Figure in the Human Species,*" *Monthly Review,* 80 (1789): 184–185. The two-paragraph review was very positive but ended with a (probably entirely facetious) jibe at the "degeneration" thesis: "He [Stanhope Smith] affirms, that the native blacks in America mend in their *colour, features,* and *hair,* in every generation. This would be controverted, no doubt, by a negro critic, who would certainly object to the word *mend;* which, however, perhaps he would candidly consider as an error of the press, and shortly say, 'for *mend,* read *degenerate:*'—[sic] and, 'for *hair,* read *wool.*'" What is interesting about this comment, beyond its nascent relativism, is that the reviewer honed in on Stanhope Smith's bare statement in 1787 that free blacks were improving in America and reversing their "degeneracy" and wrongly interpreted it as an argument for relatively quick Negro whitening. Stanhope Smith's extreme caution here, and the depth that he gave race, even in the 1787 edition of the *Essay,* does not seem to have been observed at the time, as Stanhope Smith himself complained in the 1810 *Essay* (p. 155 and see below).

8. Stanhope Smith, "Strictures," in *Essay*, 1787, p. 6.

9. Stanhope Smith, *Essay*, 1787, p. 109.

10. Ibid., pp. 8–9.

11. Anthony Pagden, *European Encounters with the New World: From Renaissance to Romanticism* (New Haven: Yale University Press, 1993).

12. Stanhope Smith, *Lectures*, vol. 1, pp. 13, 21–22.

13. Ibid., pp. 16, 103.

14. Noll, *Princeton and the Republic*, p. 65.

15. Ibid., p. 115.

16. Henry Louis Gates, *The Signifying Monkey: A Theory of African-American Literary Criticism* (New York: Oxford University Press, 1988), pp. 127–169.

17. Jupiter Hammon, "An Address to the Negroes in the State of New York," in Dorothy Porter, comp., *Early Negro Writing, 1760–1837* (Boston: Beacon Press, 1971) p. 319.

18. For early African American protest writing, see Porter, *Early Negro Writing;* Gary Nash, *Race and Revolution* (Madison, WI: Madison House, 1990); Sidney Kaplan and Emma Nogrady Kaplan, *The Black Presence in the Era of the American Revolution, 1770–1800*, rev. ed. (Amherst: University of Massachusetts Press, 1989); and James Oliver Horton and Lois E. Horton, *In Hope of Liberty: Culture, Community and Protest among Northern Free Blacks, 1700–1860* (New York: Oxford University Press, 1997).

19. Vincent Carreta, "Oulaudah Equiano or Gustavus Vassa? New Light on an Eighteenth-Century Question of Identity," *Slavery and Abolition*, 20 (1999): 96–105.

20. Vincent Harding, "Wrestling toward the Dawn: The Afro-American Freedom Movement and the Changing Constitution," *Journal of American History*, 74 (1987): 719.

21. Madison quoted in Nash, *Race and Revolution*, p. 78; Prince Hall, "A Charge," rpt. in Richard Newman, Patrick Rael, and Philip Lapsansky, eds., *Pamphlets of Protest: An Anthology of Early African American Protest Literature, 1790–1860* (New York: Routledge, 2001), pp. 44–52; James Forten, "Letters from a Man of Colour on a Late Bill before the Senate of Pennsylvania," rpt. in Nash, *Race and Revolution*, p. 196.

22. George Lawrence, *An Oration on the Abolition of the Slave Trade, Delivered on the First Day of January, 1813, in the African Methodist Episcopal Church* (New York, 1813), in Herbert Aptheker, ed., *A Documentary History of the Negro People in the United States*, 1st ed. (New York: Citadel Press, 1951), pp. 58–59.

23. African Americans had not excelled in the arts and sciences, Hamilton said, but considering their position and prospects, their talents did sometimes burst

forth: "The productions of Phillis Wheatley may not possess the requisitions necessary to stand the test of nice criticism, and she may be denied a stand in the rank of poets, yet does she possess some original ideas that would not disgrace the pen of the best poets." William Hamilton, "An Address to the New York African Society for Mutual Relief, Delivered in the Universalist Church, January 2, 1809," in Porter, *Early Negro Writing*, pp. 33–41, quotation on p. 36.

24. Benjamin Bannaker, "A Letter from Benjamin Bannaker to the Secretary of State," rpt. in Nash, *Race and Revolution*, pp. 177–181, quotations on pp. 178, 180.

25. Phillis Wheatley to Samson Occom, February 11, 1774, rpt. in *Phillis Wheatley: Complete Writings*, ed. Vincent Caretta (New York: Penguin, 2001), p. 153.

26. Albert J. Raboteau, *A Fire in the Bones: Reflections on African-American Religious History* (Boston: Beacon Press, 1995), p. 30.

27. Stanhope Smith, *Essay*, 1810, pp. 3–4.

28. John Quincy Adams, in *Monthly Anthology and Boston Review*, 4 (1807): 142. Linda K. Kerber, *Federalists in Dissent: Imagery and Ideology in Jeffersonian America* (Ithaca: Cornell University Press, 1970), discusses New England Federalist science, pp. 67–94.

29. William Linn, *Serious Considerations on the Election of a President* (New York, 1800), p. 13. Linn is discussed in Kerber, *Federalists in Dissent*, p. 55, and in Winthrop Jordan, *White over Black: American Attitudes toward the Negro, 1550–1812* (Baltimore: Penguin Books, 1969, ©1968), p. 508.

30. Clement Clark Moore, *Observations upon Certain Passages in Mr. Jefferson's Notes on Virginia, Which Appear to Have a Tendency to Subvert Religion, and Establish a False Philosophy* (New York, 1804), p. 19; Moore was actually himself a slaveholder (see Kerber, *Federalists in Dissent*, pp. 53–55).

31. Kerber, *Federalists in Dissent*, p. 75.

32. Johann Friedrich Blumenbach, *The Anthropological Treatises*, trans. and ed. Thomas Bendyshe (London: Pub. for the Anthropological Society by Longman, Green, Longman, Roberts, & Green, 1865), p. 120.

33. Blumenbach, *Contributions to Natural History* (1805) in his *Anthropological Treatises*, p. 312.

34. Blumenbach, *Anthropological Treatises*, p. 307.

35. Immanuel Kant, *Metaphysical Foundations of Natural Science*, trans. James Ellington (New York, 1970); James L. Larson discusses this passage and the relationship between Kant and Blumenbach in "Vital Forces: Regulative Principles or Constituitive Agents? A Strategy in German Physiology, 1786–1802," *Isis* 70 (1979): 234–239.

36. In *Interpreting Nature: The Science of Living Form from Linnaeus to Kant*

(Baltimore: Johns Hopkins University Press, 1994), James L. Larson takes this view, as opposed to earlier work by Peter Hanns Reill (*The German Enlightenment and the Rise of Historicism* [Berkeley: University of California Press, 1975]) and esp. Timothy Lenoir ("Kant, Blumenbach, and Vital Materialism in German Biology," *Isis,* 71 [1980]: 77–108).

37. Stanhope Smith, *Essay,* 1810, p. 10.

38. Ibid., p. 12.

39. Stanhope Smith, *Lectures,* vol. 1, p. 197.

40. Stanhope Smith, *Essay,* 1810, p. 155.

41. Ibid., p. 167.

42. Ibid., p. 152.

43. Stanhope Smith, *Lectures,* vol. 2, pp. 159–179.

44. Stanhope Smith, *Essay,* 1810, p. 167.

45. Ibid., pp. 177–179.

46. Daniel Coker, "A Dialogue between a Virginian and an African," rpt. in Newman, Rael, and Lapsansky, *Pamphlets of Protest,* pp. 52–65.

47. Ibid., p. 60.

48. Ibid., pp. 60–61. The boldness of this passage takes on further interest when one learns that Coker was in 1816 forced to decline the honor of becoming the first bishop of the newly formed African Methodist Episcopal church, the first fully independent black Christian organization, for being himself a mulatto. Many members, calling themselves "pure blacks," complained that Coker, the son of an English indentured servant mother and a black slave father, was too "light" to lead a premier black organization. If he did, whites would wonder if the church had any "African connection." In 1820, Coker led a group of eighty-six African Americans to emigrate to Liberia. See Horton and Horton, *In Hope of Liberty,* p. 141.

49. *American Review of History and Politics,* 1 (1811): 128–166; *Port-Folio,* 14 (1814): 6–33; 149–165; 252–271, 447–457. The *American Review* version, which was reprinted as the first installment (pp. 6–33) in the much more extended *Port-Folio* version, was fairly mild; the majority of the *Port-Folio* review was much harsher, but both made the same basic objection to Stanhope Smith's approach and can be considered of a piece; indeed, Caldwell claimed to have written the whole all at once, but forbore to publish his more trenchant criticisms out of respect for Stanhope Smith and public religiosity. But, he said in 1814, all the vituperation he had borne from Stanhope Smith's friends for the first review obliged him to defend himself and lay out his position fully. At any rate, the 1811 review was better reasoned and argued. In his *Autobiography* Caldwell reported with no little satisfaction that many people blamed the harshness of his 1814 critique of monogenism for Stanhope Smith's falling into a paralytic stroke and then dying five

years later (*The Autobiography of Charles Caldwell, M.D.*, ed. Harriot W. Warner [Philadelphia: Lippincott, Grambo, 1855], pp. 268–273; see also pp. 163–164).

50. Caldwell, *Port-Folio*, pp. 149–150.

51. Charles White, *An Account of the Regular Gradation in Man, and in Different Animals and Vegetables; and from the Former to the Latter* (London: C. Dilly, 1799), p. 135. This passage is quoted in, among other works, Leon Poliakov, *The Aryan Myth: A History of Racist and Nationalist Ideas in Europe*, trans. Edmund Howard (New York: Basic Books, 1974), p. 159; Jordan, *White over Black*, pp. 501–502; and William R. Stanton, *The Leopard's Spots: Scientific Attitudes toward Race in America, 1815–59* (Chicago: University of Chicago Press, 1960), p. 17.

52. White, *Regular Gradation*, pp. 137–138.

53. John Augustine Smith, "A Lecture," *New York Medical and Philosophical Journal and Review*, 1 (1809): 32–48.

54. Peter Camper, *The Works of the Late Professor Camper, on the Connexion between the Science of Anatomy and the Arts of Drawing, Painting, and Statuary, &c., &c.*, trans. T. Cogan (London: C. Dilly, 1794), p. 50. On Hunter and the facial angle, see Jordan, *White over Black*, p. 498. Stanhope Smith exclaimed of J. A. Smith's invocation of Blumenbach in support of Camper: "Can it be because Blumenbach's work is written in Latin! I will not presume any such disgraceful thing. I will, therefore, proceed to exhibit my proof, without doubting but that I shall be understood." Stanhope Smith then quoted Blumenbach's refutation of Camper, in Latin (*Essay*, 1810, pp. 178–181).

55. Stanhope Smith, *Essay*, 1810, pp. 160–161.

56. Constantine Francis Volney, *Travels through Syria and Egypt, in the years 1783, 1784, and 1785*, 3rd. ed. (London, 1805), p. 78; on Volney's role in debates over slavery, see Davis S. Wiesen, "Herodotus and the Modern Debate over Race and Slavery," *Annals of Scholarship*, 1 (1980): 31–59.

57. On Volney and geography, see Martin S. Staum, "Human Geography in the French Institute: New Discipline or Missed Opportunity?" *Journal of the History of the Behavioral Sciences*, 23 (1987): 332–340.

58. Stanhope Smith, *Essay*, 1810, p. 74.

59. Ibid., p. 73.

60. Stanhope Smith, *Lectures*, vol. 2, p. 43.

3. THE HORRORS OF ST. DOMINGUE

1. The literature on the Haitian Revolution is growing steadily. A useful recent short synthesis of Haitian events, in context of the Americas, may be found in

Lester D. Langely, *The Americas in the Age of Revolution, 1750–1850* (New Haven: Yale University Press, 1996), pp. 86–144; see also David Barry Gaspar and David Patrick Geggus, eds., *A Turbulent Time: The French Revolution and the Greater Caribbean* (Bloomington: University of Indiana Press, 1997).

2. The editor of the *Virginia Gazette and General Advertiser* observed in 1803 that "Toussaint, before the arrival of the French army could not by the most rancorous of his enemies, be accused with having spilt the blood of the innocent; he could not be reproached with requisitions and robberies, such as have marked the progress of General Leclerc" (July 3, 1803); this passage is discussed, and Pickering's remarks to Congress are quoted, in Donald R. Hickey, "America's Response to the Slave Revolt in Haiti, 1791–1806," *Journal of the Early Republic*, 2 (1982): 361–379; quotation on p. 366. See also Donald R. Hickey, "Timothy Pickering and the Haitian Slave Revolt: A Letter to Thomas Jefferson in 1806," *Essex Institute Historical Collections* 120 (1984): 149–163. On Federalist attitudes toward Haiti, see Linda Kerber, *Federalists in Dissent: Imagery and Ideology in Jeffersonian America* (Ithaca: Cornell University Press, 1970), pp. 45–52.

3. Bishop's sermon is reprinted by Tim Matthewson, "Abraham Bishop, 'The Rights of Black Men,' and the American Reaction to the Haitian Revolution," *Journal of Negro History*, 67 (1982): 148–153, and discussed in David Brion Davis, *Revolutions: Reflections on American Equality and Foreign Liberations* (Cambridge: Harvard University Press, 1990), pp. 50–52. Bishop is interesting because although beginning as a staunch Federalist, by 1802 he had become an ardent Jeffersonian, a supporter of France and of Napoleon and a critic of the mercantile instincts and interests of the Federalists, whom he excoriated as the American incarnation of all the evils of the age. Bishop dreaded some new Armageddon born of those evils. Violent Haiti, sugar island and rebel against the French, would apparently be a fitting provocation for such a disaster.

4. Atrocity stories are discussed at length in Alfred N. Hunt, *Haiti's Influence on Antebellum America: Slumbering Volcano in the Caribbean* (Baton Rouge: Louisiana State University Press, 1988), esp. pp. 37–83. For the reception of refugee planters, see Paul F. Lachace, "The 1809 Immigration of Saint-Domingue Refugees to New Orleans: Reception, Integration and Impact," *Louisiana History,* 29 (1988): 109–141.

5. Peter S. Onuf, "'To Declare Them a Free and Independent People: Race, Slavery, and National Identity in Jefferson's Thought," *Journal of the Early Republic,* 18 [1998]: 1–46; Michael Zuckerman, "The Power of Blackness: Thomas Jefferson and the Revolution in St. Domingue," in Michael Zuckerman, *Almost Chosen People: Oblique Biographies in the American Grain* (Berkeley: University of Califor-

nia Press, 1993), pp. 175–218; Tim Matthewson, "Jefferson and Haiti," *Journal of Southern History,* 61 (1995): 209–248.

6. Douglas Egerton, *Gabriel's Rebellion: The Virginia Slave Conspiracies of 1800 and 1802* (Chapel Hill: University of North Carolina Press, 1993). See also Douglas Egerton, "'Fly across the River': The Easter Slave Conspiracy of 1802," and Thomas C. Parramore, "Aborted Takeoff: A Critique of 'Fly across the River,'" both in *North Carolina Historical Review,* 68 (1991): 87–110, 111–121.

7. Quoted in Gary Nash, *Race and Revolution* (Madison, WI: Madison House, 1990), p. 79. For a collection of examples of black lionization of Toussaint, see George F. Tyson, ed., *Toussaint L'Ouverture* (Englewood Cliffs, NJ: Prentice-Hall, 1983), pp. 137–148; also Hunt, *Haiti's Influence,* pp. 97–101. Perhaps the most interesting and substantial African American treatment of Toussaint as Great Man was the stock speech of the renowned black abolitionist orator William Wells Brown, *St. Domingue: Its Revolutions and Its Patriots, A Lecture* (Boston: Bela March, 1855).

8. Prince Hall, "A Charge," 1797, rpt. in Richard Newman, Patrick Rael, and Philip Lapsansky, eds., *Pamphlets of Protest: An Anthology of Early African American Protest Literature, 1790–1860* (New York: Routledge, 2001), pp. 44–52.

9. Prince Hall, *A Charge Delivered to the Brethren of the African Lodge, on the 25th of June, 1792, at the Hall of Brother William Smith, in Charlestown, by the Right Worshipful Master Prince Hall,* rpt. in Dorothy Porter, comp., *Early Negro Writing, 1760–1837* (Boston: Beacon Press, 1971), pp. 63–69; quotations on pp. 64, 68.

10. Prince Hall, "A Charge," 1797, p. 49.

11. Ibid., p. 50.

12. Hunt, *Haiti's Influence,* pp. 38–39, 90–91. On race and Haitian politics during and after the Haitian Revolution, see David Nicholls, *From Dessalines to Duvalier: Race, Colour, and National Independence in Haiti* (New York: Cambridge University Press, 1979). Nicholls's book presents an interesting if perhaps somewhat overdrawn account of the Haitian Revolution and subsequent Haitian history as in large part a racial struggle between Haitian "blacks" and "mulattos."

13. For Federalist responses to Dessalines see Kerber, *Federalists in Dissent,* pp. 51–52.

14. Hunt, *Haiti's Influence,* pp. 107–147. The blame-the-mulattos view of slave rebellions is discussed generally in George Fredrickson, *The Black Image in the White Mind: The Debate on Afro-American Character and Destiny, 1817–1914* (Middletown, CT: Wesleyan University Press, 1987, ©1971), esp. pp. 97–129.

15. Edmund Ruffin, *The Political Economy of Slavery; or, The Institution Considered in Regard to its Influence on Public Wealth and the General Welfare* (Washington, DC: L. Towers, 1857), p. 17. Hunt surveys Toussaint's image, among whites and blacks, northerners and southerners, in the antebellum United States, in *Haiti's Influence*, pp. 84–107.

16. Onuf, "'To Declare Them a Free and Independent People,'" pp. 36–40.

17. See Nicholls, *From Dessalines to Duvalier.*

18. Nicholls discusses this in *From Dessalines to Duvalier*, pp. 32ff.

19. See also, for example, the issue of August 1, 1818, in which Niles expects the mulatto forces to give "'King Henry' a hearty drubbing."

20. Saunders early attracted notice. In 1816 the young Bostonian George Ticknor, one of the first Americans to study in Germany and later to become a prominent scholar and intellectual leader, sent to Blumenbach, whose famous course in natural history he would soon take at Göttingen, material on American Negroes and Indians. This included information about Saunders, who, Ticknor reported, had briefly run a free school in Boston for Negro children. A few months later Ticknor made Saunders's acquaintance when the two traveled on the same ship to England, where Saunders was planning to arrange the publication of the first edition of *Haytian Papers.* (George Ticknor to Johann Friedrich Blumenbach, February 17, 1816, described and quoted at length in Orie William Long, *Literary Pioneers: Early American Explorers of European Culture* [Cambridge: Harvard University Press, 1935], p. 229, n. 41.) Ticknor also gave an account of Nantucket African American Paul Cuffe's efforts to educate Africans and of the Moor and Indian School at Dartmouth College. On Saunders's career, see Arthur O. White, "Prince Saunders: An Instance of Social Mobility among Antebellum New England Blacks," *Journal of Negro History*, 60 (1975): 526–535; Julie Winch, *Philadelphia's Black Elite: Activism, Accommodation, and the Struggle for Autonomy, 1787–1848* (Philadelphia: Temple University Press, 1988), pp. 52–53; Earl Leslie Griggs and Clifford H. Prator, eds., *Henry Christophe and Thomas Clarkson: A Correspondence* (Berkeley: University of California Press, 1952), pp. 226–231, 241–244.

21. Prince Saunders, *Haytian Papers: A Collection of the Very Interesting Proclamations, and Other Official Documents; together with Some Account of the Rise, Progress, and Present State of the Kingdom of Hayti* (London: W. Reed, 1816), p. 147.

22. Banks to Saunders, August 13, 1816, rpt. in Prince Saunders, *A Memoir Presented to the American Convention for Promoting the Abolition of Slavery, and Improving the Conditions of the African Race, December 11, 1818* (Philadelphia:

Dennis Heartt, 1818), rpt. in Porter, *Early Negro Writing*, pp. 269–278; Banks's letter rpt. pp. 277–278. On the American Convention, see Richard S. Newman, *The Transformation of American Abolitionism: Fighting Slavery in the Early Republic* (Chapel Hill: University of North Carolina Press, 2002), pp. 19–20.

23. David Brion Davis, *Slavery and Human Progress* (New York: Oxford University Press, 1984), pp. 168–230.

24. See *Niles' Weekly Register,* January 18, March 22, 1817.

25. Prince Saunders, *Haytian Papers . . .* (Boston: C. Bingham, 1818).

26. Prince Saunders, *An Address, Delivered at Bethel Church, Philadelphia; on the 30th of September, 1816, before the Pennsylvania Augustine Society, for the Education of People of Colour* (Philadelphia: Joseph Rakestraw, 1818), rpt. in Porter, *Early Negro Writing*, pp. 87–95.

27. Saunders, *Memoir*, p. 224; Banks's letter rpt. pp. 277–278.

28. For Simonisse's project, see Winch, *Philadelphia's Black Elite*, pp. 183–184; for surveys of Haitian emigration projects before the Civil War, see Floyd J. Miller, *The Search for a Black Nationality: Black Emigration and Colonization, 1787–1864* (Chicago: University of Chicago Press, 1975), pp. 74–81; Rodney Carlisle, *The Roots of Black Nationalism* (Port Washington, NY: Kennikat Press, 1975), pp. 50–54; James O'Dell Jackson III, "The Origins of Pan-African Nationalism: Afro-American and Haytian Relations, 1800–1863" (Ph.D. diss., Northwestern University, 1976); Saunders to Clarkson, July 14, 1821, and May 26, 1823, rpt. in Griggs and Prator, *Henry Christophe and Thomas Clarkson;* and White, "Prince Saunders." On Boyer, see John Edward Baur, "Mulatto Machiavelli: Jean Pierre Boyer and the Haiti of His Day," *Journal of Negro History,* 32 (1947): 307–353.

29. *Resolutions and Remonstrances of the People of Colour against Colonization on the Coast of Africa* (Philadelphia, 1818), pp. 7–8; James Forten to Paul Cuffe, quoted in Sheldon Harris, *Paul Cuffe: Black America and the African Return* (New York: Simon and Schuster, 1971), p. 244. On the development of early free black attitudes toward the American Colonization Society, see Gary Nash, *Forging Freedom: The Formation of Philadelphia's Black Community, 1720–1840* (Cambridge: Harvard University Press, 1988), pp. 236–241; Winch, *Philadelphia's Black Elite,* pp. 34–39; James Oliver Horton and Lois E. Horton, *In Hope of Liberty: Culture, Community, and Protest among Northern Free Blacks* (New York: Oxford University Press, 1997), pp. 187–191; Newman, *Transformation of American Abolitionism,* pp. 86–130. On the possibly proslavery origins of the American Colonization Society, see Douglas R. Egerton, "'Its Origin Is Not a Little Curious': A New Look at the American Colonization Society," *Journal of the Early Republic* 5 (1985): 462–480.

30. Boyer to Dewey, April 30, 1824, rpt. in *Niles' Weekly Register,* June 26, 1824. The entire pamphlet was reprinted in both the *Register* and in Benjamin Lundy's *Genius of Universal Emancipation.*

31. Dewey published *Correspondence Relative to the Emigration to Hayti, of the Free People of Colour, in the United States. Together with the Instructions to the Agent Sent out by President Boyer* (New York: M. Day, 1824); much of this pamphlet was reprinted in *Niles' Weekly Register.* For the controversy within the Colonization Society, see P. J. Staudenraus, *The African Colonization Movement, 1816–1865* (New York: Columbia University Press, 1961), pp. 82–85, and Merton L. Dillon, *Benjamin Lundy and the Struggle for Negro Freedom* (Urbana: University of Illinois Press, 1966), pp. 90–91.

32. On colonization's political uses, see Paul Goodman, *Of One Blood: Abolitionism and the Origins of Racial Equality* (Berkeley: University of California Press, 1998), pp. 11–22.

33. *Niles' Weekly Register,* September 27, 1823.

34. *Genius of Universal Emancipation,* October 1824. Lundy repeatedly invoked Exodus imagery. The very first issue of the *Genius,* published in July 1821, began with an "Address to the Public" that quoted Jefferson's Query XVIII from *Notes* at length, then declared that "the same spirit that actuated the king of Egypt when he refused the Israelites their freedom, now actuates" American slaveholders, who would try to enslave whites if they could get away with it (*Genius of Universal Emancipation,* July 1821).

35. Benjamin Lundy to Isaac Barton, March 8, 1825, quoted in Henry Mayer, *All on Fire: William Lloyd Garrison and the Abolition of Slavery* (New York: St. Martin's Press, 1998), p. 73; see also p. 71.

36. Lundy's involvement in emigration began through his contacts with the North Carolina Yearly Meeting of Quakers. In 1808 North Carolina's Quakers resolved to free all their slaves and set up a gradual emancipation plan that transferred the ownership of all slaves held by Friends to the Yearly Meeting, which protected those slaves who wanted to stay in North Carolina but which tried to relocate all others elsewhere. Several were sent to Africa with Lundy's assistance. Henry J. Cadbury, "Negro Membership in the Society of Friends," *Journal of Negro History,* 21 (April 1936): 151–213; Horton and Horton, *In Hope of Liberty,* p. 103.

37. Lundy's assessment was quite correct: see Frankie Hutton, "Economic Considerations in the American Colonization Society's Early Effort to Emigrate Free Blacks to Liberia, 1816–36," *Journal of Negro History,* 68 (1983): 376–389. As Fredrickson notes, for colonization even to have made a serious attempt to succeed would have required a massive federal program on a scale unprecedented in American history up to that time. Such a program would have been anathema to the

Jacksonianism that came to dominate American political culture in the late 1820s and 30s and that, along with free black opposition and the rise of Garrisonian radical abolitionism, spelled colonization's decline as a perceived serious solution to the slavery problem. Fredrickson, *Black Image,* pp. 24–25.

38. *Genius of Universal Emancipation,* June 1825.

39. Ibid., November 1824.

40. David Brion Davis, "Reconsidering the Colonization Movement: Leonard Bacon and the Problem of Evil," and George Fredrickson, "Comment on Davis," both in *Intellectual History Newsletter,* 14 (1992): 3–16, 17–20.

41. T. R., "Observations on the Early History of the Negro Race," *African Repository and Colonial Journal,* 1 (1825): 7–12; quotations on p. 10.

42. Ibid., p. 12.

43. "Interesting Extracts, From 'An Essay on the Superstitions, Customs, and Arts, Common to the Ancient Egyptians, Abyssinians, and Ashantees,' by T. Edward Bowditch," *African Repository* 1 (1825): 204–213. This piece argued that the Egyptians civilized Ethiopia and also several other African nations, including the Ashantees. And Bowditch did not think that the Egyptians were Negroes. Indeed, he observed in his first sentence: "The traditions of emigration, not of the whole population but of particular families, so current in the Ashantee and the neighboring nations, the numerous exceptions to the negro countenance, and the striking similitude of their more extraordinary superstitions, laws, and customs to those of ancient Egypt, persuade me that most of the higher classes are descended from eastern Ethiopians who had been improved by an intercourse with the Egyptian emigrants and colonists" (p. 205).

44. *Description de L'Égypte* (Paris: De L'Imprimerie Impériale, 1809–1828), 4 vols; see Charles Coulston Gillispie and Michel Dewachter, eds., *Monuments of Egypt: The Napoleonic Edition* (Princeton: Princeton Architectural Press, 1987), "Historical Introduction," pp. 1–45. For an extensive review of material surrounding the nineteenth-century American fad for Egypt, see William B. Dinsmoor, "Early American Studies of Mediterranean Archaeology," American Philosophical Society, *Proceedings,* 87 (1944): 70–104. In particular, see "Egyptian History," *American Quarterly Review,* 4 (1828): 27–53, a long review essay on Champollion's work and the first volume of the *Description*; "Hieroglyphic System," *American Quarterly Review* 9 (1828): 339–351, a discussion of the first analysis of Champollion's decipherment; "Egyptian Mummies," *American Quarterly Review,* 18 (1835): 170–191, an attempt to demystify mummification; Edward Everett, "Hieroglyphics," *North American Review,* 34 (1831): 95–127, which stressed the mutability of human affairs. None of these pieces mentioned race, although Edward Everett's brother Alexander would in 1827 write at length about the glories of a

black Egypt as proof that Negroes were not innately inferior; see below, Chapter 4.

45. Letter from Thomas Paul, July 1, 1824, rpt. in Porter, *Early Negro Writing*, pp. 279-280.

46. Winch discusses the development of this ideology in *Philadelphia's Black Elite*, pp. 49-61.

47. Watkins's speech rpt. in *Genius of Universal Emancipation*, August 1825; see also Jacob C. Greener's address at a similar meeting two days later, in ibid., September 1825.

48. American commercial agent at Port-au-Prince quoted in Ludwell Lee Montague, *Haiti and the United States, 1714-1938* (Durham, NC: Duke University Press, 1940), p. 71; the 6,000-emigrants figure for the 1820s is Winch's estimate (*Philadelphia's Black Elite*, pp. 52-56). The white abolitionist Benjamin Hunt visited Haiti in the 1850s and found what he estimated to be 13,000 African-American emigrants and their descendants there, some of whom, particularly those well-trained in America prior to emigrating, were doing well, while others less fortunate seemed mired in poverty (Benjamin Hunt, *Remarks on Hayti as a Place of Settlement for Afric-Americans; and on the Mulatto as a Race for the Tropics* (Philadelphia, 1860), pp. 262-264). See also Charles Mackenzie, *Notes on Haiti, Made during a Residence in that Republic* (London, 1830), vol. 1, pp. 110-111.

49. J. Michael Dash, *Haiti and the United States: National Stereotypes and the Literary Imagination* (New York: St. Martin's Press, 1988), p. 15.

50. *Niles Weekly Register*, May 21, 1825.

51. The 1838 venture was small in scale and came to little; the effort in the early 1860s proved more serious but was cut off by the issuance of the Emancipation Proclamation on January 1, 1863, which led most prospective emigrants to decide to stay in the United States. See Hunt, *Haiti's Influence*, pp. 170-188; Montague, *Haiti and the United States*, pp. 66-80; Howard Bell's introduction to *Black Separatism and the Caribbean, 1860*, by James Theodore Holly and J. Dennis Harris, ed. Howard Holman Bell (Ann Arbor: University of Michigan Press, 1970), pp. 1-16; William Seraile, "Afro-American Emigration to Haiti during the Civil War," *Americas*, 35 (1978): 185-200; Jackson, "Origins of Pan-African Nationalism."

52. For a lengthy example of a proslavery tract's references to Haiti's economic deterioration, no doubt intended as an answer to Hinton Rowan Helper's numerous tables of statistics about the South's lack of productivity under slavery, see Louis Schade, *A Book for the "Impending Crisis"! Appeal to the Common Sense and Patriotism of the People of the United States; Helperism Annihilated! The 'Irrepressible Conflict' and its Consequences!* (Washington, DC: Little, Morris, 1860).

53. See Langely, p. 144.

4. THE MUTABIITY OF HUMAN AFFAIRS

1. Albert J. Raboteau, *A Fire in the Bones: Reflections on African-American Religious History* (Boston: Beacon Press, 1995), p. 56.

2. Mia Bay, *The White Image in the Black Mind: African-American Ideas about White People, 1830–1925* (New York: Oxford University Press, 2000), pp. 26–38.

3. Henri Grégoire, *An Enquiry Concerning the Intellectual and Moral Faculties and Literature of Negroes Followed with an Account of the Life and Works of Fifteen Negroes and Mulattoes Distinguished in Science, Literature and the Arts,* trans. D. R. Warden (1810; rpt. College Park, MD: McGrath, 1967), p. 39. A good introduction to Grégoire is Graham Russell Hodges's introduction to a recent reprint (Armonk, NY: M. E. Sharpe, 1997), pp. i–xxi. See as well Ruth F. Necheles-Jansyn, *The Abbé Grégoire, 1787–1831: The Odyssey of an Egalitarian* (Westport, CT: Greenwood, 1971).

4. Peter Williams, "An Oration on the Abolition of the Slave Trade, Delivered in the African Church, in the City of New York, January 1, 1808," rpt. in Dorothy Porter, comp., *Early Negro Writing, 1760–1837* (Boston: Beacon Press, 1971), pp. 343–354, quotation on p. 346.

5. William Hamilton, "An Oration, on the Abolition of the Slave Trade, Delivered in the Episcopal Asbury African Church, in Elizabeth St., New York, January 2, 1815," in Porter, *Early Negro Writing,* pp. 391–404; quotations, pp. 393, 394.

6. William Miller, *A Sermon on the Abolition of the Slave Trade: Delivered in the African Church, New York, on the First of January, 1810* (New York: J. C. Totten, 1810), pp. 33–35; see also Raboteau, *A Fire in the Bones,* pp. 43–45.

7. Prince Saunders, *Haytian Papers: A Collection of the Very Interesting Proclamations and Other Official Documents; Together with Some Account of the Rise, Progress, and Present State of the Kingdom of Hayti* (London: W. Reed, 1816), pp. 219–220.

8. On early Masonry, African Americans, and Egypt, see Wilson Jeremiah Moses, *Afrotopia: The Roots of African American Popular History* (New York: Cambridge University Press, 1998), pp. 44–51. See also "St. John's Day," *Freedom's Journal,* July 13, 1827, pp. 70–71 and "Masonic Oration," *Freedom's Journal,* July 20, 1827, p. 74.

9. On Cornish, see Tunde Adeleke, "Afro-Americans and Moral Suasion: The Debate in the 1830s," *Journal of Negro History,* 83 (1998): 127–142; David E. Swift, "Black Presbyterian Attacks on Racism: Samuel Cornish, Theodore Wright, and Their Contemporaries," in David W. Wills and Richard Newman, eds., *Black Apostles at Home and Abroad: Afro-Americans and the Christian Mission from the*

Revolution to Reconstruction (Boston: G. K. Hall, 1982); and David E. Swift, *Black Prophets of Justice: Activist Clergy before the Civil War* (Baton Rouge: Louisiana State University Press, 1989).

10. On the process of emancipation in New York City, see Shane White's imaginative study, *Somewhat More Independent: The End of Slavery in New York City, 1770–1810* (Atlanta: University of Georgia Press, 1991), which also contains an informative survey of racial thought in the Middle Atlantic states from 1770–1800, as well as an attempt to discover what middle- and low-brow racial attitudes might have been, as seen in the popular literature of the day (pp. 56–78).

11. James Oliver Horton and Lois E. Horton, *In Hope of Liberty: Culture, Community, and Protest among Northern Free Blacks* (New York: Oxford University Press, 1997), p. 168; see also Phyllis F. Field, *The Politics of Race in New York: The Struggle for Black Suffrage in the Civil War Era* (Ithaca: Cornell University Press, 1982); Paul Finkelman, "Prelude to the Fourteenth Amendment: Black Legal Rights in the Antebellum North," *Rutgers Law Journal* 17 (1986): 415–482.

12. Paul Goodman, *Of One Blood: Abolitionism and the Origins of Racial Equality* (Berkeley: University of California Press, 1998), p. 7.

13. David R. Roediger, *The Wages of Whiteness: Race and the Making of the American Working Class* (London: Verso, 1991); E. Anthony Rotundo, *American Manhood: Transformations in Masculinity from the Revolution to the Modern Era* (New York: Basic Books, 1993); Linda K. Kerber, "The Paradox of Women's Citizenship in the Early Republic: The Case of Martin vs. Massachussetts, 1805," *American Historical Review*, 97 (April, 1992): 349–378.

14. Eric Lott, *Love and Theft: Blackface Ministrelsy and the American Working Class* (New York: Oxford University Press, 1993).

15. The most intense analysis of colonization as a political movement aimed at suppressing the slavery issue is Goodman, *Of One Blood*, pp. 5–22.

16. "To Our Patrons," *Freedom's Journal*, March 16, 1827, p. 1.

17. On the *Journal*'s circulation and readership, see Lionel C. Barrow, Jr., "'Our Own Cause': 'Freedom's Journal' and the Beginnings of the Black Press," and Kenneth D. Nordin, "In Search of Black Unity: An Interpretation of the Content and Function of 'Freedom's Journal,'" *Journalism History*, 4 (1977–78): 118–122, 123–128.

18. For Cornish's involvement in the Haitian emigration scheme, see *Niles' Weekly Register*, July 3, 1824.

19. Editorial, "Christian Philanthropy," *Freedom's Journal*, March 23, 1827, p. 6.

20. "To Our Patrons," *Freedom's Journal*, March 16, 1827, p. 1.

21. Editorial from *Georgetown Columbian and District Advertiser*, May 29,

1827, rpt. and discussed in "Colonization Society," *Freedom's Journal,* June 3, 1827, pp. 50-51.

22. "Numbers of Paupers," *Freedom's Journal,* March 30, 1827, p. 11.

23. [William Watkins], "Colonization Society," letter from "A Coloured Baltimorean," *Freedom's Journal,* June 6, 1827, p. 66; see also Goodman, *Of One Blood,* p. 25 and n. 5, pp. 265-266.

24. "On the Mutability of Human Affairs," *Freedom's Journal,* April 6, 13, 20, 1827.

25. John B. Russwurm, "The Condition and Prospects of Hayti," in Philip Foner, "John Browne Russwurm: A Document," *Journal of Negro History,* 54 (1969): 393-397.

26. "Toussaint L'Ouverture," *Freedom's Journal,* May 6, May 11, May 18, 1827; "Hayti," *Freedom's Journal,* April 20, 27, May 4, June 15, 29, 1827. There was also a short piece, "Haytien Revolution," presumably by Cornish, in *Freedom's Journal,* April 6, 1827.

27. Alexander Everett, *America: or, A General Survey of the Political Situation of the Several Powers of the Western Continents, with Conjectures on Their Future Prospects, by a Citizen of the United States* (Philadelphia: Carey & Lea, 1827). *America* came out on the heels of Everett's very successful *Europe; or, A General Survey of the Present Situation of the Principal Powers* . . . (Boston: Longman, Hurst, Rees, Orme, and Brown, 1822), written in the form of letters home to his brother Edward.

28. "European Colonies in America," *Freedom's Journal,* July 13, 1827, p. 69.

29. Ibid., July 20, 1827, p. 73.

30. Ibid., July 27, 1877, p. 77.

31. Cornish, Ibid., July 27, 1877, p. 79.

32. "Africa," *Freedom's Journal,* February 7, 1829. On de Vastey, see David Nicholls, *From Dessalines to Duvalier: Race, Colour, and National Independence in Haiti* (Cambridge: Cambridge University Press, 1979), pp. 43-46; Philip D. Curtin, *The Image of Africa: British Ideas and Action, 1780-1850* (Madison: University of Wisconsin Press, 1964), pp. 242-243.

33. For an introduction into the uses of the Curse of Canaan, see Benjamin Braude, "The Sons of Noah and the Construction of Ethnic and Geographical Identities in the Medieval and Early Modern Periods," *William and Mary Quarterly,* 54 (1997): 103-142; Ron Bartour, "'Cursed be Canaan, a Servant of Servants shall he be unto his brethran': American Views on 'Biblical Slavery,' 1835-1865," *Slavery and Abolition,* 4 (1983): 41-55; William McKee Evans, "From the Land of

Canaan to the Land of Guinea: The Strange Odyssey of the Sons of Ham," *American Historical Review*, 85 (1980): 15–43.

34. James William Johnson, "Chronological Writing: Its Concepts and Development," *History and Theory*, 2 (1962): 124–145. Edith R. Sanders, "The Hamitic Hypothesis: Its Origin and Functions in Time Perspective," *Journal of African History*, 10 (1969): 521–532.

35. W. G. Browne, *Travels in Africa, Egypt, and Syria*, 2d ed. (London: T. Cadell and W. Davies, 1806), 170–175; see also Sanders, "Hamitic Hypothesis," pp. 526–528. Browne's work seems basically to have been conceived as a refutation of Napoleon's Egyptian Expedition and especially Volney. Whites who refuted the Curse of Canaan did not usually reject Noah as a prophet, not to mention condemn him as a drunkard, as so many African American writers did. Compare, for example, "The Curse of Canaan," *New York Observer*, rpt. in *Freedom's Journal*, May 4, 1827, with, for example, S. S. N., "Anglo-Saxons and Anglo-Africans," *Anglo-African Magazine*, 1 (1859): 247–254. African American clergyman and leader James W. C. Pennington, in his *Text Book of the Origin and History, &c. &c of the Colored People* (Hartford, CT: L. Skinner, 1841), made doubly sure by proving that Noah's curse could not have applied to blacks and then asking, "Is the spirit of wine the spirit of God?" (p. 18). For a rather sober refutation accepting Noah as a prophet and hardly mentioning ancient Egypt, see African American missionary and leader Alexander Crummell's paper refuting the Curse in Crummell, *The Future of Africa: Being Addresses, Sermons, Etc., Etc., Delivered in the Republic of Liberia* (New York: Scribner, 1862), pp. 327–354.

36. "The Curse of Canaan," *Freedom's Journal*, May 4, 1827, p. 29.

37. S, "On the Genealogy of the African Race," *Freedom's Journal*, August 17, 24, 31, 1827.

38. "An Apology for Pharaoh," *Freedom's Journal*, June 29, July 6, 1827, pp. 61, 65; quotation on p. 65 (July 6).

39. "Mutability," *Freedom's Journal*, April 6, 1827, p. 15.

40. Ibid., p. 15.

41. Ibid., p. 15.

42. "Mutability," *Freedom's Journal*, April 13, 1827, p. 18.

43. Ibid., pp. 18–19.

44. Ibid., p. 19.

45. "Mutability," *Freedom's Journal*, April 20, 1827, p. 28.

46. Archibald Alexander quoted in Horton and Horton, *In Hope of Liberty*, pp. 197–198.

47. For example, "Letter from Bishop Allen," *Freedom's Journal,* November 2, 1827, p. 134; this piece immediately followed a pro-colonization letter. Allen's letter was later reprinted in Walker's *Appeal.*

48. "To the Senior Editor—No I," *Freedom's Journal,* August 3, 1827, p. 82, "To the Senior Editor—No II," *Freedom's Journal,* August 10, 1827, pp. 86–87.

49. "To the Senior Editor—No. I," p. 82.

50. John B. Russwurm, "On the Varieties of the Human Race," *Freedom's Journal,* April 19, 1828, p. 26.

51. Rushwurm, "Varieties," *Freedom's Journal,* May 9, 1828, p. 51.

52. According to Russwurm, neither white nor black were as permanent as the olive or red, as cases of white or spotted Negroes or darkened whites all testified; "but who has heard of the red or olive undergoing like changes?" (Russwurm, "Varieties," *Freedom's Journal,* September 19, 1828, p. 203).

53. *Freedom's Journal,* "Our Labours," December 5, 1828, p. 283.

54. Along with the *Rights of All,* Cornish would also found *The Colored American,* which was later edited by Charles B. Ray and Philip A. Bell and ran from 1837–1842. Like the *Rights of All,* the *Colored American* devoted little space to racial theory, especially compared with *Freedom's Journal* or the place that racial theory occupied in black writing as a whole. See Donald M. Jacobs, ed., *Antebellum Black Newspapers: Indices . . .* (Westport, CT: Greenwood Press, 1976).

55. See, for example, the writing of David Walker (1829), discussed below, and, discussed in Chapter 6, the works of Hosea Easton (1828 and 1837), and the minutes of the National Convention of the American Society of Free Persons of Colour, meeting from 1830 to 1835. See also David Nickens's July 5, 1832 address to the Chillicothe, Ohio, African Methodist Episcopal Church, printed in the *Liberator,* August 11, 1832; William Whipper's 1833 eulogy of William Wilberforce, rpt. in Philip S. Foner, ed., *The Voice of Black America: Major Speeches by Negroes in the United States, 1797–1971* (New York: Simon & Schuster, 1972), pp. 49–55. There was also Native American-African American Robert Benjamin Lewis's 400-page volume, *Light and Truth . . .* (Portland, ME: D. C. Colesworthy, 1836; see also a second, enlarged edition [Boston: B. F. Roberts, 1844]), which claimed that Adam and then practically every major figure in ancient history, including Plato, Homer, and Moses, was black.

56. Robert Alexander Young, *The Ethiopian Manifesto, Issued in Defence of the Black Man's Rights in the Scale of Universal Freedom* (New York: Printed for the Author, 1828), rpt. in Richard Newman, Patrick Rael, and Philip Lapsansky, eds., *Pamphlets of Protest: An Anthology of Early African American Protest Literature,*

1790-1860 (New York: Routledge, 2001), pp. 85–89. Very little has been written on Young: see Sterling Stuckey's introduction in *The Ideological Origins of Black Nationalism*, Sterling Stuckey, ed. (Boston: Beacon Press, 1972), and Vincent E. Harding, *There Is a River: The Black Struggle for Freedom in America* (New York: Harcourt Brace Jovanovich, 1981), pp. 84–85.

57. Young, *Ethiopian Manifesto*, pp. 86–87.

58. Ibid., pp. 87–88.

59. Ibid., p. 89.

60. *David Walker's Appeal to the Coloured Citizens of the World*, ed. Peter P. Hinks (University Park: Pennsylvania State University Press, 2000); hereafter cited as Walker, *Appeal*. Hinks is now the major scholarly authority on Walker: at several points, my analysis develops his basic approach in Peter P. Hinks, *To Awaken My Afflicted Brethren: David Walker and the Problem of Antebellum Slave Resistance* (University Park: Pennsylvania State University Press, 1997).

61. Walker, *Appeal*, p. 74.

62. Hinks, *To Awaken My Afflicated Brethren;* see esp. p. 198.

63. Harrison Gray Otis to William Thorne Williams, mayor of Savannah, February 10, 1830, letter originally printed in the *Richmond Examiner*, February 18, 1830, and rpt. in Walker, *Appeal*, pp. 98–99. On Walker's death, see Hinks, *To Awaken My Afflicated Brethren*, pp. 269–272.

64. Hinks, *To Awaken My Afflicted Brethren*, p. 213.

65. Walker, *Appeal*, p. 34.

66. Ibid., p. 3.

67. See Hinks, *To Awaken My Afflicted Brethren*, p. 195.

68. Walker, *Appeal*, p. 58.

69. Ibid., p. 16.

70. Ibid., p. 19.

71. Ibid., pp. 19–20.

72. Ibid., pp. 17, 32.

73. Ibid., p. 77.

74. Scott Trafton, "Egypt Land: Race and the Cultural Politics of American Egyptomania, 1800–1900" (Ph.d. Diss., Duke University, 1998), p. 315.

75. Walker, *Appeal*, p. 10.

76. Ibid., p. 23.

77. Ibid., pp. 21–22.

78. Ibid., pp. 22–23.

79. Ibid., p. 73.

80. Hinks, "Introduction," to Walker, *Appeal*, p. xxxiv.

81. Walker, *Appeal*, pp. 20, 25, 27.

5. CONCEIVING UNIVERSAL EQUALITY

1. George Fredrickson, *The Black Image in the White Mind: The Debate on Afro-American Character and Destiny, 1817–1914* (Middletown, CT: Wesleyan University Press, 1987, ©1971), pp. 27–42.

2. James Brewer Stewart, *Holy Warriors: The Abolitionists and American Slavery*, rev. ed. (New York: Hill and Wang, 1996); Ronald G. Walters, *The Antislavery Appeal: American Abolitionism after 1830* (Baltimore: Johns Hopkins University Press, 1976), pp. 52, 67–68.

3. In my investigation, I began with Fredrickson's one major citation for Garrisonian race theory in the 1830s, "The Diversity of Men," by "M," in the *Quarterly Anti-Slavery Magazine*, 2 (1837): 199–208. A reading of the rest of the *Quarterly*, the most intellectual abolitionist organ of the day, suggested that a focus upon the relationship between West Indian emancipation and Garrison's views of Haiti, Egypt, and race theory might be revealing, especially in contrast with the proslavery literature of the day.

4. Paul Goodman, *Of One Blood: Abolitionism and the Origins of Racial Equality* (Berkeley: University of California Press, 1998), pp. 36–44; Henry Mayer, *All on Fire: William Lloyd Garrison and the Abolition of Slavery* (New York: St. Martin's Press, 1998), p. 109.

5. William Lloyd Garrison, "To the Public," *Liberator*, January 1, 1831. Richard S. Newman, *The Transformation of American Abolitionism: Fighting Slavery in the Early Republic* (Chapel Hill: University of North Carolina Press, 2002), esp. pp. 86–106.

6. Lawrence Friedman, *Gregarious Saints: Self and Community in American Abolitionism, 1830–1870* (Cambridge: Cambridge University Press, 1982), p. 21.

7. A host of studies have explored the relationship between capitalism and antislavery; without doubt the most important remains David Brion Davis, *The Problem of Slavery in the Age of Revolution, 1770–1823* (1975; New York: Oxford University Press, 1999); see also the influential debate spurred by Davis, which appears in Thomas Bender, ed., *The Antislavery Debate: Capitalism and Abolitionism as a Problem in Historical Interpretation* (Berkeley: University of California Press, 1992).

8. The strongest proponents of this defense of Garrison and his white cohorts are Goodman, *Of One Blood* (see esp. pp. 65–172) and Henry Mayer, *All on Fire*.

9. On black "uplift," see two classic early articles: Frederick Cooper, "Elevating the Race: The Social Thought of Black Leaders, 1827-50," *American Quarterly*, 24 (1972): 604-625; George A. Levesque, "Interpreting Early Black Ideology: A Reappraisal of the Historical Consensus," *Journal of the Early Republic*, 1 (1981): 269-287; see also James Oliver Horton and Lois E. Horton, "The Affirmation of Manhood: Black Garrisonians in Boston," in *Courage and Conscience: Black and White Abolitionists in Boston*, ed. Donald M. Jacobs (Bloomington: Published for the Boston Athenaeum by Indiana University Press, 1993), pp. 127-153; Patrick Rael, *Black Identify and Black Protest in the Antebellum North* (Chapel Hill: University of North Carolina Press, 2002), pp. 157-208. In a provocative recent piece, James Brewer Stewart ("The Emergence of Racial Modernity and the Rise of the White North, 1790-1840," *Journal of the Early Republic*, 18 [1998]: 181-217, and see also the "Comments" by Jean R. Soderlund, James Oliver Horton, and Ronald G. Walters, as well as Stewart's "Response," [pp. 218-236]) has argued that the 1820s and early 1830s saw the rise of an uplift ideology held in common by white evangelical immediatists and free black leaders. According to Stewart, this ideology held that a "respectable" and integrated reform community would uplift and redeem the nation, converting all whites to antislavery and uplifting all blacks from slavery's depradations. In Stewart's view, the backlash against this interracial effort at moral reform created the bitter race-mindedness that has greatly characterized American public discourse ever since. In my view, irrespective of the much-mooted question of whether one can speak of a moment of transition to "racial modernity" (discussed at length by the commentators on Stewart's essay, especially Soderlund and Walters), Stewart overplays the similarities between the ideologies expressed by white immediatists and free blacks. See below, especially discussion of "T. T."

10. Discussions of the problem of "blackness" and the Enlightenment might best begin with Frantz Fanon, *Black Skin, White Masks*, trans. Charles Lam Markham (1952; London: Pluto Press, 1986). Perhaps the two most influential recent conceptualizations of the problem have been Henry Louis Gates, Jr., *The Signifying Monkey: A Theory of African-American Literary Criticism* (New York: Oxford University Press, 1988); and especially of late, Paul Gilroy, *The Black Atlantic: Modernity and Double Consciousness* (Cambridge: Harvard University Press, 1993). William L. Andrews, *To Tell a Free Story: The First Century of Afro-American Autobiography, 1760-1865* (Urbana: University of Illinois Press, 1986), is particularly good on the problem of the Enlightenment and evangelical Christianity in early "black" writing.

11. See two articles by Donald M. Jacobs: "David Walker and William Lloyd Garrison: Racial Cooperation and the Shaping of Boston Abolition," in *Courage*

and Conscience: Black and White Abolitionists in Boston, Jacobs, ed., pp. 1–20; "William Lloyd Garrison's *Liberator* and Boston's Blacks, 1830–1865," *New England Quarterly,* 44 (1971): 259–277.

12. *Liberator,* October 29, 1831.

13. Ibid., August 11, 1832.

14. Robert B. Hall, "Slavery and the Means of Removal," delivered to New England Antislavery Society, March 26, 1832, printed in *Liberator,* April 14, 1832.

15. William Lloyd Garrison, "Some Remarks on the Former and Present State of St. Domingo and Hayti," *Liberator,* March 10, 1832. On Garrison and Haiti, see also Alfred N. Hunt, *Haiti's Influence on Antebellum America: Slumbering Volcano in the Caribbean* (Baton Rouge: Louisiana State University Press, 1988), pp. 92–93, 153–154, 156, 172.

16. *Liberator,* May 14, 1831; this article, by "V," "a gentleman of talents, whose opinion we solicited on the subject of his criticism" (Garrison introducing the piece [May 14]), appeared in three parts: April 30, May 14, May 28, 1831.

17. William Lloyd Garrison, *An Address Delivered in Marlboro Chapel, Boston, July 4, 1838* (Boston: Isaac Knapp, 1838), p. 28. For an interesting discussion of Garrison's notions of restraint and manhood and how those notions were received by free African Americans, see James Oliver Horton and Lois E. Horton, "Violence, Protest, and Identity: Black Manhood in Antebellum America," in James Oliver Horton, *Free People of Color: Inside the African American Community* (Washington, DC: Smithsonian Institution Press, 1993), pp. 80–98.

18. *Liberator,* April 14, May 5, 1832.

19. William Lloyd Garrison, *Thoughts on African Colonization* (Boston: Garrison & Knapp, 1832), p. 142.

20. Ibid., p. 142.

21. See David Brion Davis, *Slavery and Human Progress* (New York: Oxford University Press, 1984); James Walvin, "The Rise of British Popular Sentiment for Abolition, 1787–1832," in Christine Bolt and Seymour Drescher, eds., *Anti-Slavery, Religion, and Reform: Essays in Memory of Roger Anstey* (Folkestone, England: Archon Books, 1980), pp. 146–162; James Walvin, *England, Slaves, and Freedom, 1776–1838* (Jackson: University Press of Mississippi, 1986); James Walvin, ed., *Slavery and British Society, 1776–1846* (Baton Rouge: Louisiana State University Press, 1982); Seymour Drescher, *Capitalism and Antislavery: British Mobilization in Comparative Perspective* (New York: Oxford University Press, 1987).

22. "The Agricultural Code of St. Domingo," *Quarterly Anti-Slavery Magazine,* 1 (1836): 135.

23. St. Domingue, Wright declared, "once teemed with an immense population

of degraded slaves." Now it harbored a much larger number of free people who had organized themselves into an independent government and who showed no desire to give up the experiment and return to bondage. "How the intervening 'horrors,'" he wrote, "could have been conjured into an anti-liberty beacon, to scare men so proud of their own 'blood-bought liberty' as our countrymen, is a mystery worthy of solution. Does the secret lie in that portentous monosyllable, black? This deepens the mystery. The more probable hypothesis is, that truth may have met with foul play, somewhere between the two facts above mentioned." Elizur Wright, "Horrors of St. Domingue," *Quarterly Anti-Slavery Magazine*, 1 (1836): 241–306; quotation on p. 241.

24. Wright and Garrison quoted in Lawrence B. Goodheart, *Abolitionist, Actuary, Atheist: Elizur Wright and the Reform Impulse* (Kent, OH: Kent State University Press, 1990), p. 74.

25. M, "Diversities," p. 206.

26. Samuel Stanhope Smith, *An Essay on the Causes of Variety of Complexion and Figure in the Human Species*, 2d ed. (1810; rpt., ed. Winthrop Jordan, Cambridge: Belknap Press of Harvard University Press, 1965), p. 155.

27. M, "Diversities," p. 210.

28. Ibid., pp. 208–209.

29. For an interesting presentation of the case that immediatism's emergence "was as much a response to the frustrations of external opposition as it was a product of inner evangelical zeal," see David W. Blight, "Perceptions of Southern Intransigence and the Rise of Radical Antislavery Thought, 1816–1830," *Journal of the Early Republic*, 3 (1983): 139–163; quotation on p. 162.

30. *Emancipator*, November 18, 1834, discussed in Walters, *Antislavery Appeal*, p. 59.

31. Thomas Roderick Dew, *Vindication of Personal Slavery*, rpt. in Drew Gilpin Faust, ed., *The Ideology of Slavery: Proslavery Thought in the Antebellum South, 1830–1860* (Baton Rouge: Louisiana State University Press, 1981). William Jay, "Remarks on Professor Dew's Vindication of Personal Slavery," *Quarterly Anti-Slavery Magazine*, 1 (1836): 211–226.

32. Dew, *Vindication*, pp. 53–56.

33. Jay, "Remarks," p. 224.

34. Dew, *Vindication*, p. 24.

35. Eugene D. Genovese, *The Slaveholders' Dilemma: Freedom and Progress in Southern Conservative Thought, 1820–1860* (Columbia: University of South Carolina Press, 1992).

36. "T. T.," The *Liberator*, April 2, 30, 1831. Stewart, in "Racial Modernity,"

makes "T. T." into an example of early Garrisonian aspirations to create an integrated elite of "respectability" to uplift the nation and end slavery. I do not mean, by contrast, to expose T. T. as a racist, only to show how greatly his or her perspective on race and history differed from, yet likely partly derived from, that of a Walker or Cornish. For early white Garrisonians, that is, "uplift" implied transcendence of the past, even, for T. T. at any rate, racial amalgamation blending away previously real and lamentable distinctions. African Americans preaching uplift took the force of the past, its violence and terrors, more seriously; as Stewart himself elsewhere observes, they "were hardly receptive to the romantic utopianism of the white reformers' religion" (Stewart, *Holy Warriors,* p. 139).

6. BLACK IMMEDIATISM

1. Hosea Easton, *A Treatise on the Intellectual Character and Civil and Political Condition of the Colored People of the U. States; and the Prejudice Exercised towards Them: With a Sermon on the Duty of the Church to Them* (Boston: I. Knapp, 1837), rpt. in George R. Price and James Bewer Stewart, *To Heal the Scourge of Prejudice: the Life and Writings of Hosea Easton* (Amherst: University of Massachusetts Press, 1999), pp. 64–123 (hereafter cited as Easton, *Treatise*). The sermon on the duty of the church did not appear.

2. For Garrisonianism's impact on black leadership, see James Oliver Horton, *Free People of Color: Inside the African American Community* (Washington, DC: Smithsonian Institution Press, 1993), pp. 46–57.

3. See the *Liberator,* March 18, 1837, *et seq.,* for advertisements and endorsements of Easton's *Treatise.*

4. George R. Price and James Brewer Stewart, "Hosea Easton and the Agony of Race," in Price and Stewart, eds., *To Heal the Scourge of Prejudice,* pp. 1–48.

5. Hosea Easton and Henry Tyler to editor, *Freedom's Journal,* April 25, 1828. Easton and Tyler declared that "the Freedom's Journal had been conducted in a manner satisfactory to the subscribers and to the Colored community at large." They reported that at the meeting Walker declared (in terms already showing the influence of Jeffersonian language about the "wheel of fortune") that too many free blacks were passive and ignorant: "if we continue to slumber on and take our ease, our wheel of reformation will progress but slowly." Easton was also listed in the *Liberator* as one of several people convening a meeting of Boston's people of color to discuss colonization (*Liberator,* February 26, 1831).

6. Price and Stewart, "Easton and the Agony of Race," pp. 3–10; Easton, *Treatise,* pp. 110–111.

7. Hosea Easton, *An Address: Delivered before the Coloured Population, of Prov-*

idence, Rhode Island, on Thanksgiving Day (Boston, 1828), Library of Congress Rare Book Collections Theological Pamphlets, vol. 29, pp. 8, 4. I am indebted to George Price and James Brewer Stewart for having brought this pamphlet to my attention. They reprint Easton's "I tremble" in *To Heal the Scourge of Prejudice* (pp. 49–62), but Easton's "Address" passage differs and seems perhaps garbled in their version (see pp. 52–53); the passage I quote about prejudice is the same in both versions (p. 56 in Price and Stewart's edition).

8. On the convention movement, see Howard Holman Bell, *A Survey of the Negro Convention Movement, 1830–1861* (1953; rpt. New York: Arno Press, 1969), esp. pp. 10–37; also *Minutes of the Proceedings of the National Negro Conventions, 1830–1864,* ed. Howard Holman Bell (New York: Arno Press, 1969); Eddie Glaude, *Exodus! Religion, Race, and Nation in Early Nineteenth-Century Black America* (Chicago: University of Chicago Press, 2000). *The Rights of All* reported the Cincinnati situation on August 14, 1829. See also *Colored American,* October 7, 1837. Patrick Rael, in *Black Identity and Protest in the Antebellum North* (Chapel Hill: University of North Carolina Press, 2002), paints a collective portrait of the delegates' backgrounds and class status (pp. 27–44; quotation on p. 43).

9. "Conventional Address," *Minutes,* 1832, p. 36.

10. "Resolved, that this committee would recommend to the members of this Convention, to discountenance, by all just means in their power, any emigration to Liberia or Hayti, believing them only calculated to distract and divide the whole colored family." Canadian emigration was understandable if unfortunate. (*Minutes,* 1832, p. 8; see also pp. 10–20.)

11. *Minutes,* 1832, p. 12; 1833, pp. 21–24; Easton, *Treatise,* pp. 30–31.

12. On the New Haven school project see Bell, *Survey of the Negro Convention Movement,* pp. 20–26, and Price and Stewart, "Easton and the Agony of Race," pp. 16–19.

13. "Declaration of Sentiment," in *Minutes,* 1834, pp. 27–28; rpt. in *Minutes,* 1835, pp. 21ff; see also "Conventional Address," in *Minutes,* 1832, p. 36.

14. Price and Stewart, "Easton and the Agony of Race," pp. 23–24.

15. Easton, *Treatise,* p. 67.

16. Herbert Hovenkamp surveys "Biblical science" at length in *Religion and Science in America, 1800–1860* (Philadelphia: University of Pennsylvania Press, 1978).

17. William R. Stanton, *The Leopard's Spots: Scientific Attitudes toward Race in America, 1815–59* (Chicago: University of Chicago Press, 1960).

18. The literature on these subjects is immense; for some discussion of such writing with reference to race and ethnology in the United States, see Chapter 7.

19. Easton, *Treatise,* p. 68.

20. Ibid., p. 68–69.

21. Ibid., pp. 69–70.

22. Ibid., p. 72.

23. Ibid., p. 73.

24. Ibid., pp. 80–83.

25. Ibid., p. 86.

26. William Charles Wells, "An Account of a Female of the White Race of Mankind, Part of whose Skin Resembles that of a Negro, with some Observations on the Causes of the Differences in Colour and Form between the White and Negro Races of Men," in *Two Essays: Upon Single Vision with Two Eyes; the Other on Dew* (London: Archibald Constable and Co., 1818), pp. 423–439.

27. Easton, *Treatise*, p. 85.

28. Oswei Temkin, "German Concepts of Ontogeny and History around 1800," in his *The Double Face of Janus, and Other Essays in the History of Medicine* (Baltimore: Johns Hopkins University Press, 1977), pp. 373–389; Peter Hanns Reill, "Science and the Science of History in the Spätaufklärung," in H. Bödeker et al., eds., *Aufklärung und Geschichte: Studien zur deutschen Geschichtswissenschaft im 18. Jahrhundert* (Göttingen: Vandenhoeck & Ruprecht, 1986), pp. 431–451; Claude Blanckaert, "On the Origins of French Ethnology: William Edwards and the Doctrine of Race," in George W. Stocking, ed., *Bones, Bodies, and Behavior: Essays on Biological Anthropology* (Madison: University of Wisconsin Press, 1988), p. 28.

29. Johann Gottfried von Herder, *Outlines of a Philosophy of the History of Mankind,* trans. T. Churchill (London, 1800), vol. 1, pp. 260, 267. For a thoughtful evocation of this work as an example of cultural nationalism, see Frank Manuel's introduction to his abridged edition of the *Outlines,* entitled *Reflections on the Philosophy of the History of Mankind* (Chicago: University of Chicago Press, 1968).

30. Easton, *Treatise,* p. 88.

31. Ibid., p. 89.

32. Ibid., p. 89.

33. Ibid., p. 96.

34. Ibid., p. 102.

35. Ibid., p. 107.

36. Ibid., pp. 105–106.

37. Ibid., p. 108.

38. Ibid., p. 114.

39. Ibid., p. 118.

40. Ibid., p. 120.

41. Ibid., p. 119.

7. THE NEW ETHNOLOGY

1. Samuel George Morton, *Crania Americana; or, A Comparative View of the Skulls of Various Aboriginal Nations of North and South America; to Which Is Affixed an Essay on the Variety of the Human Species*. . . (Philadelphia: J. Pennington, 1839); Samuel George Morton, *Crania Aegyptiaca; or, Observations on Egyptian Ethnography, Derived from Anatomy, History and the Monuments* (Philadelphia: J. Pennington, 1844).

2. For Morton's life, see William S. Stanton, *The Leopard's Spots: Scientific Attitudes toward Race in America, 1815-59* (Chicago: University of Chicago Press, 1960), esp. pp. 24–44.

3. Henry S. Patterson, "Notice of the Life and Scientific Labors of the late Samuel Geo. Morton, M.D.," in Josiah C. Nott and George R. Gliddon, eds., *Types of Mankind: Or, Ethnological Researches* . . . (Philadelphia: Lippincott & Grambo, 1854), pp. xxxii, xxix.

4. On *Crania Americana*, see Robert E. Bieder, *Science Encounters the Indian, 1820–1880* (Norman: University of Oklahoma Press, 1986), pp. 55–103.

5. Child quoted in Charles Colbert, *A Measure of Perfection: Phrenology and the Fine Arts in America* (Chapel Hill: University of North Carolina Press, 1997), p. 215; on craniology, Stowe, and *Uncle Tom's Cabin*, see pp. 240–241.

6. Morton, *Crania Americana*, p. i; George Combe, "Phrenological Remarks on the Relation between the Natural Talents and Dispositions of Nations, and the Developments of their Brains," in ibid. Colbert, *A Measure of Perfection* discusses Morton on pp. 215–218.

7. Morton, *Crania Americana*, p. 29.

8. Scott Trafton, "Egypt Land: Race and the Cultural Politics of American Egyptomania, 1800–1900" (Ph.d. Diss, Duke University, 1998).

9. Samuel George Morton, unpaged journal of 1837 Jamaica trip, Morton Papers, American Philosophical Society (25 pp.).

10. Ibid.

11. Stanton, *Leopard's Spots*, p. 27.

12. See, for example, Communipaw [James McCune Smith], in *Frederick Douglass's Paper*, January 8, 1852, discussed in Chapter 8.

13. See Jean Baptiste Lamarck, *Zoological Philosophy; an Exposition with Regard to the Natural History of Animal*, trans. H. Eliot (London: Macmillan, 1914); *Histoire naturelle des animaux sans vertèbres* . . . , 11 vols. (Paris: Verdière, 1815–1822); Robert J. Richards, *Darwin and the Emergence of Evolutionary Theories of Mind and Behavior* (Chicago: University of Chicago Press, 1987); Pietro Corsi, *The Age of Lamarck: Evolutionary Theories in France, 1790–1830* (Berkeley: Uni-

versity of California Press, 1988); Charles Coulston Gillispie, "Lamarck and Darwin in the History of Science," in Bentley Glass, Oswei Temkin, and William L. Straus, Jr., eds., *Forerunners of Darwin: 1745–1859* (Baltimore: Johns Hopkins Press, 1959), pp. 265–291. For Lamarck as a response to "degenerationism," see the excellent summary of early nineteenth-century biological thought in David J. Depew and Bruce H. Weber, *Darwinism Evolving: Systems Dynamics and the Genealogy of Natural Selection* (Cambridge: MIT Press, 1995). For Lamarckianism's and transformationism's radicalism and uses to radicals and middle-class reformers, see Adrian J. Desmond, *The Politics of Evolution: Morphology, Medicine, and Reform in Radical London* (Chicago: University of Chicago Press, 1989); see also Philip Sloan's review of Desmond in *History of Science,* 28 (1990): 419–428.

14. For British fears, retreats, and compromises, see Depew and Weber, *Darwinism Evolving,* and also Adrian Desmond and James Moore, *Darwin: The Career of a Tormented Evolutionist* (New York: W. W. Norton, 1994).

15. For Prichard's refutation of Blumenbach and Stanhope Smith's theory that excessive bile production causes black skin, see James Cowles Prichard, *Researches into the Physical History of Man,* 1st ed. (1813: rpt., ed. George W. Stocking, Chicago: University of Chicago Press, 1973), p. 179.

16. Stocking, "From Chronology to Ethnology," introduction to Prichard, *Researches,* 1813 edition, pp. lix–lxi.

17. Prichard, *Researches,* 3d ed., vol.5, p. 374; and see Stocking, "From Chronology to Ethnology," lxxxiv–lxxxv.

18. Prichard, *Researches,* 3d ed., vol. 5, p. 552; see also Stocking, "From Chronology to Ethnology," pp. xcvii–xcviii.

19. The best short evocation of Cuvier's aims and his place in nineteenth-century biology appears in Depew and Weber, *Darwinism Evolving,* pp. 33–56. Toby A. Appel, *The Cuvier-Geoffroy Debate: French Biology in the Decades before Darwin* (New York: Oxford University Press, 1987). See also on Cuvier, Ernst Mayr, *The Growth of Biological Thought: Diversity, Evolution, and Inheritance* (Cambridge: Belknap Press of Harvard University Press, 1982); Michael Banton, *Racial Theories* (New York: Cambridge University Press, 1987); Dorinda Outram, *Georges Cuvier: Vocation, Science, and Authority in Post-revolutionary France* (Manchester: Manchester University Press, 1984).

20. Appel, *The Cuvier-Geoffroy Debate.*

21. Morton, *Crania Aegyptiaca,* p. 3.

22. The 1795 *Natural Variety* of Man and the 1805 *Contributions* both appear in Johann Friedrich Blumenbach, *The Anthropological Treatises,* trans. and ed. Thomas Bendyshe (London: Pub. for the Anthropological Society by Longman,

Green, Longman, Roberts, & Green, 1865); quote from 1795 *Natural Variety* on p. 231; for the 1805 *Contributions,* see in particular p. 312. Both these works are discussed above in Chapter 2.

23. Morton, *Crania Aegyptiaca,* p. 66. Why Morton (and Wiseman) treated Blumenbach in this way is suggested by how another prominent nineteenth-century anthropologist dealt with Blumenbach. In 1865, Cambridge University scholar Thomas Bendyshe published what remains the only translation into English of Blumenbach's anthropological works, including virtually the entire texts of the 1775 and 1795 editions of the *Natural History of Man,* as well as substantial portions of the 1806 *Contributions,* including the chapter on Negro intellect. Unlike Morton but like Prichard, Bendyshe was a monogenist and not averse to the idea of accomplished individual blacks—just to Negroes as part founders of Western civilization. In his translation, Bendyshe excluded the sections of the 1806 and 1811 *Contributions* concerning Egypt, material that, he said in his preface to the translation, "as may be supposed, is considerably behind the knowledge of the present day . . . yet the whole essay has been pronounced lately by a competent writer to be 'in some sort not worthy of that great authority.'" (Thomas Bendyshe, "Editor's Preface," in Blumenbach, *The Anthropological Treatises,* p. ix.) What made that "competent writer," who was French Egyptologist J. A. N. Perrier, deem the later *Contributions* on Egypt "unworthy" seems easy to guess: Blumenbach's claim that one third of the Egyptians resembled Negroes.

24. Morton, *Crania Aegyptiaca,* p. 66.

25. Ibid., p. 66.

26. Ibid., p. 43.

27. Ibid., pp. 64–65, 60.

28. Stephen Jay Gould, *The Mismeasure of Man,* rev. ed. (New York: Norton, 1996), pp. 82–104.

29. Stanton, *Leopard's Spots,* pp. 61–65.

30. James Cowles Prichard, *The Natural History of Man: Comprising Inquiries into the Modifying Influence of Physical and Moral Agencies on the Different Tribes of the Human Family* (London: Baillière, 1843), pp. 570–571; Prichard to Morton, February 17, 1840, Morton Papers, American Philosophical Society.

31. Prichard, *Natural History of Man,* pp. 105–106.

32. Morton's letter rpt. in Henry S. Patterson, "Notice," pp. li–lii.

33. George R. Gliddon to Ephraim George Squier, November 11, 1850, quoted in Stanton, *Leopard's Spots,* p. 143; an explorer and diplomat, Squier was a minor member of the American School and a sort of protégé of Morton's.

34. Nott, "Introduction," *Types of Mankind,* p. 52.

35. Patterson, "Notice," in Nott and Gliddon, *Types,* p. li. Trafton reads this passage somewhat differently in "Egypt Land," p. 89.

36. Josiah C. Nott, *Two Lectures on Connection between the Biblical and Physical History of Man, Delivered . . . December 1848* (New York: Bartlett & Welford, 1849), p. 80; Herbert Hovenkamp, *Science and Religion in America, 1800–1860* (Philadelphia: University of Pennsylvania Press, 1978). On Lepsius, see Suzanne L. Marchand, "The End of Egyptomania: German Scholarship and the Banalization of Egypt," pp. 3–16.

37. Moses Ashley Curtis, "Unity of the Races," *Southern Quarterly Review* 7 (1845): 372–448; see also Nott's reply, "Dr. Nott's Reply to 'C,'" *Southern Quarterly Review* 8 (1845): 148–190.

38. Nott, "Introduction," *Types,* p. 56.

39. William Harper, *Memoir on Slavery,* rpt. in Drew Gilpin Faust, ed., *The Ideology of Slavery: Proslavery Thought in the Antebellum South, 1830–1860* (Baton Rouge: Louisiana State University Press, 1981), pp. 126, 120; James Roper, *The Founding of Memphis,* 1818–1820 ([Memphis]: Memphis Sesquicentennial [1970]); John Preston Young, ed., *Standard History of Memphis, from a Study of the Original Sources* (Knoxville: Crew, 1912). To get some idea of how proslavery use of Egypt differed from that of ancient Greece and Rome, see J. Drew Harrington's survey article, "Classical Antiquity and the Proslavery Argument," *Slavery and Abolition,* 10 (1989): 60–72; also articles on the South in John Eadie, ed., *The Classical Tradition in Early America* (Ann Arbor: University of Michigan Press, 1976); and Harvey Wish, "Aristotle, Plato, and the Mason-Dixon Line," *Journal of the History of Ideas,* 9 (1949): 254–266. For the influence of the American School generally, see Reginald Horsman, *Race and Manifest Destiny: The Origins of American Racial Anglo-Saxonism* (Cambridge: Harvard University press, 1981).

40. George Fredrickson, *The Black Image in the White Mind: The Debate on Afro-American Character and Destiny, 1817–1914* (Middletown, CT: Wesleyan University Press, 1987, ©1971), pp. 88–89.

41. For *Types*'s publication history, see Reginald Horsman, *Josiah Nott of Mobile: Southernor, Physician, and Racial Theorist* (Baton Rouge: Louisiana State University Press, 1988), pp. 178–179.

42. Eugene D. Genovese, *The Slaveholders' Dilemma: Freedom and Progress in Southern Conservative Thought, 1820–1860* (Columbia: University of South Carolina Press, 1992); on Hammond's career, see Drew Gilpin Faust, *James Henry Hammond and the Old South: A Design for Mastery* (Baton Rouge: Louisiana State University Press, 1982).

8. EFFACING THE INDIVIDUAL

1. George Fredrickson, *The Black Image in the White Mind: The Debate on Afro-American Character and Destiny, 1817-1914* (Middletown, CT: Wesleyan University Press, 1987, c 1971), pp. 97-129. Fredrickson interpreted Stowe's second antislavery novel, *Dred: A Tale of the Great Dismal Swamp* (Boston: Phillips, Sampson, 1856)—which concerned a slave revolt and cast mulattoes as tortured, even Byronic figures—as an extension of white "romantic racialism." Robert S. Levine has recently argued that, on the contrary, correspondance and contact with African Americans, especially Frederick Douglass and Martin Delany, shaped *Dred*, which in his view differed substantially from *Uncle Tom's Cabin* (Robert S. Levine, *Martin Delany, Frederick Douglass, and the Politics of Representative Identity* [Chapel Hill: University of North Carolina Press, 1997], pp. 144-176). The literature on African American writing in the 1840s and 1850s (especially on Douglass) has become large; Levine's book is a good place to start for an overview.

2. Alexander Crummell, *The Eulogy on Henry Highland Garnet* (New York: 1882), reprinted in Vernon Loggins, *The Negro Author: His Development in America to 1900* (Port Washington, N.Y.: Kennikat Press, 1964), p. 182.

3. See Dov Ospovat, *The Development of Darwin's Theory: Natural History, Natural Theology, and Natural Selection, 1838-1859* (New York: Cambridge University Press, 1981).

4. Reginald Horsman, *Josiah Nott of Mobile: Southernor, Physician, and Racial Theorist* (Baton Rouge: Louisiana State University Press, 1988), pp. 113-115; William R. Stanton, *The Leopard's Spots: Scientific Attitudes toward Race in America, 1815-59* (Chicago: University of Chicago Press, 1960), pp. 147-154. Nott's paper on the Jews was printed in the American Association for the Advancement of Science, *Proceedings*, 3 (1850): 98-106.

5. For Nott's communications to Morton, see Horsman, *Josiah Nott*, pp. 117-118.

6. Josiah C. Nott and George R. Gliddon, *Indigenous Races of the Earth; or, New Chapters of Ethnological Inquiry . . .* (Philadelphia, 1857).

7. Josiah C. Nott, "The Mulatto a Hybrid—Probable Extermination of the Two Races If the Whites and Blacks are Allowed to Intermarry," *American Journal of the Medical Sciences*, 6 (1843): 252-256.

8. This notion appeared in *Types*, but was seemingly first advanced and most boldly stated by Nott in two essays of 1853: "Geographical Distribution of Animals and the Races of Man," *New Orleans Medical and Surgical Journal*, 9 (1853):

727–746, and "Aboriginal Races of America," *Southern Quarterly Review,* 8 (1853): 59–92. Nott described the Caucasian as a "cosmopolite" in "Geographical Distribution," p. 743.

9. Josiah C. Nott, *Two Lectures on Connection Between the Biblical and Physical History of Man, Delivered . . . December 1848* (New York: Bartlett & Welford, 1849).

10. Compte Arthur de Gobineau, *The Moral and Intellectual Diversity of Races . . .*, trans. H. Hotz (Philadelphia: Lippincott, 1856). The translator was a friend of Nott's. Gobineau's complaints are discussed in Michael D. Biddiss, *Father of Racist Ideology: The Social and Political Thought of Count Gobineau* (New York: Weyright and Talley, 1970) and Horsman, *Josiah Nott,* pp. 204–205.

11. *Mobile Register,* December 19, 1855; see also Horsman, *Josiah Nott,* p. 207.

12. Horsman, *Josiah Nott,* p. 210.

13. James McCune Smith to Gerrit Smith, December 28, 1846, May 12, 1848, in *Black Abolitionist Papers, 1830–1865,* comps. and eds., George E. Carter and C. Peter Ripley (Sanford, NC: Microfilming Corporation of America, 1981). David W. Blight perceptively discusses the letters to Gerrit Smith and further notes that McCune Smith's despair sometimes descended into unattractive self-pity. (David W. Blight, "In Search of Learning, Liberty, and Self-Definition: James McCune Smith and the Ordeal of the Antebellum Black Intellectual," *Afro-Americans in New York Life and History,* 9 (1985): 1–25; McCune Smith's self-pity discussed, p. 15.)

14. James McCune Smith, "Introduction," to Frederick Douglass, *My Bondage and My Freedom,* ed. William L. Andrews (Urbana: University of Illinois Press, 1987), pp. 10–11.

15. James McCune Smith, "On the Influence of Opium upon the Colonical Functions," *New York Journal of Medicine,* 2 (1844), reprinted in *Black Abolitionist Papers.* James McCune Smith, "The Fallacy of Phrenology," *Colored American,* September 23, September 30, and October 28, 1837. For McCune Smith's debates with polygenists, see W. Montague Cobb, "James McCune Smith," *Journal of the National Medical Association,* 44 (March 1952): 160–163. On McCune Smith as a doctor, see Leslie A. Falk, "Black Abolitionist Doctors and Healers, 1810–1865," *Bulletin of the History of Medicine,* 54 (1980): 258–272. McCune Smith himself chronicled his trip to Glasgow in a journal, four extracts of which appeared as "Dr. Smith's Journal," in *Colored American,* November 11, December 2, 16, 1837; June 30, 1838. On his return from Glasgow, McCune Smith found himself subject to racism from the captain of the ship that was to take him home; *Colored American,* February 17, 1838, ran the outraged letter written to the captain by one of Smith's compatriots at the University of Glasgow.

16. *Frederick Douglass's Paper,* March 25, 1852.

17. Ibid.

18. *Frederick Douglass's Paper,* June 17, 1852.

19. *Frederick Douglass's Paper,* June 17, 1852, and see Blight, "In Search of Learning," pp. 11–12.

20. Blight, "In Search of Learning," p. 8.

21. John Stauffer, *The Black Hearts of Men: Radical Abolitionists and the Transformation of Race* (Cambridge: Harvard University Press, 2002), quotation p. 283.

22. Samuel G. Morton, ["Some Observations of the Bushman Hottentot Boy"], Academy of Natural Sciences of Philadelphia *Proceedings,* 4 (1848): 5–7. William Stanton uses the incident of Morton examining the "Bushman" boy to lead off his study of the American School, *The Leopard's Spots,* pp. 1–2; Stanton does not mention the New York meeting.

23. "Annual Meeting of the Colored Orphan Asylum," *National Anti-Slavery Standard,* February 22, 1849. The *Standard* also ran a copy of a letter about Henry's history that Chase sent to the Lyceum of Natural History in New York City (later the New York Academy of Sciences).

24. "Annual Meeting of the Colored Orphan Asylum."

25. Ibid.

26. Ibid. The "Mr. Ledyard" that McCune Smith referred to must have been the British diplomat and archaeologist Austen Henry Layard, whose report on his excavations of Nineveh had just come out.

27. *Frederick Douglass's Paper,* January 1852. On Squier, see Robert E. Bieder, *Science Encounters the Indian, 1820–1880* (Norman, Oklahoma: University of Oklahoma Press, 1986), pp. 104–145.

28. *Frederick Douglass's Paper,* January 1852.

29. Ibid.

30. James McCune Smith, "Memorial to the U.S. Congress," *New York Tribune,* February 1, 17, 24, 1844; quotation, February 1. The Census controversy is too well known to be gone over in depth here. See Norman Dain, *Concepts of Insanity in the United States, 1789–1865* (New Brunswick, NJ: Rutgers University Press, 1964), pp. 104–108; Patricia Cline Cohen, *A Calculating People: The Spread of Numeracy in Early America* (1982; New York: Routledge, 1999), pp. 175–204; and Stanton, *Leopard's Spots,* pp. 58–66.

31. James McCune Smith, *The Destiny of the People of Color: A Lecture, Delivered before the Philomathean Society and Hamilton Lyceum, in January, 1841,* (New York, 1843), pp. 4, 8.

32. James McCune Smith, *A Dissertation on The Influence of Climate on Longevity,* (New York: Office of the Merchant's Magazine, 1846).

33. McCune Smith to Douglass, *Frederick Douglass's Paper,* October 16, 1861; Douglass to McCune Smith, *Frederick Douglass's Paper,* June 3, 1853. For Douglass and McCune Smith, see Stauffer, *Black Hearts of Men,* esp. p. 16.

34. "On the Claims of the Negro Ethnologically Considered: An Address Delivered in Hudson, Ohio, on 12 July 1854," *The Frederick Douglass Papers, Series One: Speeches, Debates, and Interviews,* ed. John W. Blassingame et al. (New Haven: Yale University Press, 1982), vol. 2, pp. 497–525. Although the Literary Societies' choice as speaker alarmed the colonizationists who ran Western Reserve College, more people came to hear Douglass than attended the commencement ceremony itself, and several newspapers applauded and reprinted his speech.

35. See Waldo E. Martin, Jr., *The Mind of Frederick Douglass* (Chapel Hill, NC: University of North Carolina press, 1984), pp. 229, 241.

36. Douglass, "Claims," pp. 506–507.

37. Ibid., pp. 508–509.

38. Ibid., p. 515.

39. Ibid., p. 521.

40. Ibid., pp. 521–522; 524.

41. Ibid., p. 524. For McCune Smith on Indians, see Stauffer, *Black Hearts of Men,* p. 187.

42. Mia Elizabeth Bay takes this position in *The White Image in the Black Mind: African-American Ideas about White People, 1830–1925* (New York: Oxford University Press, 1999), pp. 70–71.

43. Fredrickson would make the same point a hundred years later, when he showed how "romantic racialist" attitudes undermined white abolitionist support for aid for blacks during Reconstruciton (Fredrickson, *Black Image,* pp. 165–197).

44. William L. Andrews, "Introduction to the 1987 Edition," in Frederick Douglass, *My Bondage and My Freedom,* pp. xi–xxviii.

45. McCune Smith, "Introduction" to Frederick Douglass, *My Bondage and My Freedom,* pp. 17, 22, 39.

46. Ibid., p. 15.

47. Henry Highland Garnet, *The Past and the Present Condition, and the Destiny, of the Colored Race; A Discourse Delivered at the Fifteenth Anniversary of the Female Benevolent Society of Troy, N.Y., Feb. 14, 1848* (1848; reprint, Miami, FL: Mnemosyne Pub. 1969). By 1843, Garnet had already broken with Garrisonian moral suasion and argued not only for slave rebellion but for black political action. His "Address to the Slaves" sparked a famous confrontation at between Garnet and Douglass, who was at the time still an ardent Garrisonian moral suasionist, enemy

of political action, and pacifist. Garnet fell short one vote of having the speech published by the Convention. On Garnet's address and the convetion, see Eddie Glaude, *Exodus! Religion, Race, and Nation in Early Nineteenth-Century Black America* (Chicago: University of Chicago Press, 2000), pp. 145-161. On Garnet, see Earl Ofari Hutchinson, *"Let Your Motto Be Resistance": The Life and Thought of Henry Highland Garnet* (Boston: Beacon Press, 1972); Sterling Stuckey, "A Last Stern Struggle: Henry Highland Garnet and Liberation Theology," in Leon F. Litwack and August Meier, eds., *Black Leaders of the Nineteenth Century* (Urbana: University of Illinois Press, 1988), pp. 128-147.

48. James McCune Smith, "Civilization: Its Dependence on Physical Circumstances," *Anglo-African Magazine*, 1 (1859): 5-17.

49. Thomas Hamilton, "Apologia," *Anglo-African Magazine*, 1 (January 1859): 1-4. The two most interesting instances of mockery of race-thinking were Ethiop (William G. Wilson), "What Shall We do with the White People," *Anglo-African Magazine* 2 (February, 1860), and especially "S. S. N.," "Anglo-Saxons and Anglo-Africans," *Anglo-African Magazine*, 1 (1959): 247-254. Perhaps the fullest treatment of the *Anglo-African* appears in Patrick Rael, *Black Identity and Black Protest in the Antebellum North* (Chapel Hill: University of North Carolina Press, 2002), pp. 118-156; see also Joshi, "The Sources of American Identity: The Black Self-Image in the Pre-Emancipation Decades," *Indian Journal of American Studies*, 12 (1982): 67-87; *Anglo-African* discussed on pp. 79-82.

50. Quetelet, *A Treatise On Man and the Development of His Faculties* (1842; rpt., Gainseville FL: Scholars' Facsimilies & Reprints, 1969), pp. 100, 6. On Quetelet, see Theodore M. Porter, *The Rise of Statistical Thinking: 1820-1900* (Princeton, NJ: Princeton University Press, 1986), pp. 40-69; Stephen M. Stigler, *The History of Statistics: The Measurement of Uncertainty before 1900* (Cambridge, MA: Belknap Press of Harvard Univerity Press, 1986), pp. 161-219; Ian Hacking, "Nineteenth Century Cracks in the Concept of Determinism," *Journal of the History of Ideas* 44 (1983): 455-475; Silvan S. Schweber, "The Origin of the *Origin* Revisited," *Journal of the History of Biology* 10 (1977): 229-316; Paul F. Lazarsfeld, "Notes on the History of Quantification in Sociology—Trends, Sources and Problems," *Isis*, 52 (1961): 277-333.

51. Henry Thomas Buckle, *History of Civilization in England* (1857-1861; rpt., New York: Hearst's International Library Co., 1913), especially vo. 1, pp. 1-15. On Buckle, see Bernard Semmel, "H. T. Buckle: The Liberal Faith and the Science of History," *British Journal of Sociology* 27 (1976): 370-386; Porter, *Statistical Thinking*, pp. 60-65; 194-207; Christopher Parker, "English Historians and

the Opposition to Positivism," *History and Theory* 22 (1983): 120–145; Solomon Diamond, "Buckle, Wundt, and Psychology's Use of History," *Isis* 75 (1984): 143–152.

52. McCune Smith, *Civilization*, p. 15.

53. Ibid., p. 16.

54. Ibid., p. 17.

55. James McCune Smith, "On the Fourteenth Query of Thomas Jefferson's Notes on Virginia," *Anglo-African Magazine* 1 (1859): 225–238.

56. Ibid., pp. 234–236.

57. Ibid., pp. 237–238.